FROMMER'S
EasyGuide
TO
GERMANY

By
Donald Olson & Stephen Brewer

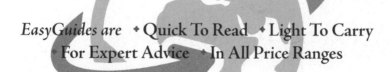

EasyGuides are ✦ Quick To Read ✦ Light To Carry
✦ For Expert Advice ✦ In All Price Ranges

FrommerMedia LLC

Published by

FROMMER MEDIA LLC

ISBN 978-1-62887-064-0 (paper), 978-1-62887-065-7 (e-book)

Editorial Director: Pauline Frommer
Editor: Arthur Frommer
Production Editor: Heather Wilcox
Cartographer: Elizabeth Puhl
Cover Design: Howard Grossman

For information on our other products or services, see www.frommers.com.

Frommer Media LLC also publishes its books in a variety of electronic formats. Some content that appears in print may not be available in electronic formats.

Manufactured in the United States of America

5 4 3 2 1

CONTENTS

ABOUT THE AUTHORS

Donald Olson is a novelist, playwright, and travel writer based in New York and Portland, Oregon. His travel stories have appeared in "The New York Times," "National Geographic," and many other national publications, and he has authored travel guides to Germany; England; Oregon; London; Vancouver, BC; and destinations throughout Europe and North America. Donald is the author of eight novels; three of them, written under the pen name Swan Adamson, have been translated into French and Russian. His plays have been produced in the United States, London, and Amsterdam. Donald's newest book, "Gardens of the Pacific Northwest," will be published in 2014 by Timber Press.

Stephen Brewer has been writing travel articles and guides for almost 3 decades. As an editor and writer, he has focused on European coverage for such magazines as "Connoisseur" and "Geo." He has written numerous guides for Frommer's, Fodor's, DK Eyewitness, Unofficial Guides, and Insight as well as authoring "Beautiful Small Coastal Towns" for Rizzoli. Stephen resides in Manhattan.

ABOUT THE FROMMER TRAVEL GUIDES

For most of the past 50 years, Frommer's has been the leading series of travel guides in North America, accounting for as many as 24% of all guidebooks sold. I think I know why.

Though we hope our books are entertaining, we nevertheless deal with travel in a serious fashion. Our guidebooks have never looked on such journeys as a mere recreation, but as a far more important human function, a time of learning and introspection, an essential part of a civilized life. We stress the culture, lifestyle, history and beliefs of the destinations we cover, and urge our readers to seek out people and new ideas as the chief rewards of travel.

We have never shied from controversy. We have, from the beginning, encouraged our authors to be intensely judgmental, critical—both pro and con—in their comments, and wholly independent. Our only clients are our readers, and we have triggered the ire of countless prominent sorts, from a tourist newspaper we called "practically worthless" (it unsuccessfully sued us) to the many rip-offs we've condemned.

And because we believe that travel should be available to everyone regardless of their incomes, we have always been cost-conscious at every level of expenditure. Though we have broadened our recommendations beyond the budget category, we insist that every lodging we include be sensibly priced. We use every form of media to assist our readers, and are particularly proud of our feisty daily website, the award-winning Frommers.com.

I have high hopes for the future of Frommer's. May these guidebooks, in all the years ahead, continue to reflect the joy of travel and the freedom that travel represents. May they always pursue a cost-conscious path, so that people of all incomes can enjoy the rewards of travel. And may they create, for both the traveler and the persons among whom we travel, a community of friends, where all human beings live in harmony and peace.

Arthur Frommer

THE BEST OF GERMANY

The word is out and maybe you've heard it: Germany is one of Europe's great travel destinations. Every year, more and more visitors from around the globe are discovering the pleasures to be found in Germany's cities, towns, and countryside. Tourist numbers have risen steadily in the 25 years since the country's dramatic reunification in 1989–1990 and show no sign of slowing down.

Germany's appeal is really no great mystery. Moody forests, jagged Alpine peaks, and miles of neatly tended vineyards are not just scenic but the stuff of legend, places that have inspired fairy tales and where much of Western history has been played out. The Germans more than anyone appreciate the soothing tonic of a hike in the Black Forest or a stroll on North Sea dunes, and just seeing these storied lands from a train window can be good for the soul. The cities are treasure-troves not just of great art and history but of culture, sophisticated lifestyles, and, from ever-changing Berlin to old-world Baden-Baden, cutting-edge architecture. Food—well, don't write off the cuisine as just a lot of heaping plates of wurst and sauerkraut and schnitzel with noodles. For one thing, these traditional dishes are delicious, and one of the pleasures of traveling in Germany is discovering time-honored regional favorites.

So, let's look a little more deeply into why your travels in Germany will be filled with pleasures that go way beyond the spectacle of dirndls, lederhosen, Alpine meadows, and half-timbered houses (although the sight of any of these can be a bit of a travel thrill, too).

Ditch Those German Stereotypes

So what about the people? Everyone seems to have an opinion about the "German character" except for the Germans themselves. The militaristic Nazi past that continues to haunt Germany has given rise to many stereotypes. But if you connect with just one German person on your trip, chances are that all the stereotypes you've heard about will crumble to dust. Germany today is the most pacifistic country in Europe, sometimes to the annoyance of its neighbors and allies. Overall, it has one of the world's highest levels of educational attainment and technological achievement. Germany never got caught up in the real-estate bubble that sent so many countries freefalling into recession, and its unemployment rate is about 5 percent, the lowest in the European Union. The Germans have their rules and ways of doing things, which sometimes seem stiff and bureaucratic, but clearly they are doing something right.

Many travelers base their notions of "national character" on their experiences with hotel employees and the waitstaff in restaurants. In that sense, Germany's hospitality industry has gone through a real sea change in the

A GUIDE TO GERMAN wine

Wine has been part of German life and culture ever since the Romans began tending vineyards some 2,000 years ago. The most famous vineyards are found in the western and southwestern parts of the country, in the Rhine Valley and along the Mosel River. The German practice of harvesting grapes at various stages of ripeness determines the official quality category that is indicated on the label. Under the German wine law, there are two categories of quality—*Tafelwein* and *Qualitätswein*.

Tafelwein Tafelwein (*taf*-fel vine; table wine) is made from normally ripe grapes. If you want a simple, inexpensive German table wine, you have two choices: *Deutscher Tafelwein* and *Deutscher Landwein*.

o **Deutscher Tafelwein** (German table wine), a simple table wine made from normally ripe grapes, is meant for everyday enjoyment and primarily consumed where it's grown. Deutscher Tafelwein comes from one of five broad Tafelwein regions.

o **Deutscher Landwein** (special table wine) is a hearty regional wine with more body and character than Tafelwein because the grapes must be riper at harvest. Dry or semidry, Landwein comes from and is named after 1 of 19 Landwein regions. If the word *Deutsch* is missing on the label, then it is not made solely of German grapes. Instead, it's a foreign wine that may or may not have been blended with German wine. It's likely to have been bottled, but not grown, in Germany.

Qualitätswein Made from ripe, very ripe, or overripe grapes, Qualitätswein (quality wine) is divided into two types: *Qualitätswein mit Prädikat* and *Qualitätswein bestimmter Anbaugebiete* (QbA). If you see QbA on the label, it means the wine comes from 1 of the 13 specified winegrowing regions and is made from approved grape varieties that have ripened sufficiently to assure that the wine will have the style and traditional taste of

past few years. Hospitality was never lacking in Germany, but it was sometimes accompanied by a manner that seemed a little less than welcoming. Today you'll find that Germans have embraced the American model of friendliness and service. What's also true is that there is a German level of professionalism in all service-related jobs that someone accustomed to the slap-dash and sloppy might find almost bewildering. A waiter in Germany does not behave like your overly familiar best friend, as is so often the case in the U.S. That's because waiters in Germany are paid a living wage and don't have to hustle for tips.

Eat Well

What about the food served in those restaurants? It's always good. Even a simple wurst, that staple of the German cuisine, is delicious. Why? Because the Germans take their food seriously and pay attention to what they eat. Sausages, by law, can have no filler added to them. Beer, by law, must adhere to strict standards of water and ingredient purity. The same is true of German wine. And the bread—well, even a humble *Brötchen,* that crusty-on-the-outside and soft-on-the-inside roll that you get for breakfast, is delicious. And the Germans have had the cautious good sense not to embrace genetically modified foods.

its region. Light, refreshing, and fruity, these wines are meant to be consumed while young, for everyday enjoyment or with meals.

Prädikatswein Qualitätswein mit Prädikat (QmP) includes all the finest wines of Germany. Referred to as *Prädikatswein*, each of these wines carries one of six special attributes *(Prädikat)* on its label. Those six attributes are *Kabinett, Spätlese, Auslese, Beerenauslese, Eiswein,* and *Trockenbeerenauslese.*

- o **Kabinett** wines are fine, usually naturally light, and made of fully ripened grapes, the lightest of the Prädikat wines generally showing the lowest alcoholic strength.

- o **Spätlese** literally means "late harvest." These superior-quality wines are made from grapes harvested after the normal harvest. Spätlese wines are more intense in flavor and concentration, but not necessarily sweet. They go well with richer, more flavorful foods, or can be drunk by themselves.

- o **Auslese** is the harvest of select, very ripe bunches. These wines are noble, intense in bouquet and taste, and usually (but not always) sweet.

- o **Beerenauslese** is the harvest of individually selected, overripe berries *(Beeren)* with a high sugar content. These are rich, sweet dessert wines.

- o **Eiswein,** or "ice wine," is made from grapes harvested and pressed while frozen to concentrate sugar and acidity. Of Beerenauslese intensity, Eiswein is truly unique, with a remarkable concentration of fruity acidity and sweetness.

- o **Trockenbeerenauslese** is made from individually selected, overripe berries dried up almost to raisins. Such wines are rich, sweet, and honeylike.

Eating local cuisine is part of any travel experience, and in Germany you'll find many regional variations of traditional German dishes. German cuisine—what you might call "traditional home cooking"—tends to be hearty and heavy on meat (particularly pork), starch (potatoes), cooked root vegetables, brined leafy vegetables (red cabbage, sauerkraut), and dairy. Fish is always available (herring is a popular delicacy), and menus are always enlivened with seasonal specialties, such *Erdbeeren* (strawberries), and game. One thing to note is that in beer-hall restaurants, the seating is often communal, so if you are shown to a table where strangers are sitting, take the opportunity to expand your experience of Germany and the Germans.

There are, of course, Michelin-starred restaurants throughout Germany where you can enjoy spectacular meals of a kind that Grandma never cooked, or at least didn't cook like this, and in cities, all manner of ethnic restaurants reflect Germany's large immigrant population (roughly 10 percent of its population of 80 million is first- or second-generation). Turkish is the most prominent "casual" ethnic food (in the form of kabobs), but you'll also find French, Italian, Chinese, Japanese, Thai, Indian, and Greek restaurants. All this information is meant to reassure you that you'll eat well in Germany wherever and whatever you eat.

Drink Well

You don't have to speak German to order a beer. It's spelled *Bier* but it's pronounced beer. And it's such a vital part of German culture that the right to drink a beer with lunch is written into some labor contracts. The traditional *Biergarten* (beer garden), with tables set outdoors under trees or trellises, remains an essential part of German culture. A *Bräuhaus* (*broy*-house) serves its own brew along with local food.

When you order a beer in Germany, you have many choices. The range of beer varieties includes *Altbier, Bockbier, Export, Kölsch, Lager, Malzbier, Märzbier, Pils, Vollbier,* and *Weizenbier.* The ratio of ingredients, brewing temperature and technique, alcoholic content, aging time, color, and taste all contribute to a German beer's unique qualities. A German law adopted in 1516 dictates that German beer may contain no ingredients other than hops, malt (barley), yeast, and water.

Dark and sweet Malzbier (*maltz*-beer; malt beer) contains hardly any alcohol. Vollbier (*fole*-beer, or standard beer) has 4 percent alcohol, Export has 5 percent, and Bockbier has 6 percent. Pils, or Pilsener, beers are light and contain more hops. Weizenbier (*vi*-tsen-beer), made from wheat, is a Bavarian white beer. Märzbier (*maertz*-beer), or "March beer," is dark and strong. The most popular beer in Germany is Pils, followed by Export.

To order a beer, decide whether you want a *dunkles Bier* (*dune*-kles beer; dark beer), brewed with darkly roasted malt fermented for a long period of time, or a *helles Bier* (*hell*-less beer; light beer), brewed from malt dried and baked by the local brewery. If you want a large glass, you ask for *ein Grosses* (ine *grow*-ses); if you want a small glass, ask for *ein Kleines* (ine *kly*-nis), and tell the waiter or tavern keeper whether you want *ein Bier vom Fass* (fum fahss; from the barrel) or in a *Flasche* (*flah*-shuh; bottle). The beer is always served cold, but not too cold, in an appropriate beer glass or mug, with a long-lasting head of white foam. A proper draft beer, according to the Germans, can't be poured in less than 7 minutes to achieve the proper head.

Sleep Well, Sweat in a Spa

What about German hotels, inns, and hostels? Here, too, there has been a shift, with a greater emphasis on friendliness, service, and comfort.

The German hotel industry uses 300 criteria to rate every hotel in Germany on a one- to five-star system, with one star being the most basic and five stars being awarded to top-of-the-line luxury hotels. (In this guide, we rate hotels with our own one- to three-star rating system that is not to be confused with the German hotel-rating system.) Although room amenities obviously vary according to the price category, you can always be assured of a superclean room. If you want to travel like a German (or like Germans used to travel), look for a *pension* (pen-see-*own*), a room in a house or apartment that provides lodgings and breakfast. You can save money in some hotels by getting a room with a shared bathroom in the hallway; never fear, the bathroom will be cleaner than yours at home. Do not expect air-conditioning except at the most expensive hotels—the Germans still believe in having windows that open for fresh air. In more expensive hotels (the type that offer fitness and wellness centers), you'll nearly always find a sauna.

Spas and saunas are a way of life in Germany—dozens of spa towns, or *Kurorte,* are scattered around the country, with thermal bath complexes where you can steam, sweat, swim, and relax. Experiencing Germany by spa is wonderful, but do keep in mind that many saunas are clothing-optional and co-ed: The Germans are not prudish when it comes to their bodies. This is part of the communal side of German life, like sharing a table at a restaurant—only, of course, you wouldn't do that nude.

Get Arty, Get Active

Germany is a country where the arts are part of life. The caliber of museums and the collections they hold can be breathtaking. Germany has a long-established musical tradition (think Bach, Beethoven, and Brahms) and is famed for the excellence of its music performances. So if you enjoy great art and music, you'll never be lacking for things to see and do in Germany. That goes for *every* kind of music, including jazz, pop, rap, hip-hop, indie, and every other genre.

A country's cultural character and heritage are also reflected in its architecture, and Germany is fascinating on that front, too. The country's visible architectural legacy spans some 1,800 years, from Roman-era walls to Ludwig's 19th-century "fairy-tale castles" in Bavaria; and the corporate skyscrapers that define Frankfurt's skyline. Less grandiosely, you'll find half-timbered inns, Bavarian chalets, ruined castles, and an imposing *Rathaus* (town hall) in just about every town or city you visit.

But this architectural heritage can also reflect the ominous side of Germany's Nazi past: the remains of Albert Speer's giant Nazi stadium in Nuremberg, the grim prison buildings at Dachau, the ruined Kaiser-Wilhelm Memorial Church in Berlin, and the numerous memorials and documentation centers that serve as reminders of the Holocaust. The Nazis excelled at destruction, but after the war, the Germans excelled at rebuilding—not just new buildings, but exact reproductions of many great palaces and churches. The Frauenkirche in Dresden is perhaps the country's greatest postwar rebuilding feat.

But maybe you're less interested in museums, music, and architecture and want to explore the German countryside. Germany has many fabled landscapes. If you're an active traveler who is interested in hiking, biking, skiing, or swimming, you can head to the Black Forest, the Bavarian Alps, or the Bodensee (Lake Constance).

All the above merely scratches the surface of what makes Germany a superb place to visit. We could also add the seasonal festivals celebrating beer, wine, music, and art. And the shopping, particularly the traditional Christmas markets with their decorated booths and regional craft and food specialties. All these examples help define who the Germans are and what you will find when you visit Germany.

GERMANY'S best AUTHENTIC EXPERIENCES

o **Exploring the New Berlin:** The fall of the Berlin Wall in 1989–90 was an event that transfixed the world and transformed the divided city into a new world capital. Berlin is still knitting itself together, but this huge, rejoined city also happens to be the most exciting city in Europe. The new Berlin is fascinating and inexhaustible, a city that invites exploration on many different fronts. See chapter 4.

o **Sipping a Beer in a Munich Beer Garden:** There's nothing more enjoyable on a balmy afternoon or evening than sitting under the trees in one of Munich's leafy beer gardens and trying to lift one of those 1-liter steins to your lips. It's a way of life and a way to meet Germans on their own turf. See chapter 6.

o **Wandering Through Munich's Viktualienmarkt:** There are markets and then there are markets like Munich's Viktualienmarkt, a hive of stalls, food stands, and specialty shops that's been around for a couple of hundred years. See chapter 6.

○ **Visiting Dachau Concentration Camp Memorial Site:** It's grim, horrifying, and unbearably poignant, but Dachau, near Munich, is also one of the most important Holocaust memorial sites in Germany. A visit gives you insight into a barbaric chapter of history and puts a human face on its victims. See p. 132.

○ **Celebrating Karneval in Cologne:** The locals call it *Fasteleer* or *Fastlovend,* but it's Karneval to most Germans, and it's celebrated in Catholic Cologne the way Mardi Gras is celebrated in New Orleans. Parades, floats, balls, parties, and plenty of food and beer characterize this pre-Lenten celebration that natives call their city's "fifth season." See chapter 9.

○ **Experiencing a German Spa:** For a quintessential German experience, visit one of Germany's spa towns—Baden-Baden, Wiesbaden, and Aachen are among the possibilities—and go through the routine of bathing, steaming, *schvitzing,* and swimming, all in one enormous complex warmed by thermal waters and dedicated to the goddess *Gesund* (health). See chapters 8 and 9.

○ **Spending Harvest Time in the German Vineyards:** Between late August and mid-October, the vineyards on the banks of the Rhine and Mosel rivers turn gold and russet, and workers gather buckets of grapes from terraced rows of meticulously pruned vines. This is the perfect time to visit charming wine towns, such as Rüdesheim and Bingen on the Rhine and Cochem on the Mosel. Sip the local vintages at a wine tavern and enjoy the scenery. See chapter 9.

○ **Ascending the Zugspitze:** The tallest mountain in Germany, soaring 2,960m (9,700 ft.) above sea level, lures view-seekers up its craggy slopes on a thrill ride via cog railway and cable car that gives new meaning to the notion that getting there is half the fun. Views from the top over the undulating Alps will quite literally take your breath away. See chapter 7.

○ **Touring the Romantic Road (Romantische Strasse):** This scenic route rambles through much of Bavaria, through an unfolding, travel-poster-worthy panorama of beautiful landscapes interspersed with small medieval cities. To the south, the road rises to the dramatic heights of the Alps and the fantasy castles of the legendary King Ludwig II. See chapter 7.

○ **Pounding the Cobblestones in Heidelberg:** This handsome old university town on the Neckar River has enchanted everyone from Goethe to Mark Twain to hordes of modern visitors, and little wonder: A half-ruined castle perched on a wooded hillside overlooks an unspoiled assemblage of medieval and Renaissance landmarks (and no small part of the appeal is that beer flows like water in the historic taverns below). See chapter 8.

GERMANY'S best MUSEUMS

○ **Alte Pinakothek,** Munich: This gigantic repository of old-master paintings could easily fill a day (or two, or three) of your time. Works by major European artists from the 14th to 18th centuries form the basis of the collection, with highlights that include a charismatic self-portrait by Albrecht Dürer and canvases by Raphael, Botticelli, Leonardo da Vinci, and Rembrandt. See p. 124.

○ **Altes Museum,** Berlin: One of the five museums on Berlin's Museum Island, this imposing neoclassical edifice houses Berlin's superlative collections of Greek, Etruscan, and Roman antiquities. Renovated to its former glory, the museum displays the full breadth of artistic expression in these ancient cultures. See p. 63.

- **Dokumentationszentrum Reichsparteitagsgelände,** Nürnberg: Displays in Hitler's monumental yet uncompleted Congress Hall chronicle the Führer's rise to power, celebrated during the Nürnberg rallies when hundreds of thousands gathered on the adjacent Zeppelinwiese (Zeppelin Field) to listen to the leader rant at more than 100,000 spectators enthralled by his violent denunciations. See p. 152.

- **Germanisches Nationalmuseum (Germanic National Museum),** Nürnberg: Germany's largest museum of art and culture spans the millennia to show off paintings, sculptures, crafts, arms and armor, early scientific instruments—if it's part of Germany's national heritage, it's here. See p. 152.

- **Grunes Gewölbe (Green Vault),** Dresden: There are two Green Vaults, old and new, in Dresden's Residenzschloss, and both display a sumptuous assortment of treasures collected by the electors of Saxony from the 16th to the 18th centuries. Precious metals, stones, porcelain, corals, and ivory were used to create this trove of decorated chests, carvings, jewelry, statuettes, and tableware. See p. 76.

- **Lenbachhaus,** Munich: Completely renovated and reopened in 2013, the 19th-century villa of portrait painter Franz von Lenbach houses a stunning collection of late-19th- and early-20th-century paintings from the Munich-based *Blaue Reiter* (Blue Rider) group, including works by Kandinsky, Paul Klee, Franz Marc, and Gabriele Münter. See p. 126.

- **Kunsthalle,** Hamburg: In Northern Germany's leading art museum, Canalettos, Rembrandts, Holbeins, and other old masters share space with modern canvases by Picasso, Warhol, Beuys, Munch, Kandinsky, Klee, and Hockney. Works by contemporary artists and those banned by the Nazis round out this fascinating and sweeping collection. See p. 92.

- **Mercedes-Benz Museum and Porsche Museum,** Stuttgart: Germany's well-earned rep for precision engineering and luxury auto travel comes to the fore in these two collections that showcase the output of world-famous hometown auto makers. Whether it's a long, lean Mercedes 500 K convertible or a Porsche 911, the gleaming showpieces turn even nondrivers into car buffs. See p. 188.

- **Museum Ludwig,** Cologne: Created in 1986 to house the modern-art collection of German collector Peter Ludwig, this museum is renowned for having one of the world's largest collections of the works of Pablo Picasso, but just about every major artist and art movement of the 20th century is represented. See p. 227.

- **Neues Museum,** Berlin: Left in ruins for decades after World War II, the Neues Museum on Museum Island underwent a remarkable restoration and renovation by British architect David Chipperfield and reopened in 2009 to great critical acclaim. The museum houses one of the world's greatest collections of Egyptian antiquities and includes the celebrated bust of Queen Nefertiti. See p. 63.

- **Schnütgen Museum,** Cologne: In the Middle Ages, Frankish Cologne was the center of a rich artistic tradition of stained-glass, painting and carving—all of which are on display in this small, superlative museum. The surprise here is the depth of expression that medieval artists achieved in their work. See p. 227.

- **Wallraf-Richartz Museum/Foundation Corboud,** Cologne: The oldest museum in Cologne presents one of Germany's grandest collections of art, covering the 14th to the 19th centuries. The collection of Gothic works, including altarpieces painted by artists of the Cologne School, is one of the finest in Europe, and the galleries are a virtual encyclopedia of art, from Flemish old masters to the French Impressionists. See p. 228.

GERMANY'S best CITIES FOR MUSIC

o **Berlin:** Germany's capital is home to seven symphony orchestras, including the famed Berlin Philharmonic, and three opera companies—Staatsoper unter den Linden, Deutsche Oper Berlin, and the Komische Oper—that share their stages with resident ballet companies. The magnificent neoclassical Konzerthaus am Gendarmenmarkt presents a year-round roster of concerts. Musically, there is more going on in Berlin than in any other city in Germany. See chapter 4.

o **Hamburg:** This northern metropolis plays host to the Hamburg State Opera, the Hamburg Ballet, and three highly regarded orchestras. See chapter 5.

o **Munich:** The capital of Bavaria is one of the great cultural centers of Germany. The acclaimed Bayerische Staatsoper (Bavarian State Opera) shares the National Theater stage with its ballet company, while the magnificent Munich Philharmonic Orchestra performs in the Gasteig Philharmonic Hall. See chapter 6.

o **Stuttgart:** The Stuttgart Ballet hit international stardom in the 1970s when John Cranko took over the company. Cranko is gone, but the company still performs at the State Theater, and so does the Staatsoper (State Opera). See chapter 8.

o **Cologne:** For a city of its size, Cologne has an amazing array of musical offerings. Major artists appear at Oper Köln (Cologne Opera), the Rhineland's leading opera house, and two fine orchestras—the Gürzenich Kölner Philharmoniker (Cologne Philharmonic) and the Westdeutscher Rundfunk Orchestra (West German Radio Orchestra)—perform in the Kölner Philharmonie concert hall. The group Musica Antiqua Köln is one of the world's foremost early-music ensembles. See chapter 9.

o **Frankfurt:** Opera Frankfurt/Ballet Frankfurt gives a big musical boost to Germany's financial center, as does the Frankfurt Philharmonic. See chapter 9.

GERMANY'S best CASTLES & PALACES

o **Heidelberg Castle,** Heidelberg: This Gothic-Renaissance 16th-century masterpiece was massively expanded as rival rulers competed for control of the Rhineland. The compound never regained its original glory after a 17th-century French attack, and today the ruins brood in dignified severity high above the student revelry and taverns of the folkloric city below. See p. 183.

o **Hohenschwangau Castle,** near Füssen: Watching its bombastic younger brother from the opposite hill, this lesser-known residence built on 12th-century ruins and finished in 1836 merits a visit. King Maximilian II lived here with his family, and the Gothic environs inspired flights of fancy in his son, the young Ludwig II. See p. 175.

o **Neuschwanstein,** near Füssen: Love it or hate it, this fairy-tale castle is nothing less than phenomenal, the romantic fantasy of "Mad" King Ludwig II. The fairy-tale allure inspired Walt Disney and attracts millions of visitors, for whom the outstanding mountain scenery alone is worth the trip. See p. 176.

o **Residenz,** Würzburg: One of the most massive baroque palaces in Germany was built between 1720 and 1744 as the official residence of the powerful bishops of Würzburg, combining gardens, a gallery of paintings, frescoes by Tiepolo, and enough decoration to satisfy the most demanding appetite for ornamentation. See p. 141.

o **Sanssouci,** Potsdam: Friedrich the Great's retreat was called Sanssouci ("Without Care"), because here he could forget the rigors of court life and exercise his intellect. Germany's most successful blend of landscape and architecture sits among intricately landscaped gardens adorned with additional buildings. See p. 72.

o **Schloss Nymphenburg,** Munich: The summer palace of the Wittelsbachs, Bavaria's ruling family, was constructed between 1664 and 1674. It's fairly modest as palaces go but contains some sumptuously decorated rooms. The surrounding gardens contain a bevy of ornamental buildings, and the former armory displays an extensive collection of carriages and sleighs. See p. 134.

o **Schloss Linderhof,** near Oberammergau: Built in the 1870s as a teenage indulgence by Ludwig II, this whimsically eclectic fantasy was inspired by Italian baroque architecture. In the surrounding park, Moorish pavilions and Mediterranean cascades appear against Alpine vistas in combinations that are as startling as they are charming. See p. 170.

o **Zwinger,** Dresden: This ornate baroque palace, with its galleries and domed pavilions surrounding a central courtyard, was completed in 1719 for Augustus the Strong, elector of Saxony and king of Poland. Salons are still hung with Augustus's art collections, the most impressive of which is the Gemäldegalerie Alte Meister (Old Masters Gallery) that contains Italian, Flemish, Dutch, and German paintings by Raphael, Van Dyck, Vermeer, Dürer, Rubens, and Rembrandt. See p. 77.

GERMANY'S best
CATHEDRALS, CHURCHES & CHAPELS

o **Dom (Cathedral),** Cologne: The largest cathedral in Germany, and one of the largest in the world, Cologne's crowning glory took more than 600 years to complete and is designated now as a UNESCO World Heritage Site. The size and stylistic unity of this Gothic marvel will astonish you. See p. 225.

o **Dom (Cathedral),** Aachen: A building of great historic and architectural significance, Aachen's cathedral consists of two parts: The Octagon, originally part of the Emperor Charlemagne palace, dates from around 800 and was the first large church to be built in western Europe since the Roman period; and the Gothic choir, where Charlemagne's remains rest in a golden reliquary. From 936 to 1531, emperors of the Holy Roman Empire were crowned here. See p. 235.

o **Dom (Cathedral),** Mainz: A sandstone structure dating from the 11th century, the Dom in Mainz is the second-most important Catholic cathedral in Germany after Cologne. Now more than 1,000 years old, the interior has Romanesque elements and later additions in the Gothic and baroque styles. See p. 217.

o **Herrgottskirche (Chapel of Our Lord),** Creglingen: Master carver Tilman Riemenschneider created this magnificent altar on which expressive figures catch the light in such a way that they seem animated and the sculpture changes in appearance throughout the day with the shifting sun. See p. 146.

o **Wieskirche,** outside Füssen: One of the world's most exuberantly decorated buildings sits in a meadow and shimmers with a superabundance of woodcarvings. See p. 174.

GERMANY'S best SPAS

○ **Aachen:** For more than 2 millennia, the warm mineral waters that flow from thermal springs below Aachen have been used for health and relaxation. Spend a couple of hours at the Carolus Therme bath complex and you'll be reinvigorated for the rest of your strenuous sightseeing schedule. See p. 233.

○ **Baden-Baden:** There's no better spa town in Germany, and certainly none more fashionable or famous than this sophisticated retreat in the Black Forest that has hosted royals and commoners alike. For a unique spa experience, shed your duds at the Friedrichsbad and follow the Roman-Irish bathing ritual that takes you through temperature-modulated saunas, steam rooms, and pools, finishing up with a cool-down and a relaxing snooze. See p. 191.

○ **Wiesbaden:** One of Germany's oldest cities, Wiesbaden attracted Roman legions to its hot springs and lures travelers today to its casino, concert halls, and the huge Kaiser Friedrich Therme. Steam, soak, bubble, sweat, and bathe your cares away and then head over to Wiesbaden's lovely beer garden on the Rhine. See p. 218.

GERMANY'S most romantic & recreational LANDSCAPES

○ **Bavarian Alps:** In perhaps the most dramatic of all German landscapes, the country's highest mountain, the Zugspitze, towers above the Alpine resort town of Garmisch-Partenkirchen. You don't have to be a sportsperson to ascend to the top on an Alpine adventure via gondola and cog railroad. See chapter 7.

○ **Black Forest (Schwarzwald):** Sophisticated health spas and recreational activities abound in the forest-clad mountains of the Black Forest, where you find lakes, hiking trails, and scenic lookouts. See chapter 8.

○ **Bodensee (Lake Constance):** This enormous swath of shimmering waters near Germany's sunny southwestern border suggests the Mediterranean, with semitropical gardens and an almost Italian languor. See chapter 8.

○ **Middle Rhine (Mittelrhein):** Cruises down the scenic midsection of the mighty Rhine take you past castle-crowned crags and legendary sites, such as Loreley rock, to charming towns in the Rheingau wine district. See chapter 9.

○ **Mosel Valley:** The Mosel Valley between Koblenz and Cochem is a scenic wine region encompassing thousands of acres of terraced and neatly tended vineyards, Roman ruins, medieval castles, and riverside towns with cobbled streets and half-timbered houses. See chapter 9.

○ **Romantic Road (Romantische Strasse):** The most romantic byway in Germany passes through small medieval towns set within a gorgeous Bavarian landscape of river valley and mountain meadow before climbing into the Alps to King Ludwig's "fairy-tale castles." See chapter 7.

GERMANY'S best RESTAURANTS

○ **Ana e Bruno,** Berlin: For some of the best Italian food outside Italy, head over to this casual yet sophisticated restaurant in Charlottenburg, where Chef Bruno Pellegrini has been perfecting and reinventing traditional Italian recipes for more than 25 years. See p. 48.

- **Beim Sedlmayr,** Munich: Take a seat at one of the communal tables and enjoy hearty, authentic Bavarian cuisine at this long-established institution in Munich's Altstadt. It's a favorite of locals—for good reason. See p. 114.

- **Curry 36,** Berlin: Who says a local neighborhood currywurst stand can't be considered a great restaurant? Berlin's favorite street food is not haute cuisine, but it sure is good—as the lines here will attest. See p. 50.

- **Die Quadriga,** Berlin: The cooking at this sophisticated dining room in the Brandenburger Hof Hotel is refined and elegant, the service is impeccable, the wine is exquisite, and the overall experience is memorable. See p. 49.

- **Fischereihafen Restaurant,** Altona, near Hamburg: Hamburgers come here for what many claim is the city's freshest fish and seafood, most of it right from the market stalls. In fact, from a window seat, you can spot the boats that hauled in your sole, eel, turbot, herring, or flounder from the seas that day. See p. 89.

- **Die Blaue Sau,** Rothenburg ob der Tauber: Foodies would find it a crime worthy of detention in the stocks in Rothenburg's Kriminalmuseum to pass through town without stopping by this grill house for a meat-heavy take on Franconian cuisine. See p. 144.

- **Früh am Dom,** Cologne: Cologne is loaded with tavern-restaurants where patrons wash down big portions of hearty Rhineland fare with rather dainty glasses of *Kölsch,* Cologne's delicious beer. Früh, near the cathedral, has been around forever and is still the best spot to sample *Kölsch* and regional cooking. See p. 224.

- **Romantik Hotel Zum Ritter St. Georg,** Heidelberg: Lovely old dining rooms on the ground floor of a landmark hotel set the gold standard for old-world cooking and service. Even liver dumplings seem fit for a prince when served by a uniformed waiter on starched linens beneath paneled ceilings and frescoes. See p. 181.

- **Tantris,** Munich: When a restaurant receives a Michelin star for something like 25 years, you can safely assume that it's a great place to eat. Tantris's Hans Haas is one of Germany's top chefs, and his restaurant serves the most innovative food in Bavaria. See p. 118.

- **Tigerpalast Gourmet Restaurant,** Frankfurt: Part of a long-running cabaret/revue, the Tigerpalast lets you combine exceptional dining with wonderful entertainment in an environment that you won't find anywhere else. See p. 209.

- **Vau,** Berlin: Chef Kolja Kleeberg took over Vau in 2002 and brought new prestige—in the form of a Michelin star—to this sleek restaurant in eastern Berlin. The cooking at Vau is refined but not fussy, and a meal here is a quiet, enjoyable event. See p. 52.

- **Weinhaus Zum Stachel,** Würzburg: The oldest (ca. 1413) wine house in a town loaded with them. The food's good, the portion's copious, the wine flows, and everyone has a wonderful time. Old-time Germany at its most appealing. See p. 139.

- **Zur Baumwolle,** Nürnberg: Pork roast with dumplings and sauerkraut and other rustic favorites keep a loyal crowd of locals happy; you'll share tables with them in lamp-lit, wood-beamed cozy surroundings. See p. 151.

GERMANY'S best HOTELS

- **Bayerischer Hof & Palais Montgelas,** Munich: Munich's oldest and largest hotel was built in the 1840s to house guests of King Ludwig I. You may feel a bit anonymous in the hallways of this enormous five-star labyrinth or want to strew breadcrumbs to find your way back to the elevators, but your room will provide you with

11

luxurious comfort, and the hotel will provide you with a huge rooftop pool, a spa complex, and all the services and amenities you could possibly want—even breadcrumbs, if you request them. See p. 109.

o **Der Europäische Hof-Hotel Europa,** Heidelberg: Gracious, stylish, and one of Germany's best offers no end of comforts in its enormous, handsomely furnished guest rooms where crystal and marble are standard equipment. Service is attentive but never stuffy, and an indoor rooftop pool rounds off a very long list of amenities. See p. 180.

o **East,** Hamburg: Style has soul in this sophisticated redo of a formidable, red-brick early-20th-century iron foundry, where edgy design elements make rooms as comfortable and functional as they are attractive. A soaring, multilevel Eurasian restaurant is just one of many exciting in-house relaxation spaces. See p. 86.

o **Excelsior Hotel Ernst,** Cologne: That luxurious breakfast buffet you have to pay for in other luxury hotels is complimentary at the Excelsior Hotel Ernst. Cologne's most convenient luxury hotel has rooms with views of the Gothic spires of Cologne Cathedral, beautiful decor, and staff members who go out of their way to make your stay worth the price. See p. 221.

o **The George,** Hamburg: Here's proof that accommodations can be urbane and soothing at the same time. One of the city's most relaxing bar/lounges, a sleek rooftop spa, and a sophisticated library are matched by dark and handsome guest rooms that come with terraces and many other nice perks. See p. 84.

o **Hotel Am Josephsplatz,** Nürnberg: Germany has no shortage of cozy little guesthouses, but it's especially refreshing to find one in the midst of a busy city. These wood-floored, nicely furnished accommodations are a great base from which to explore the surrounding streets and squares. See p. 150.

o **Hotel Anno 1216,** Lübeck: Staying in this former guildhall, where sleek, contemporary furnishings offset heavy timbers, stuccoed ceilings, frescoes, and other treasures, seems like a real privilege. The magic continues when you step outside onto streets lined with one of Europe's largest assemblages of landmarks from the Middle Ages. See p. 100.

o **Hotel Chelsea,** Cologne: It's not grand, it's not luxurious, and it's not quite in the center of Cologne, but the rooms have been smartly designed in a modern, minimalist style, staff members are friendly and helpful, and there's a cozy cafe attached to the hotel. See p. 222.

o **Louis Hotel,** Munich: This chic urban inn with rooms overlooking Munich's Viktualienmarkt features a wonderful Japanese restaurant and a summertime roof terrace. See p. 112.

o **Lux 11,** Berlin: An excellent location near Alexanderplatz; large, modern, comfortable rooms and suites with kitchenettes; and a hip, youthful vibe make Lux 11 a great choice for longer stays in Berlin. See p. 47.

o **The Mandala,** Berlin: Just off Potsdamer Platz, this quietly elegant luxury hotel is a winner on many fronts. The location is central, the decor is calm and comfortable, the rooms are among the largest in Berlin, there's a spa with sauna, and the on-site bar and restaurant are both noteworthy. See p. 47.

o **Mandarin Oriental,** Munich: Comfort and service is what this memorable boutique hotel tucked into Munich's Altstadt is all about, and it excels at both. Large, comfortable, high-ceilinged rooms; a Michelin-starred restaurant; and a rooftop swimming pool are among its amenities, and the location across from the Hofbräuhaus and steps from Marienplatz couldn't be more central. See p. 112.

o **Orphée Grosses Haus,** Regensburg: A trio of related accommodations in one of Germany's most beautiful medieval cities combine opulence, style, comfort, Bavarian hospitality in an enchanting collection of accommodations. See p. 160.

o **Wedina,** Hamburg: A good hotel makes its guests feel at home, and these moderately priced accommodations do so in four townhouses on a dignified St. Georg district street just off the Alster. You can choose the surroundings that suit you best, be it a comfy room facing an urban garden or a snazzy tri-level modernist suite. A library is one of many other homey touches. See p. 85.

GERMANY ITINERARIES

2

Wondering where to go in Germany? That, of course, depends on what you want to see and do. But here are some ideas—some show off the highlights, others focus on a few regions, others cater to some special interests, whether that's tasting wine or showing the kids medieval castles.

GERMAN HIGHLIGHTS IN 1 WEEK

This 7-day tour begins in Munich and ends in Berlin, showing off the best of southern and northern Germany and introducing the country's two greatest cities, two of King Ludwig II's castles, and a mighty river, the Rhine, as it flows past the lively city of Cologne. Our preferred mode of transport is train, a comfortable and efficient way to get anywhere you want to go in Germany.

Day 1: Munich

Spend your first day in marvelous **Munich** (see chapter 6). Head first for **Marienplatz** (p. 119), the city's main square. You can go up to the top of the **Rathaus** (p. 119) tower for a bird's-eye view, watch the **Glockenspiel,** and visit the nearby **Frauenkirche** (p. 122), Munich's largest church. Then walk over to the adjacent **Viktualienmarkt** (p. 127), one of the greatest food markets in Europe. Browse around and find a place for lunch from among the dozens of possibilities in the area. Afterward, make your way to the **Asamkirche** (p. 119) for a glimpse of the rococo ornamentation for which southern Germany is famous. In the afternoon, choose a museum: If you're an art lover, you may want to see the priceless collection of old masters at the **Alte Pinakothek** (p. 124); if you're interested in science and technology, make your way to the famous **Deutsches Museum** (p. 126). If you're in the mood for oom-pah-pah, have dinner at the fun-loving **Hofbräuhaus am Platzl** (p. 115). Munich is one of Germany's top cultural capitals, so you may want to end your evening at a concert or the opera.

Day 2: More Munich

Start your second day in a palace. You need the entire morning to wander through the enormous **Residenz** (p. 123) in central Munich. Or make an easy excursion to beautiful **Schloss Nymphenburg** (p. 134) which you can reach by streetcar. If you choose Nymphenburg, allow some extra time to wander through the gardens, and be sure to visit the collection of carriages, which includes the ornate sleighs and coaches used by King Ludwig II of Bavaria, creator of Neuschwanstein Castle. Have lunch near Marienplatz. In the afternoon, choose another museum to visit. Two possibilities are the **Neue Pinakothek** (p. 124), a showcase for 19th-century German and European art, and the newly restored **Lenbachhaus** (p. 126), with its stunning collection of early German Expressionist art. At some point, fit in a stroll in the bucolic **Englischer Garten,** Munich's oldest, largest and prettiest park. You can relax at the park's famous beer garden.

Day 3: Bavarian Alps

Head to the **Bavarian Alps** (see chapter 7), just south of Munich. Arrive in **Garmisch-Partenkirchen** in time to ascend the **Zugspitze,** Germany's highest peak, for a spectacular view of the Alps. No exertion required: You'll make the trip on cog railway and cable car.

Day 4: Füssen

Make your way to **Füssen,** jumping off point for Neuschwanstein and Hohen-schwangau castles. Try to arrive early, and make **Neuschwanstein** your first stop; Germany's most popular tourist attraction quickly fills up with tourists as the day wears on. You can easily make the 6.5km (4-mile) trip from Füssen to the castle by bus. Tours of King Ludwig II's fairy-tale castle take about 1 hour. If you're still in a "royal" mood, visit adjacent **Hohenschwangau Castle,** Ludwig's child-hood home. Enjoy a nice stroll around medieval Füssen before settling into a weinstub for dinner.

Day 5: Cologne

Hop on the train and make your way to **Cologne** (see chapter 9) on the River Rhine in western Germany. By fast train, the trip from Munich takes about 5 hours. You'll see Cologne's greatest sight—the enormous **Dom** (**Cathedral;** p. 225)—as soon as you step out of the train station. Enjoy the afternoon in this lively Rhine-side city by visiting the awe-inspiring cathedral and one of its many fine museums, such as the **Römisch-Germanisches Museum** (**Roman-Germanic Museum;** p. 227), dedicated to the Romans who made Cologne one of their strategic forts nearly 2,000 years ago; the **Wallraf-Richartz Museum** (p. 228), displaying old and modern masters; and **Museum Ludwig** (p. 227), entirely devoted to 20th-century and contemporary art. You can also take a sight-seeing **boat ride** (p. 230) along the Rhine. Stay overnight in Cologne and have dinner at one of the city's famous beer halls (be sure to sample *Kölsch,* Cologne's delicious beer). The city has an excellent music scene, too, so you may want to see an opera or attend a concert.

Day 6: Berlin

In the morning, take one of the sleek, superfast trains to **Berlin** (see chapter 4). The trip takes about 4½ hours. Huge, sophisticated Berlin has endless things to do (for additional ideas, see "Northern Germany in 1 Week," below). Settle into your hotel and then take one of the sightseeing **bus tours** (p. 64) of the city—oth-erwise you'll see only a fraction of this enormous metropolis. After your tour, make your way over to the **Brandenburg Gate** (p. 57), the symbol of the city, and the nearby **Reichstag** (p. 62), the country's parliamentary headquarters. Take the elevator up to the modern dome on top of the Reichstag for a fabulous view over Berlin (the dome is open late, so you can come back later if the line is long).

From the Reichstag, walk east down **Unter den Linden** (p. 41) to **Museumsinsel (Museum Island),** and stop in at the **Pergamon Museum** (p. 64) for a look at the massive Pergamon Altar, and/or the **Neues Museum** (p. 63), with its world-class collection of Egyptian antiquities, including the celebrated bust of Queen Nefertiti, one of Berlin's greatest treasures. Berlin is famed for its nightlife, so when darkness falls you may want to attend an opera, a concert, or a cabaret.

Day 7: Berlin

Here's hoping your flight home departs sometime in the afternoon, so you can take advantage of the morning by going over to the western side of Berlin to stroll down **Kurfürstendamm,** the renowned boulevard known locally as Ku'Damm, before making your way to the airport.

NORTHERN & SOUTHERN GERMANY IN 2 WEEKS

This itinerary makes a clockwise circuit of Germany, from Berlin, to Hamburg in the far north, south to Munich and its scenic surroundings, and finally west to the romantic town of Heidelberg and the Schwarzwald (Black Forest).

Day 1: Berlin

Germany's capital and largest city, is the starting point of your 2-week tour of Deutschland. Follow the suggestions for Berlin in the 1-week itinerary until late afternoon and then from Museumsinsel, you can walk to **Friedrichstrasse,** the upscale shopping street of eastern Berlin, or visit the **East Side Gallery,** the longest preserved section of the Berlin Wall. Or, if the day is clear, you might want to walk over to Alexanderplatz and zoom up to the observation deck of the **Fernsehturm (Television Tower),** the tallest structure in western Europe.

Day 2: Berlin

Spend your second day on the western side of the city. Head over to the Charlottenburg neighborhood for a tour of **Schloss (Palace) Charlottenburg** (p. 56) and a stroll through the palace gardens. Make your way back to the **Kurfürstendamm** (known as Ku'Damm; p. 40), the most famous boulevard in western Berlin, for lunch or to find a cafe for *Kaffee und Kuchen* (coffee and cake). Stop by the **Kaiser-Wilhelm Gedächtniskirche (Kaiser Wilhelm Memorial Church;** p. 53), left as a colossal ruin after the devastation of World War II. Then spend a while strolling in the **Tiergarten,** Berlin's most famous park. Have something fun lined up for the evening: Berlin has three opera houses, seven symphony orchestras, cabarets, variety shows, and countless bars and clubs.

Day 3: Day Trip to Potsdam

Give yourself at least 4 hours for this excursion (take the S-Bahn), which includes a tour of and **Schloss Sanssouci** (p. 72), Frederick the Great's rococo palace, and a stroll through the landscaped grounds. You can eat near the palace or in the charming town of Potsdam. In the afternoon, visit one of Berlin's great museums, such as the **Gemäldegalerie (Painting Gallery;** p. 53) or the **Jüdisches Museum (Jewish Museum;** p. 60), where Germany's Jewish life is chronicled and commemorated through art and artifacts.

Day 4: Day Trip to Dresden

On the Elbe River about 2 hours south of Berlin by train, Dresden is one of the great art cities of Germany. You want to focus your attention on the **Albertinum** (p. 76), a vast collection of treasures accrued by Saxon rulers; the famed treasury known as the **Grünes Gewolbe** (**Green Vault;** p. 76) in the Residenzschloss; and the **Zwinger** (p. 77), a restored royal palace that is home to four museums, the most important being the **Gemäldegalerie Alte Meister** (**Old Masters Gallery;** p. 77). Make it a point to see the **Frauenkirche** (**Church of Our Lady;** p. 76), which reopened in 2006 after being painstakingly restored.

Day 5: Hamburg

From Berlin, head north to **Hamburg** (see chapter 5), about 1½ hours by fast train. You don't have a lot of time to see this spread-out metropolis, so sign onto to two tours: A hop-on, hop-off bus tour will show off the sights and gets you to some of the places you want to see and a cruise takes you through the harbor, one of the world's busiest, that has kept Hamburg on the map of commerce for centuries. Where you choose to spend time depends on your tastes, but top stops are the **Kunsthalle** (p. 92), an outstanding collection of old masters and modern works, and **HafenCity** (p. 94), a new waterside quarter that's transforming the city. Come nightfall, there's only one place to go: Any one who comes to Hamburg must make at least one foray into **St. Pauli,** where the Reeperbahn, Europe's most famous red-light district, is ground zero for salacious nightlife.

Day 6: Lübeck

A short trip from Hamburg, this port on the Baltic Sea boasts more buildings from the 13th to the 15th centuries than any other city in northern Germany—more than just about anywhere else in Europe, for that matter, since it's said that within an area of 5 sq. km (2 sq. miles) around the Marktplatz stand 1,000 medieval houses.

Day 7: Munich

The trip from Hamburg takes fewer than 6 hours by train and is a wonderful way to sit back, relax, and watch the scenery change from north to south. With only an evening and day in Munich, you have to make some decisions about what to see. Start your explorations at **Marienplatz** (p. 119), the city's main square, and then head over to the adjacent **Viktualienmarkt** (p. 127) to wander through this wonderland of an outdoor market. Choose a museum you'd especially like to visit: Most visitors make the **Alte Pinakothek** (**Old Masters Gallery;** p. 124) their top priority, but the **Deutsches Museum** (p. 126), devoted to science and industry, is one of the most popular museums in the country. Stay overnight in Munich. You have innumerable ways to spend the evening in this cultural mecca: opera, symphony, pop concerts, theater, beer halls, beer gardens, and clubs.

Day 8: More Munich

Start the day with a self-guided tour of the **Residenz** (p. 123), the gigantic "city palace" of Bavaria's former rulers, the Wittelsbachs. You need at least 2 hours to visit the entire complex. After lunch near Marienplatz, stroll in the lovely **Englischer Garten** (p. 122) and stop for a drink or a meal at the park's famous beer garden. There are many other museums to choose from in Munich, including **Lenbachhaus** (p. 126), with its superb collection of German Expression art, and the Greek and Roman antiquities on display in the **Glyptothek** (p. 126).

Day 9: Regensburg

A bit off the beaten path, this is one of Germany's best-preserved medieval cities and the only one to remain completely unscathed by World War II bombings. Some 1,400 medieval buildings have survived and create a jumble of steep, red-tiled roofs above narrow lanes and lively squares next to the Danube. Spend the day here taking it easy as you poke around the Altstadt.

Day 10: Füssen

Make your way back to Munich and on to **Füssen** (see chapter 7), 6.5km (4 miles) from the most famous tourist attraction in all of Germany: Ludwig II's **Neuschwanstein Castle** (p. 176). Give yourself some leeway with time because the crowds (especially in summer) can be dense (you might want to visit the castle early on the morning of Day 11 before the crowds arrive). You can also tour neighboring **Hohenschwangau Castle** (p. 175), where Ludwig spent his childhood. If local bus connections work in your favor, squeeze in a visit the nearby **Wieskirche (Church in the Meadow),** a baroque masterpiece.

Day 11: Heidelberg

The trip today takes about 4 hours and will get you to this ancient university town on the Neckar River by mid- to late afternoon—just in time for a stroll through the **Altstadt (Old Town),** which looks much as it did a century ago, with a mixture of architectural styles ranging from the Gothic to the Neoclassical. Find your way up to **Heidelberg Castle** (p. 183), a romantic hilltop ruin with a view down to the tiled roofs of the Altstadt nestled alongside the river. Back in the Altstadt, a stop at the **Kurpfälzisches Museum (Museum of the Palatinate;** p. 184) gives you a look at Tilman Riemenschneider's masterful wooden altarpiece of Christ and the Apostles, dating from 1509.

Day 12: Heidelberg & a Side Trip to Baden-Baden

Begin the day in the **Marktplatz** (p. 182), the Altstadt's main square, dominated by the Gothic **Heiliggeistkirche (Church of the Holy Spirit;** p. 182). Cross the **Alte Brücke (Old Bridge)** and stroll along Philosophenweg (Philosopher's Way), a 250-year-old promenade that provides a view of romantic Heidelberg from the other side of the Neckar. Then head south to Baden-Baden, the glamorous spa resort at the edge of the Black Forest where people were getting into hot water as far back as the Roman era, when the emperor Caracalla came to soak his arthritic bones in the thermal pools. You can "take the waters" at **Friedrichsbad,** a 125-year-old mineral-bath establishment; the experience takes about 3½ hours.

Day 13: Nuremberg

Hop on the train in Heidelberg and in about 3 hours, you're in **Nuremberg** (see chapter 7), one of the most attractive mid-size cities in Germany, where the entire **Altstadt** is a pedestrian zone. Squares with lovely fountains, Gothic churches, and the picturesque precincts alongside the Pegnitz River are below the **Kaiserburg (Imperial Castle;** p. 152). Collections at the Germanisches Nationalmuseum (Germanic National Museum) include works by Renaissance great Albrecht Dürer, whose house is here, and the Dokumentationszentrum Reichsparteitagsgelände (Nazi Rally Grounds Documentation Center), housed in the former Nazi Congress Hall, provides a chronological overview of the rise of Nazism.

Day 11: Berlin

Head back to **Berlin,** where your tour began, to catch your flight home. The train ride from Nuremberg is about 5½ hours. (Alternatively, you can fly home from Frankfurt, a little more than 2 hr. by train from Nuremberg, or from Munich, under 2 hr. from Nuremberg.)

NORTHERN GERMANY IN 1 WEEK

This week-long itinerary includes Berlin, the most exciting city in Europe (and the third-most popular after London and Paris), and the Hanseatic cities of Hamburg and Lübeck. We're adding Dresden, a good day trip from Berlin. These northern cities are relatively close to one another but worlds apart in terms of culture and atmosphere.

Days 1, 2 & 3: Berlin

When it comes to exploring the endlessly fascinating city of **Berlin** (see chapter 4), 3 days is hardly enough, but even a short visit will provide you with an introduction and make you want to return. This itinerary presents different options from the Berlin itineraries in the 1-week and 2-week itineraries above; have a look at those, too, for more ideas on how to spend your 2 days.

Germany's capital is celebrating the 25th anniversary of the fall of the Berlin Wall in 2014, with a year-long roster of events that culminates on November 9, the actual anniversary date. If you are interested in the rise and fall of the Wall, there are many places you can visit to gain a better understanding of what it was and what it meant. The longest remaining section of the Wall is the **East Side Gallery** (p. 62), a veritable outdoor art gallery painted by dozens of international artists. Another spot to visit is the **Berlin Wall Memorial/Berliner Mauer Dokumentationszentrum** (p. 62), a reconstructed stretch of the Wall with a memorial building that documents where the Wall stood and what it actually looked like. A third possibility is the **Mauermuseum Haus am Checkpoint Charlie (Berlin Wall Museum at Checkpoint Charlie;** p. 61), a small museum at the former crossing into East Berlin. Finally, for a glimpse—albeit a somewhat nostalgic one—of what life in the Deutsche Demokratische Republik (DDR) of East Berlin, spend an hour or two in the **DDR Museum** (p. 57), devoted to the Soviet-inspired objects in everyday use in the DDR. Visiting all four of these sites will take up an entire day.

On one of your 3 Berlin days you'll want to make a stop at the iconic **Brandenburger Tor (Brandenburg Gate;** p. 57) and nearby **Reichstag** (p. 62), where you can ascend to the glass dome for a great view of the city. Afterwards, art lovers should allow at least 2 hours to visit the European masterworks on display in the **Gemäldegalerie (Painting Gallery;** p. 53), in the Kulturforum complex. You probably won't have time to visit all five museums comprising Berlin's **Museumsinsel (Museum Island;** p. 63), so concentrate on two of them: the **Neues Museum** (p. 63), with its superlative collection of Egyptian antiquities and the 2,500-year-old bust of Queen Nefertiti, one of Berlin's greatest treasures; and the **Pergamon Museum,** with its famous Greek altars, Roman city gates, and Babylonian processional walls.

Day 4: Day Trip to Potsdam

Head here to see **Schloss Sanssouci** (p. 72), Frederick the Great's beautiful baroque palace. Give yourself at least 4 hours to tour the palace, stroll through the landscaped grounds, and explore a bit of Potsdam, the 1,000-year-old city that is the capital of Brandenburg. In the evening, back in Berlin, consider attending a concert, an opera, or just chill out at a nice bar or café.

Day 5: Day Trip to Dresden

You can get there by train from Berlin in a couple of hours, but make certain you leave Berlin early because there is so much to see in Dresden. Concentrate on three places, all of them loaded with art treasures: the **Albertinum,** the **Grünes Gewolbe (Green Vaults),** and the **Zwinger** palace with its **Gemäldegalerie Alte Meister (Old Masters Gallery).**

Day 6: Hamburg

Board a train at Berlin's Hauptbahnhof for the 2-hour trip to **Hamburg** (see chapter 5). You'll have an afternoon to take in some sights, and to get an idea of what this appealing port city is all about, take a harbor cruise to see the wharves, cranes, and huge ships that keep Hamburg on the map as Europe's second-largest port (after Rotterdam). For your last evening in Germany take a walk on the wild side down the Reeperbahn, the city's famous (or infamous) Red Light district.

Day 7: Flight Home

From Hamburg, board a fast train back to Berlin or Frankfurt.

THE SCENIC SOUTH IN 1 WEEK

This itinerary highlights a clutch of towns and cities along and just off the Romantic Road, a scenic route the rambles through much of rural Bavaria, past meadows and forests to medieval towns and cities before ascending into the Alps. Give yourself an unhurried day and night in each place. You can easily do this trip by train in a week.

Day 1: Würzburg

For many Germans, the south begins in this small, lively city stretching along the River Main. University students add life to the narrow lanes and bright squares and lend a German version of joie de vivre. Würzburg's appreciation of the good life become clear as soon as you notice the town is swathed in vineyards that climb the surrounding hillsides above its gabled rooftops and produce a dry, fruity white wine. On an easy walk through the Altstadt you'll come upon the **Residenz** (p. 141), one of the largest and most impressive Baroque palaces in Germany; the 10th-century **Dom St. Kilian** (p. 140); and the **Rathaus (Town Hall;** p. 140), a 13th-century building with a 16th-century painted facade. The nearly 500-year-old **Alte Mainbrücke (Old Main Bridge;** p. 140) crosses the Main River to a path that climbs the vineyard-covered slopes to **Festung Marienberg (Marienberg Fortress;** p. 140), the hilltop stronghold where the prince-bishops lived and now home to the **Mainfränkisches Museum (Franconian Museum of the Main;** p. 141) worth visiting primarily to see the collection of remarkably expressive wood sculptures by Tilman Riemenschneider, a 16th-century master woodcarver

Day 2: Rothenburg-ob-der-Tauber

For sheer historical panache, no other city in Germany can match **Rothenburg-ob-der-Tauber,** a little over an hour from Würzburg by train. For an introduction to this walled medieval city located on a high promontory above the Tauber River, take a walk on a portion of the town ramparts from the massive 16th-century **Spitalbastei** (a medieval tower-gate) to the **Klingenbastei** (another tower-gate). Down at street level there are plenty of picturesque nooks and crannies to explore, as well as the Gothic **St.-Jakobskirche (Church of St. James),** with a masterful altarpiece created by the Würzburg sculptor Tilman Riemenschneider. As you're walking, look for a Rothenburg specialty called Schneeballen (snowballs)—crisp, round pastries covered with powdered sugar. You can buy them in bakeries all across town.

Day 3: Nürnberg

This fascinating city of half a million residents is about 70 minutes by train from Rothenburg. It's large enough to offer several worthwhile attractions, small enough so that you can see everything in a day, and has a nice urban buzz. As you wander through the streets of this ancient capital of the Holy Roman Empire, you'll find reminders of Nuremberg's brightest period–the Renaissance, when it bloomed as an artistic powerhouse–and its darkest, when it was the site of massive Nazi rallies.

Looming over the city is the Kaiserburg (Imperial Castle), the official residence of German kings and emperors from 1050 to 1571. The city's one must-see museum is the **Germanisches Nationalmuseum (Germanic National Museum;** p. 152), with collections that include works by Renaissance greats Veit Stoss and Albrecht Dürer, who lived in Nürnberg from 1509 to 1528. The colorful, cobblestoned Hauptmarkt (Market Square) is filled with stalls selling fruit, flowers, vegetables, and Lebkuchen, the delicious honey-and-spice cakes first created in Nuremberg over 500 years ago. On the square's eastern side is the **Frauenkirche (Church of Our Lady;** p. 153), whose 16th-century mechanical clock chimes the noontime hours as figures appear and pay homage to Emperor Karl IV. Just off the **Hauptmarkt** is the Altes Rathaus (Old Town Hall) and nearby are the twin-towered **St. Lorenz-Kirche (Church of St. Lawrence),** the largest and most beautiful Gothic church in Nuremberg, and the 13th-century **St. Sebaldus Kirche (St. Sebald Church;** p. 154), dedicated to Nuremberg's patron saint. Nuremberg's war-time history comes chillingly alive in the **Dokumentationszentrum Reichsparteitagsgelände (Nazi Rally Grounds Documentation Center;** p. 152), housed in the former Nazi Congress Hall and providing a chronological overview of the rise of Nazism.

Day 4: Regensburg

With some 1,400 medieval buildings, **Regensburg** (about an hour by train from Nurnberg with good connections) is the largest medieval city in Germany and the only one to survive World War II completely intact. Situated at the northernmost point of the Danube River, it's a lovely little city slightly removed from the restless hustle of modern life. Your explorations inevitably lead to the 12th-century **Steinerne Brücke (Stone Bridge;** p. 161), spanning the Danube and providing panoramic views of the Altstadt (Old Town).

Day 5: Augsburg

A stroll through **Augsburg,** 2½ hours by train from Regensburg, reveals an attractive urban landscape loaded with historic buildings, charming corners, and the lively ambience of a university town. Rathausplatz, the city's main square, is dominated by the 17th-century **Rathaus (Town Hall; p.** 164) and adjacent **Perlachturm (Perlach Tower),** capped by a distinctive dome called an "Augsburg onion." The Fuggerei, the world's first almshouse-complex, was built in 1523 and still in use today. **Dom St. Maria** (p. 163), Augsburg's cathedral, displays paintings by Hans Holbein the Elder and contains some of the oldest stained glass in Germany.

Day 6: Füssen

By train you can get from Augsburg to **Füssen** in about 2 hours. The town has lovely squares and narrow cobblestone streets, and is a place to headquarter while exploring the nearby fairy-tale castle of **Neuschwanstein** (p. 176) built by King Ludwig II. You can easily make the 6.5km (4-mile) trip from Füssen to the castle by bus. Tours of Germany's most popular attraction take about 1 hour. If you're still in a "royal" mood, visit adjacent **Hohenschwangau Castle** (p. 175), Ludwig's childhood home.

Day 7: Garmisch-Partenkirchen

Your final stop are the two side-by-side villages of **Garmisch-Partenkirchen** that make up Germany's top Alpine resort to ski, to hike, to climb, or simply to gaze at some spectacular mountain scenery. Unless you plan on strapping on a pair of skis to test your meddle on a high-altitude run, the biggest thrill you're likely to have is ascending the **Zugspitze,** Germany's highest mountain, via cog railway and cable car.

DISCOVERING GERMANY WITH KIDS

Taking a train, visiting a castle, walking through market, even riding the U-Bahn—a lot about Germany will appeal to kids, and to their parents, too. Many hotels let children stay for free in their parents' room, or for a few euros more; public transportation offers reduced rates for kids; and all museums and attractions offer at least a half-price reduction for children.

Days 1 & 2: Munich

Spend your first days in **Munich** (see chapter 6). The entire inner city is a car-free pedestrian zone where you and your kids can stroll with ease. There are plenty of outdoor cafes around **Marienplatz** (p. 119), the city's main square; while there, be sure to catch the **Glockenspiel** show (p. 124) at 11am on the spire of the **Rathaus.** Right next to Marienplatz is the **Viktualienmarkt** (p. 127), the best outdoor market in Germany and a great place to have a casual lunch. Later, you may want to take a tram or subway over to the **Englischer Garten (English Garden;** p. 122), one of the largest and most beautiful city parks in Europe, where you can wander along the tree-shaded walks, run in the meadows, or sit in the famous beer garden (nonalcoholic refreshments available for the kids). You should also head over to the kid-friendly **Deutsches Museum,** the largest science and technology museum in the world. It's loaded with interesting stuff for kids and adults, including a room with an elaborate model train. On a visit to the **Spielzeugmuseum (Toy Museum;** p. 119), in the Altes Rathaus on Marienplatz, your technologically savvy offspring can marvel (or not) at historic toys that have nothing to do with computers or flashy animation.

Day 3: More Munich

Schloss Nymphenburg (p. 134) is on the top of your list today. The *Schloss* (palace) is a breeze to get to (it's right in the city on the streetcar line), and **Nymphenburg Park** (p. 134) behind the palace is grand and inviting, with gardens and an English-style park with forested paths, and some intriguing buildings, including an 18th-century swimming pool and a baroque hunting lodge. There's also a museum with ornate carriages and sleighs that might trigger memories or fantasies of fairy tales. If you didn't make it to the Deutsches Museum the day before, you might want to head over there in the afternoon, or to the **Deutsches Museum Verkehnszemtrum (Transportation Museum;** p. 127), where your kids can see how people got around in the days before cars, and also what early bicycles and cars looked like.

Day 4: Garmisch-Partenkirchen

Take the train to **Garmisch-Partenkirchen** (see chapter 7) in the Bavarian Alps south of Munich. First order of business is to ascend the **Zugspitze** (p. 168), Germany's highest peak (2,960m/9,720 ft.). A cog railway and a cable car take you up and bring you back—a fascinating treat for kids. The view from the summit is—what else?—spectacular. If you and your kids enjoy hiking, the area around Garmisch-Partenkirchen is great hiking country, with all levels of trails. Most hikes take an energetic 4 to 5 hours, but some of them are shorter and easy enough for children. Stay overnight in Garmisch. Good skiing and ice-skating in the enormous **Eiszentrum** (p. 168), used for the 1936 Winter Olympics, are available all winter.

Day 5: Füssen

Take the train to **Füssen,** near Garmisch-Partenkirchen, and from there a bus to **Neuschwanstein** (p. 176), "Mad" Ludwig's fairy-tale castle. Germany's most-visited tourist attraction perches on a rocky spur that requires a good uphill hike to reach. You also can also reach the castle by bus or horse-drawn cab. The forested hills all around Neuschwanstein and neighboring **Hohenschwangau Castle** (p. 175) are full of excellent hiking paths. Stay overnight in Füssen and explore the charming old town on foot.

Days 6 & 7: Freiburg

Ride the train to **Freiburg** (see chapter 8), your headquarters in the **Schwarzwald (Black Forest).** Consider renting a car for just 1 day: From Freiburg you can make an easy 145km (90-mile) circuit through a scenic part of the Schwarzwald, with stops for short hikes and cable-car rides to the top of the **Belchen,** a famous mile-high peak with spectacular views of the Rhine plain, and to the 1,450m (4,750-ft.) summit of a peak called **Seebuck.** You can also stop at two Black Forest lakes, the **Schluchsee** and **Titisee.**

Day 8: Head Home

Make your way back to Frankfurt or Munich for the trip home. How about that—the kids actually had a good time!

PROSIT! GERMANY FOR WINE LOVERS

When you raise a glass of wine in Germany, the toast is a simple *"Prosit!"* (pronounced *prohst*). This itinerary takes you to the wine regions in western Germany and begins and ends in Frankfurt. On boat rides on the Rhine and Mosel rivers you will cruise past some of Germany's most noted vineyards.

Day 1: Freiburg

From Frankfurt airport, hop on a train for the 2-hour trip to **Freiburg** (see chapter 8), a lively university town in the Black Forest. Freiburg is surrounded by 1,600 acres of vineyards, more than any other city in Germany. On the last weekend in June, the city celebrates with a **4-day wine festival** that includes public tastings. **Weinkost** is another wine-tasting event in mid-August. Most of the grapes grow on the warm lower slopes of the nearby **Kaiserstühl (Emperor's Throne),** a volcanic massif. The young, light Silvaner wine is an ideal accompaniment to *Spargel* (white or green asparagus) in May. For a great meal with regional wines, dine at **Zum Roten Bären,** the oldest inn in Freiburg.

Day 2: Cologne

The train trip to Cologne takes about 4 hours. In the adjacent **Rheingau wine district,** a 45km (27-mile) stretch of the Rhine between the towns of **Wiesbaden** and **Bingen,** wine has been produced since Roman times, and Rheingau Rieslings rank among the best white wines made anywhere. You can take a Rhine cruise through the scenic winegrowing region between Koblenz and Rüdesheim or Bingen (see "Day Trips from Cologne," in chapter 9), stopping at either one of those towns to sample the local vintage and enjoy traditional Rhineland fare.

Days 3 & 4: The Mosel Valley

Southwest of Cologne, this is another scenic winegrowing region. You can easily make this a day trip from Cologne. The valley follows the course of the Mosel River for more than 160km (100 miles) between Koblenz and Trier. Beautiful scenery and fine wines make this a prime area for leisurely exploration. The easiest way to enjoy a **cruise on the Mosel River** is to take a train to Koblenz. Between late April and the third week in October, cruises depart daily from Koblenz to **Cochem,** a picturesque wine village surrounded by vineyards and a popular spot for wine tastings and festivals. **Mosel-Wein-Woche (Mosel Wine Week),** which takes place the first week in June, celebrates the region's wines with tasting booths and a street fair; **Weinfest** takes place the last weekend of August. The half-timbered **Alte Thorschenke** in Cochem, both a hotel and a wine restaurant, is one of the oldest and best-known establishments along the Mosel.

Day 5: Frankfurt

From Cochem, Cologne, or Freiburg, make your way back to **Frankfurt.** If you have a few more days, you can continue your tasting tour of Germany. Wherever you go, look for the local *Weinstube* (wine tavern), a convivial spot to sample Germany's many fine vintages.

GERMANY IN CONTEXT

E very country and every culture offers a unique opportunity— and sometimes a challenge—to enlarge one's personal experience and understanding of the world. Germany is no exception. The more you know about German life and German culture, the more enjoyable and rewarding your trip to Germany will be. This chapter provides useful background information to help you plan your trip and understand the country. Check out the major festivals and events to find out what's going on when. A section on German history arranges the country's long and complicated past into a concise, easy-to-digest chronology. We cross-reference highlights of German art and architecture to specific cities and sites to help you place these works in context, and introduce the best of German food, beer. Finally, we provide suggestions for other books and movies that deal with all aspects of German life.

3

WHEN TO GO

Peak travel months in Germany are May through October, with another boost in December when the Christmas markets are held and skiers head to the Bavarian Alps.

Weather

As in many parts of the world, the weather in Germany has become less predictable. Locals in northern Germany will tell you that they now get less snow and more rain, in southern Germany they'll tell you that the climate is hotter and drier than it used to be. So be prepared for variations. Recent summers brought record-breaking heat waves and even in autumn many parts of Germany can be warmer than expected. A hurricane-like storm swept over parts of northern Germany in October 2013.

Overall, Germany has a predominantly mild, temperate climate. Average summer temperatures range from 20°C–30°C (72°F–80°F). The average winter temperature hovers around 0°C (32°F). That said, bear in mind that the climate is constantly affected by colliding continental and maritime air masses from the Baltic and North seas, resulting in plenty of unpredictable weather, especially in the north.

Festivals & Special Events

There's more to Germany than Oktoberfest. Germany hums year-round with festivals and special events of all kinds, and these can add an additional sparkle to your trip. Below are a few of the major festivals and special events.

JANUARY

New Year's Day International Ski Jumping in Garmisch-Partenkirchen (p. 165) is one of Europe's major winter sporting events. www.gapa.de. January 1.

FEBRUARY

Berlin International Film Festival lasts for a week and showcases the work of international film directors in addition to the latest German films. www.berlinale.de. Second week in February.

Fasching (Carnival) festivals take place in Catholic cities throughout Germany, reaching their peak on the Tuesday (Mardi Gras) before Ash Wednesday. Celebrations in Cologne (see chapter 9) and Munich (see chapter 6) are particularly famous. A week in February.

MAY

Hamburg Sommer is the umbrella name given to a summer-long series of cultural events in Hamburg (see chapter 5), including concerts, plays, festivals, and special exhibitions. www.hamburg.de/dom. May through July.

Historisches Festspiel (History Festival), Rothenburg ob der Tauber (p. 142), celebrates the story of how a brave citizen saved the town from destruction by drinking a huge tankard of wine (an event called *Der Meistertrunk*). www.meistertrunk.de. Events take place over a 4-day period every Whitsuntide (Pentecost, the seventh Sunday after Easter), in early September, and twice in October.

Oberammergau Passionspiele (Passion Play), a world-famous religious spectacle performed in the small Bavarian town of Oberammergau (p. 169) every decade, will next be performed in 2020. www.oberammergau-passionplay.com. May through October.

JUNE

Heidelberg Castle Illumination During this week, fireworks enliven the sky in the romantic university city of Heidelberg (p. 178). www.schloss-heidelberg.de. One Saturday in early June, mid-July, and early September.

Mozart Festival in Würzburg (p. 135) is a major cultural event in Germany. www.mozartfest.de. Early June to early July.

Gay Pride festivals, featuring parades, performances, and street fairs, take place in Berlin (see chapter 4), which hosts the largest such fest in Germany and Cologne (see chapter 9). Berlin's celebration is the last weekend in June; Cologne, first weekend in June.

JULY

Schleswig-Holstein Music Festival One of the best music festivals in Europe, classical concerts take place in venues in and around the lovely old city of Lübeck (p. 99). www.shmf.de. Mid-July through August or early September.

Weinfest (Wine Festival) Enjoy vintages from the surrounding Black Forest area during this celebration in Freiburg (p. 195). Events take place in the Münsterplatz surrounding Freiburg's magnificent cathedral. www.weinfest.freiburg.de. First week of July.

Bayreuther Festspiele One of Europe's major opera events, the Bayreuther Festspiele (also known as the Richard Wagner Festival) takes place in the composer's famous Festspielhaus (opera house) in Bayreuth. www.bayreuther-festspiele.de. July through late August.

AUGUST

Weinkost (Food and Wine Fair) During this yearly event in Freiburg (p. 195), local residents and visitors enjoy the first vintages from grapes grown in the Black Forest district and regional food specialties. www.freiburg.de. Late July to early August.

Nürnberger Herbsvolksfest (Fall Folk Festival), a big Frankish folk festival in Nuremberg (p. 147), features folk music, jazz concerts, and events for the whole family. www.volksfest-nuernberg.de. Last week in August to the first week in September.

Rotweinfest (Red Wine Festival), held in the village of Assmannshausen on the scenic Mittelrhein (see "Day Trips from Cologne," chapter 9), celebrates the wines it is most famous for. www.assmannshausen. mittelrhein.net. Late August.

Musikfest Berlin, spread out over more than 2 weeks, plays host to orchestras, ensembles, conductors, and soloists from around the world. www.berlinerfestspiele. de. Late August to mid-September.

Alstervergnügen (Alster Pleasures) Arts and abound during in Hamburg's august fete (p. 79). Events, which take place around Binnenalster Lake, include food stalls, fireworks, and shows. www.alstervergnuegen. info. Last weekend in August.

Stuttgart Wine Festival Wine lovers converge on Schillerplatz in Stuttgart (p. 185) to taste a selection of more than 350 Württemberg wines and sample regional food specialties. www.stuttgart-tourist.de. Last week in August.

SEPTEMBER

Oktoberfest Germany's most famous beer festival, happens mostly in September, not October, in Munich (see chapter 6). Most activities occur at Theresienwiese, where local breweries sponsor giant tents, each holding up to 6,000 beer drinkers. www.oktoberfest.de. Mid-Sept to first Sunday in October.

Beer Festival Dating back to 1818, the 16-day Stuttgart's (p. 185) beerapalooza is the second largest in Germany after Munich's Oktoberfest. It begins with a grand procession of horse-drawn beer wagons and people in traditional costumes and features food, rides, and tents for beer drinkers. www.stuttgart-tourist.info. Late September.

OCTOBER

Frankfurt Book Fair The largest book fair in Europe, it's a major event in the world of international book publishing. www.buchmesse.de. Mid-October.

NOVEMBER

Jazz-Fest. Staged at various venues in Berlin, this annual music event attracts some of the world's finest jazz artists. www.berliner festspiele.de. First week in November.

Hamburger Dom (also called Winter Dom), an annual amusement fair at Heiligengeistfeld in Hamburg is the biggest public event in northern Germany. www.hamburg.de/dom. November through December.

DECEMBER

Christmas Markets, sometimes called a *Weihnachtsmarkt* (*Weihnachten* means Christmas) or a *Christkindlmarkt* (literally, "Christ Child Market"), take place in town squares throughout Germany. You find them in Berlin, Cologne, Dresden, Frankfurt, Heidelberg, Munich, Nuremberg, Rothenburg ob der Tauber, and Stuttgart, among other cities. www.visitgermany.com. Last weekend in November through Christmas.

Holidays

Public holidays are January 1, Easter (Good Fri and Easter Mon), May 1 (Labor Day), Ascension Day (10 days before Pentecost/Whitsunday, the seventh Sun after Easter), Whitmonday (day after Pentecost/Whitsunday), October 3 (Day of German Unity), November 17 (Day of Prayer and Repentance), December 25 (Christmas), and December 26. In addition, the following holidays are observed in some German states: January 6 (Epiphany), Corpus Christi (10 days after Pentecost), August 15 (Assumption), and November 1 (All Saints' Day).

A BRIEF HISTORY OF GERMANY

Germany Today

Germany's long and tumultuous history remains clouded by the horrors of World War II and the Holocaust. How a civilized European nation slipped into the state of barbaric inhumanity that existed during the Nazi era is a question that continues to haunt survivors, occupy historians, and shadow the Germans themselves. Memorials to the victims of the Holocaust are scattered throughout Germany, perhaps most poignantly at the sites of the Dachau and Auschwitz concentration camps.

As a result of that harrowing chapter in its modern history, which resulted in the devastation of its cities, the disarmament of its military machine, and the deaths of millions of people, Germany became a strongly pacifist country, and the use of military force in world conflicts always arouses controversy amongst its citizens.

The other big political issue that has affected Germany's contemporary consciousness is the separation of the country into two opposing regimes: capitalist West, communist East–from 1961 to 1989. The fall of the Berlin Wall in November, 1989, signaled an enormous shift in German life. Though most East Germans embraced the democratic changes that came with reunification, there were many who resented what they saw as a wholesale takeover of their country and who were suddenly exposed to the uncertainties and economic ruthlessness of a free-market economic system. By the time the Wall came down, East Germany was in many respects a broken country, a corrupt police-state with dwindling resources, decaying infrastructure, and a legacy of environmental pollution that will be a long-term challenge to clean up. The cost of reunification was far higher than predicted and took a toll on people's economic and emotional lives. Outdated, state-controlled industries that could not compete in a free market economy were scrapped, jobs were lost, crime–most troublingly, neo-Nazi hate crimes–rose. Yet Germany moved forward.

Today, it's one of the most prosperous country in Europe and has been for many years. A nation of savers, it never gave in to the easy-credit credo and had stronger

DATELINE

A.D. 1st century The Roman sphere of influence extends well into the borders of present-day Germany (Germania to the Romans), with garrisons established at Cologne, Koblenz, Mainz, and Trier.

A.D. 400 The Romans withdraw from Germany; in the following centuries, the empire of the Franks represents the transition from a loose conglomeration of German tribes into what eventually would become the German Empire.

ca. 800 Charlemagne (Karl der Grosse; 768–814) is responsible for the earliest large-scale attempt to unite the lands of Germany under one ruler.

ca. 900–1500 The power struggles and invasions of the Middle Ages continually disrupt the unity hammered out by Charlemagne. Until the demise of the Holy Roman Empire in 1806, Germany remains a collection of small principalities and free cities. An upswing in international commerce from the 11th to 13th regulations and more oversight in its banking industry. Germany is a country where labor unions remain strong despite attempts to whittle away their power.

And when it comes to sponsoring and supporting arts and culture, Germany is right there at the top. The generous subsidies that once helped every town and city to operate its own opera house and theatre have been reduced, in some cases eliminated, but the arts scene remains vigorous, part of a long tradition the Germans regard as essential.

Germany's Architecture

Germany's buildings span some 1,200 years of architectural history and were created in a number of different styles. (The Porta Nigra, a 1,800-year-old arched gateway in Trier, is Germany's only remaining Roman-era structure of any significance.) But Germany's rich architectural heritage suffered a devastating blow during World War II, when Allied bombing raids leveled entire cities and left many important buildings and churches in ruins. Some areas escaped damage, such as the medieval towns along the Romantic Road (see chapter 7), but the overall devastation affected nearly the entire country. Many historic buildings are painstaking postwar reconstructions. Here are examples from around Germany of the major architectural trends.

CAROLINGIAN & OTTONIAN (9TH–11TH C.)   The earliest manifestations of a discernibly Germanic architecture date from the period of Charlemagne's rule as king of the Franks (768–814) and Emperor of the West (800–14)—called the Carolingian era after Charlemagne. Constructed around 800, Charlemagne's Palatinate or Octagonal chapel in Aachen (p. 233) harkens back to earlier Byzantine models of building. During the Ottonian dynasty architecture developed more complex ground plans and a rational system was devised for dividing churches into a series of separate units, a method that was to be of consequence in Romanesque design.

ROMANESQUE (11TH–12TH C.)   Simple, clear forms, thick walls, and rounded arches signal Romanesque architecture, a building style adapted from earlier Roman models. The cathedral in Mainz (p. 217) and Dom St. Kilian (p. 140) in Würzburg are two of the largest Romanesque churches in Germany.

centuries leads to the foundation of "Free Imperial Cities" like Hamburg and Lübeck. The Gothic architectural style is imported from France and used for building Cologne Cathedral.

1500–1700   A time of social unrest and religious upheaval throughout Germany. Martin Luther (1483–1546) battles against the excesses of the Catholic Church and his work has far-reaching implications. As the Protestant Reformation spreads, the Catholic Church launches a Counter-Reformation that culminates in the bloody Thirty Years' War (1618–48), pitting the Protestant north against the Catholic south and affecting the whole of Europe. Albrecht Dürer (1471–1528) and Hans Holbein the Younger (1497–1543) are among the artists who spark an artistic Renaissance in Germany.

1700–1800   Under Frederick the Great (Friedrich der Grosse; 1740–86), Prussia gains status as a great European power. During this period, the works of German artists, writers, composers, and philosophers usher in the Age of Enlightenment.

continues

GOTHIC (13TH–16TH C.)   Cologne Cathedral (p. 225) is Germany's greatest example of Gothic architecture, a style developed in France and diffused throughout Europe. Compared to Romanesque, Gothic style is slender and daring, with pointed arches, soaring vaults and spires, and enormous windows. A simpler and more monumental kind of Gothic architecture, built of brick, predominates in northern Germany in cities such as Lübeck (p. 99).

RENAISSANCE (LATE 15TH–17TH C.)   Augsburg (p. 162) is one of the best cities in Germany to see Renaissance architecture, a style characterized by calm precision, orderly repeating lines, and classical decoration over windows and doors. Renaissance architecture was imported from Italy into southern Germany.

BAROQUE (17TH–18TH C.)   A decorative exuberance in curvy Baroque architecture sets it apart from the more sober Renaissance style. The Baroque flourished in Catholic, Counter-Reformation areas in the south of Germany. The Residenz (p. 141) in Würzburg and the palace of Sanssouci (p. 72) in Potsdam are two of the best examples in Germany. Munich abounds in the Baroque.

ROCOCO (18TH C.)   Notch up the elements of Baroque and you have Rococo, exemplified by curving walls and staggering amounts of gilded and stucco decoration. One of the most famous examples of flamboyant Rococo church architecture in Germany is the Wieskirche (p. 174) in Bavaria. The Rococo style was used in theatres of the time: The Altes Residenztheater (p. 123) in Munich is one of the best examples.

NEOCLASSICAL/NEO-GOTHIC (19TH C.)   The Neoclassical style was meant to be a rebuke to the excesses of Baroque and Rococo. As the century wore on, Neoclassicism gave way to the more ponderous Neo-Gothic style. This faux-medievalism is what Ludwig's Neuschwanstein castle (p. 176) is all about.

JUGENDSTIL (LATE 19TH–EARLY 20TH C.)   Jugendstil is the German name for Art Nouveau, an early-20th-century European movement that emphasized flowing, asymmetrical, organic shapes. Many Jugendstil villas line the streets of lakeside neighborhoods in Hamburg,

Early 1800s After defeating the Austrian and Prussian armies, Napoleon occupies several German cities and abolishes the Holy Roman Empire. In 1813, Prussian, Austrian, and Russian armies fight the French emperor in Leipzig, which is followed by the decisive Battle of Waterloo.

Mid- to late 1800s Following Napoleon's defeat, the country's military and political rulers are determined to return to a system of absolute monarchy. The question of independence and national unity comes to a head in the 1848 revolution. When that effort fails, the Austrian Hapsburg monarchy reimposes its sovereignty over Prussia and other parts of Germany. Prussian statesman Otto von Bismarck (1815–98) advocates consolidation of the German people under Prussian leadership. After triumphs in the Franco-Prussian War (1870–71), Bismarck succeeds in winning over southern German states and, in 1871, becomes first chancellor of the German Empire (Reich).

1914–1918 For many observers, the Great War represented a German attempt to dominate Europe. Military conflict on the eastern front results in the

BAUHAUS (1913–33)   A rigorously modern style, free of frills and unnecessary decoration, Bauhaus was championed by Walter Gropius (1883–1969), who founded the Bauhaus school to create functional buildings and furnishings. The school was banned by the Nazis because it didn't promote "German-looking" architecture. The Bauhaus aesthetic was taught and practiced in the United States by European expatriates and their disciples. The Neue Nationalgalerie (p. 56) in Berlin, dating from 1968 and the last building designed by former Bauhaus teacher Mies van der Rohe, exemplifies the timeless Bauhaus style.

MODERNISM (1948 ONWARD)   A major housing shortage and rebuilding effort in bombed cities in Germany followed the devastation of World War II. If you walk down the streets or pedestrian zones in just about any major German city, you'll see modernist buildings all around you. It's a simple, functional style with straight lines and square windows, and it learned quite a few lessons from the Bauhaus. One of the most famous architects of the period since World War II is Hans Scharoun, whose daring Philharmonie (p. 69) concert hall in Berlin was completed in 1963.

POSTMODERNISM (1980S ONWARD)   Postmodernism is a style practiced by architects who plunder the past and apply old styles to the buildings of today. James Stirling's Neue Staatsgalerie (p. 188) in Stuttgart is a reminder of just how uninspired and dated most postmodern buildings are.

A Brief History of German Art

Germany abounds in art museums. You can't escape them, nor should you try. The country's rich artistic heritage is on display in even the smallest cities, while cities like Berlin and Munich boast world-class collections. The chronology below paints the major trends and artists with a brief, broad brushstroke.

CAROLINGIAN & OTTONIAN (9TH–10TH C.)   During the Carolingian period mosaics based on earlier Roman and Byzantine models were used to decorate Charlemagne's Palatine or Octagon chapel (p. 235) and palace in Aachen, and carved ivory book covers were notable. The first outstanding examples of German painting

defeat of Russia, while fighting on the western front ultimately leads to German defeat and the abdication of Kaiser Wilhelm II. Although the war isn't fought on German soil, it results in severe food shortages throughout the country and intensifies political unrest.

1919–1932 In its attempt to establish a democratic and republican government, the so-called Weimar government represents a break in dominant traditions of German history. Residual issues from World War I and hostility from conservative groups conflict with reformist and radical impulses

of the left and with the cultural avant-garde. During the "Golden Twenties," Berlin — capital of the Weimar Republic — blossoms into Germany's economic and cultural center.

1933–1945 Economic crisis in Germany is a major factor in the rise of the Nazi movement, but old authoritarian, nationalistic, and imperialistic attitudes also provide a ripe environment for the National Socialist Party to take control. As the brutal anti-Semitic political agenda of Adolf Hitler (1889–1945) becomes

continues

(illuminated manuscripts) and sculpture were created during the Ottonian dynasty (ca. 960–1060). Carved in Cologne in the late 10th century, the Gero cross in Cologne cathedral (p. 225) is believed to be the oldest existing large-scale crucifix in the Western world. Fine craftsmanship is apparent in the metalwork of this period as well.

ROMANESQUE (11TH–12TH C.) Romanesque art flourished in Germany, exemplified more in church building with incised decorative stonework. Little remains of Romanesque fresco painting, although there is an example from about 1000 at the Kloster St. Mang (p. 173) in Füssen.

GOTHIC (13TH–14TH C.) With the diffusion of the French Gothic style throughout Europe, notable contributions were made by the Germans, particularly in the field of sculpture, which was used to adorn the portals of Cologne cathedral (p. 225), and the doors of Augsburg's Dom St. Maria (p. 163). In Cologne, the Wallraf-Richartz Museum (p. 228) has galleries devoted to the Cologne school of painting from this period, and the Schnütgen Museum (p. 227) has superb examples of medieval stained-glass and sculpture.

RENAISSANCE (15TH–16TH C.) German sculpture, particularly carved wooden altarpieces, reached an artistic highpoint in the late 15th century with the powerfully expressive works of Peter Vischer (1460–1529), Viet Stoss (1439–1533), Adam Kraft (1460–1508), and Tilman Riemenschneider (1460–1531; see p. 140). Manuscript illumination and fresco painting declined as stained-glass technique and panel painting became more highly developed. Flemish influence is seen in the paintings of Stephan Lochner (1400–51), whose Adoration of the Magi altarpiece graces Cologne cathedral (p. 225). Hans Holbein the Elder (1465–1524) is another major 15th-century figure, but the artistic genius of the century was Albrecht Dürer (1471–1528), who visited Venice and brought elements of the Italian Renaissance style to Germany. Dürer's paintings, woodcuts, and engravings influenced all European art of the time; his work's on view in Munich's Alte Pinakothek (p. 124), Berlin's Gemäldegalerie (p. 53), and Nuremberg's Germanisches Nationalmuseum (p. 152).

Painting was at its height in the 16th century. The great masters of the age—all of whose work can be seen in Munich's Alte Pinakothek (p. 124)—were Hans Holbein

apparent, thousands of German Jews, including many prominent artists, scientists, and politicians, flee the country to escape persecution. Millions of Jews and other "undesirable" minorities throughout Germany and the rest of Nazi-occupied Europe are systematically exterminated in one of the most horrifying chapters in world history. At the end of the war, with its major cities in smoldering ruins, Germany ceases to exist as an independent state.

1948   West German recovery gets underway with U.S. assistance in the form of the Marshall Plan. The Soviet blockade of West Berlin results in the Anglo-American Berlin airlift, which continues until 1949.

1949–1961   Intending at first to govern conquered Germany as one unit, the war's victors divide it into two states as the Cold War intensifies. The Federal Republic of Germany in the western half of the country has its capital in Bonn, and the Soviet-ruled German Democratic Republic (GDR) in the eastern half has its capital in East Berlin. Two Germanys develop with highly different political, economic, and social systems.

the Younger (1497–1543); Mathias Grünewald (d. 1528); Albrecht Altdorfer (1480–1538), who brought pure landscape painting into vogue; Lucas Cranach the Elder (1472–1553); and Hans Baldung (1484–1545).

BAROQUE & ROCOCO (17TH–18TH C.)   Ceiling paintings and swirling, often gilded stuccowork is part and parcel of the decoration in the exuberant Baroque and Rococo churches and palaces that are found throughout southern Germany. Two notable examples are the Wieskirche (p. 174) and the Asamkirche (p. 119) in Munich. At this time, too, small Dresden china figures and groups became popular, with the workshops at Meissen producing exquisite miniature statuettes of genre subjects.

ROMANTICISM (19TH C.)   In the early part of the century, a school of German historical painting emerged and the period brought to the fore genre painters such as Moritz von Schwind (1804–71) and Carl Spitzweg (1808–85). The greatest artist of the Romantic period was Caspar David Friedrich (1774–1840), whose famous "Cross in the Mountains" (1808) hangs in Dresden's Gemäldegalerie Alte Meister (p. 77).

EXPRESSIONISM (EARLY 20TH C.)   In the early years of the 20th century, the sentimental and derivative genre and landscape scenes of the previous century were replaced by a fresh, dynamic and highly personalized sensibility. The wave of 20th-century artists who emerged created an art known as Expressionism for its purposeful distortion of natural forms and attempt to express emotion. The expressionist movement came in three waves. The first, Die Brücke (the Bridge) founded in Dresden in 1905 included Ernst Kirchner 1880–1938), Emil Nolde (1867–1956), and Karl Schmidt-Rottluff (1884–1976); you can see their work in Dresden's Albertinum (p. 76). It was followed in 1911 by the Munich-based Der Blaue Reiter (Blue Rider) group, which included Franz Marc (1880–1916), Gabriele Münter (1877–1962), and several foreign artists, including Swiss-born Paul Klee (1879–1940) and Russian-born Wassily Kandinsky (1866–1944); their work can be seen in the In Munich's Lenbach-haus (p. 126). Die Neue Sachlichkeit (the New Objectivity), a movement founded in the aftermath of World War I by Otto Dix (1891–1969) and George Grosz (1893–1959), was characterized by a more realistic style combined with a cynical, socially critical philosophical stance that was vehemently anti-war. The brilliant, bitter

1961   The Berlin Wall is constructed, sealing off East Berlin from West Berlin and, on a larger scale, East Germany from West Germany.

1989   The opening of the Berlin Wall marks for East Germany the culmination of a wave of previously suppressed revolutionary sentiment across central and eastern Europe. Reforms by Soviet leader Mikhail Gorbachev and underground, grassroots communication between citizens in East Germany lead to massive demonstrations against the repressive, Stalinist government of the GDR.

1991   East and West Germany unite under one government. Berlin is made the new capital of a reunified Germany.

2006   Angela Merkel, who grew up in the GDR, becomes Germany's first female chancellor.

2013   Angela Merkel is re-elected for a third term as chancellor and is the most politically powerful leader in Europe.

2014   Germany, and especially Berlin, celebrates the 25th anniversary of the fall of the Berlin Wall.

continues

canvases of Dix and Grosz hang in the Neue Nationalgalerie (p. 56) in Berlin. Artists working in related styles included Oskar Kokoschka (1886–1980) and Käthe Kollwitz (1867–1945), whose haunting sculptures, drawings and prints can be seen at the Käthe Kollwitz Museum in Cologne (p. 225).

Several of these same artists taught at the Bauhaus, which espoused functionalism and encouraged experimentation and abstraction with the ideal of combining artistic beauty with usefulness.

NAZI ERA (1933–45)   The Nazi regime, which regarded all abstract and expressionist works as degenerate, discouraged and destroyed any but heroic, propagandistic art, and the Germany of the 1930s and early 1940s produced nothing of artistic significance. As a recent discovery in Munich revealed, the Nazis may have condemned abstract art but they also stole it from collectors and museums and sold the canvases for hard currency outside of Germany.

POST–WORLD WAR II (1945–PRESENT)   Germany hasn't had one predominant school or movement to define its art since World War II, but it has produced internationally recognized artists such as the iconoclastic sculptor Josef Beuys (1921–86), the painter Anselm Kiefer (b. 1945), and the painter-sculptor Georg Baselitz (b. 1938), and the painter and visual artist Gerhard Richter (b. 1932). All four of these artists are represented in Stuttgart's Staatsgalerie (p. 188), and stained-glass windows created by Richter can be seen in Cologne cathedral (p. 225). Anyone interested in contemporary German art should also visit Cologne's Museum Ludwig (p. 227). In the 25 years since the Wall fell, Berlin has seen an explosion of artistic expression—some 10,000 artists are now living in Berlin.

Germany's Great Musical Tradition

Some of the greatest works of Western music have been written by German composers. The roster includes Hildegard of Binger, Bach, Handel, Beethoven, Brahms, Mendelssohn, Schumann, and Wagner, as well as 20th-century greats Richard Strauss, Alban Berg and Kurt Weill. The country's rich musical history dates back to 12th-century *Minnesängers* (troubadours) and religious chants. Over the centuries, Germany's musical traditions were fostered in convents, monasteries and churches where composers were hired to write sacred songs, cantatas and oratorios. Eventually, as opera houses and concert halls became a fixture in German cities, a wider public clamored for musical performances. Classical music remains an important part of German culture today.

GERMANY IN BOOKS & FILMS
Books

The books listed below can help you gain a better understanding of German history, culture, personalities, and politics.

o **"Before the Deluge: A Portrait of Berlin in the 1920s"** by Otto Friedrich: A fascinating portrait of the life of Berlin between the wars.

o **"Berlin Diaries, 1940–1945"** by Marie Vassilchikov: The secret journals of a young Russian aristocrat who lived and worked in Berlin throughout World War II

o **"Berlin Journal, 1989–1990"** by Robert Darnton: An eyewitness account of the events that led to the opening of the Berlin Wall and the collapse of East Germany's Communist regime.

neoclassical buildings OF NOTE IN BERLIN & MUNICH

Neoclassical architecture has its stylistic roots in the Classical era of Greece. There are several great examples in Berlin (see chapter 4), where the Prussian architect Karl Friedrich Schinkel (1781–1841) created a Neoclassical avenue called Unter den Linden and an island of museums, the Museumsinsel (p. 63). In Munich (see chapter 6), the architect Leo von Klenze (1784–1864) designed museums like the Glyptothek (p. 126) and monuments like the Propyläen at Königsplatz, inspired by Greek temples. This style can also be called Greek Revival.

- "Berlin Noir" by Philip Kerr. Bernie Gunther is the dyspeptic Berlin detective in these three thought-provoking crime novels set in Nazi Germany and post-war Berlin and Vienna.
- "Billiards at Half-Past Nine" by Heinrich Böll: A compelling novel by one of Germany's best-known writers about the compromises made by a rich German family during the Hitler years.
- "Bismarck" by Edward Crankshaw: An objective and highly readable life of the first chancellor of the German Empire.
- "Buddenbrooks" by Thomas Mann: A classic of German literature, this novel deals with the transition of a merchant family in Lübeck from 19th-century stability to 20th-century uncertainty.
- "Europe Central" by William T. Vollman: A bold, brilliant novel that examines the authoritarian cultures of 20th-century Germany and Russia and creates a mesmerizing picture of life during wartime from many different perspectives.
- "Five Germanys I Have Known" by Fritz Stern: The well-known historian chronicles the five distinct eras of Germany's modern history that his Jewish family has experienced.
- "Frederick the Great" by Nancy Mitford: Frederick, statesman, scholar, musician, and patron of the arts, sketched with wit and humor.
- "German Family Research Made Simple" by J. Konrad: If you're interested in tracing your German roots, this easy-to-follow guide makes the task easier.
- "The German Lesson" by Siegfried Lenz: A bestseller from 1971, this powerful novel explores Nazism and its aftermath in the north German provinces.
- "Germany, 1866–1945" by Gordon Craig: One of the best single accounts of the turbulent political, cultural, and economic life in Germany from the foundation of the German Reich through the end of the Third Reich.
- "The Good German" by Joseph Cannon: A war correspondent returns to post-war Berlin in search of a story and a past love.
- "Here I Stand: A Life of Martin Luther" by Roland Bainton: A fascinating and meticulously researched account of the Protestant reformer.
- "Hitler: 1936–1945: Nemesis" by Ian Kershaw: Several good biographies about Hitler have been written, including works by Robert Payne, Joachim Fest, and John Toland, but Kershaw's is one of the best.
- "My Life in Politics" by Willy Brandt: The political memoirs of Willy Brandt (1913–92), winner of the Nobel Peace Prize in 1971, mayor of cold-war West Berlin (1957–66), and chancellor of West Germany (1969–74).

THE bauhaus INFLUENCE

Founded in Weimar in 1919 by Walter Gropius (1883–1969), the Bauhaus was forced to move to Dessau and finally to Berlin before it was banned by the Nazis in 1933 for being "too modernist." But in its brief and beleaguered 14 years of existence (it reemerged after World War II), the Bauhaus managed to revolutionize architecture and design. The banal historicism that dominated architecture and the kitschy overdecoration of everyday objects was swept away and replaced with unadorned exteriors and clear forms that focused on the utility and functionality of the object. Everything from houses to factories and cradles to teapots was radically re-imagined, and the Bauhaus creations that emerged have now become icons of modern design. Teachers in the school included artists like Paul Klee and Wassily Kandinsky, and architects like Gropius and Mies van der Rohe.

- **"The Tin Drum"** by Günter Grass: Perhaps the most famous novel about life in post-World War II Germany, written by a Nobel Prize winner who kept his own Nazi past a secret until 2006.
- **"A Tramp Abroad"** by Mark Twain: Twain's account of his travels in Germany is as fresh today as when it first was published in 1899.
- **"The Wall in My Backyard"** by Dinah Dodds and Pam Allen-Thompson: In this collection of interviews, East German women describe the excitement, chaos, and frustration of the transitional period between the fall of the Berlin Wall in 1989 and the reunification of Germany less than a year later.
- **"When in Germany, Do as the Germans Do"** by Hyde Flippo: A short, entertaining crash course in German culture, customs, and heritage.
- **"Witness to Nuremberg"** by Richard Sonnenfeldt: The chief American interpreter at the war-crimes trials tells his story of dealing directly with Hermann Göring, the powerful Nazi official who was subsequently executed for war crimes.

Films

As with literature, World War II and the Holocaust have dominated the subject matter of recent films about Germany–so much so that German-made films about contemporary German life rarely get a showing outside of Germany unless they win a top prize at a film festival. The list below includes a selection of German and Germany-themed films available in many formats.

- **"Berlin Alexanderplatz"** (1980): Rainer Werner Fassbinder's 15-part television adaptation of the novel by Alfred Döblin follows the life of a man released from prison between the two world wars.
- **"The Blue Angel"** (1930): The film that shot Marlene Dietrich to international stardom remains stark, startling, and provocative.
- **"Cabaret"** (1972): A musical based on Christopher Isherwood's Berlin Stories and set in Berlin at the brink of World War II.
- **"The Counterfeiters"** (2007): Based on a true story, this Oscar-winning film (Best Foreign Language Film) tells the story of master forger Salomon "Sally" Sorowitsch and his fellow criminals who were assigned the job of forging massive amounts of fake dollars and pounds in an effort by the Nazi regime to weaken the Allies.

- **"A Foreign Affair"** (1948): Billy Wilder's cynically hilarious look at postwar occupied Berlin, starring Marlene Dietrich as an amoral cabaret singer.
- **"Goodbye, Lenin!"** (2004): A wry comedy about a young man in East Berlin who tries to keep his bedridden mother, a loyal Communist, from learning that the wall has come down and Germany has been reunited.
- **"Heimat"** (1984–2005): This series created for West German television begins in 1919 with the return of a soldier from the Great War to his village in the northwestern corner of Germany, a rural region known as the Hunsrück, and ends 63 years later; the history of modern Germany is refracted through the experiences of an extended family, the Simons.
- **"The Lives of Others"** (2006): An Academy Award winner for Best Foreign Language Film, this haunting film reveals how the East German secret police (the Stasi) spied on the country's citizens, destroying and dehumanizing lives.
- **"The Marriage of Maria Braun"** (1979): Hanna Schygulla stars as a woman married to a soldier in the waning days of World War II.
- **"Metropolis"** (1927): Fritz Lang's classic of German cinema, in which the Workers plan a revolt against the aloof Thinkers that dominate them in a future dystopia.
- **"Olympiad"** (1936): Leni Riefenstahl's super-Aryan take on the 1936 Olympic games in Berlin.
- **"On the Other Side"** (2007): This well-acted and well-received contemporary drama explores the lives of Turks and Germans living in the multicultural Germany of today.
- **"The Reader"** (2008): Hollywood adaptation of a novel set in postwar Germany and dealing with the life of an illiterate woman who worked in a concentration camp.
- **"Triumph of the Will"** (1934): Leni Riefenstahl filmed the gigantic 1934 Nazi conference and rally in Nuremberg as "image-control" propaganda for the Third Reich.
- **"Wings of Desire"** (1988): An angel roaming the streets of Berlin and recording the angst and joy of ordinary life falls in love with a mortal.

BERLIN

4

n 2014, **Berlin ★★★** marks the 25th anniversary of the fall of the Berlin Wall. It's a momentous occasion, full of symbolism and emotion for those who had lived with the gruesome concrete barrier that kept Berlin—and, symbolically, all of Germany—divided for more than 40 years. In the quarter-century since the Wall came tumbling down, Berlin has re-established itself as Germany's capital and gone through an urban and social transformation that has made it, once again, one of the most exciting cities in Europe (many would say, *the* most exciting). Superlative museums, grand (and grandiose) monuments, a nightlife that's both glamorous and gritty, a performing arts scene that has no equal in Germany, fascinating neighborhoods to explore, fabulous parks and green spaces to enjoy, cafes, beer gardens, shopping, elegant restaurants and on-the-go street food—Berlin truly does have something for everyone. And although Berlin is a fast-paced, forward-looking city, it is also a city full of memorials and reminders of its haunted and harrowing Nazi and Communist past. Berlin has seen it all and lived to tell the tale—a tale that makes this city perpetually fascinating and endlessly exciting as it reinvents itself again and again.

One thing to note: There is a great deal of construction still going on in Berlin, both above and below ground, as formerly divided city continues to knit itself together. You'll notice this especially along Unter den Linden and around Alexanderplatz.

This chapter also includes day trips to **Dresden,** an art-filled city in eastern Germany that is now on many visitors' must-see list; and to **Potsdam,** where Frederick the Great's glorious palace of **Sanssouci** is now a UNESCO World Heritage Site.

ESSENTIALS

Arriving

BY PLANE   At press time Berlin still had two airports, Tegel and Schöne-feld, and the opening of what will become Berlin's major new international airport, **Berlin-Brandenburg International Airport (BBI),** was officially rescheduled to open in 2014 after many delays—but insider's say the new airport will not be ready until 2018. When it opens, most international flights will arrive at the new BBI, 20km (12 miles) from the city center. The new airport will have a rail station under the main terminal, so you can reach the center of Berlin in 20 minutes. For current information on BBI and the two airports currently serving Berlin, go to www.berlin-airport.de.

Tegel (TXL) airport, 8km (5 miles) northwest of the center, currently serves European and long-haul destinations. **Buses** 128, X9, 109, and the **Jet Express TXL** depart for Berlin from stops outside the terminal every 10 or 20 minutes from 6am to 11pm. The journey takes between 15 and 40 minutes; tickets cost 2.60€ and can be purchased at the BVG kiosk close to the airport exit or from the ticket machines at the bus station. Validate your ticket by stamping it in the machine on the bus. A **taxi** ride costs approximately 35€; taxis depart from ranks outside the terminal.

Schönefeld (SFX) airport, 18km (11 miles) southeast of the center, connects with destinations across Europe, Asia, and Africa, and is served by low-cost airlines like **easyJet, Ryanair,** and **Germanwings.** A regular **S-Bahn** service (S45 and S9) departs from the airport and takes about 45 minutes to reach central Berlin. Alternatively take the **Airport Express** train, departing every half-hour from 4:30am to 11pm and taking about 30 minutes to reach Hauptbahnhof (Berlin's main train station), stopping en route at Ostbahnhof, Alexanderplatz, and Friedrichstrasse. Tickets for either service cost 3.20€ and can be purchased from the machines on the platforms. Expect to pay around 40€ for the 45-minute **taxi** journey into town.

BY TRAIN   You can reach Berlin by train from everywhere in Europe. All long-distance high-speed trains now arrive at and depart from the **Hauptbahnhof** (main train station), Europa Platz 1 (© **0800-15-07-090** for train schedules; www.hbf-berlin.de), Europe's newest and largest train station. Unless you arrive by a local, regional train, you'll be pulling into this new, user-friendly terminal. On the main floor there's a BERLIN infostore, the name given to Berlin's tourist information centers (see "Visitor Information," below). Whether you're staying in western or eastern Berlin, getting to your hotel from the Hauptbahnhof couldn't be easier. The entrance to the S-Bahn (elevated train) is on the second floor of the station; the entrance to the U-Bahn (subway or underground train) is on the first floor, and there are buses right outside.

BY CAR   Four Autobahn (freeway) routes enter Berlin from western Germany; three enter from the east. The drive from Frankfurt or Munich takes about 8 hours, depending on traffic. After you're in Berlin, however, a car is a nuisance. Unless you know this huge city well, getting around by public transportation is far easier than by car

Visitor Information

At a **BERLIN infostore** you can find information, book a hotel room, buy the money-saving Berlin Welcome Card, bus and subway tickets, and half-price music and theater tickets. Berlin has five walk-in infostores:

○ **Tegel Airport,** Terminal A, Gate 2, open daily 6am to 9pm.

○ **Hauptbahnhof** (main train station), Europaplatz, open daily 8am to 10pm (U-/S-Bahn: Hauptbahnhof).

○ **Brandenburg Gate,** Pariser Platz, open daily 9:30am to 6pm (U-Bahn: Brandenburger Tor).

○ **Neues Kranzler Eck,** Kurfürstendamm 21, open Monday through Saturday 9:30am to 8pm, Sunday 10am to 6pm (U-/S-Bahn: Zoologischer Garten).

○ **Fernsehturm** (Television Tower), Panoramastrasse 1a (U-/S-Bahn: Alexanderplatz), open late-May through Oct daily 10am to 8pm

The infostores operate one **information line** (© **030-25-00-25**), open Monday through Friday 8am to 7pm, weekends 9am to 6pm; it costs a minimum of 0.50€ per minute.

For online info, go to **www.visitberlin.de**; all the information is available in English.

City Layout

Covering some 60 square miles, Berlin is one of the world's largest cities. For first-time visitors, getting a handle on this sprawling metropolis can be difficult. Even though the Wall has been down since 1989, the first and simplest way to understand Berlin is still to think in terms of the old political boundaries of West and East.

WESTERN BERLIN NEIGHBORHOODS

Western Berlin's glitziest artery was—and remains—the 4km-long (2½-mile) boulevard known as **Kurfürstendamm,** or **Ku'Damm** for short. The train station **Bahnhof Zoologischer Garten** (**Bahnhof Zoo** for short), near the Ku'Damm, is the major transportation hub on the western side of the city and a good landmark for orienting yourself.

Tiergarten The area known as Tiergarten includes Berlin's massive Tiergarten park and a business-residential district of the same name that is located near Bahnhof Zoo. Tiergarten park, originally intended as a backdrop to the grand avenues laid out by the German kaisers, stretches east and ends at the cultural center known as the **Kulturforum,** home of the **Philharmonie (Philharmonic Hall),** the famed **Gemäldegalerie (Painting Gallery),** the **Neue Nationalgalerie (New National Gallery),** and other museums. The park contains the **Berlin Zoo** in its southwest corner, and the landmark **Siegessäule (Victory Column).** Tiergarten's eastern border ends at the **Brandenburg Gate** and the **Reichstag (Parliament)** building. This is one of the best areas in western Berlin for hotels and restaurants.

Charlottenburg The Charlottenburg district is the wealthiest and most commercialized in western Berlin. Along the famous **Ku'Damm,** which runs through it, you find the best concentration of hotels, restaurants, theaters, cafes, nightclubs, shops, and department stores. The 22-story **Europa Center,** a shopping center and entertainment complex (Berlin's first, dating from the 1960s), rises just across the plaza from the **Kaiser-Wilhelm-Gedächtnis Kirche (Memorial Church).** Charlottenburg's regal centerpiece is **Schloss Charlottenburg (Charlottenburg Palace),** with its lovely gardens and nearby museums: the **Bröham Museum** and the **Berggruen Sammlung**

(Collection). Charlottenburg also is the home of the **Deutsche Oper Berlin (German Opera House),** one of Berlin's three opera houses. Upscale shops, restaurants, and cafes fill the neighborhood around **Savignyplatz,** a tree-lined square a short walk north of Kurfürstendamm. Charlottenburg, which has plenty of hotels and pensions (B&Bs), makes a convenient base for visitors.

Kreuzberg For a long time the Kreuzberg neighborhood was the poorest and most crowded of western Berlin's districts. Today, about 35 percent of its population is composed of *Gastarbeiter* (guest workers) from Turkey, Greece, and the former Yugoslavia, many of whom have now lived in Kreuzberg for 40 years or more. Starting in the 1960s and 1970s, the district became home to the city's artistic countercultural scene. Although gentrification has changed Kreuzberg's character, the neighborhood remains funky around the edges, with lots of bars and clubs. Kreuzberg is where you find the new **Jüdisches (Jewish) Museum** and the **Mauermuseum Haus am Checkpoint Charlie,** dedicated to the history of divided Berlin.

Schöneberg Like Kreuzberg, Schöneberg developed in the 19th century as an independent suburb for workers. After World War II, the area was rebuilt as a middle-class neighborhood. The borough is centrally located, close to the Ku'Damm, with good U-Bahn connections and many hotels and pensions. Berlin's densest concentration of gay bars and clubs is in Schöneberg between Nollendorfplatz and Victoria-Luise-Platz.

Wilmersdorf The huge park called the **Grünewald** takes up the western portion of the borough of Wilmersdorf. This 38-sq.-km (15-sq.-mile) lake-filled forest begins just beyond the western edge of the Kurfürstendamm and is Berlin's largest uninterrupted wooded area. **Wannsee** is the most popular lake for swimming and boating. Closer in, toward the Ku'Damm, Wilmersdorf is a quiet residential neighborhood filled with an assortment of hotels and pensions and plenty of low-key restaurants and cafes.

Dahlem Now the university district, Dahlem originally was established as an independent village to the southwest of Berlin's center. You may want to come here to visit the **Brücke Museum** or the **Ethnologisches (Ethnology) Museum.**

MITTE & EASTERN BERLIN NEIGHBORHOODS

Mitte Called **Berlin-Mitte, Stadtmitte (City Center),** or just plain **Mitte (Center),** this is the central section of former East Berlin. Before the war and the division of the city, this area was, in fact, the center of Berlin and it has regained its former pre-eminence to such an extent that many visitors never visit the western side of the city. The oldest and most historic part of Berlin, Mitte has numerous cultural attractions and ever-expanding restaurant, club and arts scenes. If you really want to be where the action is, stay in Mitte.

Mitte symbolically begins at **Potsdamer Platz** and the **Brandenburg Gate,** on the east side of Tiergarten park (the **Reichstag** is here, too). The grand boulevard called **Unter den Linden,** which starts at the Brandenburg Gate and extends east, is lined with 18th- and 19th-century palaces and monuments. (A new U-Bahn/subway line is being built on Unter den Linden, so expect construction for the next few years.) The **Staatsoper Unter den Linden** is the main opera house in eastern Berlin, and the **Komische Oper,** Berlin's third opera house, is also located here. The elegantly proportioned, neoclassical square called **Gendarmenmarkt,** just off Unter den Linden, is home to the restored early-19th-century **Konzerthaus am Gendarmenmarkt.**

Magnificent **Museumsinsel (Museum Island),** site of five major museums, anchors the eastern end of Unter den Linden and has been designated a UNESCO World Heritage Site. At the eastern terminus of Unter den Linden stands the grandiose **Berliner Dom (Berlin Cathedral);** across from it, on the site of the demolished GDR Palast der Republik, the city is now rebuilding the Prussian City Palace.

Friedrichstrasse, which intersects Unter den Linden, has regained its prewar status as eastern Berlin's preeminent shopping street. U-Bahn and S-Bahn lines converge at **Friedrichstrasse train station,** the transportation hub of eastern Berlin (equivalent to Bahnhof Zoo in western Berlin). **Hauptbahnhof,** Berlin's new main train station, is just north of Mitte in the Government Quarter.

Alexanderplatz, a square named for Russian Czar Alexander I, was the center of activity in the Soviet era. It's now in the process of being completely redone and completely commercialized. One of Berlin's Soviet-era landmarks, the **Fernsehturm** (TV tower), rises from Alexanderplatz; at 368m (1,207 ft.), it is still the highest structures in Europe. The **Nikolaiviertel (Nicholas Quarter),** just south of Alexanderplatz along the Spree River, is a charming area restored to look as it did (with some contemporary touches) in Berlin's medieval and baroque eras. Taverns and riverside restaurants make this quarter ideal for a leisurely and picturesque stroll.

Prenzlauer Berg and Friedrichshain Prenzlauer Berg, northeast of Mitte, is now the hippest neighborhood in eastern Berlin, and a favored spot for young Berliners to live, with a burgeoning cafe and club scene. Friedrichshain, to the southwest of Prenzlauer Berg, is another old and formerly decrepit eastern Berlin neighborhood that is rapidly gentrifying and attracting young Berliners.

Getting Around

BY PUBLIC TRANSPORTATION   Berlin is an enormous city, but it has an excellent public transportation system. Taking the **S-Bahn** (elevated train), **U-Bahn** (underground), or **bus** will get you anywhere you want to go. All of them use the same fare

MONEY-SAVING TRANSPORTATION strategies

If you're planning more than two trips on public transportation in Berlin, you'll save money by buying a **Tageskarte (day pass)** for 6.70€–7.20€, depending on the number of zones you want. The Tageskarte is good for unlimited transportation within the zones you purchase it for. You can save euros on transportation and sightseeing with a **Berlin WelcomeCard,** which covers unlimited public transport in zones AB and gives reductions on 160 sights and attractions. A 48-hour, 72-hour, 5-day pass costs 19€/25€/32€. A 72-hour pass including admission to Museum Island's galleries and museums costs 34€. The Tageskarte and Berlin WelcomeCard can be purchased at any Berlin Infostore (see "Visitor Information," above). For more information visit **www.berlin-welcome-card.com**.

system. Berlin is divided into three **tariff zones:** AB (2.60€ for a single fare), BC (2.90€ for a single fare), and ABC (3.20€ for a single fare). A single AB ticket is good for most journeys in central Berlin. Buy your tickets at any U-Bahn or S-Bahn station and validate them in the station machines before you board. (The entire system runs on an honor system.) Tickets are good for 2 hours. For information on all forms of Berlin's public transportation, call ✆ **030/19-449,** or visit **www.bvg.de**.

BY S-BAHN   Speedy and efficient, **S-Bahn** trains (www.s-bahn-berlin.de) provide an enjoyable way to explore Berlin. The service comprises 15 routes, which feed into three main lines going east–west, north–south, and circling around central Berlin. Purchase and validate your ticket at one of the red or yellow ticket-validation machines on the platform before boarding. The S-Bahn operates from 4am to 12:30am, later at weekends. S-Bahn entrances are marked with an S in a green background. Some S-Bahn lines intersect with U-Bahn lines, so you can transfer from one to the other. The S-Bahn is particularly handy if you are traveling from Bahnhof Zoo in western Berlin to Mitte in eastern Berlin or southwest to Grunewald and the lakes.

BY U-BAHN   **U-Bahn** underground trains (www.bvg.de) provide another fast and efficient way to get around Berlin. Ten lines run to more than 170 stations from 4am until midnight, later at the weekend. At peak times, trains depart every 3 to 5 minutes. U-Bahn entrances are marked with a U in a blue background. Validate your ticket in one of the validation machines before boarding.

BY BUS   If you're not in a hurry, Berlin's **buses** are a great way to get about and enjoy the views, especially from the upper deck. Routes 100 and 200 are particularly scenic and travel from Bahnhof Zoo east to Mitte, passing many Berlin landmarks along the way. Buy your ticket before boarding, not on the bus. You can download routes from www.bvg.de.

BY TAXI   **Taxis** wait outside major hotels, stations, and airports round the clock. Most drivers speak some English. There's a minimum charge of 3.20€, plus 1.65€ per kilometer. If you're going less than 2km (1¼ miles) and flag down the cab, ask for the *Kurzstreckentarif* (short-route fare); the driver should switch off the meter and charge no more than 4€. Reputable companies include **TaxiFunk Berlin GmbH** (✆ **030-44-33-22**) and **Funk Taxi Berlin** (✆ **030-26-10-26**).

BY CAR   Once in central Berlin, there's no need for a **car;** it's cheaper, quicker, and more carbon friendly to use the excellent public transport network, even for day trips.

Pay-and-display parking costs around 2.50€ per hour from 9am to 6pm or 8pm. Clearly display your ticket on the dash.

BY BICYCLE Berlin's network of cycling trails makes biking a popular way to get around. Bikes are a fun, eco-friendly way of exploring the sights. Most S-Bahn and U-Bahn trains have a dedicated car for bikes, but you need to buy an additional reduced fare ticket to take the bike on public transportation.

ON FOOT With its grand avenues, pedestrian-only streets, leafy parks, squares, and riverside and canalside promenades, Berlin is a city best enjoyed and discovered on foot. For information on guided walking tours, see "Exploring Berlin," below.

[FastFACTS] BERLIN

ATMs There are plenty of ATMs for withdrawing cash 24/7. Maestro, Cirrus, and Visa cards are widely accepted, but be aware that your bank usually charge a hefty fee for withdrawals from a foreign bank.

Business Hours Most banks are open Monday through Friday 9am to 3pm. Most other businesses and stores are open Monday through Friday 9 or 10am to 6 or 6:30pm and Saturday 9am to 4pm. Some stores are open late on Thursday (usually 8:30pm).

Dentists If you need a dentist, ask your hotel concierge. For a dental emergency, call ✆ **030/ 89004333.**

Doctors & Hospitals You'll find a list of Berlin hospitals and English-speaking doctors at www.doctorberlin.de. You can also locate an English-speaking doctor by calling ✆ **01804/22552362.** In case of a medical emergency, call ✆ **030/310031.** To summon an ambulance, dial ✆ **112.**

Emergencies To call the police, dial ✆ **110.** To summon an ambulance, dial ✆ **112.**

Internet Access Nearly all hotels and hostels offer Wi-Fi, often (but not always) free. Many bars and cafes also offer Wi-Fi (sometimes, as at Starbucks, free to customers). The Sony Center at Potsdamer Platz is a free Wi-Fi hotspot. For a list of other free hotspots, visit www.hotspot-locations.de.

Police The national police emergency number is ✆ **110.** For local police, dial ✆ **030/46644664.**

Newspapers & Magazines Newsstands carry "Zitty" and "Berlin-Programm," both of which list current events taking place around the city. You can also check online at www.visitberlin.de.

Pharmacy Pharmacies (Apotheken) operate during normal business hours and post details of the nearest 24-hour pharmacy on their front door. At least one per district stays open all night. Central pharmacies include **Pluspunkt Apotheke,** Friedrichstrasse 60 (✆ **030/ 20-16-61-73**), and **Apotheke Berlin Hauptbahnhof**

(✆ **030/20-61-41-90**). The website www.berlin.de lists pharmacies by district.

Post Office You'll find post offices scattered throughout Berlin, with large branches at Bahnhof Zoo and Hauptbahnhof (main train station). Most post offices are open Monday through Friday 8am to 6pm and Saturday 8am to 1pm.

Safety Berlin is generally a safe city, but use common sense when you're out and about. Keep an eye on your valuables in crowded places and public transportation and don't walk alone at night, in parks and on dimly lit streets. If you're driving, park your car in a secure lot or garage.

Telephones To make a local call, dial 030 (the three-digit city prefix in Berlin) followed by the number.

Toilets Clean public toilets are found throughout Berlin and at all train stations. In most of them you need a .50€ or 1€ coin to get through the turnstile or to unlock the stall door. It's customary to tip attendants .50€.

WHERE TO STAY

Finding a hotel room in Berlin is easy, as prices are lower than in other major European cities. But, you'll save precious time by booking a hotel before you arrive, and you'll usually save money, too, by going through a web discounter. **Note** The prices listed in this chapter are undiscounted rack rates; unless a big event is happening in town, you'll likely be able to get lower prices than those listed here.

If you arrive in Berlin without a hotel room, you can go to the **BERLIN infostore** at **Hauptbahnhof, Tegel Airport,** or **Kranzler Eck** (for locations and opening hours see "Visitor Information," above), where the staff will help you find a hotel room in your price range. You can also book hotels by calling ℂ **030/25-00-25** or by going online at **www.visitberlin.de**.

Hotels in Western Berlin

Arco Hotel ★   A four-story, turn-of-the-century building, on a quiet street near the Ku'Damm, houses this comfortable, small hotel. Rooms are reasonably large and have high, light-giving windows and modern furniture. The private bathrooms (showers, no tubs) are on the diminutive side, however. One of the nicest features here is the airy breakfast room, which looks out on a courtyard garden (you can eat outside in warm weather). The English-speaking staff, too, is friendly and helpful.

Geisbergstrasse 30. ℂ **030/2351480.** www.arco-hotel.de. 23 units. 69€–117€ double with breakfast. U-Bahn: Wittenbergplatz. **Amenities:** Wi-Fi (3€/day).

Bleibtreu Hotel ★★   Chic, central, contemporary digs near the Ku'Damm? Head to this trend-conscious boutique hotel that emphasizes healthy comfort (no chemicals are used for cleaning and the natural fabrics used are hypoallergenic). The rooms aren't particularly large but they're artfully designed and furnished in a way that "uncramps" the space by using clear, simple shapes, bright splashes of color, and original artwork. You can customize and control your room lighting by remote control and adjust the window shades with the touch of a button. One especially nice feature is the free minibar in every room. Need another treat? Head to the on-site Wellness Center where you can take a pore-cleansing sauna in the herbal steam bath or book a special reflexology, acupuncture or beauty treatment. The on-site Deli 31 lays out a healthy breakfast buffet (an extra 19€) and morphs into a New York-inspired deli that serves vegetarian dishes, sandwiches and burgers as well as traditional German specialties. There are usually special weekend offers available on the hotel's website.

Bleibtreustrasse 31. ℂ **030/884740.** www.bleibtreu.com. 59 units. 120€–210€ double. U-Bahn: Uhlandstrasse. **Amenities:** Restaurant; bar; exercise room; room service; sauna, free Wi-Fi.

Brandenburger Hof ★★★   Think Bauhaus, baby! This unique hotel takes its design cues from that 1920s German design school, which was famous for its streamlined chrome-and-leather furniture and form-equals-function aesthetic. And happily, it combines those now-classic forms with everything necessary for modern hotel comfort. Guest rooms and suites are unusually large and give guests a delicious sense of an earlier era, one that was just moving into modernism. Bathrooms have finely crafted wood and granite finishes. Centrally located in western Berlin, the tony Brandenburger Hof is close to the Ku'Damm and the Tiergarten. For an additional 36€ you can enjoy a sumptuous champagne breakfast buffet in the glass-walled conservatory built around a Japanese garden.

Eislebener Strasse 14. ℂ **030/214050.** www.brandenburger-hof.com. 86 units. 265€–315€ double. U-Bahn: Kurfürstendamm or Augsburger Strasse. **Amenities:** 2 restaurants; bar; spa; access to nearby health club; room service, business center, free Wi-Fi.

Hotel Artemisia ★★ If you are a woman looking for a safe, affordable hotel, this women-only establishment in Wilmersdorf should fit the bill. Located on the top floors of a large apartment building, Artemisia is comfortable and refreshingly free of froufrou. The rooms are large, light, and simply furnished but still have a warm ambience heightened by splashes of color. Ten of the 12 rooms have toilets and small showers. You can save money by renting a dorm bed or one of the two rooms that share a toilet and shower. A private roof terrace with views over Berlin becomes a gathering spot on warm afternoons and evenings. Breakfast buffet available for 10€.

> ## Rental Apartments
>
> Check out www.all-berlin-apartments. com, www.ferienwohnungberlin.com, www.apartmentsapart.com, www. roomorama.com, airbnb.com and vrbo. com for short-term apartment rentals in Berlin that are sometimes remarkably inexpensive.

Brandenburgischestrasse 18. ⓒ **030/8738905.** www.frauenhotel-berlin.de. 12 units. 64€–109€ double. **Amenities:** Bike rentals (12€/day), free Wi-Fi.

Hotel Domus ★★ Set in an unusually pretty section of Wilmersdorf, down the street from St. Ludwig's Church and within walking distance of the Ku'Damm, this modern, frill-free, and newly renovated hotel has a calm, appealing simplicity. The rooms, which face an inner courtyard or the street, are comfortable and quiet (thanks to soundproof windows) and tastefully decorated with contemporary furniture. The bathrooms are unusually large and have either a shower or a tub. Breakfast is served in a lovely dining room. All in all, this is a real find.

Uhlandstrasse 49. ⓒ **030/318797270.** www.hotel-domus-berlin.de. 73 units. 58€–88€ double. U-Bahn: Hohenzollernplatz or Spichernstrasse. **Amenities:** Bar; free Wi-Fi in lobby

Hotel-Pension Elegia ★ This modest, well-run pension in Charlottenburg is one of the best deals in western Berlin, and its location couldn't be more convenient to the cafe-restaurant-shopping streets around Savignyplatz and the Ku'Damm. The 12 rooms, all on the second floor of a turn-of-the-century apartment building (no elevator), are simple and clean with contemporary furniture and the charm of wooden floors and stucco ceilings. Three street-facing rooms have balconies; the rooms facing the courtyard can be a bit dark, but they're very quiet. There's also a 2-bedroom apartment. Share a bathroom and you'll save even more. Breakfast is not offered here, but there are lots of cafes and bakeries in the area.

Niebuhrstrasse 74. ⓒ **030/49807220.** www.hotel-pension-elegia.de. 12 units. 39€–59€ double. S-Bahn: Savignyplatz. **Amenities:** Free Wi-Fi.

Hotel-Pension Funk ★ The former home of silent-movie star Asta Nielsen is a flashback to an earlier era. Rooms and public spaces are old-fashioned and comfortable, replete with original features such as Art Nouveau windows, plasterwork ceilings, and the kind of sturdy, made-to-last furnishings that once defined German comfort and elegance. It also boasts a top location off Ku'Damm. You can save money by booking a room with shared bathroom.

Fasanenstrasse 69. ⓒ **030/8827193.** www.hotel-pensionfunk.de. 14 units. 52€–129€ double w/ breakfast. U-Bahn: Kurfürstendamm or Uhlandstrasse.

Pension Nürnberger Eck ★ An atmospheric pension on the second floor of a building near the Europa Center, the Nürnberger Eck features high-ceilinged rooms with heavy doors that open off a long, dark hallway. Although the eight rooms are stylistically something of a mishmash—with patterned wallpaper, Oriental rugs, and big pieces of furniture—the pension does convey an Old Berlin charm. The lower rates are for rooms with shared bathrooms.

Nürnberger Strasse 24A. ℂ **030/2351780.** www.nuernberger-eck.de. 8 units, 5 with bathroom. 70€–90€ double with breakfast. U-Bahn: Augsburgerstrasse.

Hotels in Mitte & Eastern Berlin

Arcotel Velvet ★★   Smack-dab in the middle of Mitte's most vibrant, round-the-clock area, the Arcotel Velvet is modern, exciting, and inviting—and you can find some terrific deals on the website. The building's glass façade and the floor-to-ceiling and wall-to-wall windows in the rooms create a sense of openness and light and, just as importantly, make you feel like you're part of the exciting city just outside. The views over the rooftops of Berlin from the suites and junior suites on the upper floors are romantic and memorable. Throughout the hotel you'll encounter original pieces of art created by artists who live in the area. Start you evening out in the hip Velvet Lounge, known for its excellent cocktails. Breakfast costs an addition 17€ but there are lots of cafes in the area where you can eat out for less.

Oranienburger Strasse 52. ℂ **030/2787530.** www.arcotel.at. 85 units. 89€–230€ double. S-Bahn: Oranienburger Strasse. **Amenities:** Restaurant; bar; bikes; room service, Wi-Fi (5€/day).

Baxpax Downtown Hostel Hotel ★   Nothing fancy here: The rooms have been simply designed and furnished and there's a cafe and a roof terrace for relaxing and meeting fellow backpackers and explorers. But if your goal is a really inexpensive place to stay in Berlin, this clean, friendly hostel/hotel in Mitte should do. You can stay in an 8-bed dorm room, a more private double room with a shower and toilet, or a small studio with a bathroom. Baxpax has two other hostels in eastern Berlin in addition to this one: **Baxpax Kreuzberg Hostel Berlin,** Skalitzer Strasse 104 (ℂ **030/69-51-83-22;** S-Bahn: Schlesisches Tor), and **Baxpax Mitte Hostel Berlin,** Chausseestrasse 102 (ℂ **030/28-39-09-35;** U-Bahn: Oranienburger Tor). Breakfast at all of them costs an additional 5.50€, and they all share the same website.

Ziegelstrasse 28. ℂ **030/27874880.** www.baxpax.de. S-Bahn: Oranienburgerstrasse. 17€–28€ dorm bed without bathroom; 35€–60€ double w/shower and toilet.

Circus Hotel ★   For a virtuous, and highly "green" stay, head to this modestly priced, youth-oriented boutique hotel. Everything possible here is recycled, most of the lamps have energy-saving bulbs, and there's no A/C (but there is heat in the winter). Local artists have put up installations in some of the common areas. As for the rooms, they're far more style savvy than one usually gets in this price bracket, mixing cheerily colorful walls (think orange, acqua or deep red, off-set by white), 1960s-esque furniture created by the hotel's designer (Sandra Ernst) and homey bric-a-brac for an added dash of personality. Rainfall showers in the bathrooms are another unexpected luxury. The on-site restaurant emphasizes local produce (it offers a generous breakfast buffet for 8€); guests gather there and in the lovely garden courtyard. Circus also operates a hostel right across the street from the hotel at Weinbergsweg 1A (ℂ **030/20-00-39-39**) with 16 simple bedrooms, costing 29€ to 31€ for a dorm bed, 29€ to 43€ for a double.

Rosenthalerstrasse 1. ℂ **030/20003939.** www.circus-berlin.de. 60 units. 85€–95€ double. U-Bahn: Rosenthaler Platz. **Amenities:** Restaurant; bar; bike rentals, free Wi-Fi.

Honigmond Garden Hotel ★★   Yes, there's a garden here and romantics will fall in love with its creeping vines, potted plants and trees. This 19th-century hotel's gracious, high-ceilinged rooms are also a period-pieces of pleasure, with hardwood floors, stucco walls, antiques, and even some canopied four-poster beds. All in all, there's a warm, welcoming, old-fashioned charm and atmosphere here that's lacking in many of eastern Berlin's glossier and trendier hotels.

Invalidenstrasse 122. ☏ **030/284455077.** www.honigmond-berlin.de. 44 units. 125€–230€ double w/ breakfast. U-Bahn: Berlin-Nordbahnhof Tor. **Amenities:** Restaurant; bar; room service, free Internet.

Lux 11 ★★   This unusual design hotel in the hip heart of Mitte, offers centrally located digs that reflect the "new" Berlin. It's casual and trendy at the same time, with comfy, low-to-the-floor sofas and coffee tables, room dividers with flat-screen TVs, and wonderfully comfortable beds with gleaming white linens offset by bright pink-and-fuchsia spreads. My only kvetch is that the lighting in the hallways is too artfully dim. But that's a small complaint, and I have to give the Lux points for its suites with small kitchens, the open bathrooms equipped with rainshowers, and the property's large closets (always a plus). Some of the rooms are more like apartments, making them perfect for longer stays. At street level you'll find an Aveda spa, a fashion boutique…and an intriguing new area of rapidly gentrifying East Berlin to explore. You can easily walk to Hackescher Markt or Museum Island from here, or get anywhere in the city from the Alexanderplatz train station.

Rosa-Luxemburg-Strasse 9–13. ☏ **030/9362800.** www.lux-eleven.com. 72 units. 149€–229€ double. S-Bahn: Alexanderplatz. **Amenities:** Restaurant; bar, free Wi-Fi.

The Mandala Hotel ★★★   The Mandala, which opened on Potsdamer Platz in 1999, is a stand-out among Berlin's many new hotels. It is dedicated to calm, and in a big, busy city like Berlin, that's a winning concept. You can chill out with a cocktail at the chic **Qui** lounge, dine on-site without missing out at the highly regarded **FACIL** restaurant, or enjoy a sauna or spa treatment at the top floor **Ono** spa. The large rooms and suites have a quiet, soothing, contemporary decor with natural finishes of wood and stone and larger-than-average bathrooms that feature high-quality i+m toiletries and bathrobes. The ambience is both understated and very luxe. As in most hotels, the Mandala offers an array of room options at varying prices, from simple doubles to executive suites with balconies to a fabulous penthouse. The opulent breakfast buffet is served in the lovely FACIL restaurant, a glass-walled structure surrounded by bamboo and greenery. Check the hotel website for special offers.

Potsdamer Strasse 3. ☏ **030/590050000.** www.themandala.de. 167 units. 180€–800€ double. U-Bahn: Potsdamer Platz. **Amenities:** Restaurant; bar; exercise room; room service; spa, Wi-Fi (10€/day).

Ostel Hostel ★   If you're curious about life in the now-defunct GDR (that is, former Communist East Berlin), here's your chance to indulge in what Berliners call *Ostalgia,* a kind of kitschy nostalgia for Soviet culture (without the Stasi spying on you and better food). This tower-block hotel wafts you back to the recent yesteryears of Russian bad taste. A picture of a beaming East German official adorns the reception, where clocks show the time in Commie Moscow, Havana, and Beijing. You can choose to snooze in a prefab apartment decorated with Soviet-era furnishings and portraits of vanished politicians, check into the Stasi suite complete with bugging devices (inoperable), or bed down in the budget pioneer dorm like a good little apparatchik. Don't expect the luxuries of the decadent West because you won't find any—except for bed linen and towels. But you will probably have a good time, a decent night's sleep, and wake up glad that the Wall fell. Plus the staff is nicer than anyone ever was during the GDR days.

Wriezener Karree 5. ✆ **030/5768660.** www.ostel.eu. 32€–37€ double with shared/private bath S-Bahn: Ostbahnhof. **Amenities:** Free Wi-Fi.

WHERE TO EAT

Berlin offers every kind of international cuisine and, at last count, 19 Michelin-starred restaurants. As for the local culinary tradition it's fairly basic and *very* filling. Typical Berlin dishes include grilled or pickled herring with onions, fried potatoes, and bacon; pickled or roast pork *(Schweinefleisch)* or pork knuckles *(Eisbein)* with red cabbage and dumplings; meatballs *(Buletten)* with boiled potatoes; and pea soup *(Erbsen-suppe)*. A plate with various cold meats is called a *Schlachteplatte.* Game like venison, duck, and wild boar appears seasonally, as does goose; carp and trout often are available. Fancier restaurants often serve what's called *neue Deutsche Küche* (New German Cuisine), which uses the old standbys as a starting point but dresses them up with unusual ingredients and international touches. Berlin is a city that likes street food, too, especially the ubiquitous currywurst, the fast-food of choice for many Berliners; it's a sausage (usually cut into bite-size pieces) in a spicy sauce with curry powder sprinkled on top. *Note:* If a restaurant bill says *Bedienung,* then a service charge has already been added, so just round up to the nearest euro.

Restaurants in Western Berlin

Ana e Bruno ★★★ ITALIAN   It may seem counter-intuitive to come to Berlin for a fabulous Italian meal, but this charming restaurant is worth the trip. It's a bit out of the center, in Charlottenburg, but if you make the trek, you won't be disappointed. This is Italian cuisine of the highest order—what you might find at the finest restaurants in Italy—served in a lovely, contemporary setting. For over 25 years Chef Bruno Pellegrini, who hails from Lake Como, has been putting a modern spin on Italian classics, creating his own distinctive versions of *nuova cucina.* Traditional family recipes are offered too. Ingredients are absolutely fresh and authentic. The linguine with shaved truffle is divine, but all the pastas here are divine. The menu changes seasonally and always features fish, meat and game—but you can also dine on fabulous vegetarian dishes. If everything is making your mouth water, choose one of the chef's tasting menus and sample a bit of everything. So dress up and join adventurous diners who like to linger over their food and wine, the Italian way. Service is friendly, helpful and professional.

Sophie-Charlotten-Strasse 101. ✆ **030/3257110.** www.a-et-b.de. Main courses 19€–34€; fixed-price menus 65€–95€. Daily 5–10:30pm. S-Bahn: Sophie-Charlotte-Platz.

Arlecchino ★ ITALIAN   It's not that easy to find a good restaurant that lets you enjoy a satisfying meal at an affordable price, but this Italian eatery does just that. If you find yourself longing for a plate of homemade pasta—maybe linguine with zander (a fish) and fresh basil pesto, or penne with lamb ragu, or fettuccine with spinach and mushrooms—head to this cheery, unpretentious place just off the Ku'Damm. You'll be dining with other Berliners, including Italians who want a taste of home cooking. You can order wine by the glass for just 3€, or an inexpensive fixed-price lunch for under 10€. The pizzas are made in a wood-fired oven. All in all, an enjoyable place to enjoy a good, unfussy meal.

Meinekestrasse 25. ✆ **030/8812563.** Main courses 8€–20€. Daily noon–10pm. U-Bahn: Uhlandstrasse.

Die Quadriga ★★★ MODERN CONTINENTAL   Small and elegant, Die Quadriga restaurant in the Bauhaus-inspired Brandenburger Hof Hotel offers a truly memorable dining experience, but you need to reserve in advance because the restaurant seats only 28 diners. Everything is of the finest quality, including the diners, so dress up and treat yourself to a special night out. Chef Sebastian Voetz prepares seasonally fresh dishes that are both classically and nouvelle French. You might start with variations of Coquille St.-Jacques with mango and beetroot, or green risotto with baby vegetables, followed by roasted yellowfin mackerel or saddle of venison. The superlative wine list includes several wines available by the half-bottle or by the carafe. The service is impeccable in the best sense of the word.

In the Hotel Brandenburger Hof, Eislebener Strasse 14. ℂ **030/214050.** www.brandenburger-hof. com. Reservations required. Main courses 32€–42€. Daily lunch Tues–Sat 6–10:30pm. Closed 2 weeks in Jan and 2 weeks in Aug. U-Bahn: Kurfürstendamm or Augsburgerstrasse.

Lubitsch ★ CONTINENTAL/GERMAN/MEDITERRANEAN   Like Arlecchino (described above), Lubitsch is a comfortable restaurant where you can get a good meal at a surprisingly affordable price. Named for Ernst Lubitsch, the German film director of the 1920s, this minimalist cafe and restaurant (paneled walls, tables with white tablecloths and flowers) is popular with Berlin's television and film folk as well as locals and tourists. You can drop in for just a coffee and pastry or a glass a wine, or order a meal like Wiener schnitzel with cucumbers and fried potatoes, or the Lubitsch burger. All the ingredients are fresh, local and seasonal.

Bleibtreustrasse 47. ℂ **030/8823756.** www.restaurant-lubitsch.de. Main courses 12€–18€, 3-course meal 10€. Mon–Sat 10am–midnight; Sun 6pm–1am. U-Bahn: Kurfürstendamm.

Marjellchen ★★ EAST PRUSSIAN   Old East Prussian recipes prepared by the owner's grandmother inspired the dishes that are served at this restaurant, which celebrated its 25th anniversary in 2010. For an appetizer, try homemade aspic, smoked Pomeranian goose, or fried chicken legs. Other starters include *Beetenbartsch,* a delicious red-beet soup with beef strips and sour cream, and a tasty potato soup with shrimp and bacon. Main courses are something of an adventure: stewed pickled beef with green dumplings and stewed cabbage; smoked ham in cream sauce, pork kidneys in sweet-and-sour cream sauce, or roast of elk with chanterelle mushrooms; or, for the less adventurous, that old Berlin favorite, *Königsburger Klöpse* (meatballs with parsley potatoes and beetroot). You also find vegetarian dishes, such as broccoli soufflé. This isn't the kind of place foodies flock to, but the cooking is honest, reliable, and authentic in a way that's quite satisfying. The dining room evokes a bit of Old German charm, with oil lamps and vested waiters.

Mommsenstrasse 9. ℂ **030/8832676.** www.marjellchen-berlin.de. Main courses 11€–24€. Daily 5pm–midnight. Closed Dec 23, 24, and 31. U-Bahn: Adenauerplatz or Uhlandstrasse.

Paris Bar ★ FRENCH   In terms of decor, this French bistro tucked in between Savignyplatz and the Kaiser-Wilhelm Memorial Church in Charlottenburg, hasn't changed much since it opened just after World War II, which is what makes it so charmingly atmospheric. But in the past couple of years, the restaurant has expanded its classic French bistro menu to include a seasonally adjusted assortment of Austrian and Mediterranean-inspired dishes. You can still get a good omelet or a streak with frites, but you'll also find dishes like asparagus with hollandaise sauce, ham, and new potatoes; risotto with porcini mushrooms; and Wiener schnitzel.

Kantstrasse 152. ℂ **030/3138052.** Main courses 13€–32€. Daily noon–2am. U-Bahn: Uhlandstrasse.

Restaurants in Mitte & Eastern Berlin

Curry 36 ★ BRATWURST   Here's your chance to line up with the locals and eat like a real Berliner—wolfing down the city's most famous street food: currywurst, from a street stand. You can't say you've been to Berlin until you've tried one of these bratwurst sausages covered with a spicy sauce, sprinkled with curry powder, and traditionally served with *pommes frite,* cabbage salad, or a Brötchen (white roll). You'll see currywurst stands all over Berlin, but the most famous one is Curry 36 in Kreuzberg. After you've tried one, you can say, as JFK did, "Ich bin ein Berliner." Other fast-food snacks are available, too, but why bother?

36 Mehringdamm. ⓒ **030/2517368.** Bratwurst 2€–7.50€. No credit cards. Daily 9am–5pm; Sat 10am–4pm; Sun 11am–3pm.

Fischers Fritz ★★★ FRENCH/SEAFOOD   At this elegant palace of haute cuisine, in the tony Regent Hotel, the creative cooking of chef de cuisine Christian Lohse has earned two Michelin stars every year since 2008. Dining here is a gourmet adventure that utilizes the freshest produce and products of land and sea—but the sea predominates and if you love fish you will always find it on the menu. Start with carpaccio of halibut and fennel salad, and then savor Icelandic sea trout with pea emulsion, or steamed filet of sea bass. And the dessert menu ranges from classic (fresh white chocolate mousse) to downright exotic (bittersweet artichoke ice cream, anyone?). The wine cellar is outstanding, and the service is deft. There's a smart-casual dress code, so leave your running shoes at the hotel. The prices for lunch are the most reasonable, given the quality of the cooking.

Charlottenstrasse 49. ⓒ **030/20336363.** www.fischersfritzberlin.com. Reservations required. Main courses 28€–78€; fixed-price dinner menus 110€ and 180€; 3-course lunch menu 47€. AE, DC, MC, V. Daily noon–2pm and 6:30–10:30pm. U-Bahn: Französische Strasse.

Ganymed ★★ FRENCH   Berlin is full of trendy restaurants serving trendy food, but sometimes it's the long-established and resolutely "old-fashioned" places that leave the most lasting impression. Take Ganymed—it's been around since 1929, lived through war and Wall, and even in the GDR days, when dining out was rare. The brasserie-style food that it offers is hearty, wholesome and delicious. Try that old Berlin favorite, green pea soup, if you want something hot, filling and authentic. Most of what's offered, however, is traditionally French. The fixed-price dinner might include lamb knuckles braised in Beaujolais and served on broad beans and minced potatoes, or whole grilled sea bream with fennel. The interior is cozy and charming, with checkered tablecloths and candlelight.

Schiffbauerdamm 5. ⓒ **030/28599046.** www.ganymed-brasserie.de. Main courses 12€–28€; 3-course fixed-price dinner 33€. Daily noon–midnight. U-Bahn: Friedrichstrasse.

Henne ★ GERMAN   If you don't like chicken, stay away from Henne in Kreuzberg, because chicken is almost the only thing they serve. But boy, is that crispy corn-fed poultry, with sides of coleslaw and potatoes, ever good. Chicken cooked to a special recipe is what Henne has been serving since 1908; a few other traditional dishes like sausages and meatballs are also on the limited menu. The price of a fulling and satisfying meal here may leave you clucking with pleasure. Henne is basically a working-class beer tavern housed in a late-19th-century building.

Leuschnerdamm 25. ⓒ **030/6147730.** Main courses 6€–8€. Tues–Sun 6–11pm. U-Bahn: Moritzplatz.

Käfer's Restaurant Dachgarten ★★★ MODERN GERMAN   Dining in a landmark like the Reichstag, Germany's Parliament building, is a memorable experience, perhaps as much for the setting as for the cuisine. But you need to deal with security issues if you want to dine in to this popular rooftop restaurant adjacent to the famous glass dome that crowns the building. When you call for a reservation you'll have to give your date of birth and then you'll be given a reservation number. Present this number and a photo I.D. to the attendant at the Reichstag's entrance facing the Platz der Republik, and you'll be shown to an elevator that goes directly to the restaurant, avoiding the lines of sightseers waiting to visit the dome. It's worth it: The modern German food is *almost* as good as the view. Be different and come for breakfast, before the crowds appear. The lunch menu features some surprisingly old-fashioned Berlin favorites. The dinner menu is rich and meant to be paired with fine wines: marinated saddle of venison on apple-celery salad with cream of smoked trout and radish, ragout and fried fillet of pigeon…you get the picture, and the fabulous view that goes with it.

In the Reichstag, Platz der Republik. ℭ **030/22629900.** www.feinkost-kaefer.de. Reservations necessary. Main courses 20€–30€, 4-course dinner menu 117€. Daily 9am–midnight. S-Bahn: Unter den Linden.

Kartoffelkeller ★ GERMAN
Let us now praise the potato. Yes, that humble tuber may not be considered very sexy, but for centuries it has been the staple food in countries around the world, including Germany. The potato (*Kartoffel* in German) is celebrated at this cozy basement (*Keller* in German) restaurant in Mitte. When you want something fast, filling and inexpensive to eat, venture down and choose from the 100 spud-inspired dishes. The potato-packed menu encompasses everything from herby potato pancakes to Swiss *rösti,* plus baked taters with toppings of various kinds. There's a beer garden in summer to help you digest the starch.

Albrechtstrasse 14b. ℭ **030/282-85-48.** www.kartoffelkeller.com. Main courses 10€–14€. Daily 11am–11pm. S-Bahn: Friedrichstrasse.

Katz Orange ★★★ INTERNATIONAL
Located on the courtyard of an old brick brewery building, Katz Orange is a foodie favorite that serves vegan and organic meat dishes using responsibly sourced ingredients. The menu is small, the cooking creative and satisfying. This is what "slow cuisine" is all about. When dinner is over, Katz Orange becomes a late-night lounge.

Bergstrasse 22. ℭ **030/98-32-08-430.** www.katzorange.com. Main courses 15€–26€. Mon–Sat 6pm–3am. U-Bahn: Oranienburger Strasse.

La Riva ★ ITALIAN/SEAFOOD
One of the prettiest buildings in the restored Nikolaiviertel (Nicholas Quarter), just south of Alexanderplatz, is the Ephraim-Palais, a richly ornamented 1765 mansion. Part of the building is a museum, while another section contains this Italian-influenced restaurant, which sits right next to the Spree River. You'll want a table outside if the weather is fine. And you'll probably want to order fish, because that's what this place does best. Choices include salmon with white-wine sauce; grilled trout; swordfish with fresh tomatoes, onions, and basil; and grilled or baked crayfish. Pasta is made fresh daily, and the pizzas are good, too. The restaurant also has a well-stocked wine cellar.

Spreeufer 2. ℭ **030/2425183.** Main courses 7.50€–23€. Daily 11am–midnight. S-Bahn: Alexanderplatz.

Maultaschen Manufaktur ★ GERMAN/SWABIAN
Everyone and his brother knows and loves pasta, and thinks that it's a food exclusive to Italy or Italian restaurants. But did you know that Germany has its own delicious kind of pasta? Called *Maultaschen,* it originated in the southwestern part of Germany known as Swabia. Maultauschen is a kind of ravioli traditionally filled with minced meat, herbs, spinach,

and breadcrumbs. There's a vegetarian version that you can order at this restaurant, filled with sun-dried tomatoes and feta cheese, or spinach and mozzarella. In this simple, inexpensive, specialty restaurant, the Maultaschen is freshly prepared and served either in a broth or browned in butter. It couldn't be simpler or tastier, and it's a great way to expand your pasta repertoire.

Lützowstrasse 22. (*) **017/85647645.** www.maultaschen-manufaktur.de. Main courses 8€–11€. Mon–Sat 6pm–midnight. U-Bahn: Kurfürstenstrasse.

Restaurant Zur Nolle ★ GERMAN   A hundred years ago, Zur Nolle was a busy working-class beer hall beneath the Friedrichstrasse S-Bahn station. The place closed in 1968 but reopened in 1993 as a sign of post-reunification nostalgia for a bit of Old Berlin. It looks snazzier now than it did during its working-class days, but still evokes a kind of 1920s ambience and it's a great, unpretentious spot to enjoy a filling and inexpensive meal. The menu is loaded with traditional Berlin favorites served in hearty portions. Try the jacket potatoes with herring, yogurt, apple, or onion fillings. Vegetarian offerings include vegetable lasagna and roasted broccoli with cheese served on pasta. If you want a taste of Old Berlin, try the homemade *Buletten* (meatballs), which come with a variety of sauces, spices, and additions (fried egg, bacon, onions, or mushrooms), or the roast bratwurst. Wash everything down with a cold, foamy *Bier von Fass* (beer from the tap).

Georgenstrasse, S-Bahnbogen 203 (beneath the arches of Friedrichstrasse S-Bahn station). (*) **030/2082645.** Main courses 7€–13€. Mon–Thurs 11:30am–midnight; Fri–Sat 11:30am–1am; Sun 11:30am–6pm.

Treffpunkt Alt-Berliner Kneipe ★ GERMAN/BERLINER   It's become almost impossible to find a simple, old-fashioned, inexpensive *Kneipe,* or neighborhood tavern-restaurant, in ever-upward and always-gentrifying Mitte, so this is a great place to know about if you want a taste of old Berlin. There is no "decor" to speak of, just tables (some of them shared) and the bar. The food is simple, hearty, and delicious. The menu is limited to a few traditional Berlin favorites: cabbage rolls, pea and lentil soup, herring with onions, pickled eggs, *Buletten* (meatballs), sausages and a few others. Accompany your meal with a glass of beer *vom Fass* (on tap) and enjoy this unfussy bit of old Berlin—while it lasts.

Mittelstrasse 35. (*) **030/2041819.** Main courses 5€–10€. Mon–Fri 11am–1am; Sat noon–1am; Sun noon–midnight. U-Bahn: Friedrichstrasse.

Vau ★★★ INTERNATIONAL   This upscale gastronomic showcase, which was one of the first high-profile gourmet restaurants to open in the former East Berlin after reunficiation, has earned a Michelin star for its refined cooking. Under the direction of Kolja Kleeberg, Vau emphasizes classic French cruisine such as marinated lobster in yellow turnip and tuffles, and confit of breast of veal, but it stretches the culinary boundaries to include modern German cooking and seasonal specialties. The menu choices are deftly prepared and can be surprisingly unfussy. You might find pork with bok choi, artichokes and onion ketchup; pastrami with baked onions and mustard; and various fish choices. In this long, rather narrow room with an arched ceiling, everything is very precise, very modern, and very beautiful. It's a good choice for a memorable meal.

Jägerstrasse 54–55 (near Gendarmenmarkt). (*) **030/2029730.** www.vau-berlin.de. Reservations necessary for dinner. All courses 40€; fixed-price menus 100€–120€. Mon–Sat noon–2:30pm and 7–10:30pm. U-Bahn: Hausvogteiplatz.

Zur Letzten Instanz ★★ GERMAN Berlin's oldest restaurant, dating from 1525, occupies two floors of a much-restored baroque building in the Nikolaiviertel (Nicholas Quarter), and has a series of wood-paneled dining rooms, including one with an old-fashioned Kachelofen (ceramic stove) where Napoleon supposedly warmed his tootsies one cold Berlin day. The menu is as traditional and atmospheric as the dining rooms or the quick-witted waiters who have worked here for decades. Main courses include Old Berlin staples like grilled herring, meatballs, and braised lamb knuckles with green beans and dumplings. For dessert, try the chocolate-covered pancakes filled with blueberries, vanilla ice cream, and whipped cream.

Waisenstrasse 14–16 (near the Alexanderplatz). ✆ **030/2425528.** www.zurletzteninstanz.de. Main courses 12€–20€. Mon–Sat noon–1am. U-Bahn: Klosterstrasse.

EXPLORING BERLIN

No other city in Germany can match Berlin for the sheer number of attractions and diversions it offers. The city is particularly rich in museums (170 of them at last count) and you could build your entire trip around visiting them. But Berlin the living city is fascinating wherever you go, filled with historic monuments, gut-wrenching memorials, picturesque parks and lakes, famous avenues and riverside promenades, and lots of new architecture. In fact, Berlin has more new buildings than any other city in Europe. And, the building—or rebuilding—continues apace, so that some parts of Mitte, especially along Unter den Linden and near Museum Island, are still giant construction sites and will remain so at least until 2016.

Western Berlin Attractions

Gemäldegalerie (Painting Gallery) ★★★ MUSEUM The Gemäldegalerie houses Berlin's greatest collection of European painting, with an emphasis on medieval German and Dutch art and 16th-century Italian and 17th-century Dutch painting. Several Italian masterpieces are on display, including Raphael's "Virgin and Child with the Infant St. John" and Bronzino's "Portrait of Ugolino Martelli." The gallery contains one of the world's largest collections of Rembrandts. This is a huge collection and to see it in any depth you should give yourself at least 2 hours.

Mattäiskirchplatz 4. ✆ **030/266423040.** www.smb.spk-berlin.de/gg. Admission 10€ adults, 5€ students, free for children 16 and under. Tues–Sun 10am–6pm (Thurs until 8pm). U-/S-Bahn: Potsdamer Platz.

Kaiser-Wilhelm Gedächtniskirche (Kaiser Wilhelm Memorial Church) ★★ LANDMARK/MEMORIAL/CHURCH One of Berlin's most famous landmarks, the Gedächtniskirche (Memorial Church) is a ponderous neo-Romanesque structure from the late 19th century. Built to commemorate the 1871 establishment of the German Empire, the church was blasted by a bomb in World War II, and its ruined shell was preserved as a symbol of the ravages of war. You probably won't want to spend more than a few minutes inside. The small modern church beside the Gedächtniskirche is an octagonal hall designed by Egon

> ### Never on a Monday
>
> Many (but not all) of Berlin's museums are **closed Mondays** throughout the year. They're also closed January 1; December 24, 25, and 31; and the Tuesday after Easter. The biggies on Museum Island—the Pergamon Museum, the Neues Museum—are now open daily.

Western Berlin

HOTELS ■

Arco Hotel **9**

Bleibtreu Hotel **6**

Brandenburger
Hof **12**

Hotel Artemisia **7**

Hotel Domus **8**

Hotel-Pension Elegia **3**

Hotel-Pension Funk **10**

Pension Nürnberger
Eck **13**

RESTAURANTS ◆

Ana e Bruno **2**

Arlecchino **11**

Die Quadriga **12**

Lubitsch **4**

Marjellchen **5**

Paris Bar **15**

ATTRACTIONS ●

Gemäldegalerie (Painting Gallery) **21**

Kaiser-Wilhelm-Gedächtniskirche
(Kaiser Wilhelm Memorial Church) **14**

Neue Nationalgalerie
(New National Gallery) **20**

Schloss Bellevue (Bellevue Palace) **19**

Schloss Charlottenburg
(Charlottenburg Palace) **1**

Siegessäule
(Victory Column) **17**

Tiergarten **18**

Zoologischer Garten–
Aquarium **16**

Eierman in 1961. The modern church, with its gorgeous deep-blue stained glass, is a venue for weekend concerts.

Breitscheidplatz. © **030/2185023.** www.gedaechtniskirche-berlin.de. Free admission. Daily 9am–7pm. U-Bahn: Zoologischer Garten.

Neue Nationalgalerie (New National Gallery) ★★ MUSEUM A monumentally modern building in the Kulturforum complex, the New National Gallery was designed in 1968 by famed German architect Ludwig Mies van der Rohe. The museum, an enormous expanse of glass windows and simple symmetry, contains a small but impressive collection of international 20th-century painting and sculpture, including works by de Chirico, Dalí, Miró, Mark Rothko, and Frank Stella. Of special interest are the paintings by early- to mid-20th-century German artists Max Beckmann, Max Ernst, and Otto Dix, and two bitter and brilliant oils by George Grosz that capture the decadent despair of the Weimar years in the 1920s. The gallery also is used for special traveling exhibitions.

Potsdamerstrasse 50. © **030/2662651.** www.neue-nationalgalerie.de. Admission 8€ adults, 4€ students, free for children 16 and under. Tues–Sun 10am–6pm (Thurs until 10pm). S-Bahn: Potsdamer Platz.

Schloss Charlottenburg (Charlottenburg Palace) ★★★ PALACE/CASTLE The oldest section of this lovely baroque palace was built in 1699 as a breezy summer retreat for Sophie Charlotte, the wife of Elector Friedrich III. Its present form dates from 1790. Much of the palace was destroyed in World War II and painstakingly reconstructed. You can see the palace only on a tour, given only in German (you can buy an English-language guidebook at the ticket counter), that includes the historical rooms, the living quarters of Friedrich I and Sophie Charlotte, the eye-catching porcelain room, and the royal chapel. In the Schlossgarten (palace garden), you'll find the charming Schinkel Pavilion, an Italianate summer house designed in 1825 by Karl Friedrich Schinkel, the leading architect of the day. At the far end of the Schlossgarten, close to the Spree River, is the Belvedere. This former royal teahouse contains exquisite Berlin porcelain, much of it from the 1700s. To see the palace and gardens, you need at least 2 to 3 hours.

Luisenplatz. © **030/320911.** www.spsg.de. 12€ adults, 7€ students and children 13 and under. Tues–Sun 10am–6pm (Nov–Mar until 5pm). U-Bahn: Richard-Wagner-Platz.

Tiergarten ★★★ PARK/GARDEN Berlin's largest urban park, the popular Tiergarten (literally, "animal garden") is a favorite spot for Berliners to stroll and enjoy a number of attractions. (Tiergarten also is the name of Berlin's smallest neighborhood.) With lawns, canals, trees, and miles of meandering paths, the Tiergarten park was originally laid out by Peter Josef Lenné, one of the great landscape architects of the early 19th century, as a private park for the electors of Prussia. The **Zoologischer Garten (Berlin Zoo)** and **Aquarium** occupy the park's southwestern corner. In the northwestern corner is the **Hansaviertel (Hansa Quarter),** a residential area where architects were invited to build projects in the 1950s, and dignified **Schloss Bellevue,** the palatial residence of Germany's president. Erected in 1873 to commemorate the Prussian victory in the Prussian-Danish war, the **Siegessäule (Victory Column)** is the most famous of the Tiergarten's many monuments. A golden goddess of victory (dubbed "Golden Elsie by Berliners) perches high atop the red-granite column that stands in the center of the Grosser Stern traffic circle on the Strasse des 17 Juni, a wide boulevard that bisects the Tiergarten and is the western extension of Unter den Linden. The column's observation platform, reached by climbing up 290 stairs in a spiral staircase, offers memorable views of the park and city and is open daily (Apr–Oct Mon–Fri 9:30am–6:30pm, Sat–Sun 9:30am–7pm; Nov–Mar Mon–Fri 10am–5pm, Sat–Sun 10am–5:30pm; 3€ adults, 2.50€ students and children).

Tiergarten Park. Bounded on the west by Bahnhof Zoo and the Europa Center, on the east by Berlin-Mitte, the Brandenburg Gate, and Potsdamer Platz. U-Bahn: Zoologischer Garten or Hansaplatz. S-Bahn: Tiergarten or Bellevue.

Mitte & Eastern Berlin Attractions

Brandenburger Tor (Brandenburg Gate) ★★★ LANDMARK/ARCHITECTURAL SITE Berlin's most famous and potent symbol, the Branenburg Gate is a neoclassical triumphal arch completed in 1791 and crowned by the famous Quadriga, a four-horse copper chariot drawn by the goddess Victoria. The revolutionary events of 1848 and 1918, like those in 1989, saw the gate used as a symbolic gathering place for Berliners. When the Wall came down, hundreds of thousands of East Germans walked freely through the gate into West Berlin for the first time since 1961. In the Room of Silence, built into one of the guardhouses, visitors still gather to meditate and reflect on Germany's past.

Pariser Platz at Unter den Linden. Free admission. Room of Silence daily 10am–6pm. S-Bahn: Unter den Linden.

DDR Museum ★★ MUSEUM For a hands-on experience of daily life in the Deutsche Demokratische Republik (DDR, usually called GDR—German Democratic Republic—in English), nothing beats this museum by the River Spree. Laid out like a prefab housing estate, 17 themed rooms transport you back to the former East Germany, which existed from 1949 until 1990. Everything on display can be touched: Answer the phone in the Soviet-era living room, rummage through closets, or rev the engine of a Trabant. From typical food brands to the famous FDJ (Freie Deutsche Jugend, or Free German Youth) shirts, Erika typewriters to table football, the museum takes a fond look at everyday lives of ordinary East Germans. There's even a dedicated exhibition on the classlessness and freedom of *Freikörperkultur* (FKK), or nudism, in the DDR. There's a lot of Ostalgia here, and the chilling workings of the DDR's police-state aren't overly emphasized.

Karl-Liebknecht-Strasse 1. ✆ **030/847123731.** www.ddr-museum.de. Admission 6€ adults, 4€ students. Daily 10am–8pm. U-/S-Bahn: Alexander-Platz.

Deutsches Historisches Museum (German History Museum) ★★ MUSEUM From the Neanderthals to the Nazis and beyond, the entire saga of German history is presented in this museum housed in the old Zeughaus (Armory). Like many German museums, this one is exhaustive and can be exhausting because it attempts to cover 2,000 years of German history in pictures and documents. The rooms are set up chronologically. I would recommend that you visit the sobering, first-floor galleries devoted to World War II; they have the most impact. On the 2nd floor, seek out Napoleon's bicorn hat and sword, which Prussian soldiers discovered after he ran from the Battle of Waterloo in 1815. A noteworthy architectural addition is the adjacent glass spiral exhibition space designed by architect I.M. Pei.

Unter den Linden 2. ✆ **030/203040.** www.dhm.de. Admission 8€, free for 17 and under. Daily 10am–6pm. U-Bahn: Französische Strasse.

Deutsche Kinemathek Museum für Film und Fernsehen (German Film and Television Museum) ★★ MUSEUM Anyone who has an interest in German film or film in general will find lots of fascinating exhibits in this museum. The

Mitte & Eastern Berlin

ATTRACTIONS ●

Alte Nationalgalerie **39**
Altes Museum **36**
Berliner Dom (Cathedral) **37**
Berlin Wall Memorial/Berliner Mauer Dokumentations- zentrum **1**
Bode-Museum **42**
Brandenburger Tor (Brandenburg Gate) **14**
DDR Museum **38**
Deutsches Historisches Museum (German History Museum) **33**
Deutsche Kinemathek Museum (German Film Museum) **17**
East Side Gallery **25**
Fernsehturm (Television Tower) **43**
Gendarmenmarkt **28**
Humboldt University **12**
Jüdisches Museum (Jewish Museum) **21**
Mauermuseum Haus am Checkpoint Charlie (Berlin Wall Museum at Checkpoint Charlie) **27**
Memorial to Homosexuals Persecuted Under Nazism **16**
Memorial to the Murdered Jews of Europe **15**
Neues Museum **40**
Neue Wache (New Guardhouse) **32**
Pergamonmuseum **41**
Reichstag **13**
Staatsoper Unter den Linden **29**
Topography of Terror **20**

HOTELS ■

Arcotel Velvet **6**
Baxpax Downtown Hostel Hotel **7**
Baxpax Kreuzberg Hostel Berlin **23**
Baxpax Mitte Hostel Berlin **5**
Circus Hotel **2**
Honigmond Garden Hotel **4**
Lux 11 **44**
The Mandala Hotel **18**
Ostel Hostel **26**

RESTAURANTS ◆

Curry 36 **22**
Fischers Fritz **30**
Ganymed **8**
Henne **24**
Käfer's Restaurant Dachgarten **13**
Kartoffelkeller **9**
Katz Orange **3**
La Riva **34**
Maultaschen Manufaktur **19**
Restaurant Zur Nolle **10**
Treffpunkt Alt-Berliner Kneipe **11**
Vau **31**
Zur Letzten Instanz **35**

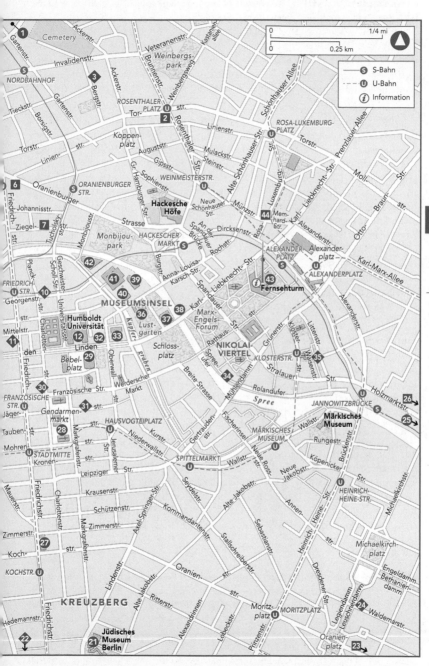

entire history of German cinema is documented in rare film clips from the silent era up to the present. One wing is devoted to the legendary Marlene Dietrich, a native Berliner who catapulted to international fame in 1930 in Josef von Sternberg's "Der Blaue Engel" ("The Blue Angel") and went on to become Germany's only major star in Hollywood. The fascinating Marlene memorabilia includes photos, costumes, props, letters, and documents. You need at least an hour here.

Sony Center, Potsdamer Strasse 2. © **030/3009030.** www.filmmuseum-berlin.de. Admission 6€ adults; 4.50€ students, seniors, and children 15 and under. Tues–Sun 10am–6pm (Thurs until 8pm). U-/S-Bahn: Potsdamer Platz.

Fernsehturm (Television Tower) ★★ VIEW/LANDMARK/ARCHITEC-TURAL SITE

You can't miss this weird-looking television tower built by the Communists back in 1968 because it's the tallest structure in Europe (368m/1,208 ft.) and visible from almost everywhere in Berlin. Berliners call it "the speared onion" because of its shape, or the "Pope's Revenge" because what looks like a cross appears on the silvery surface when light is reflected in a certain way. With its metallic glint and revolving silver sphere, it's definitely got a presence, and it's a great choice for a view of Berlin by day or night. An elevator zooms you up to the viewing platform in 40 seconds as the elevator operator rattles off facts and figures. At the top there's a sweeping view over the city extending some 40km (25 miles) on a clear day. The sphere has "the world's highest bar," where you can order an expensive beer, and there's a restaurant even higher up. The lines to get in can be long and slow, so arrive early or later in the afternoon if you're in a hurry.

Panoramastrasse 1A. © **030/2423333.** www.berlinerfernsehturm.de. Admission 13€ adults, 8€ children under 16. Mar–Oct 9am–midnight; Nov–Feb 10am–midnight. U-/S-Bahn: Alexanderplatz.

Gendarmenmarkt ★★★ PLAZA/SQUARE/ARCHITECTURAL SITE

Twin churches inspired by Rome's Piazza del Popolo flank this monumentally graceful baroque square—the most beautiful architectural ensemble in Berlin. Looking at the square today, it's hard to imagine that at the end of World War II, the Gendarmenmarkt had been reduced to a pile of smoldering rubble and remained in ruins until 1977, when East Berlin finally began this reconstruction. The square was named for the Gens d'Armes regiment, which had its guardhouse and stables here from 1738 to 1782. The centerpiece of the square is Friedrich Schinkel's imposing, neoclassical **Schauspielhaus,** or theater (now called the **Konzerthaus am Gendarmenmarkt;** for concert information, see "Performing Arts"), completed in 1821. On the north side of the square is the **Französicher Dom (French Cathedral),** built for the influx of French Huguenots (Protestants) who settled in Berlin after being forced to flee Catholic France in 1685. Facing this church like a mirror image on the south side is the **Deutscher Dom (German Cathedral).** Surrounding the square is a bevy of chic restaurants and hotels.

U-Bahn: Französische Strasse.

Jüdisches Museum (Jewish Museum) ★★★ MUSEUM

One of Berlin's newer and most interesting museums is located in Kreuzberg, just south of Mitte. Designed by American architect Daniel Libeskind, the zinc-clad building is shaped like a stretched-out Star of David and houses Europe's largest Jewish museum. Items on display include historical and ceremonial objects; portraits of prominent Jewish figures; works of Jewish artists; documents; photos; and memorabilia. You follow a chronological pathway occasionally interrupted by deliberately disorienting memorial spaces like the Axis of Holocaust, where the spotlight is on the fate of individuals, and

EXPLORING mitte's MUSEUMS, MONUMENTS & MEMORIALS

Before the Wall went up, Mitte was the historic center of Berlin. It wasn't called Mitte (or Center) until after reunification, when a massive urban readjustment shifted attention (and money) back to this historic area.

Mitte's two main commercial thoroughfares are Friedrichstrasse and Unter den Linden. Laid out in 1647 and extending about 1km (¾ mile) east from the Brandenburg Gate, **Unter den Linden** is one of Berlin's most famous and historically significant boulevards. The name, which means "under the lindens," came from the linden trees that were originally planted along the street. This boulevard is the oldest and royalest in central Berlin, with several monumental buildings and palaces from the 18th and 19th centuries. On it stands **Humboldt University,** a renowned seat of learning whose scholars and scientists, including Albert Einstein, have won some 29 Nobel prizes. A 19th-century equestrian statue of Prussian king Frederick the Great stands in front of the university. Friedrich Schinkel's 1818 **Neue Wache (New Guardhouse),** which originally served as headquarters for the King's Guard, is now dedicated to victims of war and tyranny and contains the Tomb of the Unknown Soldier, the Tomb of the Unknown Resistance Fighter, and the remains of a concentration camp victim; a powerful sculpture called "Grieving Mother" by the great German artist Käthe Kollwitz sits in the center of the otherwise bare room. **Gendarmenmarkt,** Berlin's most beautiful square, lies just south of Unter den Linden. The **Zeughaus (Armory),** Berlin's largest baroque building and the first (1706) major building to be constructed on Unter den Linden, houses the **Deutsches Historisches Museum** (described below). The **Staatsoper Unter den Linden,** the oldest of Berlin's three opera houses, is also located here (see "Performing Arts"). The giant **Berliner Dom (Berlin Cathedral)** squats at the end of Unter den Linden.

Museumsinsel (Museum Island, described below), Berlin's greatest collection of museums is just north of Unter den Linden. In historically and culturally rich Mitte you will also find several significant memorials, particularly the **Memorial to the Murdered Jews of Europe,** near the Brandenburg Gate at Cora-Berliner-Strasse 1 (www.holocaust-mahnmal. de) and the **Gay Holocaust Memorial to Homosexuals Persecuted Under Nazism** right across the street from it in Tiergarten park.

the Holocaust Tower, with its heavy iron door that gives you the terrifying sense of being trapped inside. Other poignant creations include Menashe Kadishman's Shalechet (Fallen Leaves), a triangular void filled with 10,000 screaming iron faces that clank as you cross them.

Lindenstrasse 9–14. © **030/25993300.** www.jmberlin.de. Admission 5€, free for children 6 and under. Daily 10am–8pm (Mon until 10pm). U-Bahn: Hallesches Tor or Kochstrasse.

Mauermuseum Haus am Checkpoint Charlie (Berlin Wall Museum at Checkpoint Charlie) ★ MUSEUM

If you're interested in the history of the Berlin Wall, this small museum in Kreuzberg is well worth an hour of your time. Located near what once was Checkpoint Charlie, the most frequently used traffic crossing into Communist East Berlin, the museum documents the wall's history from its construction in 1961 to its fall in 1989. The photographs, newspaper clippings, and attempted

REMEMBERING THE berlin wall

In 2014 Berlin celebrates the 25th anniversary of the fall of the Berlin Wall. While Berliners won't forget this monstrous concrete symbol of political division and paranoia, the majority of it was torn down in the early 1990s. But there are still a few places to see remnants of the Wall.

The **East Side Gallery** ★★★ (U-Bahn: Warschauerstrasse Strasse), a 2km (¾-mile) section of the Wall along the Spree River southeast of Alexanderplatz, is the longest and best preserved section left standing. It was painted by an international group of artists in the 1990s and is considered an outdoor art gallery. The Wall is still a political flashpoint for many Berliners. Controversy recently erupted when the city tried to restore some of the sections of the East Side Gallery that that had been damaged by weather and graffiti, and again when a real-estate developer removed two sections and began constructing an incongruous luxury apartment building behind the old Wall.

The **Berlin Wall Memorial/Berliner Mauer Dokumentationszentrum** ★★★ (Bernauer Strasse 111; www.berliner-mauer-dokumentationszentrum.de; Tues–Sat 10am–6pm, Nov–Mar to 5pm; free admission; U-Bahn: Bernauer Strasse), created by the government as a memorial center, is a 230-ft.-long (70m) reconstructed stretch of the Wall at Bernauer Strasse and Ackerstrasse. The memorial consists of two mirrorlike stainless-steel walls that include fragments of the original wall, and a memorial building with photos of the area pre-1989 and eyewitness testimonies of what it was like when the wall stood. Part of the memorial is the Chapel of Reconciliation (*Kapelle der Versöhnung*), a contemporary building set on the site of a church that was blown up in 1985 in order to widen the border strip at this spot.

escape devices (chairlifts, false passports, hot-air balloons, even a minisub) used by East Germans may give you a new take on the meaning of freedom, and how much the 25th anniversary of the Wall's demise means to Berliners.

Friedrichstrasse 43–45. ℂ **030/2537250.** www.mauermuseum.de. Admission 13€ adults, 9.50€ students, free for children 16 and under. Daily 9am–10pm. U-Bahn: Kochstrasse or Stadtmitte.

Reichstag (Parliament) ★★★ LANDMARK/ARCHITECTURAL SITE   The Reichstag is the seat of the German Parliament. Built in a pompous High-Renaissance style between 1884 and 1894, the building was partially destroyed by a fire in 1933 that probably was set by the Nazis, who, blaming the fire on the Communists, used the incident as an opportunity to seize power. Allied bombs destroyed part of the Reichstag in World War II. Today, a striking glass dome designed by English architect Sir Norman Foster crowns the building. After a security check, you can take an elevator up to the dome, where a sweeping vista of Berlin opens out before you. The dome also has an outdoor observation area and a rooftop restaurant (p. 50). Because this is one of Berlin's most popular attractions, lines can be long so arrive early. Check the website guided tour reservations.

Platz der Republik 1. ℂ **030/2270.** www.bundestag.de. Free admission. Tours daily when Parliament is not in session. S-Bahn: Unter den Linden.

Topography of Terror ★★ MEMORIAL/MUSEUM   Located on the grounds of Hitler's SS and the Gestapo Headquarters, this modern concrete and glass building provides historical information on National Socialism and its crimes against humanity.

From this site between 1933 and 1945, the Nazi regime orchestrated the genocide of European Jews, gypsies, homosexuals, and political opponents. It's a site of "remembrance and learning," with a documentation center that opened in 2010, 65 years after the end of World War II.

Niederkirchnerstrasse 8. *℃* **030/254509950.** Free admission. May–Sept daily 10am–8pm; Oct–Apr daily 10am–6pm. U-Bahn: Potsdamer Platz.

MUSEUMSINSEL (MUSEUM ISLAND)

Five museums on an island in the River Spree form the oldest museum complex in Berlin and are listed as a UNESCO World Heritage Site. The buildings were constructed after Frederick William III issued a decree stipulating that the privately owned artwork of the royal family needed to be made accessible to the public. If your time is limited, concentrate on the Pergamon Museum and the Neues Museum.

Alte Nationalgalerie ★★ MUSEUM   Perched high on its base and looking like an ancient Greek temple, this museum is known for its collection of 19th-century German and French and European Impressionists, including Pissarro, Cezanne, Delacroix, Degas and Van Gogh. The museum also has a large collection of the works of Berlin artist Adolph von Menzel, Caspar David Friedrich, and others representing the Romantic and Classical movements in 19th-century German art.

Bodestrasse 1–3. *℃* **030/20905577.** www.smb.museum.de. Admission 8€ adults, 4€ students, free for children 16 and under. Tues–Sun 10am–6pm (Thurs until 10pm). S-Bahn: Hackescher Markt.

Altes Museum ★★★ MUSEUM   Karl Friedrich Schinkel, the city's greatest architect, designed this structure, which resembles a Greek Corinthian temple, in 1822. On its main floor is the **Antikensammlung (Museum of Antiquities),** a vast repository of classical antiquities including Greek sculptures, jewelry and silverware, and a world-renowned collection of Etruscan and Roman art. The upper floor showcases treasures from late-Hellenistic cremation urns and sarcophagi to mosaics, mummy portraits, and other treasures, A small side gallery is devoted to ancient erotic art and artifacts.

Am Lustgarten, Museumsinsel. *℃* **030/20905577.** www.smb.museum. Admission 10€ adults, 5€ students, free for children 16 and under. Daily 10am–6pm (Thurs until 10pm). S-Bahn: Hackescher Markt.

Bode-Museum ★★ MUSEUM   The Bode-Museum, anchoring the north end of Museum Island, reopened its doors in 2006 after undergoing a massive renovation that turned a rather dark and dull building into a museum showplace. Here you'll find a rich collection of German, French, Dutch, and Italian sculpture (marble, wood, bronze) from the Gothic to the Neoclassical periods. The museum also contains galleries with late-antique and Byzantine works and a major coin collection. The audio guide will help you navigate; give yourself at least a full hour just to graze the highlights.

Monbijoubrücke, Bodestrasse 1–3. *℃* **030/20905577.** www.smb.museum. Admission 10€ adults, 5€ students and children. Tues–Sun 10am–6pm (Thurs until 8pm). U-Bahn: Friedrichstrasse.

Neues Museum ★★★ MUSEUM   There's nothing new about the "New Museum," a Neoclassical building built between 1843 and 1855, except that it's undergone a complete renovation/rebuilding by English architect David Chipperfield and reopened to great acclaim in 2009 after being closed for over 60 years. The new New Museum is a triumph of museum design. Much of the building was destroyed in World War II but portions of its interior survived and were incorporated into Chipperfield's new design. The museum houses a glorious Egyptian collection, which includes papyruses, mummy masks, hieroglyphics, and statuary. Make a beeline for Berlin's most

Saving Money on Museumsinsel

Each of the five museums here charges a separate admission, but if you are going to be visiting more than one museum on Museumsinsel over a 3-day period, consider getting a **Museum Pass Berlin** for 24€ adults, 12€ seniors and students. The Museum Pass, available at the central ticket kiosk on Museum Island, will get you into all five museums on Museum Island for 3 days, and into every other museum in Berlin as well. Another money-saving option is the 3-day **Berlin Welcome Card Museumsinsel,** which costs 34€ for adults and provides entry to all five museums plus unlimited public transportation in Berlin's central fare zone. Check out www.visitberlin.com to find out about other money-saving passes.

famous antiquity, the entrancing and enigmatic **bust of Queen Nefertiti** (1350 B.C.), who holds crowds spellbound in her own gallery. The museum is also home to the Museum for Prehistory and Early History, with highlights such as the Neanderthal skull from Le Moustier and Heinrich Schliemann's collection of Trojan antiquities and the golden mask of Agamemnon.

Bodestrasse, Museumsinsel. ℰ **030/266424242.** www.neues-museum.de. Admission 12€ adults, 6€ students and children. Daily 10am–6pm (Thurs until 8pm). S-Bahn: Hackescher Markt.

Pergamon Museum ★★★ MUSEUM   Of all the museums on Museum Island, the renowned Pergamon Museum is the must-see (okay, along with the Neues Museum). And what you must see is the **Pergamon Altar,** considered one of the Seven Wonders of the Ancient World and still holding its own today. Part of the enormous Temple of Zeus and Athena, dating from 180 to 160 B.C., the altar was discovered in 1876 in western Turkey. Another showpiece is the ornate two-storied **Market Gate of Miletus,** a Roman building facade from the time of Emperor Marcus Aurelius (around A.D. 165). The **Near East Museum** in the museum's south wing contains one of the largest collections anywhere of antiquities from ancient Babylonia, Persia, and Assyria.

Am Kupfergraben 5, Museumsinsel. ℰ **030/20905577.** www.smb.spk-berlin.de. Admission 12€ adults, 6€ students, free for children 16 and under. Daily 10am–6pm (Thurs until 8pm). U-Bahn/S-Bahn: Friedrichstrasse.

Guided Tours

WALKING TOURS   For an excellent introduction to Berlin and its history, try one of the themed walking tours offered by **Berlin Walks** (ℰ 030/3019194; www.berlin walks.de). "Discover Berlin" is a 4-hour introductory tour; "Infamous Third Reich Sites" focuses on the sites of major Nazi buildings in central Berlin; "Jewish Life in Berlin" takes you through the prewar Jewish community; Reservations are unnecessary—simply meet the guide at the appointed starting point, which will be listed on the website. Tours (in English) cost 12€ for adults, 10€ for 14- to 25-year-olds.

BUS TOURS   Berlin is a sprawling metropolis and an organized bus tour can be the best way to get a good overview of the entire city and its many neighborhoods and sights you might not otherwise have time to see. **Severin+Kühn,** Kurfürstendamm 216 (ℰ **030/88-04-190;** www.severin-kuehn-berlin.de; U-Bahn: Kurfürstendamm), offers a half-dozen tours of Berlin and its environs. Check their website for current tours, times and prices.

4

Exploring Berlin

BERLIN

BOAT TOURS   Berlin is a city of rivers (the Spree and Havel) and canals, and a boat tour opens up a different side of this endlessly fascinating metropolis. The city's best-known boat operator is **Stern und Kreisschiffahrt,** Pushkinallee 15 (✆ **030/53-63-600;** www.sternundkreis.de). The most popular of their cruises, "Historische Stadtfahrt" (Historic City Tour), offered daily from March through October, takes you for a 1-hour ride on the Spree; see their website for departures times and prices.

SHOPPING

Berlin is a great shopping city and you can find anything you want. But keep in mind that you'll pay less for goods made in Germany and the European Union than for goods imported to Germany from the United States. German porcelain, china, crystal, and cutlery, for example, are prized for their quality, and their prices are lower here than in the United States.

The main shopping boulevard in the western part of Berlin is the famous **Ku'Damm** (short for Kurfürstendamm). Quality stores, in addition to stores carrying souvenirs and T-shirts, line the street. The specialty stores on the side streets around the Ku'Damm, especially between **Breitscheidplatz** and **Olivaer Platz,** are good shopping grounds.

Another good shopping street in western Berlin, close to Ku'Damm, is **Tauentzienstrasse** and its intersecting streets: **Marburger Strasse, Ranke Strasse,** and **Nürnberger Strasse. Europa Center (Tauentzienstrasse),** Berlin's first shopping mall, dating back to the 1960s, contains dozens of shops joined by restaurants and cafes. **Neues Kranzler Eck,** an upscale, outdoor retail "passage" created right on the Ku'Damm at Joachimstaler Strasse, is newer and trendier.

The **Uhland-Passage,** at Uhlandstrasse 170, has some of the best boutiques and big-name stores in Berlin. Shoppers interested in quality at any price head to **Kempinski Plaza** (Uhlandstrasse 181-183), home to some of the most exclusive boutiques in the city, including haute-couture women's clothing. You find trendier boutiques along **Bleibtreustrasse.**

The **Potsdamer Platz Arkaden** (U-/S-Bahn: Potsdamer Platz), one of the most comprehensive shopping malls in Berlin, contains over 100 shops scattered over three levels. Unter den Linden is emphatically not a shopping street, but **Friedrichstrasse** is. This was the main shopping street in eastern Berlin (now Mitte) before World War II and before the Wall. It has regained its former prominence and is decidedly upscale.

Candy & Confections

Bonbonmacherei ★ FOOD SPECIALTIES   You can't help but love an old-fashioned candy store like this one in Mitte, where the sweets (*bonbons,* in German) are still made by hand in small btches. Sweet treats, from sour limes to the famous leaf-shaped Maiblätter (candies shaped by tiny leaves and flavored with woodruff) with woodruff are available here. Heckmannhöfe, Oranienburger Strasse 32. ✆ **03044055243.** No credit cards. S-Bahn: Oranienburger Strasse.

Königsberger Marzipan ★ FOOD SPECIALTIES   At this family-run store in Charlottenbrg marzipan is made the old-fashioned way and then lovingly hand-wrapped. Pestalozzistrasse 54a. ✆ **030-323-82-54.** U-Bahn: Wilmersdorfer Strasse.

China & Porcelain

KPM (Königliche Porzellan-Manufaktur) ★★★ CHINA & GLASSWARE
For 250 years, KPM has been producing fine porcelain (called "white gold"),

BERLIN flea MARKETS

A flea market in Germany is called a *Trödelmarkt* or a *Flohmarkt*. There are over 50 of them scattered around the city, some dedicated to antiques and books, others to clothes, kitsch, and whatnots. The **Flohmarkt Boxhagen Platz** (Boxhagen Platz; S-Bahn: Frankfurter Tor), is a favorite Sunday shop-and-stroll spot for Berliners, who come to find pieces of kitsch, nostalgia, sort-of antiques, and used clothing. The market is open every Sunday from 10am to 6pm. In Mitte, behind the Bode Museum on Museum Island, the **Antik- und Buchmarkt am Bode Museum** (Kupfergraben 1; S-Bahn: Friedrichstrasse), is open Saturday and Sunday from 10am to 5pm and sells a mishmash of books, antiques and collectibles. Another market to check out if you're in Mitte on Sunday between 10am and 4pm is **Flohmarkt am Arkonaplatz** (Arkonaplatz; U-Bahn: Bernauer Strasse), where you can browse for clothing and bric-a-brac. If nothing catches your fancy, just take a seat at one of the many cafes around Arkonaplatz and enjoy the scene in one of Berlin's hippest neighborhoods. For the locations of other Berlin flea markets, visit **www.visitberlin.de**.

including pieces that are hand-painted and hand-decorated with patterns based on traditional 18th- and 19th-century KPM designs. There are sales outlets throughout Berlin, including at KaDeWe department store (see below), at Friedrichstrasse 158 in Mitte, and iat Kurfürstendamm 27 (in the Kempinski Hotel Bristol). The best selection is at the **KPM flagship store and manufactory,** where you can take a guided tours (12€; Sat 3pm) and see the craftspeople at work, or buy pieces in the showroom. Wegelystrasse 1. *©* **030/39009215.** www.kpm.de. U-Bahn: Tiergarten.

Department Stores

Galeries Lafayette ★★ DEPARTMENT STORE   Paris in Berlin is found at this modern department store, right off Friedrichstrasse. You'll find women's fashion, beauty products, children's clothes, and a gourmet food department. Französische Strasse 23. *©* **030/209480.** www.galeries-lafayette.de. U-Bahn: Französische Strasse.

Kaufhaus des Westens (KaDeWe) ★★ DEPARTMENT STORE   This huge department store was established nearly a century ago and contains six floors of upscale merchandise, including men's and women's fashion, accessories, linens, housewares and a sixth-floor food department with sit-down counters and the tastiest herring sandwiches in Berlin. Tauentzienstrasse 21. *©* **030/21210.** www.kadewe.de. U-Bahn: Wittenbergplatz.

Design

Bauhaus Archive ★★★ DESIGN/LIFESTYLE   The shop at the landmark Bauhaus Archive Museum of Design offers an intriguing variety of well-designed items in contemporary styles, some designed by artists of the Bauhaus movement. More than 250 items, which incorporate not only design, but also utility, are available for the home and office. Klingelhöferstrasse 14. *©* **030/2540020.** www.bauhaus.de. U-Bahn: Nollendorfplatz.

Stilwerk ★★★ DESIGN/LIFESTYLE   This temple of design in Charlottenburg is spread out over four floors and carries high-end brands like Bang & Olufsen, Mösch, and Niessing. Whether you're looking for understated jewelry or ultra-sleek home furnishings, this is the place. Kantstrasse 17. *©* **030/315150.** www.stilwerk.de. S-Bahn: Savignyplatz.

Fashion

Buckles & Belts ★ FASHION It's a cinch to cinch your waist—just visit this glam store in Mitte where buckles and Italian leather belts have been turned into an art form. The range of buckles is staggering, and stretches from one-of-a-kind artists' creations to those inspired by nature motifs. Alte Schonhauserstrasse 14. ℭ **030/28093070.** U-Bahn: Rosa-Luxemburg-Platz.

Claudia Skoda ★★ FASHION You'll find the latest collection of Berlin designer Claudia Skoda at this chic boutique in Mitte. From chunky sweaters to snug-fitting dresses, her colorful knitwear is elegant, feminine, and modern. Alte Mulackstrasse 8. ℭ **030/40041884.** www.claudiaskoda.com. U-Bahn: Weinmeisterstrasse.

EASTBERLIN ★ FASHION Durable yet eye-catching urban basics for men and women, from hand-printed hoodies to T-shirts and bags in bold colors and street-cool designs, are what this store in Mitte is all about. Alte Schönhauser Strasse 33–34. ℭ **030/24723988.** www.eastberlinstore.com. U-Bahn: Weinmeisterstrasse.

Hut Up ★ FASHION/SPECIALTY SHOPPING Felt lovers unite! Or at least check out the selection of distinctive hats, bags, dresses, and baby booties made from raw wool using felting and blocking techniques. Everything's one-of-a-kind; great German-made gifts. Heckmannhöfe. ℭ **030/28386105.** S-Bahn: Oranienburger Strasse.

Koko von Knebel ★ FASHION/SPECIALTY SHOPPING This fashion boutique in Charlottenburg is not for you—unless you happen to walk on all fours, bark, and eat from a dish on the floor. No, it's for your pampered pooch, the one you insist on dressing up in clothes s/he hates but you find adorable. Designer Udo Waltz has created a line of canine clothing including gem-encrusted collars (from punk to Playboy bunny), raincoats, and even lingerie. Uhlandstrasse 181. ℭ **043/19970868.** www.kokovonknebel.com. U-Bahn: Uhlandstrasse.

FASHION—VINTAGE

Made in Berlin ★ FASHION Trawl through the racks at this fun and fashionable vintage shop in Mitte for high-quality secondhand clothes, shoes, and accessories (like oversize 1960s sunglasses the size of computer screens). Shop during Wednesday's Happy Hour from 10am to 3pm and you'll get a 20 percent discount. Friedrichstrasse 114a. ℭ **030/24048900.** U-Bahn: Friedrichstrasse.

Glanzstücke ★ FASHION This glittery boutique in Mitte's Hackesche Höfe carries vintage costume jewelry, evening bags, feather boas and more. Hackesche Höfe. ℭ **030/2082676.** www.glanzstuecke-berlin.de. S-Bahn: Hackescher Markt.

Waahnsinn ★ FASHION What would you expect to find in a store whose name means "crazy" or "nonsense"? A bit of everything with an emphasis on fun, right? Come here to search out vintage and new fashion, and kitschy gifts like miniature Fernsehturms, beaded ball gowns, retro lamps, and authentic lederhosen. Rosenthaler Strasse 17. ℭ **030/2820029.** www.waahnsinn-berlin.de. U-Bahn: Rosenthaler Platz.

Gifts

Ach Berlin ★ GIFTS/SOUVENIRS Berlin rules—in a cheeky way—at this Gendarmenmarkt shop. Magnets, T-shirts printed with city landmarks, USB sticks shaped like the Fernsehturm, retro bags, and skyline keyrings, edibles—you'll find plenty of gift inspiration in this fun souvenir store. Alte Markgrafenstrasse 39. ℭ **030/92126880.** U-Bahn: Hausvogteiplatz.

Ampelmann ★ GIFTS/SOUVENIRS When the traffic lights in the old DDR turned green, Ampelmann was the "walk" figure you saw—a little man in a hurry (perhaps to escape from the Stasi). This Hackesche Höfe store pays tribute to this much-loved symbol of East Germany by turning him into a design logo. He's emblazoned on retro lamps, T-shirts, umbrellas, everything you can think of. Hof V, Hackesche Höfe. ℂ **030/44726438.** www.ampelmann.de. S-Bahn: Hackescher Markt.

Erzgebirgshaus ★ SPECIALTY SHOPPING For those who never want Christman to end, this traditional store offers a year-round selection of hand-carved wooden decorations from the Erzgebirge, a region in Saxony. Pick up nutcrackers, incense-smoking carved figures, and candelabras. Friedrichstrasse 194–199. ℂ **030/20450977.** U-Bahn: Stadtmitte.

Kwik Shop ★ GIFTS/SOUVENIRS The sharp-eyed owners of this quirky kiosk in Prenzlauer Berg have searched the world for the oddities you just can't live without and the unusual gift that you want to give to a loved one. Breton mussel baskets, brightly colored Wellington boots, dachshund-shaped doorstops—you get the idea. Kastanienallee 44. ℂ **030/41997150.** U-Bahn: Rosa-Luxemburg-Platz.

NIGHTLIFE

In Berlin, "nightlife" runs round-the-clock, and there's plenty to do at any hour. No matter what your tastes and interests, you will find something to do when the sun goes down. The caliber and variety of of Berlin's performing arts scene is extraordinary, and the club scene is—and has been since the 1920s—legendary.

The monthly English-language newspaper, **"The ExBerliner"** (www.exberliner.com), provides a witty, informative guide to the city's culture and entertainment. This magazine is available at newsstands and tourist offices. Tourist offices also distribute a free magazine called **"New Berlin"** providing tips and recommendations to visitors.

Discounted Tickets

Unsold, day-of-performance tickets for music, dance, and theater venues throughout Berlin are sold for up to 50 percent off at the **BERLIN infostores;** for locations and opening hours, see "Visitor Information," above. A **Berlin Welcome Card** (described under "Getting Around," above) allows you to buy reduced-price tickets (usually 25 percent off) at several major performing-arts venues, including the opera houses.

The German-language **"Berlin Programm"** (www.berlin-programm.de) is available at newsstands. The most detailed listings are found in **"zitty"** (www.zitty.de), a biweekly publication in German.

You can buy tickets at the venue's box office *(Kasse).* Tickets can usually be purchased right up to curtain time. Tickets for more than 100 venues, including opera, classical concerts, musicals, and cabarets are available at **Hekticket** (www.hekticket.de), with outlets in the Deutsche Bank foyer at Hardenbergstrasse 29 ℂ **030/230-9930;** U-Bahn: Zoologischer Garter) and Karl-Liebknecht-Strasse 12, on the S-Bahn bridge at Alexanderplatz (ℂ **030/230-9930;** U-/S-Bahn: Alexanderplatz); both are open Monday through Saturday from 10am to 6pm.; the Zoo location is also open Sundays from 2 to 6pm. For some of the larger opera, ballet, and classical-music venues, you can buy tickets online.

Opera & Classical Music

Berliner Philharmoniker (Berlin Philharmonic) ★★★ THE PERFORMING ARTS The Berlin Philharmonic is one of the world's premier orchestras and performs under the baton of Sir Simon Rattle in the acoustically superb **Philharmonie** in the Kulturforum. Herbert-von-Karajan-Strasse 1. ℰ **030/25488999.** www.berlin-philharmonic. com. U-Bahn: Potsdamer Platz.

Deutsche Oper Berlin ★★★ THE PERFORMING ARTS This opera company performs in Charlottenburg in one of Germany's great post-war opera houses, presenting a full repertoire of classic and contemporary operas, recitals, and ballet. Bismarckstrasse 35. ℰ **030/34384343.** www.deutscheoperberlin.de. U-Bahn: Deutsche Oper. S-Bahn: Charlottenburg.

Komische Oper Berlin ★★★ THE PERFORMING ARTS The Komische Opera has become one of the most highly regarded theater ensembles in Europe, presenting many contemporary productions of operas, operettas, ballets and musical theater. Behrenstrasse 55–57. ℰ **030/202600.** www.komische-oper-berlin.de. U-Bahn: Französische Strasse. S-Bahn: Friedrichstrasse or Unter den Linden.

Konzerthaus Berlin ★★★ THE PERFORMING ARTS This splendid neoclassical building on Gendarmenmarkt offers two venues for classical concerts. The **Berlin Symphony Orchestra** and **Deutsches Sinfonie Orchestra** both perform in this glittering, pitch-perfect hall. Gendarmenmarkt. ℰ **030/203092101.** www.konzerthaus.de. U-Bahn: Französische Strasse.

Staatsoper Unter den Linden ★★★ THE PERFORMING ARTS Berlin's oldest opera house provides a stage for opera, chamber concerts, recitals, and ballet of remarkable quality. While the house is currently closed for restoration and not set to reopen until 2015, the company performs at the Schiller Theater on Bismarkplatz. Unter den Linden 7. ℰ **030/20354555.** www.staatsoper-berlin.org. U-Bahn: Französische Strasse.

Cabaret & Variety Shows

Friedrichstadt Palast ★★ CABARET/REVUE For access to talent that includes multilingual comedians and singers, jugglers, acrobats, musicians, plenty of coyly expressed sexuality, and lots of costume changes, consider an evening here. Although showtimes may vary with whatever revue is featured at the time of your visit, they tend to begin Tuesday to Saturday at 8pm, with additional performances every Saturday and Sunday at 4pm. Friedrichstrasse 107. ℰ **030/23262326.** www.friedrichstadt palast.de. U-/S-Bahn: Friedrichstrasse.

Wintergarten Varieté ★★★ CABARET/REVUE The largest and most nostalgic Berlin cabaret, the Wintergarten offers a variety show every night, with magicians, clowns, jugglers, acrobats, and live music. Potsdamer Strasse 96. ℰ **030/588433.** www. wintergarten-variete.de. U-Bahn: Kurfürstenstrasse.

Dance & Music Clubs

A Trane ★★ JAZZ VENUE This small and smoky jazz house is an excellent choice for beginning or ending an evening of barhopping in Charlottenburg. It features topname and top-talent musicians from all over the world. It's open daily at 9pm; music begins around 10pm. Pestalozzistrasse 105. ℰ **030/3132550.** www.a-trane.de. S-Bahn: Savignyplatz.

4

BERLIN | Nightlife

Clärchens Ballhaus ★★★ DANCE CLUB A landmark in old East Berlin, Clärchens Dance Hall opened in 1913 and has reemerged as a fun and fabulous place for all-age ballroom dancing in an atmosphere complete with bow-tied waiters and silver tinsel. There's salsa, swing, waltz, and tango every night and you can brush up your footwork at one of the regular dance classes; see the website for details. Auguststrasse 24. ✆ **030/2829295.** www.ballhaus.de. S-Bahn: Oranienburger Strasse.

Club der Visionäre ★★ BAR Relaxed and effortlessly cool, this canal-side shack in Kreuzberg is the place to be on balmy summer evenings. When the weather's warm, young hipsters laze on the deck area, gulp cold beer, and drift away to chill-out music. Am Flutgraben 1. ✆ **030/69518944.** www.clubdervisionaere.com. U-Bahn: Schlesisches Tor.

Delicious Doughnuts ★ DANCE CLUB Acid jazz and other delights are available here, but the doughnuts are long gone. A scarlet-red decor with black-leather booths and a pocket-size dance floor is just part of the allure, along with hot DJs. Rosenthalerstrasse 9. ✆ **030/28099274.** www.delicious-doughnuts.de. U-Bahn: Rosenthaler Platz.

SO36 ★★ DANCE CLUB The lines begin to form here about 30 minutes before this witty and unconventional club opens its doors. Its name derives from the postal code for this district in Kreuzberg before World War II. Inside, you'll find two very large rooms, a stage, an ongoing rush of danceable music, and a mixed gay-lesbian-straight scene with a varied musical line-up from Asian house to techno, punk, and funk. It also stages regular concerts and campy themed events. Oranienstrasse 190. ✆ **030/61401306.** www.so36.de. U-Bahn: Kottbusser Tor.

The Bar, Beer Garden & Cafe Scene

Café Aedes ★★★ CAFE Trendy, convivial, and very hip, Café Sedes is a place to elax with a cup of coffee and a dessert, or enjoy a simple meal that's not too expensive. Rosenthaler Strasse 40–41. ✆ **030/285-8278.** Daily 10am–midnight. U-Bahn: Weinmeisterstrasse.

Café Einstein ★★★ CAFE This legendary Viennese-style cafe in an old townhouse serves mellow house-roasted *Kaffee* and freshly made *Kuchen* (cakes) as well as breakfast, lunch and dinner. There is another branch at Unter den Linden 42. Kurfürstenstrasse 58. ✆ **030/2615096.** www.cafeeinstein.com. Daily 9am–1am. U-Bahn: Wittenbergplatz

Café Silberstein ★★★ CAFE This one of the best places to see the "new" eastern Berlin in all its up-to-the-nanosecond trendiness. The cafe is housed in a long, tall, narrow room with original 1920s wall paintings and modern furniture. On the menu, you find sushi, salads, miso soup with noodles, and an all-day breakfast. Oranienburger Strasse 27. ✆ **030/281-2095.** Mon–Fri 10am–4am; Sat–Sun 10am–5am. S-Bahn: Oranienburger Tor.

Golgatha ★★★ BEER GARDEN In the heart of Kreuzberg's Viktoriapark, this leafy beer garden becomes an open-air club after 10pm, with DJs spinning electro, rock, and pop. You can come to dance or just for relaxed drinks on the terrace. Top-notch German brews including the local Kreuzberg Monastery dark beer go well with snacks from the charcoal grill. Dudenstrasse 40. ✆ **030/7852453.** www.golgatha-berlin.de. Apr–Sept daily 9am–6am; closed Oct–Mar. U-Bahn: Platz der Luftbrücke.

Prater Garten ★★★ BEER GARDEN This 600-seat beer garden in Prenzlauer Berg is the city's oldest, dating from 1837, and attracts a wonderfully diverse Berlin crowd. A selection of local beers and hearty meals is available. Kastanienallee 7–9. ✆ **030/4485688.** www.pratergarten.de. Apr–Sept Mon–Sat 6pm–midnight, Sun noon–10pm. U-Bahn: Eberswalder Strasse.

The Liberate ★★ BAR   With its glittering chandeliers, tufted banquettes and black-and-gold wallpaper, this over-the-top cocktail bar in the hot new Monbijou Park area evokes Hollywood glamor in the 1950s, and coincidentally serves great cocktails. Kleine Präsidentenstrasse 4. ℭ **030/8867778.** www.theliberate.com. Wed–Sun. S-Bahn: Hackescher Markt.

Solar ★★★ BAR/VIEW   Arguably the best view of Berlin by night is to be had from this sleek, glass-walled lounge on the 17th floor of a nondescript high-rise in Mitte. Kick back with a drink as the city's landmarks twinkle below. There's a fancy fusion restaurant as well, if you want a meal with a view. It ain't cheap, but it sure is pretty. Stresemannstrasse 76. ℭ **0163/765225700.** www.solarberlin.com. Daily. S-Bahn: Anhalter Bahnhof.

Gay & Lesbian Bars

Kumpelnest 3000 ★★ BAR/DANCE CLUB   Gay or straight, you're welcome here. All that's asked is that you enjoy a good time in what used to be a brothel. This crowded and chaotic place is really a bar now, but there's also dancing to disco classics. Lützowstrasse 23. ℭ **030/2616918.** www.kumpelnest3000.com. Daily 7pm–5am. U-Bahn: Kurfürstenstrasse.

Prinzknecht ★ GAY & LESBIAN BAR   It's large, brick-lined, and mobbed with ordinary guys who just happen to be gay. If you want a place that manages to be both classy and down-to-earth, within walking distance of lots of other gay bars, this is a good choice. Fuggerstrasse 33. ℭ **030/23627444.** www.prinzknecht.de. Daily 3pm–3am. U-Bahn: Viktoria-Luise-Platz.

SchwuZ ★★ GAY & LESBIAN BAR/DANCE CLUB   Hidden behind the conventional-looking facade of the Café Sundström is this basement club where the mostly gay, mostly male, and mostly under 35-year-old crowd comes to dance the night away. Mehringdamm 61. ℭ **030/6290880.** www.schwuz.de. Daily 11pm–4am. U-Bahn: Mehringdamm.

DAY TRIPS FROM BERLIN

No one would ever blame you for spending all of your time in Berlin, but if you want to see something more of the region, consider a day trip to Potsdam or Dresden. Both of these cities are urban treasure troves that reveal the scope of Germany's artistic, architectural and cultural heritage.

Potsdam & Sanssouci Palace ★★★

24km (15 miles) SW of Berlin

The best day trip from Berlin is to the baroque town of Potsdam on the Havel River, site of Frederick the Great's **Schloss Sanssouci (Sanssouci Palace),** often called Germany's Versailles and the architectural signature of one of Germany's most dominating personalities. Allow yourself at least half a day to visit this remarkable palace and its beautiful grounds. Potsdam, a former garrison town and now the capital of the state of Brandenburg, celebrated its 1,000th anniversary in 1993 and has historic sites of its own, but be sure to make Sanssouci your top priority.

Either before or after your tour, spend some time wandering through **Sanssouci Park,** the palace's magnificent landscaped gardens, with their bevy of historic buildings. All of the buildings on the grounds charge a separate admission, but the only one truly worth your time is the **Bildergalerie (Picture Gallery).** All of these places are signposted within Park Sanssouci and share the same information number and website as the palace.

GETTING THERE

BY TRAIN   From Berlin, **S-Bahn line S7** stops at the **Potsdam Hauptbahnhof (train station).** Hop on **bus no. 695** in front of the station and ride nine stops to the Schloss Sanssouci stop. Cross the road, turn left, and you'll almost immediately come to a flight of stairs leading up to the palace. If you don't want to hassle with transportation, you can take one of the **Potsdam-Sanssouci bus tours** offered by the Severin + Kuhn sightseeing bus companies on Ku'Damm (see "Bus Tours," above); the cost is generally about 45€ for a half-day fast-track tour.

GETTING AROUND

BY PUBLIC TRANSPORTATION   If you don't have a Berlin Welcome Card with Potsdam included, you can buy a **Premium Day Ticket** for 21€ that is good for all transportation and museums in Potsdam, including Sanssouci. Buy your ticket at the Potsdam Information center, which can also help you with walking tours, boat tours, and Tourist Tram tours.

VISITOR INFORMATION

Potsdam-Information, Brandenburgerstrasse 3, Am Brandenburger Tor (℗ **0331/27-55-88-99;** www.potsdam-tourism.com), is open Monday through Friday 9:30am to 6pm and Saturday through Sunday 9:30am to 4pm (Nov–Mar Sat–Sun until 2pm.)

ROYAL POTSDAM

Schloss Sanssouci ★★★ PALACE/CASTLE/PARK/GARDEN   One of the greatest and most beautiful examples of European rococo, Sanssouci was built between 1745 and 1747 as Frederick's summerhouse, a place where he could let his wig down, discuss weighty matters with French philosopher Voltaire, and make music with composer Carl Philip Emanuel Bach. In short, Sanssouci ("without cares") was a sort of summer resort for an enlightened monarch. The long, one-story building is crowned by a dome and flanked by two round pavilions. Fred the Great created the original design for the grounds, and his planning still is evident in the restored vineyard terraces and the area immediately around the palace. The elliptically shaped **Marble Hall** is the largest in the palace, but the **Music Salon** is the supreme example of the rococo style. All kinds of rococo treasures fill the palace, which you see on a tour that lasts about 45 minutes. The tour is given only in German, but information sheets in English are available from the guide.

Park Sanssouci. (℗ **0331/9694200.** www.spsg.de. Admission 8€ adults, 5€ seniors/students. Apr–Oct Tues–Sun 10am–6pm (Nov–Mar to 5pm).

Bildergalerie (Picture Gallery) ★★ GALLERY/MUSEUM   Set on the eastern side of the palace grounds, this building was completed in 1763 and displays Frederick the Great's collection of works from the Italian Renaissance and baroque eras. The building's unassuming facade hides a sumptuous marble and gold interior with paintings by Peter Paul Rubens (1577–1640), Caravaggio (1571–1610), and Anthony van Dyck (1599–1641). Pick up a flyer in English detailing the most important works and give yourself at least 30 to 45 minutes to see the lightlights.

Park Sanssouci. Admission 6€ adults, 5€ seniors/students. May–Oct Tues–Sun 10am–6pm.

Chinesische Teehaus (Chinese Teahouse) ★ ARCHITECTURAL SITE   This little gem of a rococo building in Sanssouci park resembles a Chinese pagoda. Ornamental "Oriental" buildings like this were all the rage in 18th-century Europe. The privileged classes would retire here to drink a new beverage called tea. This building is not open to the public.

Neues Palais (New Palace) ★ PALACE/CASTLE   The largest building in Sanssouci park was completed in 1769 and used by the Hohenzollern royal family. Inside you can see rococo rooms filled with paintings and antiques.

Park Sanssouci. Admission 8€ for guided tour. Sat–Thurs 9am–5pm (Nov–Mar until 4pm).

Orangerie ★ GALLERY   The mid-19th-century Orangerie, west of the palace, contains copies of paintings by Raphael and features ornately decorated salons.

Park Sanssouci. Admission 3€. Mid-May to mid-Oct Fri–Wed 10am–5pm.

Schloss Cecilienhof (Cecilienhof Palace) ★★ PALACE/CASTLE   Built to look like an English country manor, this palace was a royal residence from 1917 until 1945. At the end of World War II, the palace was used as headquarters for the Potsdam Conference attended by the heads of the Allied powers, including U.S. President Harry Truman, British Prime Minister Winston Churchill, and Russian dictator Joseph Stalin. Now the palace serves as a hotel and conference center. On a guided tour, you can visit the private rooms used by Crown Prince Wilhelm and Princess Cecelie. More interesting are the rooms used for the Potsdam Conference.

Park Sanssouci. Admission 8€ for tour. Tues–Sun 9am–5pm (Nov–Mar until 4pm).

MORE OF POTSDAM

Although your priority when visiting Potsdam will probably be Sanssouci, the city of Potsdam itself has many charming streets and historic areas and structures that you can explore before or after your visit to the palace and gardens.

Nikolaikirche ★★ CHURCH   Rising above Potsdam's cobblestoned marketplace square, this mighty neoclassical church, completed in 1837 and inspired by Santa Maria Maggiore in Rome, is the handiwork of the prolific 19th-century German architect Karl Friedrich Schinkel (1781–1841), whose buildings are also found along Unter den Linden and at Charlottenburg Palace in Berlin.

Am Alten Markt. ℂ **0331/2708602.** www.nikolai-potsdam.de. Admission free to the church, tower 5€. Daily 9am–5pm.

Altes Rathaus (Old Town Hall) ★ MUSEUM   The Greco-Roman-inspired town hall beside the Nikolaikirche dates from the mid–18th century and has a noteworthy Corinthian colonnade. Perched on top of the cupola is the Greek Titan Atlas, bent under the weight of the Earth. The Altes Rathaus underwent a complete transformation and reopened in 2013 as the **Forum for Art and History** with a permanent exhibit that walks visitors through Potsdam's 1,000-year history.

Am Alten Markt 9. ℂ **0331/2896868.** Admission 5€ adult, free for children under 18. Tues–Fri 10am–5pm; Sat–Sun 10am–6pm.

Holländisches Viertel (Dutch Quarter) ★★ NEIGHBORHOOD   Centered around Am Bassin and Benkerstrasse, the picturesque Dutch Quarter is named after the Dutch craftsmen who came to Potsdam in the mid–18th century at the invitation of "Soldier King" Frederick Wilhelm I. As you wander the cobbled lanes past gabled houses, look for Am Bassin 10, where Mozart lived in 1789, and the Italianate belfry of nearby St. Peter und Paul Kirche (1870). Antiques shops, boutiques, and galleries line Benkerstrasse. A bit farther to the northwest, the neo-Gothic Nauener Tor (1755) is one of the last remaining city gates.

WHERE TO EAT

La Maison du Chocolat ★ DESSERTS On warm days, the terrace here is the best place to enjoy the Holländisches Viertel's Dutch ambiance. The old-world cafe is famed for its smooth hot chocolate and fruit tarts.

Benkertstrasse 20. ✆ **0331/2370730.** Desserts and snacks 5€–8€.

Specker's Gaststätte zur Ratswaag ★★ CONTINENTAL Located midway between Potsdam's railway station and its historic core, this is one of Potsdam's finest restaurants, with a menu that emphasizes fresh, local, seasonal ingredients.

Jägerallee 13. ✆ **0331/2804311.** www.speckers.de. Main courses 16€–35€; fixed-price menu 30€. Tues–Sat noon–2pm and 6–11pm.

Dresden ★★★

198km (123 miles) S of Berlin

Dresden celebrated its 800th anniversary in 2006. Perhaps the most important celebratory event was the reopening of the famous domed **Frauenkirche (Church of Our Lady),** destroyed in the bombings of World War II. The Frauenkirche is a symbol of what Dresden once was—a city known as "Florence on the Elbe," and renowned for its architecture and art treasures—and hopes to become again. Under the rule of Elector Augustus the Strong (1670–1733), the preeminent personality in the town's history, Dresden flourished as one of the great cultural centers of Europe. But on the night of February 13, 1945, Allied firebombs destroyed three-quarters of Dresden's Altstadt, the beautiful old core of the city. Historic buildings have since been rebuilt, but the work has taken decades and uninspired architecture from the Soviet GDR days still remains. After reunification in 1990, Dresden emerged as the top contender for tourists in the former East Germany. Dresden, the capital of Saxony, is an expensive city, top-heavy with upmarket luxury hotels and restaurants, which is another reason why you may want to visit as a day trip from Berlin rather than stay overnight.

> ### Save Money with a Dresden City-Card
>
> Admission prices to Dresden's many museums can quickly add up. To save money, buy a **Dresden City-Card** (26€) at the tourist information office. This card is good for all public transportation and admission to most of the city's museums.

GETTING THERE

BY TRAIN To make Dresden work as a day trip, you'll need to start early and take a fast Eurocity (EC) train. On an EC train, the trip time from Berlin's hauptbahnhof to **Dresden Hauptbahnhof** is about 2 hours. For train information and schedules visit www.bahn.com.

GETTING AROUND

BY PUBLIC TRANSPORTATION You can walk everywhere in the historic core, or use the bus and tram lines. A 24-hour pass for all forms of public transportation costs 5€. Maps and tickets are sold at machines outside the main rail station.

BUS TOURS City tours by **Stadtrundfahrt Dresden,** Königstrasse 6 (✆ **0351/89-95-650;** www.stadtrundfahrt.com), depart from Theaterplatz, adjacent to the Augustusbrücke (Augustus Bridge) at 30-minute intervals for circular tours of the city that incorporate all the major museums and monuments. Visitors can hop on or off the bus

ATTRACTIONS ●
Albertinum **1**
Frauenkirche (Church of Our Lady) **2**
Grünes Gewölbe (Green Vault) **5**

Katholische Hofkirche (Catholic Court Church) **4**
Zwinger **7**

RESTAURANTS ◆
Café Schinkelwache **6**
Café zur Frauenkirche **3**

Information ⓘ
Pedestrians only

at any of 22 points along the way. The stops are keyed to multi-lingual descriptions in a brochure. The price is 20€ for adults, 18€ for students and seniors.

VISITOR INFORMATION

There's a branch of the **Dresden Tourist Information Office** (ⓒ **0351/50-15-01;** www.dresden.de) in the **Hauptbahnhof (main train station),** open daily 9am to 7pm. They can provide you with with all the information you need about the city, bus and walking tours, and public transportation.

EXPLORING DRESDEN

The Elbe River divides Dresden more or less in half. All the major cultural attractions, including art museums, the newly restored Frauenkirche, churches in the **Altmarkt (Old Market)** and **Neumarkt (New Market)** squares, the Zwinger Palace museums, and the Semper Opera House, are on the south side of the Elbe. **Prager Strasse,** a wide pedestrian street lined with shops, hotels, and restaurants, is the main thoroughfare. **Dresden-Neustadt** occupies the north side of the river. Pretty 19th-century houses reconstructed to hold shops, apartments, and restaurants line **Hauptstrasse** and **Königstrasse,** its main streets.

Albertinum ★★★ MUSEUM Between 1884 and 1887, King Albert of Saxony (1828–1902)—whose full name was (are you ready?) Frederick Augustus Albert Anton Ferdinand Joseph Karl Maria Baptist Nepomuk Wilhelm Xaver Georg Fidelis—cconverted the royal arsenal into a home for his vast collection of art and precious jewelry. The **Gemäldegalerie Neue Meister (New Masters Gallery)**, taking up two floors, is a rich collection of 19th- and 20th-century art. The collection concentrates on German art, starting with moody works by Caspar David Friedrich (1774–1840), the great German Romantic artist, and going up to the brilliant works of Dresden-born Otto Dix (1889–1969), a painter who ran afoul of the Nazis. Allot at least an hour to see the highlights. The **Skulpturen-Sammlung (Sculpture Collection)** includes examples from over 5 millennia, starting with the ancient cultures of the Mediterranean region through all epochs of European sculpture to the present.

Brühl Terrace. ℂ **0351/49142000.** www.skd-dresden.de. Admission 10€ adults, 7.50€ seniors and students, free for children 17 and under. Tues–Sun 10am–6pm. Tram: 1, 3, 5, 7, or 8.

Frauenkirche (Church of Our Lady) ★★★ CHURCH Built between 1726 and 1743, the Frauenkirche on the southeast side of Neumarkt (New Market Square) was the most important Protestant church in Germany and had one of the most famous domes in Europe. The 1945 Allied bombing of Dresden destroyed 80 percent of the city, including the Frauenkirche. After the war, the East German government let the charred ruin remain as a memorial. A painstaking restoration project began in 1993 and was finally completed in 2006. The reopening of the church was an event of major symbolic importance. The new golden cross atop the dome, an exact replica of the 18th-century original, was built by the son of a British bomber pilot who took part in the original bombing raid. Once again this baroque church dominates the historic center of Dresden; step inside the brilliant white interior to admire the immaculate restoration work.

Neumarkt. ℂ **0351/6560670.** www.frauenkirche-dresden.de. Free admission. Daily 10am–noon and 1–6pm, except during Sunday concerts. Tram: 4 or 8.

Grünes Gewölbe (Green Vault) ★★★ MUSEUM The fabulous assortment of treasures displayed in the Residenzschloss consists of two collections, each requiring a separate admission. The **Neues Grünes Gewölbe (New Green Vault)** features ten rooms of selected masterworks from the huge collection of 16th- to 18th-century objects, including rococo chests, ivory carvings, gold jewelry, bronze statuettes, intricately designed mirrors, and priceless porcelain. Allow yourself at least an hour to browse this treasure-trove (be prepared for crowds), and take advantage of the free audio guide. Unless you're a nut for *objets d'art* nut, this dazzling selection of highlights will more than satisfy your curiosity. But there's more, if you want it. The **Historisches Grünes Gewölbe (Historic Green Vault)** features a larger selection of the collection and can only be visited with a prebooked timed-entry ticket, available in advance by going online at www.skd-dresden.de.

Residenzschloss, Sophienstrasse. ℂ **0351/49142000.** www.skd-dresden.de. Admission: New Green Vault 10€ adults, 7.50€ seniors and students, Historic Green Vault 12€; both free for children 17 and under. Wed–Mon 10am–6pm. Tram: 4 or 8.

Katholische Hofkirche (Catholic Court Church) ★ CHURCH The restored Hofkirche, also known as the Cathedral of St. Trinitas, is the largest church in Saxony. Built by the son of Augustus the Strong, Frederick Augustus II (ruled 1733–63), the church was constructed in a lavish Italian baroque style with a curving facade and a 86m (282-ft.) bell tower decorated with statues of saints and apostles. Inside, you can see the crypt with the tombs of 49 kings and princes of Saxony.

Schlossplatz. ℂ **0351/4951133.** Mon–Fri 9am–4:30pm; Sat 10am–4pm; Sun noon–4pm. Tram: 4 or 8.

4

Day Trips from Berlin

BERLIN

Zwinger ★★★ PALACE/CASTLE Augustus the Strong, elector of Saxony and king of Poland, built this magnificent baroque palace in 1719. He wanted the Zwinger to be his Versailles and a place where he could show off his incredible art collections. The architect, M. D. Pöppelmann (1662–1736), designed a series of galleries and domed pavilions to enclose a large rectangular courtyard with formal gardens, fountains, and promenades. The semicircular **Wallpavillon** at the west end and the adjacent **Nymphenbad,** with its graceful fountains and mythological figures, are notable buildings that rely on the exuberant sculptures of the Bavarian artist Balthasar Permoser (1651–1732). On the northeast side is the Semper Gallery, a Renaissance-style two-story pavilion linked by one-story galleries; Gottfried Semper added the pavilion in 1846. Today, this entire complex of buildings contains a stunning collection of museums. They all charge separate admissions (another good reason to buy a **Dresden City-Card,** described above) and they are all open Tuesday through Sunday, 10am to 6pm; for more information go to www.skd-dresden.de.

The most important museum in the Zwinger is the **Gemäldegalerie Alte Meister (Old Masters Gallery)** ★★★ in the Semper Gallery (entrance at Theaterplatz 1). This gallery, one of the best in the world, has as its showpiece Raphael's "Sistine Madonna." The collection also includes Flemish, Dutch, and German paintings by Van Dyck, Vermeer, Dürer, Rubens, and Rembrandt. Galleries 2 through 4 display a series of detailed Dresden townscapes painted by Canaletto in the mid–18th century. Canaletto's views of Dresden are so true to life that they were used as reference works during the post-WWII reconstruction of the city. Allow at least 2 hours for unhurried browsing. Admission is 10€ adults, 7.50€ seniors and students.

The **Porzellansammlung (Porcelain Collection),** with its entrance in the Glockenspiel Pavillon (Carillon Pavillion), displays Japanese, Chinese, and Meissen porcelain from the 18th and 19th centuries. The "giant animal room" on the second floor has a collection of 18th-century Meissen animals. Depending on your interest, you can see everything 30 minutes or less. Admission is 6€ adults, 4.50€ seniors and students.

On the west side of the Zwinger, to the left of the Wallpavillon, is the intriguing **Mathematische-Physikalischer Salon (Salon of Mathematics and Physics),** with all manner of clocks and scientific instruments of the 16th to 19th centuries. Admission is 6€ adults, 4.50€ seniors and students.

WHERE TO EAT

Café Schinkelwache ★ CONTINENTAL This sandstone structure in the center of Theaterplatz was built in 1832 by architect Karl Friedrich Schinkel to house soldiers and guards. In 1995, the building was rebuilt and reconfigured into a cafe with outdoor tables on the terrace. If you're daytripping to Dresden and want an easy, convenient spot to have lunch, this is a good choice. Menu selections include pastries, meal-size salads, soups, crepes with mushrooms and chicken, and veal stew. You can also sit and enjoy wine, beer, or coffee.

Sophienstrasse am Theaterplatz. ✆ **0351/4903909.** Main courses 7€–12€; fixed-price menu 13€–20€. Daily 9am–midnight. Tram: 1, 2, 4.

Café zur Frauenkirche ★ GERMAN/INTERNATIONAL This street-side corner cafe, located directly across from the Frauenkirche, is a good place to sit outside and eat or have a drink. The menu typically has dishes such as grilled lamb cutlet with asparagus, pastas, and pork goulash with cabbage and dumplings. For dessert try the homemade *Quarkkeutchen,* a baked dumpling filled with cheese and raisins.

An der Frauenkirche 5. ✆ **0351/4989836.** Main courses 10€–20€. Daily 10am–1am. Tram: 4 or 8.

SHOPPING

Weihnachtsland am Zwinger, Kleine Brüdergasse 5 (© **0351/86-21-230;** www. weihnachtsland-dresden.com), is the best-stocked and most interesting gift shop in Dresden, with a selection of Christmas, New Year's, and Easter ornaments that are handmade in the nearby Erzgebirge region.

The oldest manufacturer of porcelain in Dresden is **Wehsener Porzellan,** 5km (3 miles) southeast of the center at Dohnaerstrasse 72 (© **0351/47-04-370;** Tram: 13; Bus: 72 or 76). Its handpainted objects are the most charming and interesting in Dresden. You can also take a free tour of the studios and factory.

Dresden's **Weihnachtsmarkt** (also called the **Striezelmarkt**) is the oldest Christmas market in Germany. This December event, which began in 1434, takes place in the Altmarkt and features handmade regional crafts and gift items and homemade foods. Look for woodcarvings from the Erzgebirge Mountains, indigo-printed cloth and pottery from Lusatia, gingerbread from Pulsnitz, filigree lace from Plauen, Advent stars from Hermhut, and blown-glass tree decorations from Lauscha.

HAMBURG & THE NORTH

E very nation seems to have a north–south divide, and Germany is no exception. Travel up here from even northerly Berlin and you'll notice a difference—the salt tinged breezes off the Baltic Sea, the distinctive brick gabled houses favored by Hanseatic merchants and seafarers, a preference for herring and other fish, the long winter nights and long summer days, the palpable presence of Scandinavia. Our coverage focuses on two of northern Germany's standouts, the dynamic port city of Hamburg and medieval Lübeck, an architectural treasure trove.

HAMBURG ★★

285km (177 miles) northwest of Berlin

Hamburg's is a tale of two cities…or three, or four. Germany's second largest city, after Berlin, and Europe's second-largest port, after Rotterdam, has so many facets that visitors stumble into one fascinating cityscape after another. The copper-roofed tower of old baroque Hauptkirche St. Michael's rises next to glass and steel office buildings. The port, with its wharfs, cranes, dry docks, and a flotilla of ships coming and going day and night rambles along the banks of the Elbe River as far as the eye can see. A maze of canals laces through the old city, lined with sturdy brick warehouses where Hamburg merchants once stashed carpets, tea, and the other lucre of trade. These days boldly designed high-rise corporate headquarters—Hamburg is a media capital and industrial center—are the powerhouses of wealth and influence. Elegant 19th-century facades along the shores of the Alster, the shimmering lake at Hamburg's center, and Jugenstil (art nouveau) villas scream bourgeois comforts; smart-phone-toting Armani clad execs carry on the legacy of well-fed Middle Age burghers who made fortunes after Frederich Barbarossa declared the city a free port in 1193. Then there's Hamburg's underbelly—the infamous Reeperbahn, the sleazy avenue where "Hiya sailor" is the anthem of easy virtue. The stag partiers and other denizens of the night who dip into this slice of lowlife are onto something—Hamburg might be business-minded, even stuffy in places, but it can also be a lot of fun, whatever your notion of a good time is. That might also mean gazing at an Expressionist canvas in the Kunsthalle, or watching Hamburgers haggle over the price of cod at the Fischmarkt, or cruising past architectural stunners in HafenCity, a brand new waterfront quarter. As you get to know Hamburg, you will be surprised at just how easy it is to succumb to this city's charms and how many there are.

Essentials

GETTING THERE

BY PLANE   Hamburg-Fuhlsbüttel, 8km (5 miles) north of the city center, is served by frequent flights to and from major German airports and many European and intercontinental destinations. **Lufthansa** (© **01803/805805;** www.lufthansa.com) flies into Hamburg from most major German and European cities, and many national carriers also serve Hamburg, including Air France from Paris and British Airways from London. United Airlines offers nonstop service from the United States (from Newark) but on most carriers a flight from the U.S. requires a change in Frankfurt or another European hub. For flight information in Hamburg, call © **040/50750** or visit www.ham.airport.de.

The ultramodern terminal, with a roof shaped like an enormous airplane wing, is well-equipped wth shops and boutiques—even a branch of Harrods of London—as well as restaurants and other establishments.

During the day the S-Bahn (suburban rail network) line S1 operates every 10 minutes between the airport and Hamburg's central railway station, Hauptbahnhof (the trip takes 25 min.). The airport (Flughafen) S-Bahn station is directly in front of the air terminals. The one-way fare to the center is 3€, or 1.50€ for ages 11 and under.

BY TRAIN   There are two major rail stations, the centrally located **Hamburg Hauptbahnhof,** Hachmannplatz 10 (© **040/39183046;** www.bahn.com), and **Hamburg-Altona** (© **040/39182387;** www.bahn.com), at the eastern edge of the Altstadt. Most trains arrive at the Hauptbahnhof, although trains from the north of Germany, including Westerland and Schleswig, arrive at Altona. The two stations are connected by train and S-Bahn. Hamburg has frequent train connections with all major German cities, and is a hub for international routes as well. From Berlin, 15 trains arrive daily (trip time: 2½ hr.), 37 from Bremen (trip time: 54 min. to 1 hr., 16 min.), and 33 from Hannover (trip time: 1½ hr.). For information, call © **01805/996633** (www.bahn.com).

BY BUS   Information about short-haul buses from surrounding towns and villages is available from **Hamburger Verkehrsverbund** (© **040/19449;** www.hvv.de).

BY CAR   The A1 Autobahn reaches Hamburg from the south and west, the A7 from the north and south, the A23 from the northwest, and the A24 from the east.

VISITOR INFORMATION

Tourist-Information, in the Hauptbahnhof, Kirchenallee exit (© **040/30051300**), is open Monday to Saturday 8am to 9pm, Sunday 10am to 6pm (phone inquiries are accepted Mon–Sat 9am–7pm). Another office, **Port Information,** near the harbor landing stage in St. Pauli on Landungsbrücken (© **040/30051300**), is open April to October daily 8am to 6pm, and November to March daily 10am to 6pm. There is another tourist office at the airport, at terminals 1 and 2 (arrivals area), open daily 6am to 11pm. You may also contact the visitor information hot line at © **040/30051300** or see www.hamburg-tourism.de.

CITY LAYOUT

A couple of things to keep in mind. One, Hamburg is not compact and can't be easily covered on foot; you'll probably have to depend on public transportation or taxis. Two, think water. Hamburg lies on the Elbe River, 109km (68 miles) from the North Sea, and water seems to be everywhere in this city that is centered around a lake, the Alster; faces a busy harbor; and is laced with canals. (These canals are commercial and

Around Hamburg

industrial waterways, lined with docks and warehouses; don't fall for the touristic mumbo jumbo that Hamburg is the Venice of the North, because busy, business-minded Hamburg in no way resembles that Italian city.)

The **Alster,** often sparkling with white sails, is divided by bridges into the Binnenalster (Inner Alster) and the larger Aussenalster (Outer Alster). Busy avenues, including the elegant, shop-lined Ballindamm, flank the Binnenalster, as do such noteworthy landmarks as the Colonnaden, an arcade of shops and cafes, and the Hamburgische Staatsoper, the opera house.

The **Altstadt (Old Town)** is south of the Binnenalster, tucked between the lakeshore and the Elbe River waterfront. The Hauptbahnhof is on the eastern fringe of the Altstadt, and the Rathaus, the Renaissance-style city hall, and adjacent Rathausmarkt are on the western edge. Two major shopping streets run between the Hauptbahnhof and the Rathausmarkt, the Spitalerstrasse (a pedestrian mall) and Mönckebergstrasse, paralleling it to the south.

A new district, **HafenCity,** is growing up south of the Altstadt in former docklands that extend 3km (2 miles) along the Elbe River. At the moment much of HafenCity looks like a forest of cranes rising above construction sites, but it's predicted that by

2020 or so a concert hall, bars, slick office buildings, and hundreds of waterfront apartments will have transformed the docklands into the city's new pride and joy.

St. Pauli, west of the Altstadt, is the Hamburg's famous red light district, where shops and clubs line the lurid Reeperbahn, a street where sex is sold over-the-counter, not under.

The Neighborhoods in Brief

CENTRAL HAMBURG

Hamburg's commercial and shopping districts are on the southernmost shores of the Alster (the lake at the city center) and in the Altstadt (Old City), around the Rathaus (City Hall). Don't look for a lot of historic charm—there certainly is some, though World War II laid waste to much of it. Notable survivors include the city's distinctive red-brick warehouses that line canals near the waterfront, and some noble landmarks, such as St. Petri Church with its skyline-piercing dome. St. Georg, an inner city neighborhood running alongside the lake just north of the Hauptbanhof, is one of many old quarters that have been gentrified in recent years. Parts are still a bit dodgy, but leafy streets near the lake, especially the Langhe Reihe, are lined with cafes and restaurants, some catering to gays, and some of the city's most character-filled hotels are in this old neighborhood.

THE WATERFRONT

The Port of Hamburg is the world's fifth-largest harbor, stretching for nearly 40km (25 miles) along the Elbe River. Hamburg has been one of the busiest centers of trade on the Continent for almost ten centuries and is, largely as a consequence of this maritime trade, one of Germany's wealthiest cities. HafenCity, Europe's largest inner-city urban development project extends for 3km (2 miles) along the Elbe River. The emerging district is expected to double the population of central Hamburg with thousands of waterfront apartments, and includes a concert hall, bars, and slick office buildings.

ST. PAULI

Hamburg's infamous nightlife and red-light district centers on the Reeperbahn, neon-lit and garrish and offering all sorts of pleasures—cafes, sex shows, bars, dance clubs, and music halls. This maritime quarter is a lot less raucous than it once was and these days many habitues are more intent on drinking and dancing than paying for companionship.

ALTONI

Once populated mainly by Jews and Portuguese, this western district is the scene of some great dining and nightlife. Those in search of more traditional pursuits can wake at the crack of dawn on Sunday to check out what's happening in the stalls of the historic Altona Fischmarkt.

AROUND THE LAKE

Many villas dating from the 1800s and some stunning *Jugendstil* buildings line the streets of tree-filled residential districts around the Aussenalster. A particularly attractive lakeside enclave is Harvestude, since the 19th-century home to Hamburg's wealthy burghers and whose villas are now occupied by many foreign consulates.

GETTING AROUND

A word to the wise: Park your car and use public transportation to avoid traffic and the hassle and expense of parking.

BY PUBLIC TRANSPORTATION Hamburg's **U-Bahn,** one of the best subway systems in Germany, connects with the **S-Bahn** surface trains. This network is the fastest means of getting around, though buses are also fast and efficient and travel in special lanes throughout the city center. For information, call ✆ **040/19449.**

Single tickets for the U-Bahn, S-Bahn, and the bus cost 2.80€ for citywide service and 1.30€ for trips within the center city. A 3-day pass for 1 person costs 17€.

The Hamburg Card offers unlimited travel on all public transport in Hamburg, as well as discounts to museums, other attractions, and city tours. A 1-day card costs 8.90€ for individuals or 15€ for families (one adult and up to three children 14 years old and under). A 3-day card costs 22€ for individuals and 39€ for families, and a 5-day card costs 38€ for individuals and 64€ for families. You can get these cards at some hotels, major U-Bahn stations, and the tourist office, or go to www.hamburg-travel.com or call ✆ **040/30051300.**

The U-Bahn (subway), S-Bahn (city rail), A-Bahn (commuter rail), buses, and harbor ferries are run by Hamburger Verkehrsverbund (HVV), Steinstrasse 12. For information, call ✆ **040/19449** (www.hvv.de). Tickets are sold at machines in U-Bahn and S-Bahn stations, on buses, and at railroad ticket counters.

BY TAXI   Taxis are available at all hours; call ✆ **040/211211** (www.taxi211211.de). Taxi meters begin at 2.70€ and charge 1.70€ per kilometer after that.

[Fast FACTS] HAMBURG

Business Hours   Most businesses and stores are open Monday to Friday 9am to 6pm and Saturday 9am to 2pm (to 4 or 6pm on the first Sat of the month). Note that most stores are not open on Sunday or in the evenings.

Car Rentals   We don't recommend that you rent a car for touring Hamburg, and you can easily reach Lübeck and other outlying towns by train. If you do require a car, you'll find all the major agencies at the airport; see p. 239 for info on car rentals in Germany.

Consulates   Consulate General of the U.S., Alsterufer 27–28 (✆ **040/ 41171415**); British Consulate-General, Neuer Jungfernstieg 20 (✆ **040/4480326**).

Currency Exchange
You'll find ATMS throughout Hamburg. If you require the services of a bank, try the **ReiseBank** at the Hauptbahnhof (✆ **040/ 323483**), which is open daily 7:30am to 10pm and has a number of English-speaking staffers. The same bank maintains a branch at the Altona Station (✆ **040/ 3903770**), open Monday to Friday 7:30am to 8pm, and Saturday 9am to 2pm and 2:45 to 5pm. There's also a branch in Terminal 2 of Hamburg's airport (✆ **040/ 50753374**), open daily 8am to 9pm.

Doctors & Dentists
Ask at the British or American consulates, or go to the large medical center in St. Georg, **Allgemeines Krankenhaus Sankt Georg,** Lohmühlenstrasse 5, 20099 Hamburg (✆ **040/ 1818850;** U-Bahn: Lohmühlenstrasse), where you'll find an English-speaking staff.

Drugstores   Large pharmacies with English-speaking staff include **Roth's Alte Englische Apotheke,** Jungfernstieg 48 (✆ **040/ 343906;** U-Bahn: Jungfernstieg), open Monday to Friday 8:30am to 8pm and Saturday 9am to 6pm.

Emergencies   Dial ✆ **110** for the police; for an ambulance, an emergency doctor or dentist, or the fire brigade, dial ✆ **112.**

Post Office   The post office at the Hauptbahnhof, Hachmannplatz 13, is centrally located. You can make long-distance calls here far more cheaply than from your hotel. It's open Monday to Friday 8am to 8pm, Saturday 8am to 6pm, and Sunday 10am to 4pm. A branch office located at the airport is open Monday to Friday 6:30am to 9pm, Saturday

8am to 6pm, and Sunday 10am to 6pm. For information on either post office, call (C) **01802/3333.**

Safety Hamburg, like all big cities of the world, has its share of crime. The major crimes that tourists encounter are pickpocketing and purse/camera snatching. Most robberies occur in the big tourist areas, such as the Reeperbahn and the area around the Hauptbahnhof, which can be dangerous at night.

Toilets There are decent public facilities in the center of Hamburg, and the Hauptbanhof has several.

Expect to pay about 1€ to use them.

Transit Information
For U-Bahn and S-Bahn rail information, call the **Hauptbahnhof,** Hachmannplatz 10 ((C) **01805/996633;** www.bahn.com).

Where to Stay

It seems that just about every major international chain on earth has an outpost in Hamburg, so if familiar surroundings are what you want, you won't have any trouble finding them. But Hamburg also has some truly distinctive lodgings, from legendary landmarks to hip hostels. Some are in your face with over-the-top design, others stress low-key comfort. You'll probably want to stay near the center of this far-flung metropolis—choice locales are the cental city in the Altstadt and around the Alster, and near the waterfront, around the port and St. Pauli. A hotel in any of these spots will put you within easy reach of sights, restaurants, and nightlife. If you need a room last minute, stop by **Hamburg's Tourismus Centrale** (Tourist Information Office) in the Hauptbahnhof ((C) **040/30051300;** www.hamburg-tourism.de), where a counter can book accommodations. Rooms in more than 200 hotels in all price categories are available. There's a fee of 5€ per reservation. You can use this agency on a last-minute basis, but no more than 7 days in advance of the time you'll need the room. Hotel-booking desks can also be found at the airport in Arrival Hall A.

CENTRAL CITY

The George ★★   A handsome library and some other clubby touches play off the English-sounding name, but for the most part these lodgings at the edge of the St. Georg neighborhood give off a chic, contemporary vibe. More than half of the handsome guest rooms open to balconies, as do most of the corner suites. In all, dark carpeting, subdued lighting, and sleek furnishings enhanced with rich fabrics ensure a nice refuge from the busy city. Especially relaxing are the friendly, ground-floor Ciao bar and the top-floor spa and sauna, where a lounge and terrace overlook the Alster.

Barcastrasse 3. (C) **040/2800300.** Fax 040/28003030. www.thegeorge-hotel.de. 125 units. 155€–216€ double. Rates include buffet breakfast. Parking 16€. U-Bahn: Uhlandstrasse. **Amenities:** Restaurant; bar; bikes; concierge; health club and spa; room service; free in-room Wi-Fi.

Kempinski Hotel Atlantic ★★   The first thing to know about this gleaming white palace on the shores of the Alster, built for transatlantic passengers in the early 1900s, is that it's one of the world's truly legendary hotels. The second is that with a little internet sleuthing you can book one of the commodious, high-ceilinged guest rooms, not too many of which are alike, for not much more than what you'd pay for a business-oriented hotel in Hamburg. Of course, many of the guests could care less about costs: Madonna, Mick Jagger, Elton John, and a long roster of other notables stay here when in town, as do savvy travelers who feel at home in the surprisingly cozy lounges, sophisticated art deco bar, and guest rooms well stuffed with comfy arm chairs and plump bedding. No doubt they all enjoy the sweeping staircases, lake views, indoor pool, meticulous service, and atmosphere that is a lot more laid back than you'd expect from such regal surroundings.

An der Alster 72–79. ✆ **800/426-3135** in the U.S., or 040/28880. Fax 040/247129. www.kempinski. atlantic.de. 252 units. 179€–400€ double; from 423€ suite. Parking 32€. U-Bahn: Hauptbahnhof. Near the Aussenalster. **Amenities:** 2 restaurants; bar; babysitting; bikes; concierge; exercise room; indoor heated pool; room service; spa; Wi-Fi (fee).

Hotel SIDE ★ Offbeat and postmodern, built around an elliptical atrium, this design statement in steel and glass puts you right in the heart of Hamburg while giving you a break from the typical chain hotel circuit. Matteo Thun, the well-known Milan designer, left nothing to chance in creating neutral-toned bedrooms that are not only airy and stylish but also extremely comfortable, with lots of surfaces and places to tuck clutter away and equipped with commodious, snazzy bathrooms embellished with glass sinks and big windows; suites float above the city in special glass-enclosed quarters cantilevered above the main structure. A rooftop lounge and terrace and spa with an indoor pool add even more pizazz to a stay in this haven of high style.

Drehbahn 49. ✆ **040/309990.** www.side-hamburg.de. 178 units. 150€–300€ double. Parking 20€. U-Bahn: Gänsemarkt or Stephansplatz. Amenities: Restaurant; bar; babysitting; bikes; concierge; exercise room; indoor heated pool; room service; spa; Wi-Fi (fee).

Superbude It's a little too cool for it's own good sometimes—montages made from newspaper clippings on the walls, funky furnishings fashioned from crates, lots of high-tech lighting. But if that's the only snarky thing to be said about an incredibly fair-valued hostel, the place must be okay. And Hamburg's best lodging deal has plenty to commend it. Functional though colorfully stylish lounges and rooms are spotless, fridges are stocked with cheap beer, the breakfast is substantial, the beds are super comfortable, and bathrooms are modern and spiffy. A lot of rooms are cozy doubles and can be let as singles, though young backpackers and young at hearts on a budget often opt for a bunk in a four-bedded room. There are two Superbudes: This one's in the St. Georg district, where you'll be not too far from the lake and some good ethic restaurants, and another one is in the midst of St. Pauli nightlife.

Spaldingstrasse 152. ✆ **040/3808780.** www.superbude.de. 64 units. 59€–133€ double. Parking 5€. U-Bahn: Berliner Tor. **Amenities:** Cafe; bikes; free in-room Wi-Fi.

Wedina ★★★ You can chose from a lot of options at this stylish and low-key retreat near the shores of the Alster: a choice of pillows and bedding, the style of decor (traditional or soothing minimalist), which of four buildings you prefer (from a 19th-c. villa to a sleek concrete and glass modern annex), even where you want to enjoy breakfast—in a conservatory that, like many rooms, overlooks a lovely Italianate garden or, in good weather, the garden itself. Many famous writers like to lay low in these soothing surroundings while in Hamburg on book tours and to lecture, and autographed copies of many modern masterpieces are proudly on display. You'll find plenty of other reading matter lying around the cozy library, or you can rent a bike for a spin around the lake. There are no elevators, and some especially spacious and attractive units are multilevel, so if stairs are an issue, ask for a room that requires a minimum of climbing.

Gurlittstrasse 23. ✆ **040/2808900.** www.wedina.de. 59 units. 118€–170€ double. Rates include buffet breakfast. Bus: 6. Near the lake, a 5-min. walk from the Hauptbahnhof. **Amenities:** Bar; bikes; free in-room Wi-Fi.

NEAR THE WATERFRONT

East ★★ Style has soul in this sophisticated redo of a formidable, red-brick early 20th-century iron foundry where minimalist design is accented with exposed brick, wrought iron, and natural fabrics to create a transporting environment that is surprisingly warm and welcoming and vaguely exotic. Nattily curved headboards separate even the smallest rooms into lounging and sleeping areas, while bathrooms are tucked away behind floating curtains and have separate WC and showers cabins with rainfall shower heads. A modernistic candlelit bar, soaring Eurasian restaurant, leafy courtyard, rooftop terrace, and gym and spa provide plenty of in-house diversions, and St. Pauli nightlife is just outside the door.

Simon-von-Utrecht Strasse 31. *℃* **040/309930.** www.east-hotel.de. 78 units. 155€–290€ double. Parking 14€. U-Bahn: St. Pauli. **Amenities:** Restaurant; bar; babysitting; concierge; exercise room; room service; spa; A/C, T hair dryer, minibar, Wi-Fi (in most; free).

Hafen Hamburg ★ This waterside complex does not have a lot of designer flash and flair but the modern, businesslike accommodations put you within easy walking distance of St. Pauli nightlife. Best of all, a room with a view here provides a front row seat for the comings and goings in the busy harbor below, and many city sights are an easy stroll or short U-Bahn ride away. This sprawling complex encompasses a 19th-century seafarer's residence and two modern towers—rooms in all are functionally comfy and enlivened with nautical prints, but only some have water views—that's why you're staying here, so make sure to request one when booking.

Seewartenstrasse 9. *℃* **040/311130.** www.hotel-hafen-hamburg.de. 355 units. 100€–200€ double. Parking 14€. U-Bahn: Landungsbrücken. **Amenities:** Restaurant; 3 bars; sauna; Wi-Fi (free, in lobby).

25hours Hotel HafenCity ★ If you're smack dab in the middle of Hamburg's new waterfront district you'd better make the most of your surroundings, and that's exactly what this trendy outpost of a Hamburg-based, design-oriented hotel group does. Shipping crates, old timbers, and stacks of Oriental carpets (a nod to the surrounding warehouses that once stored the bounty of Eastern trade) fill the lounge areas, while bedrooms are cabin style, varying in size from snug to commodious enough for a captain and carrying out the nautical theme with tattoo-emblazoned wallpaper, crate-like furnishings, portholes, and logbooks in which you can follow the story of seafarers. It's all great fun, creature comforts are not spared, and many rooms have phenomenal harbor views. If all this design gets to be a bit much, head up to the rooftop sauna to chill out while taking in the city below. The in-house bar serves simple meals, including a delicious and generous breakfast, and the desk will turn over the keys of an Austin Mini so you can take a spin around town.

Paul-Dessau-Strasse 2. *℃* **040/855070.** www.25hours-hotel.com. 89 units. 125€–155€ double. V. Free parking. S-Bahn: Bahrenfeld. **Amenities:** Restaurant; 2 bars; babysitting; bikes; free in-room Wi-Fi.

Fritzhotel ★ Hamburg doesn't get much more hip than it does in the arty Sternschanze quarter, and here's a hotel that cooly—as in quietly and tastefully—suits the surroundings. Bright, high-ceilinged guest rooms on a floor of a 19th-century apartment house are done in soothing neutrals with bold splashes of color. Some open to balconies, but the quieter ones face a leafy courtyard off the street. There are few amenities—and no bar or restaurant—but fresh fruit and coffee are on hand and the neighborhood, at the edge of lively St. Pauli, is chockablock with cafes and bars.

Schanzenstrasse 101–103. *℃* **040/82222830.** Fax 040/822228322. www.fritzhotel.com. 17 units. 90€ double. Free parking. U-Bahn: Sternschanze. **Amenities:** Free in-room Wi-Fi.

Where to Dine

Hamburg is married to the sea, and all sorts of denizens of the deep end up on the table: lobster from Helgoland; shrimp from Büsum; turbot, plaice, and sole from the North Sea; and huge quantities of fresh oysters. It's no accident many of the Hamburg's best and most popular restaurants are seafood houses—and they're reasonably priced, since seafood is not exorbitantly expensive in this port city. But Hamburgers are carnivores, too, hence their eponymous contribution to world cuisine, here known as *Stubenküchen* (hamburger steak). A traditional sailor's dish, *Labskaus,* is made with beer, onions, cured meat, potatoes, herring, and pickles, but brace yourself for at least a taste of the city's iconic treat, *Aalsuppe* (eel soup). Whatever your epicurean appetite, you can probably satisfy it in this city that's long had ties with exotic lands—ethnic restaurants do a brisk business in almost every neighborhood. While dining can be a fine art and a costly pursuit in this expense-account-oriented city, you can also eat well without breaking the bank. No matter how much you spend, in many places your meal will probably be seasoned with an ingredient that Hamburg seems to care a lot about, a generous dash of trendiness.

CENTRAL CITY

Bullerei MEAT   An old cattle hall in the Schanze meatpacking district, just north of St. Pauli, has been transformed into an industrial-looking dining room geared to some serious meat eating (dried beef hangs in a glass display case and menus are covered in the plastic strips that hang over the doors to meat lockers). Graffiti art, exposed brick walls, and lots of wood furnishings create comfortable surroundings for enjoying pork cheeks, veal knuckles, salty ham, or maybe just some old-fashioned German sausages, even fresh fish—washed down with a selection from the excellent wine list or a wide choice of German beers.

Lagerstrasse 34b. ℂ **040/33442110.** www.bullerei.com. Main courses 20€–30€. Mon–Sun 11am–11pm. U-Bahn: Sternschanze.

Die Bank ★★ NORTHERN GERMAN/CONTINENTAL   You'll feel like a robber baron on the marble-columned trading floor of this former bank. Imaginatively backlit photos of money might get you in the mood to part with some yours for the richly satisfying Banker's Plate, an embarrassment of crustacean riches, or foie gras and other traditional French indulgences; you can also dine simply on wurst or steak frites, or explore the kitchen's forays into some adventurous Asian-fusion dishes. The lounge-music-infused space is hopping at all times, with diners crowded onto communal tables and a long, long bar, but stick around after dessert and you'll see this former temple of commerce turned into a rather riotous dance club.

Hohebleichen 17. ℂ **040/2380030.** www.diebank-brasserie.de. Reservations required. Main courses 14€–30€. Mon–Sat noon–3pm and 6:30–10:30pm. U-Bahn: Gasenmarkt.

Fillet of Soul ★ INTERNATIONAL   The Deichtorhallen is a turn-of-the-20th-century gem, two adjoining steel-and-glass structures near the harbor that once served as market halls and these days house temporary art and photography exhibitions. Tucked into a wing of the vast spaces is an intimate, minimalist dining room where chefs in an open kitchen do nouvelle takes on German standards that are works of art in themselves, along the lines of pink-roasted breast of goose with saffron-flavored rice and pan-fried zanderfish with bacon-studded *Sauerkraut.* Coffee, pastries, and light fare are available in the adjoining cafe throughout the day, and any daytime visit should coincide with a walk through the galleries, open Tuesday through Sunday from 9 to 6 (admission is 9€).

In the Deichtorhallen Museum, Deichtorstrasse 2. *℮* **040/70705800.** www.fillet-of-soul.de. Reservations recommended. Main courses lunch 8.50€–12€, dinner 14€–28€. No credit cards. Cafe and bar Tues–Sun 11am–midnight; restaurant Tues–Sun noon–3pm and 6–10pm. U-Bahn: Steinstrasse.

Restaurant Nil INTERNATIONAL   The name is a reference to some innovative spicing in such classics as beef bourguignon, but that's about as exotic as this classic French bistro gets. A regular clientele (many are in publishing and the arts) can count on the kitchen to serve heartier northern-style dishes in the colder months then dip into the south for inspiration come spring. Any time of year, mirrored walls and lots of brass and plush upholstery will probably transport you to Paris.

Neuer Pferdemarkt 5. *℮* **040/4397823.** www.restaurant-nil.de. Reservations recommended. Main courses 18€–22€; fixed-price menu 41€. No credit cards. Wed–Mon 6pm–midnight. U-Bahn: Feldstrasse.

NEAR THE WATERFRONT

Fischküche Karin Brahm ★ SEAFOOD   An unpretentious, brightly lit fish house near the harbor works hard to satisfy Hamburg's unquenchable appetite for seafood, serving the freshest catch in many variations. To get a taste of some local favorites, start with smoked eel and move on to cod, served with potatoes and mustard sauce—but there's plenty else on the large, ever-changing menu. Nothing that comes out of the kitchen is trendy or haute, service is of the no-nonsense school, and there's nothing stylish, cozy, or otherwise notable about the modern surroundings, but fresh ingredients deftly prepared make this a surefire hit with piscivores.

Kajen 12. *℮* **040/365631.** www.die-fischkueche.de. Reservations recommended. Main courses 15€–40€. Mon–Fri noon–midnight; Sat 4pm–midnight. U-Bahn: Rödingsmarkt.

IN ALTONA

Eisenstein ★ INTERNATIONAL/PIZZA   The crowd of stylish regulars doesn't let the clamor and clatter deter them from enjoying a fusion of Italian, Mediterranean, and German fare in one of Hamburg's most appealing dining spaces. A restored factory envelops diners in brick walls, rough-hewn timbers, and daylight streaming through huge windows (and candlelight by night). Southern Europe meets the north in dishes like Atlantic cod flavored with provencal spices and Italian-style thin crust pizza topped with gravalax. An excellent selection of beer and light fare makes this a popular stop on the late-night circuit.

Friedensallee 9. *℮* **040/3904606.** www.restaurant-eisenstein.de. Reservations recommended. Main courses 18€–25€; fixed-price dinners 33€–37€; pizzas 8€–14€. No credit cards. Daily 11am–11pm. U-Bahn: Altona Bahnhof.

Das Weisse Haus ★ GERMAN/SEAFOOD   Unlike the Washington landmark with which it shares a name, Hamburg's famous White House is a cramped old fisherman's cottage. That doesn't keep eager diners away, and you'll have to book well in advance for the privilege of submitting yourself to the whims of the kitchen, which, aside from catering to allergies and strong dislikes, sends out whatever it wants, basing meals on what looked good in the market that day. A Hamburg classic, *aalsuppe* (eel soup), often makes an appearance, followed by some creative seafood preparations, though the kitchen is just as comfortable with meat and even vegetarian meals.

Neumühlen 50. *℮* **04/309016.** www.das-weisse-haus.de. Reservations required. 2-course menu 28€; 3-course menu 34€; 4-course menu 42€. Mon–Sat noon–3pm and 6–9pm. U-Bahn: Altona.

Fischereihafen Restaurant ★★ SEAFOOD   A harborside perch near the fish market is a fortuitous locale for this long-standing Hamburg favorite, an institution that's popular with a well-dressed crowd who looks like they're used to fancier surroundings. What matters here is freshness, and fish and shellfish are right out of the market stalls and show up in some simple but memorable renditions, along the lines of Arctic trout with wild garlic and rare tuna steak with peppercorns and honey-laced soy sauce. A nice view of the Elbe, through large picture windows and from a small terrace in good weather, nicely tops off a memorable meal.

Grosse Elbstrasse 143. ℂ **040/381816.** www.fischereihafenrestaurant.de. Reservations required. Main courses 18€–46€; fixed-price menu 60€. Sun–Thurs 11:30am–10pm; Fri–Sat 11:30am–10:30pm. S-Bahn: Königstrasse.

Landhaus Scherrer ★★★ NORTHERN GERMAN/CONTINENTAL   A converted white-brick, cozy-looking brewery in Altona soothes at first sight, surrounded as it is by lawns shaded by trees. Wood paneled walls and low lighting do nothing to disrupt the mellow mood, the inventive menu combines northern German and international flavors to satisfying effect, and the kitchen throws in an emphasis on locavore ingredients. Crispy whole north German duck with seasoned vegetables is a feast for two, but you can dine solo on roast goose with rhubarb in cassis sauce and other hearty classics. You can eat lightly in the adjoining bistro.

Elbchaussee 130. ℂ **040/8801325.** www.landhausscherrer.de. Reservations required. Main courses 28€–39€; fixed-price menu 111€. Mon–Sat noon–3pm and 6:30–10:30pm. Bus: 135.

Exploring Hamburg

Hamburg is large and spread out, but geography won't put a damper on your sightseeing. Most of what you'll want to see is in or near the central city, and even if a cold wind off the Baltic Sea deters you from walking it's easy to get around town on the U-bahn or bus.

Unless you have a big appetite for clicking off sights, you may be pleased to know that Hamburg has far fewer landmarks and stellar museums than Berlin or Munich do. You can probably see what you want in a full day. Even if your appreciation of art is on the low side, you'll want to step into the **Kunsthalle** (p. 92), at least to see the weird creations of the German expressionists. The façade of the over-the-the-top neo-Renaissance-style **Rathaus** (p. 92) is a must-see, and so is **Hauptkirche St-Michaelis** (below), where you should make the ascent to the dome for a view over the far-flung metropolis at your feet. The city itself is the main attraction. You can't leave town without catching a glimpse of the Alster, the lake in the city center, and you'll want to see the port—best viewed from the deck of a tour boat (see below). Two neighborhoods to check out are **HafenCity,** an emerging waterside quarter where some of the world's leading architects are in a contest to see who can create the most stunning glass tower, and, of course, **St. Pauli.** Whether you come to this red-light district dedicated to debauchery to partake or observe, you'll never think of Germany as uptight and strictly businesslike again.

IN & AROUND THE ALTSTADT

Hauptkirche St-Michaelis ★ CHURCH   You'll want to soak in the sumptuous Baroque interior, admire the pipe organs (maybe playing if you come for a morning service or evensong), and pay homage at the tombs of esteemed Hamburgers in the huge crypt. But save your energy for the climb up the 449 steps of the twisting, narrow

Hamburg

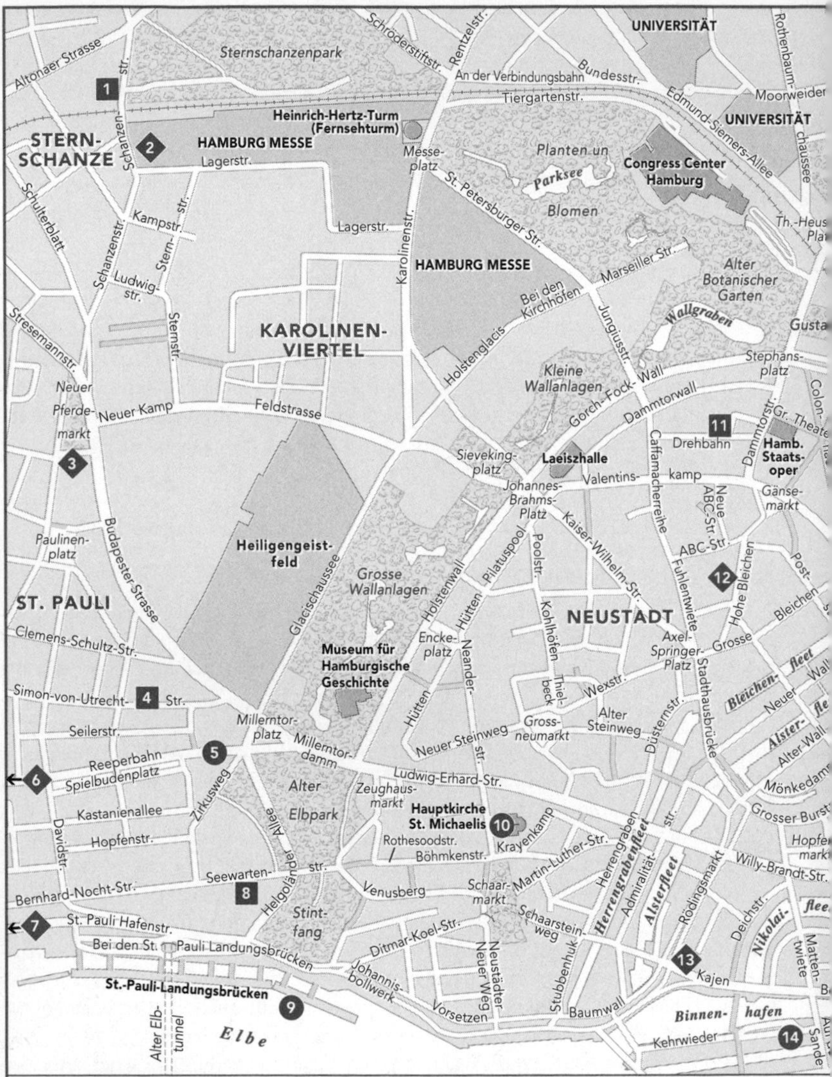

Map labels (streets, districts, landmarks):

Altonaer Strasse · Schrödertiftsstr. · Rentzelstr. · UNIVERSITÄT · Rothenbaumchaussee · Moorweider · Sternschanzenpark · An der Verbindungsbahn · Bundesstr. · Tiergartenstr. · Edmund-Siemers-Allee · UNIVERSITÄT · Heinrich-Hertz-Turm (Fernsehturm) · STERN-SCHANZE · HAMBURG MESSE · Messe-platz · Planten un · Congress Center Hamburg · Th.-Heus Pla · Lagerstr. · St. Petersburger Str. · Parksee · Blomen · Schulterblatt · Schanzenstr. · Kampstr. · Stern-str. · Lagerstr. · Karolinenstr. · HAMBURG MESSE · Bei den Kirchhöfen · Marseiller Str. · Alter Botanischer Garten · Gusta · Ludwig-str. · Stresemannstr. · Stern-str. · KAROLINEN-VIERTEL · Holstenglacis · Jungiusstr. · Wallgraben · Stephans-platz · Colon- · Neuer Pferde-markt · Neuer Kamp · Feldstrasse · Kleine Wallanlagen · Gorch-Fock-Wall · Dammtorwall · Gr. Theate · Budapester Strasse · Sieveking-platz · Laeiszhalle · Valentins- · Caffamacherreihe · kamp · Drehbahn · Hamb. Staats-oper · Gänse-markt · Paulinen-platz · Heiligengeist-feld · Johannes-Brahms-Platz · Kaiser-Wilhelm-Str. · Neue ABC-Str. · Fuhlentwiete · ABC-Str. · ST. PAULI · Grosse Wallanlagen · Glacischaussee · Encke-platz · Holstenwall · Platuspool · Poolstr. · Hütten · NEUSTADT · Hohe Bleichen · Post- · Clemens-Schultz-Str. · Museum für Hamburgische Geschichte · Neander- · Kohlhöfen · Thiel-beck · Wexstr. · Axel-Springer-Platz · Grosse · Stadthausbrücke · Bleichen · fleet · Simon-von-Utrecht-Str. · Seilerstr. · Millerntor-platz · Millerntor-damm · Hütten · Neuer Steinweg · Alter Steinweg · Bleichen · Neuer · fle · Alter Wall · Reeperbahn · Spielbudenplatz · Zirkusweg · Ludwig-Erhard-Str. · Gross-neumarkt · Düsternstr. · Mönkeda · Kastanienallee · Alter Elbpark · Zeughaus-markt · Hauptkirche St. Michaelis · Krayenkamp · Grosser Burst · Hopfenstr. · Davidstr. · Reeperbahn · Helgoländer Allee · Rothesoodstr. · Böhmkenstr. · Herrengraben · Grosser Burst · Willy-Brandt- · markt · Bernhard-Nocht-Str. · Seewarten-str. · Venusberg · Schaar-markt · Martin-Luther-Str. · Admiralität · Alsterfleet · Rödingsmarkt · Deichstr. · Nikolai- · St. Pauli Hafenstr. · Stintfang · Schaarstein-weg · Neustädter Neuer Weg · Stubbenhuk · Herrengrabenfleet · Marten- · twiete · fleet · Bei den St. Pauli Landungsbrücken · Ditmar-Koel-Str. · Johannis-bollwerk · Vorsetzen · Baumwall · Kajen · St.-Pauli-Landungsbrücken · Alter Elb-tunnel · Elbe · Binnen-hafen · Kehrwieder · Sande · Au

HOTELS ■

- East **4**
- Fritzhotel **1**
- The George **25**
- Hafen Hamburg **8**
- Hotel Side **11**
- Hotel Wedina **24**
- Kempinski Hotel Atlantic **23**
- Superbude **26**
- 25Hours Hotel HafenCity **16**

RESTAURANTS ◆

- Bullerei **2**
- Das Weisse Haus **7**
- Die Bank **12**
- Die Fischküche Karin Brahm **13**
- Eisenstein **6**
- Fillet of Soul **18**
- Fischereihafen Restaurant **7**
- Landhaus Scherrer **7**
- Restaurant Nil **3**

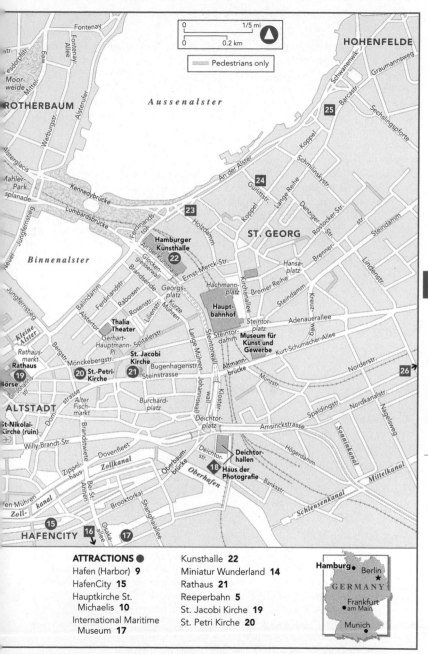

ATTRACTIONS ●

Hafen (Harbor) **9**
HafenCity **15**
Hauptkirche St.
  Michaelis **10**
International Maritime
  Museum **17**

Kunsthalle **22**
Miniatur Wunderland **14**
Rathaus **21**
Reeperbahn **5**
St. Jacobi Kirche **19**
St. Petri Kirche **20**

staircase (there's also an elevator for the less adventurous) for a sweeping view of Hamburg from the top of the **copper-roofed tower ★**.

Michaeliskirchplatz, Krayenkamp 4C. © **040/376780.** www.st-michaelis.de. Free admission. Daily 8am–6pm. U-Bahn: Rodginsmarkt or St. Pauli.

Kunsthalle ★★★ GALLERY A walk through the bright, handsome galleries of one of Germany's outstanding art museums provides a head-spinning look at Western masterpieces. For many Hamburgers, pride of place in the two buildings belongs to the Bertram altarpiece, painted for the St. Petri Church in 1379. The 24 scenes depict the history of humankind as told in the Bible, from creation to the flight into Egypt. Look for some sardonic touches, like the little fox chewing the neck of the lamb next to it, a sad comment perhaps on the fate of the meek. Continue through the Canalettos, Rembrandts, Holbeins, and other old masters to German Romanticism. Among these works is Caspar David Friedrich's "The Wall of Mist," the object of a much publicized heist in which the painitng was stolen from a train and later returned. The new wing by O. M. Ungers houses the Galerie der Gegenwart, Art of the Present, with an impressive collection of canvases by Picasso, Warhol, Beuys, Munch, Kandinsky, Klee, Hockney, and many other leading contemporary artists currently making waves in the art world, among them installation artist Rebecca Horn, photorealist Gerhardt Richter, and conceptualist Jenny Holzer. A large showing of German Expressionism is a credit to the museum's effort to rebuild a collection of "degenerate" art banned and often destroyed by the Nazis.

Glockengiesser Wall. © **040/428131200.** www.hamburger-kunsthalle.de. Admission 12€ adults, 6€ children 4–12, free for children 3 and under, 18€ family ticket. Tues–Sun 10am–6pm (Thurs until 9pm). U-Bahn: Hauptbahnhof.

Rathaus ★ LANDMARK It's new by German standards—late 19th century—but the neo-Renaissance City Hall with 647 rooms makes quite an impression nonetheless, a sandstone testimony to Hamburg's wealth and importance. The 49m (161-ft.) clock tower looms high above the Rathausmarkt and the Alster Fleet, the city's largest canal. Tours through grandiose staterooms embellished with tapestries and glittering chandeliers are given hourly, but this pile is just as satisfyingly admired from the outside—unless you are detail-oriented and might enjoy hearing about the 3,780 pinewood piles upon which the block-long structure rests or the 8,605 souls who perished in the 1897 cholera epidemic and are commemorated by a gurgling fountain. The 16th-century **Börse** (Stock Exchange), Adolphsplatz 1 (© **040/361-3020**), stands back to back with the Rathaus; guides conduct free tours (in German) of the Börse on Tuesday and Thursday at 11am and noon. Should this brush with capitalism inspire you to disperse some of your own wealth, cross the Alster Fleet to the Alsterarkaden, an arched passageway lined with fashionable clothing and jewelry shops.

Rathausplatz. © **040/428310.** Rathaus tours 3€. Mon–Fri 10am–3pm and Sat–Sun 10am–1pm (no tours during official functions). U-Bahn: Rathausmarkt.

St. Jacobi Kirche ★ CHURCH Medieval altars and sculptures evoke the church's 14th-century founding, but most of the Gothic exterior is a 1950s reconstruction. Germany's premier organ manufacturer Arp Schnitger, who made instruments for Johan Sebastian Bach, crafted the massive organ with 4,000 pipes in 1693. To hear its sonorous sounds you may attend Sunday services or, better yet, stop in at noon on Thursdays to enjoy a free concert.

Jakobikirchhof 22, with an entrance on Steinstrasse. © **040/3037370.** www.jacobus.de. Free admission. Mon–Sat 10am–5pm. U-Bahn: Mönckebergstrasse.

A BIT OF beatlemania

John Lennon once said, "I was born in Liverpool, but I grew up in Hamburg." As Beatles fans know, the group got its start here in the early 1960s, when they played gigs at a string of sleazy St Pauli clubs. When the group returned to Liverpool in 1960 they were billed as "The Beatles: Direct from Hamburg." They soon returned to Germany and introduced such hits as "Love Me Do" in St. Pauli clubs. Though a museum to the Fab Four has been shuttered, the city has not lost interest in the sensation it nurtured. A corner on the Reeperbahn has been designated "Beatles-Platz," where effigies of the five are enshrined in glass (the fifth wheel is bassist Stuart Sutcliffe, who left the group to study art and died of a cerebral aneurism soon afterward). The boys stand in the middle of a circle of paving stones blackened to look like a vinyl record.

St. Petri Kirche ★ CHURCH Hamburg's favorite church deserves a quick stop just because it's so venerable, founded in 1192 and in continuous use since. The lion-head knocker on the main door dates from 1342, making it the oldest piece of art in Hamburg, though little else in the church can claim similarly notable provenance or artistic merit. The present structure itself dates from the mid–19th century, when the early church was raised by a fire—a feat World War II bombers attempted to repeat many times but failed to achieve, making St. Peter's one of old Hamburgers proud survivors. The best time to visit is Wednesday afternoon at 5:15, when the organ pumps out a *Stunde der Kirchenmusik* (Hour of Church Music).

Speersort 10. ℂ **040/3257400.** www.sankt-petri.de. Free admission. Mon–Fri 10am–6pm; Sat 10am–5pm; Sun 9am–9pm. U-Bahn: Rathausmarkt.

ALONG THE WATERFRONT

Hafen (Harbor) ★★★ NEIGHBORHOOD Ever since the emperor Friedrich Barbarossa issued an edict granting free-trading privileges to Hamburg in 1189, the city has earned fame and riches from its busy harbor, one of the largest in the world. Hamburg commemorates Frederic's gesture in early May with 3 days of windjammer parades, fireworks, and other celebrations, and these days most of the maritime activity takes place in a vast swath of riverside docks and warehouses just southwest of the city, where the Elbe splits into two arms as it nears the North Sea. The only real way to see the docklands is on a harbor cruise that departs from the city's main passenger landing stage, **St. Pauli-Landungsbrücken.** Don't board the 19th-century clipper ship *Rickmer Rickmers* and expect to get anywhere; docked just east of the landing at Pier 1, the magnificent vessel is now a museum of maritime history (ℂ **040/319-5959;** daily 10am–5:30pm; 3€/$4 for adults, 2.50€/$3.50 for children ages 4–12).

You can also join the cadre of old salts who regularly make the trip out to **Willkomm-Höft (Welcome Point)** in outlying Wedel, where each day more than 50 arriving and 50 departing ships pass a maritime station that stands on the tip of the peninsula off which crews first catch sight of the cranes and slipways of the Port of Hamburg. From sunrise to sunset (8am–8pm in summer) arriving ships are greeted with the national anthem of the country where the vessel is registered. The station master lowers the Hamburg flag in salute, and the passing ship dips its flag in response. You can get to Wedel by S-Bahn; the point is a 15-minute walk from the stop. While in Wedel, you might want to step into the cellars of **Schulauer Fährhaus,** a restaurant at Parnastrasse 29 (© **04103/92000;** www.schulauer-faehrhaus.de), and pay a visit to the **Buddelschiff-Museum** (© **04103/920016;** www.buddel.de), where more than 200 little vessels are carefully preserved in bottles. The museum is open March to October, daily 10am to 6pm; November to February, hours are Saturday and Sunday only 10am to 6pm. Admission is 3€ for adults and free for children.

HafenCity ★★ NEIGHBORHOOD   The largest urban inner-city urban renewal project in Europe is dazzling even before it's completed. More than 400 acres of former docklands along the River Elbe will eventually increase the size of the inner city by almost half and double the amount of housing in Hamburg. While it's estimated that it will be 2020 before finishing touches are put on the streets, plazas, and riverside promenades, some stunning glass towers are already transforming the skyline. Check out the shiplike Unilever building at Strandkai 1, and the Elbphilharmonie, the new philharmonic hall slated to debut, after many delays, in 2015—even unfinished it's a stunning addition to the cityscape, an undulating wedge of frosted glass that seems to rise from the water like the prow of a ghost ship. You can find out more at the **Hafen-City InfoCenter,** Sandtorkai 30 (© **040/3690-1799;** www.hafencity.de), open Tuesday through Sunday from 10am to 6pm (May–Sept until 8pm). To reach the InfoCenter, take the U3 U-Bahn line to Baumwall, Bus 3, or Bus 6.

International Maritime Museum ★ MUSEUM   In a tribute to Hamburg's longstanding relationship with the sea, ten floors of a formidable old red-brick neo-Gothic warehouse near the waterfront in HafenCity are stacked chockablock with all things nautical. The vast spaces are literally crammed with memorabilia, and eclectic holdings run the nautical gamut from a 3,000-year-old dugout unearthed on the banks of the Elbe to 47 letters of Lord Horatio Nelson, hero of the Battle of Trafalgar, to photographs and drawings of ships to uniforms and navigation equipment. If the 15,000 menus from ocean liners seem overwhelming, wait until you get to the top floor and come across the 26,000 model ships, stacked tightly side by side in row after row of glass cases as if they were moored in the world's most impossibly crowded harbor. (If this quirkily exhaustive collection whets your appetite to stock up on some maritime memorabilia, make your way across town to St. Pauli, where the **Captain's Cabin,** Bei Dim St. Pauli Landungsbrücken 3 [© **040/316373;** www.captains-cabin. de; S-Bahn: Landungsbrücken], sells ship models, telescopes, barometers, figureheads, lamps, nautical clothing for the whole family, prints, posters, and more.)

Koreastrasse 1. (© **040 3009 3300.** www.internationales-maritimes-museum.de. Admission 13€, 15€ small family (1 adult and 2 children), 25€ large family (2 adults and 3 children). Tues–Sun 10am–6pm. U-Bahn: Überseequartier.

Miniatur Wunderland ★ MUSEUM   Wunderland bills itself as the world's largest model railway, but it's a lot more than Lilliputian trains chugging through snowy Alpine peaks—even though there are plenty of such charming scenarios, with 900 trains and a total of 12,000 cars traveling through landscapes from Scandinavian forests to American deserts. Planes descend from the sky and make a smooth landing at Hamburg airport, trucks roar down highways, and fire trucks and police cars race through city streets. Even the miniaturized human activity is fascinating to witness: Body builders lift weights, prostitutes stand alluringly in windows, and pop-concert-goers light up cigarettes, making Wunderland one of the few public places in Hamburg where smoking is tolerated.

Kehrwieder 2. www.miniatur-wunderland.de. Admission 12€ adults, 6€ children. Sun 8:30am–6pm; Mon and Wed–Fri 9:30am–9pm; Tues 9:30am–9pm; Sat 8am–9pm. U-Bahn: Baumwell.

THE WORLD'S oldest profession

Hamburg's official line is that the Reeperbahn is the city's second-greatest attraction and asset (after the port). The well-regulated approach to prostitution and sex solicitation is similar to Amsterdam's, even though the Reeperbahn is a lot more seedy-looking than Amsterdam's red-light district. In Hamburg every officially sanctioned working girl must submit to a medical examination every 2 weeks—and pay income tax on her profits. The district's police station, Davidwache, at the corner of the Davidstrasse and the Reeperbahn, provides highly visible and omnipresent police protection. No amount of police presence is going to protect you from paying exorbitant prices for watered-down cocktails or astronomical cover charges, and a little common sense will help you enjoy a walk on the wild side without losing your shirt.

Reeperbahn ★★ NEIGHBORHOOD   The St. Pauli district (U-Bahn: St. Pauli; S-Bahn: Reeperbahn), just west of the center, is where it all hangs out in Hamburg. St. Pauli's midsection—the "genital zone," as it's sometimes called—is the district's main drag, the Reeperbahn, a 1km (½-mile) thoroughfare whose name literally translates as "rope street," referring to the massive amounts of hempen rope produced here during the 18th and 19th centuries for ships in Germany's biggest harbor. Hamburg's first theater opened on the Reeperbahn in 1842, and from there it was all downhill into any manner of licentiousness. By the 1860s, the question, "Whatcha doing, sailor?" became the unofficial motto of an army of prostitutes who set up shop (with the legal sanction of municipal authorities) in the district. These days, by mid-evening the bars and theaters (legitimate and otherwise) are roaring away and you'll find thousands of women and men in drag, strutting their stuff along the turf. German enterprise has honored these women (and their reputation for a good time) by naming one of Hamburg's native beers in their honor—the famous "St. Pauli Girl."

The most exclusive and expensive area is Herbertstrasse, where women display their charms to window-shoppers from behind plate-glass. By city ordinance, this street is open only to men 19 and over (women are officially banned, but this does not seem to be enforced). Less expensive rents can be found on the streets near Herbertstrasse: Gunterstrasse, Erichstrasse, Friedrichstrasse, Davidstrasse, and Gerhardstrasse. If it's erotic theater you're looking for, you'll have to move a few blocks away to Grosse Freiheit, a street whose name appropriately translates as "Great Freedom." Any act of sexual expression, with every conceivable permutation, except those that involve animals (bestiality is one of the few things expressly forbidden), is shown in these theaters. Be it joyful, be it disgusting, it's all here, often performed by artists who can barely conceal their boredom.

Outdoor Activities

The Alster ★★ LAKE   Top spot for a jog or power walk is the pedestrian walkway around this lake in the city center. It's about 7km (4 miles) all the way around, but you can do a shorter circuit around the smaller, inner lake, the Binnenalster, in about 1½km (1 mile). On a nice day you can take to the waters of the outer lake, the **Aussenalster. H. Pieper** (✆ **040/247578;** www.segelschule-pieper.de), a boathouse just off Kennedybrucke in front of the Atlantic Kempinski Hotel, rents rowboats, paddle boats, and one-occupant sailing dinghies; prices begin at 15€ per hour. This outfitter is open April to late September, daily 10am to 8pm.

Carl Hagenbeck's Tierpark ★★ ZOO/AQUARIUM   It's easy to forget that Hamburg's zoo, 5km (3 miles) southwest of the city center, is home to some 2,500 animals, so appealing are the landscaping and architectural attractions. The Nepalese temple and Japanese garden are especially transporting, as are the animal enclosures themselves—the Tierpark was the first zoo in the world to recreate environments similar to the creatures' habitats in the wild, separated from onlookers by pools and moats. These have been shored up a bit since 1956, when in one of the biggest "zoo breaks" in history 45 rhesus monkeys escaped from their quarters and ran wild through the streets of Hamburg.

Hagenbeckallee at Steilingen. ℂ 040/5300330. www.hagenbeck.de. Admission 16€ adults, 11€ children 4–16, free for children 3 and under, 49€ family ticket. Parking 2.50€. Mar–Oct daily 9am–5pm (closes later in nice weather); Nov–Feb daily 9am–4:30pm. U-Bahn: Hagenbeck's Tierpark.

Wallringpark ★★ PARK/GARDEN   While Hamburg has no shortage of greenery, the most beautiful stretches are these four adjacent, meticulously maintained parks and gardens west of the Altstadt and Alster Lake. Planten und Blomen (Plants and Flowers), laid out in 1936, contains the largest Japanese garden in Europe, with rock gardens, flowering plants, miniature trees, and winding pathways. The Alter Botanischer Garten (Old Botanical Garden) south of Planten and Blomen nurtures rare plant specimens in greenhouses bursting with tropical flora. The Kleine (small) and Grosse (large) Wallanlagen parks are geared to recreation, with a roller-skating rink, playgrounds, and an ice-skating rink in winter. You can chug through the quartet on a miniature railway and cap off a summertime visit with an evening concert in in the Planten und Bloomen, where colorfully illuminated fountains keep time to classical and pop music; daily from June to August at 10.

Entertainment & Nightlife

Hamburg is famous and infamous for nightlife. You can go high-brow, as the city has excellent opera and dance companies and symphonies; middle brow in chic bars and homey rathskellers; or lowbrow on and around the Reeperbahn, in Hamburg's notoriously sex-oriented St. Pauli district. Hamburg's gay scene is almost as robust as that in Berlin, and centers in St Georg, just to the east of the Haupthbanhoff, where most of the district's gay venues are along and around two main streets, Lange Reihe and Steindamm. **Visitor information centers** in the Wandelhalle of the Hauptbahnhof (ℂ **040/30051300**) and on the St. Pauli-Landungsbrücken are usually littered with fliers announcing goings-on around town and counters sell tickets to mainstream events. The **Ticketmaster** affiliate in Hamburg is Kartenhaus at Schanzenstrasse 5 (ℂ **040 43 59 46;** www.kartenhaus.de; Mon–Fri 10am–7pm, Sat 10am–2pm).

THE PERFORMING ARTS

Hamburgische Staatsoper (Hamburg State Opera) ★★★ THE PERFORMING ARTS   One of the world's leading opera houses, built after World War II, its known for excellent acoustics and advanced technical facilities. It's home to the **Hamburg State Opera** and the **Hamburg Ballet.** Grosstheaterstrasse 25. ℂ **040/356868.** www.hamburgische-staatsoper.de. Tickets 10€–146€. U-Bahn: Stephansplatz. S-Bahn: Dammtor.

Musikhalle ★★ THE PERFORMING ARTS   This survivor of Germany's romantic age, painstakingly restored after World War II, hosts concerts by the **Hamburg**

Symphony, the **Hamburg Philharmonic,** the **NDR Symphony,** and the **Monteverdi-Chor,** known for its interpretations of baroque and Renaissance music. Touring orchestras also perform here. For tickets, call either the number listed below or the number listed for the Staatsoper (see above). Johannes-Brahms-Platz 1. ℰ **040/357666.** www.laeiszhalle.de. Tickets up to 45€. U-Bahn: Stephansplatz. S-Bahn: Dammtor.

THEATER The **English Theatre of Hamburg,** Lerchenfeld 14 (ℰ **040/2277089;** www.englishtheatre.de; U-Bahn: Mundsburg), is the only English-speaking theater in the northern Germany and actors present popular plays and the classics.

The **Deutsches Schauspielhaus** ★, Kirchenallee 39 (ℰ **040/248713;** www.schauspielhaus.de; U-Bahn: Hauptbahnhof), is one of the largest and most important theaters in the German-speaking world, performing both classics and modern plays—but you'll need to understand German to appreciate fully the genius of these productions.

NIGHTLIFE

Café Gnosa ★★ COFFEE HOUSE Laid-back and art deco-inspired, this gay-friendly bar and restaurant is a popular place to sip coffee or wine and enjoy breakfast and a nice selection of salads and more substantial meals throughout the day. The real reason to come is to mingle with the locals, many of whom have been hanging out here for years. It's open until 1am. Lange Reihe 93. ℰ **040/243034.** www.gnosa.de. U-Bahn: Hauptbahnhof.

Club Grosse Freiheit 36/Kaiserkeller ★ CLUB & MUSIC SCENE The Beatles performed here in the basement Kaiserkeller in their earliest days, and Prince and Willie Nelson have been on the bill at the larger club upstairs. Today the venue is best known as a cultural landmark, though some of the pop and rock concerts pull in big crowds. Grosse Freiheit 36. ℰ **040/31777811.** www.grossefreiheit36.de. Cover 4€–20€. S-Bahn: Reeperbahn.

Cotton Club ★ CLUB & MUSIC SCENE Hamburg's oldest jazz club hosts jazz and Dixieland bands from throughout Europe and the United States. Hours are Monday to Saturday 8pm to 1am. Alter Steinweg 10. ℰ **040/343878.** www.cotton-club.de. Cover 6.50€–15€. S-Bahn: Stadthausbrücke.

Fabrik ★ CLUB & MUSIC SCENE An old ammunition depot turned factory hosts musician of every stripe and an eclectic schedule offers something different almost every night and features club music, classical, African bands, jazz, and blues, along with film and stage events. Barnerstrasse 36 (5 min. from Bahnhof Altona). ℰ **040/391070.** www.fabrik.de. Cover 10€–35€. U-Bahn: Altona.

Le Lion ★★ BAR So intimate you might not get in—try though, by ringing the buzzer hidden inside the lion's head on the door. Better yet, make a reservation to enjoy serious cocktails in a grown-up, subtly lit room. Rathaustrasse 3. ℰ **040/334753780.** www.lelion.net. S-Bahn: Rathaus.

Meanie Bar ★ DANCE CLUB One of the few places along the Reeperbahn that caters to locals attracts a lot of artists and musicians. Spielbudenplatz 5. ℰ **040/4301110.** www.molotowclub.com. S-Bahn: Reeperbahn.

Molotow ★★ DANCE CLUB This much-beloved venue in the cellar of the Meanie Bar is the place to dance to funk and alternative. Opening hours may vary, but usually it opens Wednesday and Sunday at 8pm, Thursday to Saturday at 11pm;

BAR ROOMS with a view

You can enjoy the spectacle of Hamburg's port while keeping warm and dry and slacking your thirst at 20Up, on the 20th floor of the **Empire Riverside Hotel,** Bernhard-Nocht-Strasse 97 (*©* **40/311190;** www.empire-riverside. de). A similarly dramatic view is to be had from the 14th-floor **Tower Bar** of the Hafen Hotel, Seewartenstrasse 9 (*©* **040/311130;** www.hotel-hafen-hamburg.de). The perspective of the maritime activity and sprawling city is eye-catching by day, and downright dazzling at night.

closing time is usually when the crowd feels like dispersing. Spielbudenplatz 5. *©* **040/4301110.** www.molotowclub.com. Cover 5€–16€. S-Bahn: Reeperbahn.

Tom's Saloon ★★ BAR   Hamburg's landmark gay bar, named for gay icon Tom of Finland (once a regular) has a street-level dance club, a friendly cocktail lounge, and a cellar bar where leather is derigeur. Men of all ages mix here, and women won't feel comfortable anywhere but the crowded dance floor, and even there aren't a terribly welcome presence. At least one part of this place is open every night 10pm until dawn; every Wednesday to Sunday, additional sections open for greater space. The 5€ cover includes one drink. Pulverteich 17. *©* **040/25328943.** www.toms-hamburg.de. U-Bahn: Hauptbahnhof.

Spielbank Hamburg ★ GAMBLING   Hamburg's low-key casino occupies attractive but fairly unremarkable surroundings and offers roulette, blackjack, and poker. You can also enjoy a drink at the bar, taking in the panoramic view over the roofs and lakes of Hamburg. The minimum stake for roulette is 2€, for blackjack 5€. Men should wear jackets and ties. Everyone needs a passport to get in (you must be 18 or over to enter and gamble). The casino is open daily 3pm to 3am. Stephansplatz 10. *©* **040/4501760.** www.spielbank-hamburg.de. U-Bahn: Stephansplatz.

Tours

Guided tours are a good way to see spread-out Hamburg, and plenty of operators are on hand to show you around. To get a sense of the lay of the land and see the far-flung landmarks and neighborhoods, hop on one of the Top Tour double-decker buses operated by **Hamburger Stadtrundfahrten** (*©* **040/641-3731;** www.top-tour-hamburg. de) that leave from the main train station, Kirchenallee entrance, every 30 minutes from 9:30 a.m. to 5 p.m. (hourly in winter). The 90-minute tours cost 18€ for adults, 15€ for children up to 14.

For a look at Hamburg's port, a fascinating hubbub of maritime activity, climb aboard one of the pleasure craft operated by **HADAG Seetouristik und Fährdienst AG,** Bei den St. Pauli, Fischmarkt 28 (*©* **040/3117070;** www.hadag.de). The 75-minute tours, in German and English, depart the Landungsbrücken, Pier 3, in St. Pauli at hourly intervals every day April to September 10:30am to 4:30pm, and from October to March 11am to 3:30pm. The fare is 17€ for adults, 8€ for children 13 and under, and 25€ for a family ticket.

Relaxing, but a lot less colorful, are tours of the Inner and Outer Alster operated by **ATG-Alster-Touristik,** Am Anleger Jungfernstieg (*©* **040/3574240;** www.alster touristik.de). In good weather departures are daily about every 30 minutes from 10am to 6pm, with trips lasting 50 minutes—just about the right amount of time to get your fill of pleasant vistas of the tree-lined shores, church spires, and sailing boats. November to March, tours depart daily at 10:30am, noon, 1:30, and 3pm. Boats leave from the Jungfernstieg quayside (U-Bahn: Jungfernstieg). Trips cost 15€ for adults and 7€ for children 15 and under.

LÜBECK ★★★

66km (41 miles) NE of Hamburg

Along the ancient streets of Lübeck's *Altstadt* you'll find more buildings from the 13th to the 15th centuries than in any other city in northern Germany—more than just about anywhere else in Germany or in Europe, for that matter, since it's said that within an area of 5 sq. km (2 sq. miles) around the Marktplatz stand 1,000 medieval houses. The overall effect of all these high-gabled houses, massive gates, strong towers, and towering steeples is outrageously picturesque, providing a dip into the past when Lübeck was one of the founding cities of the mighty Hanseatic League, a confederation that controlled trade along the Baltic as far as Russia.

The Hanseatic merchants decorated their churches with art treasures and gilded their spires to show off their wealth. Much of this remains, earning the city a place on the United Nations Educational, Scientific and Cultural Organization (UNESCO) World Heritage list of international monuments. You'll want to work a day trip to Lübeck into your Hamburg itinerary, but the city is so captivatingly picturesque, with quite a bit to see and do, that you might want to spend the night.

Essentials
GETTING THERE
BY TRAIN The Lübeck Hauptbahnhof lies on major rail lines linking Denmark and Hamburg, and on the Hamburg-Lüneburg-Lübeck-Kiel-Flensburg and Lübeck-Rostock-Stralsund lines, with frequent connections. From Hamburg, 32 trains arrive daily (trip time: 48 min.), 23 from Berlin (trip time: 3–4 hr.). For information, call ℭ **01805/996633** (www.bahn.com).

BY BUS Long-distance bus service to and from such cities as Berlin and Kiel is provided by **Autokraft GmbH** (ℭ **0431/6660;** www.autokraft.de).

BY CAR Access to Lübeck is via the A1 Autobahn north and south.

GETTING AROUND
The Altstadt and most of the city's attractions can be reached on foot from the Hauptbahnhof, about a 15-minute walk from the Marktplatz. You can also take bus no. 1, 5, 11, or 21. Fare is 2.20€.

VISITOR INFORMATION
For tourist information, contact the Lübeck-Informations-Zentrum, just next to the entrance to the medieval city, **Holstentor** (Holsten Gate), at Holstentorplatz 1–5 (ℭ **0451/8899700;** www.luebeck-tourismus.de), January to May and October to December Monday to Friday 9:30am to 6pm and Saturday 10am to 3pm; June to September Monday to Friday 9:30am to 7pm, Saturday 10am to 3pm, and Sunday 10am to 2pm. Admission to each of Lübeck's museums is 6€ for adults and 3€ for children and students. *Tip:* If you're going to visit two museums, you'll save 50 percent off your admission to the second one by showing your receipt from the first.

SPECIAL EVENTS Lübeck is the center of the **Schleswig-Holstein Music Festival** (✆ **0451/389570**; www.shmf.de), with performances during July and August every year. At the Christmas market, vendors from northwestern Germany sell their wares—many of them handmade items from toys to pottery—during the 3 weeks before Christmas on the Rathausplatz.

Where to Stay

Lübeck spreads well beyond the banks of the Trave River, connecting canals that once formed the perimeter of the old city. You'll find some chains in these outlying areas, but the atmospheric Altstadt is the place to stay, and a hotel here puts you within walking distance of all the sights you want to see. Any of the Altstadt hotels are also within walking distance of the train station.

Hotel an der Marienkirche ★★

Everything is sparse and uncluttered in this old house across from Marienkirche, where rooms are done in crisp Scandinvian style and neutral tones with nice bursts of color and contemporary art here and there. All of the rooms are furnished to be allergy free, and some have dust-preventing cork flooring; on the aesthetic side, from some of those in front of the house you'll be staring right into the brick towers of Marienkirche. A healthful and substantial breakfast is served in the sunny breakfast room, opening to a small terrace.

Schüsselbuden 4. ✆ **0451/799410.** www.hotel-an-der-marienkirche.de. 18 units. 75€–95€ double. Rates include buffet breakfast. Parking 7€ nearby. Bus: 1, 3, or 11. **Amenities:** Free in-room Wi-Fi.

Hotel Anno 1216 ★★★

The name dates the premises, one of the oldest brick houses in Lübeck and so beautifully restored that staying in this former guildhall and residence seems like a real privilege. The spacious quarters keep the historic surroundings intact, and sleek, contemporary furnishings offset heavy timbers, stuccoed ceilings, frescoes, and other treasures. The handsome singles and doubles are commodious and attractive, while three suites installed in former salons are as impressive as the surroundings were meant to be. An excellent breakfast (extra) tops off a stay in these distinctive lodgings, and amenities include free phone calls within Europe and to the United States.

Alfstrasse 38. ✆ **0451/4008210.** www.hotelanno1216.de. 11 units. 138€ double suites 198€–228€. Parking 7€ nearby. Bus: 1 or 3. **Amenities:** Free in-room Wi-Fi.

Ringhotel Jensen ★

A gabled 15th-century patrician townhouse on the banks of the Taber provides atmospheric lodging near the heart of town. The somewhat plain accommodations aren't as historically authentic as the gabled exterior, but they are pleasantly comfortable, many face the Holstenstor gate, and a generous buffet breakfast is served in a sunny room overlooking the river.

An der Obertrave 4–5. ✆ **0451/702490.** www.ringhotel-jensen.de. 42 units. 93€–115€ double. Rates include buffet breakfast. Parking 7€ nearby. Bus: 1, 3, or 11. Near the Holstentor. **Amenities:** Restaurant; room service; free in-room Wi-Fi.

Where to Eat

Brauberger ★ NORTHERN GERMAN

Drink from the source at this in-town brewery that has been making pale ale since 1225. You'll have to make your way around the huge copper brewing kettles as you look for a seat at one of the communal tables in the cavernous, multilevel space, where customers put down their steins long enough to discover some excellent food of the schnitzel and sausage variety. Service, despite a nightly crush, is friendly and fast.

Alfstrasse 36. ✆ **0451/71444.** www.brauberger.de. Main courses 7€–14€. Daily 5pm–midnight. Bus: 1 or 3.

Lübeck

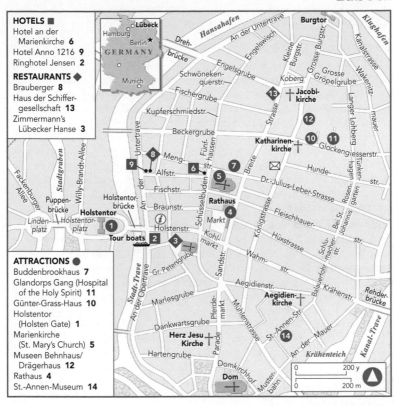

Haus der Schiffergesellschaft ★ NORTHERN GERMAN It's hard not to fall under the magical spell of this former sailor's haunt from 1535, where ship models, lanterns, and other nautical memorabilia hang from paneled walls and ceilings above scrubbed-oak plank tables and high-backed wooden booths carved with the coats of arms of Baltic merchants. You can share a table in the main dining hall to enjoy baked black pudding with slices of apple and lamb's lettuce (and other local favorites), or take a seat at the long bar. Wherever you sit, take a look at what might be the most enchanting artifacts of all, revolving lamps painted with scenes in which ships sail across the seas. Reservations recommended.

Breitestrasse 2. ℗ **0451/76776.** www.schiffergesellschaft.com. Main courses 12€–20€. Daily 10am–midnight. Bar Tues–Sat 5pm–4am. Bus: 1 or 2.

Zimmermann's Lübecker Hanse ★★ SEAFOOD/GERMAN Ask Lübeckers where to eat, and they'll probably steer you this time-honored favorite, where warmly lit, dark-paneled rooms are an especially welcome and atmospheric refuge on a chilly evening. Fresh Baltic fish and seafood are the menu standouts (and hearty fish soup is a meal in itself), though chef Patrick Marquand also prepares a lot of beef and game, including an aromatic roast duck and a delicious currywurst made from deer. Desserts couple Lübeck's love of chocolate and the kitchen's skill with pastry. Be sure to get a reservation.

Kolk 3–7. © **0451/78054.** www.luebecker-hanse.com. Main courses 14€–23€. Tues–Sat noon–3pm and 6pm–midnight. Closed Jan 1–14. Bus: 1, 3, or 11.

Exploring Lübeck

Your sightseeing will be concentrated in Lübeck's remarkable Altstadt, surrounded by the Trave River and its canals to lend an island-like appearance and atmosphere. Walking from the Hauptbahnhof, you'll cross into the Altstadt on the Puppenbrücke (Puppets Bridge), a stone span that got its irreverent name from the seven statues of classical gods and goddesses that stand on its railings.

The city mandated the use of brick after fires in the 13th century destroyed many wooden structures, creating a remarkably pleasing uniformity throughout the old town. You'll notice that some of the medieval redbrick buildings are decorated with black glazed bricks. The black glaze comes from salt that was sprinkled onto the bricks before they were put in the kiln and is a measure of the wealth of the builder—salt was considered to be "white gold."

Buddenbrookhaus ★★ MUSEUM   Readers well versed in the works of author Thomas Mann (and everyone should be) might recognize this commodious, stone house with a gabled roof, recessed doorway, and leaded-glass fan over heavy double doors. This is the house Mann (1875–1955) described as the family home in "Buddenbrooks." Mann's grandparents lived here, and the novelist spent much of his childhood in the large, gracious rooms, a few of which have been reconstructed. Most galleries in the rebuilt and modernized interior displays photographs, letters, and documents chronicling Mann's life, and that of his family, including their flight from Nazi Germany in 1933. Thomas's brother, Heinrich Mann (1871–1950), also a novelist and author of "Professor Unrat," the inspiration for the movie "The Blue Angel," is also well memorialized. Displays are in German with English translations in small type; more accessible are video recordings of Mann and other family members, including the author's speech in Hollywood denunciating McCarthyism and his son Klaus's recollection of returning to bomb-shattered Munich after the war.

Mengstrasse 4. © **0451/1224192.** www.buddenbrookhaus.de. Admission 6€ adults, 3€ students, free for children 13 and under, 10€ for a family ticket. Daily 10am–5pm. Bus 1 or 3.

Glandorps-Gang (Hospital of the Holy Spirit) ★ LANDMARK   One of the oldest social-welfare institutions in Europe occupies one of the most important monumental buildings of the Middle Ages, with a belfry and four turreted spires. Philanthropic local citizens founded the hospital in 1230. In the early 19th century, when the building was converted to a shelter for elderly men and women, 130 tiny wooden cabins without ceilings were built within its enormous main hall. The cabins remain intact, and you can poke your head inside them.

2 Grosse Gröpelgrube 2. Free admission. Tues–Sun 10am–5pm.

Günter Grass-Haus ★ MUSEUM   One of Germany's most-esteemed postwar authors was born in Danzing, now Gansk, Poland, in 1927 and has lived outside Lübeck for many years. Grass is best known for "The Tin Drum," published in 1959. Anyone who's read the novel or seen the film can't help but to think of the eels-in-the-horsehead scene when traveling along the broad, marshy shores of the Baltic Sea around Hamburg and Lübeck. Grass unleashed a torrent of criticism in 2006 when he revealed, in advance of the publication of his autobiography, that he had served in the

THE sweet side OF LÜBECK

Lübeck is the world capital of Marzipan, a sweet almond paste. According to legend, Lübeckers ran out of flour during a long siege and started grinding almonds to make bread. They were so pleased with the sweet results that they've been making Marzipan ever since. To sample Lübeck's famous product, stop in at **Cafe Niederegger,** Breitestrasse 98 (*© **0451/53010**), located right across

from the main entrance to the Rathaus since 1806. On the ground floor, you can purchase bars and boxes of Marzipan to take away (an excellent gift idea), or you can go upstairs to the pleasant cafe for dessert and coffee; they also have seating across the street in the arcades behind the Rathaus facing Marktplatz. Niederegger's is open daily from 9am to 6pm.

Nazi Waffen SS at age 17; some critics suggested the Nobel Prize committee should revoke Grass's prize. Grass is also a sculptor, watercolorist, printmaker, and charcoal artist, and renderings of eels and fish fill these rooms in an old printing plant, alongside many of his original manuscripts and the machines, from an Olivetti manual typewriter to computers, on which he wrote them. Some of his elegant bronzes grace the courtyard. Next door, at no. 25, step through the baroque portal of the **Füchtingshof,** an almshouse built in the 17th century for the widows of seamen and merchants (open 9am–noon and 3–6pm); you'll enter a tranquil courtyard with houses still occupied by widows. Down the street are two more former almshouses, testimony to how well Renaissance Lübeck treated its citizens: the **Glandorps-Gang,** at no. 41, and the **Glandorps-Hof,** at nos. 49 and 51.

Glockengiesserstrasse 21. *© **0451/1224190.** www.grass-haus.de. Admission 6€ adults, 3€ students, 2.50€ children 13 and under. Apr–Dec daily 10am–6pm; Jan–Mar daily 11am–5pm.

Holstentor (Holsten Gate) ★★ LANDMARK The first monument you encounter when you emerge from the train station was for centuries the main entrance to town, looming over a bridge leading into the Altstadt. The twin cylindrical towers rising above a steeped gable are mightily impressive, which is the point—built in the 15th century, the gate was meant to announce Lübeck's power and prestige rather than defend the city. An inscribed motto brings home the city's traditionally noncombattive nature and reads, "Harmony at home and peace abroad." Within the tower is the Museum Holstentor, worth a quick stop to see a made-to-scale replica of mid-17th-century ü, along with some beautifully made scale models of Hanseatic Kogge (cogs, or single-sail vessels). Just to the south are the **Salzspeicher (Salt Lofts),** a group of six gabled Renaissance buildings; the oldest dates from 1579, the newest from 1745. Merchants stored salt (considered "white gold") from nearby Lüneburg in these buildings before shipping it to Scandinavia, where it was used to preserve fish. Each of the six buildings is different, reflecting trends in Renaissance gabled architecture.

Holstentorplatz. *© **0451/1224129.** www.die-luebecker-museen.de. Admission 5€ adults, 2€ children under 16. Tues–Fri 10am–4pm; Sat–Sun 11am–5pm. Bus: 1, 3, or 11.

Marienkirche (St. Mary's Church) ★ CHURCH Soaring flying buttresses and towering windows seem to dwarf the rest of the rest of Lübeck, all the more so since this remarkable assemblage rises on the highest point in the Altstadt. One of Germany's most remarkable and picturesque churches was an easy mark for World War II bombers, who leveled the bell towers in 1942, inadvertently creating a conversation piece—the shattered bells remain embedded in the church floor, a testament to the horror and ludicrousness of war. You may contemplate this as you sit in the soaring nave, with the world's tallest brick vaulting, enjoying one of the summertime organ concerts, a tradition established by esteemed 18th-century master organist Dietrich Buxtehude. Just outside the entrance a rather cherubic devil with shiny horns polished by the touch of many hands sits atop a block of stone. Legend has it that the workers building the cathedral told the devil they were constructing a winestub, and the devil gladly joined in the construction, knowing the establishment would help bring many souls over to the dark side. When Satan realized he had been duped he attempted to smash the walls with the stone, but workers appeased him by pointing out that the rathskeller in the adjoining Rathaus would send him many clients.

Schusselbuden 13. (✆ **0451/397700.** www.st-marien-luebeck.de. Free admission. Daily 10am–6pm (closed when services are being conducted). Bus 1 or 3.

Museen Behnhaus/Drägerhaus ★★ GALLERY Two patrician houses portray prosperous Lübeck life in a suites of rooms furnished and decorated in the styles of different periods, from lavish Rococo to restrained neoclassical. On the walls of adjoining galleries is an outstanding collection of 19th- and 20th-century paintings; those by Edward Munch, who lived and worked in Lübeck, get the spotlight, though many of the German Romantic and Impressionist works are outstanding; look for the colorful painting of Lübeck's St. Jacobkirch by Austrian artist Oskar Kokoshka (1886–1980) who also lived and worked in Lübeck briefly. "Self Portrait with Family" (1820), by Lübeck native Johan Friedrich Overbeck eerily evokes a Renaissance painting of the Holy Family; it's one of several works by like-minded artists who left Germany to lead a life of virtue and nobility in Rome, taking their artistic inspiration from the Renaissance masters.

Königstrasse 9–11. (✆ **0451/1224148.** www.museum-behnhaus-draegerhaus.de. Admission 6€ adults, 3€ students and children 6 to 18, 2€ for children 5 and under. Apr–Sept Tues–Sun 10am–5pm; Oct–Mar Tues–Fri 10am–4pm, Sat–Sun 11am–5pm.

Rathaus ★ HISTORIC BUILDING Aracades, towers, gables, redbrick walls embellished with black glazing and coats of arms,—everything about this 13th-century landmark conspires to present a fairytale appearance. Tours in English and other languages show off some rather somber and pompous staterooms that are not nearly as appealing as the architectural flourishes on the exterior.

Rathausplatz. (✆ **0451/1221005.** Tickets 3€ for adults and 1.50€ for children. Tours Mon–Fri at 11am, noon, and 3pm.

St.-Annen-Museum ★ MUSEUM/RELIGIOUS SITE A 16th-century convent originally housed nuns, who came here (and to other medieval convents) not necessarily with a religious calling but out of practicality—the surroundings provided a home to unmarried women whose families could not afford dowries to marry off their daughters. They enjoyed a fair amount of freedom in these common rooms, cloisters, and refectories that later served simultaneously as a prison and almshouse. They now house religious art, including several altar pieces and, quite appropriately, five sculptures of the wise virgins of biblical parable who had the foresight to be prepared when some fellows arrived looking for wives and hence got their men—a medieval warning to be prepared for the Day of Judgement.

St-Annen Strasse 15. (✆ **451/1224137.** Admission 6€ for adults, 3€ for students and children 6–18. Tues–Sun 10am–6pm (Jan–Mar 11am–5pm).

MUNICH

Munich (München, pronounced *Mewn*-shin, in German), the capital of Bavaria, is a town that likes to party. Walk through the Altstadt (Old City) on a sunny day or a balmy evening and you'll see people sitting outside, in every square, drinking, eating, and enjoying life. And there is a lot of life to enjoy in this attractive city, which seems to epitomize a certain beer-drinking, oom-pah-pah image many people still have of Germany (an image, by the way, that makes most Germans laugh or cringe). The beer and oom-pah-pah is definitely here—you'll find it at the famous Hofbräuhaus and other beer halls—but suds and songs sung in swaying unison are only one part of Munich. The other part is rich, cultured and sophisticated, with a kind of proud, purring prosperity that supports the arts on a grand scale and appreciates the finer things in life (such as the BMWs that are produced here). In addition to having several world-class museums, it can lay claim to having the richest cultural, gastronomic and retail life in southern Germany. It's softer and not as gritty as Berlin or Hamburg, at least not in its lovely and lively inner core, where church bells chime and the streets are paved for people, not cars.

Historically Catholic, and associated with the Italian Counter-Reformation, Munich's (and Bavaria's) architectural legacy includes exuberantly decorated baroque and rococo churches and palaces of a kind rarely seen in northern Germany (one notable exception being Sanssouci palace outside Berlin); and grand neoclassical monuments and buildings from the time of Ludwig I (1786–1868), who wanted to make his capital city a "new Athens." (Much of the city had to be rebuilt after World War II bombing, however.) Munich's wholehearted embrace of traditional feasts and festivities is also aligned to its Catholic heritage, and it's these seasonal events that still bring Münchners together and make visitors feel welcome. The kingdom of Bavaria, created by Napoleon in 1806, lasted until 1918, and a sense of that privileged royal past still lingers in Munich. But this is also a city where it's a tradition to share a communal table in a beer hall and enjoy the company of complete strangers.

Think of Munich as the capital of *Gemütlichkeit,* that not-quite-translatable adjective that means something between cozy and good-natured. Once you visit, you'll understand why it's long been called Germany's "secret capital"—the place where most Germans would live if they could.

ESSENTIALS

As one of Germany's major cities, Munich has no lack of transportation options. Like Frankfurt, Munich has an international airport, so you can fly

HOW TO "do" OKTOBERFEST

The world's greatest beer festival starts in September and runs to the first Sunday in October. All the *trinken und essen* (drinking and eating) at this giant 2½-week party takes place at the traditional **Theresienwiese** ("Wiesn" for short) festival grounds, where different beers are sold in 14 different tents, each with its own atmosphere and food (sausage and sauerkraut prevail). If you've got kids with you (they'll love the rides), the Augustiner tent is considered to be the most family-friendly tent. The best food is found at Käfer's Wiesn'n-Schanke. Oktoberfest beer is delicious but strong, with a 5 to 7 percent alcohol level, and it's served in 1-liter portions. Translation: Pace your beer drinking and drink plenty of water, or you may find yourself on the floor instead of at the table. The Wiesn welcomes millions of visitors, but only has seating for about 100,000, so if you want to sit, especially on busy weekend evenings, it's imperative to arrive early—the gates open at 10am—and claim your space.

there directly from the U.S. and the U.K., and is easily accessible from anywhere within Germany or Europe.

Getting There

BY PLANE   Munich's **Franz Josef Strauss International Airport** (℗ **089/9752-1313;** www.munich-airport.com) is located 29km (18 miles) northeast of the city center. Opened in 1992, the airport is among the most modern and efficient in the world. The S-8 **S-Bahn light-rail train** (℗ **089/4142-4344**) connects the airport with the **Hauptbahnhof** (main train station) in downtown Munich. Trains leave from the S-Bahn platform beneath the airport every 20 minutes daily between about 4am and 10:45pm, less frequently through the night. The fare for the 40-minute trip is 10€ adults. (If you are going to be using public transportation once in the city, you'll save money by buying an **All-Zone Tageskarte/Day Ticket** for 11€ and using it to get into the city.) The **Lufthansa Airport Bus** (℗ **0180/583-8426;** www.airportbus-muenchen. de) runs between the airport and the main train station in Munich every 20 minutes from about 6:30am to 10:30pm The trip takes about 40 minutes and costs 11€. A **taxi** to the city center costs about 70€ and can take more than an hour if traffic is heavy.

BY TRAIN   You can easily reach Munich by train from any city in Germany or Europe. Daily trains arrive from Frankfurt (trip time: 3¾ hr.) and Berlin (trip time: 6 hr.). Munich's **Hauptbahnhof,** on Bahnhofplatz near the city center, is one of Europe's largest train stations, with a hotel, restaurants, shopping, and banking facilities. A train information office on the mezzanine level is open daily from 7am to 8pm; you can also call **Deutsche Bahn** (German Rail; ℗ **11861** for train information and schedules [an English speaker will be available to help you]; www.bahn.com). Connected to the rail station are the city's extensive **S-Bahn** rapid-transit system and the **U-Bahn** (subway) system.

BY CAR   Think twice about driving to or in Munich. Most of downtown is a pedestrian-only area—wonderful if you're a walker, a nightmare if you're a driver. Traffic jams are frequent, and parking spaces are elusive and costly. If you plan on making excursions into the countryside, renting a car in the city center instead of trekking out to the airport is more convenient. Car-rental companies with windows at the main train station include **Avis** (℗ **089/1260-000;** www.avis.com), **Hertz** (℗ **089/1295-001;** www.hertz.com), and **Sixt Autovermietung** (℗ **089/550-2447;** www.sixt.com).

Visitor Information

Munich's tourist office, **Fremdenverkehrsamt München** (© **089/233-96500;** www. muenchen.de), operates two **tourist information centers** where you can pick up a map of Munich and get information on cultural events. The one located in the **Hauptbahnhof** (main train station) at Bahnhofplatz 2 is open Monday through Saturday 9am to 8pm and Sunday from 10am to 6pm; this office offers a hotel-booking service. A second branch of the tourist office is located in the city center at Marienplatz in the **Neues Rathaus (New Town Hall);** hours are Monday through Friday 9am to 7pm, Saturday 9am to 4pm, and Sunday 10am to 2pm.

The Neighborhoods in Brief

INNENSTADT (INNER CITY)

The Innenstadt encompasses central Munich west of the Isar River, the area of most interest to visitors. Within the Innenstadt is the **Altstadt (Old City),** an oval-shaped pedestrian-only district. Munich's **Hauptbahnhof** (main train station) lies just west of the Altstadt. **Marienplatz,** dominated by the **Altes Rathaus** and **Neues Rathaus** and with several major churches in the vicinity, is the Altstadt's most important square. **Kaufingerstrasse,** a pedestrian-only shopping street, starts at the west end of Marienplatz, and Tal, a retail and restaurant street, begins at east side of the square. Just to the south of Marienplatz is the **Viktualienmarkt,** a wonderfully lively outdoor market. Between Marienplatz and Odeonsplatz is the **Platzl** quarter, famed for its nightlife, restaurants, and the landmark **Hofbräuhaus,** the most famous beer hall in the world. **Odeonsplatz,** to the north of Marienplatz, is one of Munich's most beautiful squares, site of the **Residenz** (former royal palace) and the giant **National Theatre,** home of the famed Bavarian State Opera. Running west from Odeonsplatz is Briennerstrasse, a wide shopping avenue that leads to **Königsplatz (King's Square).** Flanking this large square are three neoclassical buildings constructed by Ludwig I and housing Munich's antiquities: the **Propyläen,** the **Glyptothek,** and the **Antikensammlungen.** Another trio of world-famous art museums—the **Alte Pinakothek (Old Masters Gallery),** the **Neue Pinakothek (New Masters Gallery),** and the **Pinakothek Moderne Kunst (Gallery of Modern Art)**—are located in the **Museum Quarter,** just northeast of Königsplatz. **Theresienwiese,** where Oktoberfest is held, is located southwest of the Altstadt.

SCHWABING

Ludwigstrasse connects the Altstadt with Schwabing, a former artists' quarter located north of the Altstadt and known for its cafes, restaurants, and nightlife.

BOGENHAUSEN & HAIDHAUSEN

East of the Isar River, outside the city center, lie **Bogenhausen** and **Haidhausen,** leafy residential neighborhoods where you find some hotels and restaurants.

SCHWABING

The northern section of the city, with **Leopoldstrasse** as its artery, had a Bohemian heyday before World War I and has become a restaurant and entertainment area popular with students and tourists. The **Englischer Garten** spreads out along its eastern border and **Olympiapark** and Josephsplatz mark its western border.

OLYMPIAPARK

Site of the 1972 Olympics, the entire park is now a multipurpose complex hosting concerts, sporting events, fairs and more. **BMW Welt,** the car maker's showroom, museum and factory, is located here.

NYMPHENBURG

Nymphenburg, about a 20-minute tram ride northwest of the city center, is of interest to tourists primarily because of **Schloss Nymphemburg,** the summer palace of Munich's long-ruling family, the Wittelsbachs. The ornately decorated palace with its adjacent museums and beautifully landscaped grounds make a trip here worthwhile.

Saving Money on Transportation

A **Tageskarte** (day ticket) good for a day of travel within the inner city costs 5.80€ for one adult; a **Partner Tageskarte** costs 11€ and is good for up to 5 people traveling together. A **3-Tageskarte** (3-day ticket) costs 14€; the **partner 3-tages-karte,** good for up to 5 people traveling together, costs 25€. You can buy these cards from the ticket vending machines or at station ticket windows.

Getting Around

Munich is a large city, only slightly smaller than Berlin or Hamburg. The best way to explore is by walking and using the excellent public-transportation system. In the Altstadt, you can walk to all the attractions—in fact, you have to, because the Altstadt is a car-free zone.

BY PUBLIC TRANSPORTATION   An extensive network of **U-Bahn** (subway), **S-Bahn** (light-rail), **Strassenbahn** (trams), and **buses** makes getting anywhere in the city relatively easy. You'll probably use the underground U-Bahn and the aboveground **Strassenbahn** systems most frequently. The same ticket entitles you to ride U-Bahn, S-Bahn, trams, and buses. Purchase tickets from vending machines in U-Bahn and S-Bahn stations; the machines display instructions in English. You also can buy tickets in the tram or from a bus driver. Tickets must then be **validated** in the machines found on U-Bahn and S-Bahn platforms and in buses and trams; stick your ticket into the machine, which stamps it with the date and time. A validated ticket is valid for 2 hours. You can transfer as often as you like to any public transportation as long as you travel in the same direction.

Munich has **four concentric fare zones.** Most, if not all, of your sightseeing will take place in Zone 1, which includes the city center. A **single ticket** *(Einzelfahrkarte)* in Zone 1 costs 2.60€.

For information, call the public-transportation authority, **MVV,** at ℂ **089/41424344,** or visit it on the Web at www.mvv-muenchen.de.

BY TAXI   Taxis are cream-colored, plentiful, and expensive. You can get a taxi at one of the stands located all across the city, or you can hail a cab on the street if its rooftop light is illuminated. Taxi fares begin at 3.30€ and rise by 1.60€ per kilometer; there's an additional 1.20€ charge to order a taxi by phone. Call **Taxizentrale** at ℂ **089/21610** for a radio-dispatched taxi.

BY BICYCLE   Munich is a bike-friendly city. One of the most convenient places to rent a bike is **Radius Bikes** (ℂ **089/5434877740;** www.radiustours.com), at the far end of the Hauptbahnhof at Arnulfstrasse 2. The charge is 3€ per hour, or 15€ to 18€ per day. A deposit of 50€ or a credit card number is required; students receive a 10 percent discount. Radius Bikes is open mid-March through October Monday through Friday 9am to 6pm and Saturday through Sunday 9am to 8pm.

[FastFACTS] MUNICH

ATMs   You'll find bank ATMs all over Munich.

City Telephone Code For Munich, **089.** Use 89 if you're calling Munich from outside Germany; 089 if you're within Germany but not in Munich. If you're calling within Munich, leave off the city code and dial only the regular phone number.

Dentists & Doctors

For an English-speaking dentist, go to the **Klinik und Poliklinik für Kieferchirurgie der Universität München,** Lindwurmstrasse 2A (✆ **089/51600;** U-Bahn: Goetheplatz), the dental clinic for the university. It deals with emergency cases and is always open. For 24-hour medical service, go to **Schwabing Hospital,** Kölner Platz 1 (✆ **089/ 30680;** U-Bahn: Scheidplatz).

Emergencies

For emergency medical aid or the police, phone ✆ **110.** Call the fire department at ✆ **112.**

Internet Access

Chances are, Wi-Fi will be available either free or for a nominal charge at your hotel. WiFi is free at any **Starbucks.** You can send e-mails or check your messages at the **EasyEverything Internet Café,** Bahnhofplatz 1 (✆ **089/ 55999696;** U-Bahn: Hauptbahnhof). It's open daily 7:30am to 11:45pm. For a current list of internet cafes sorted by location, go to **www.muenchen.de/ internetcafes**.

Pharmacy/Drugstores

For an international drugstore where English is spoken, go to **Bahnhof Apotheke,** Bahnhofplatz 2 (✆ **089/594119;** www. hauptbahnofapo.de; U-Bahn/S-Bahn: Hauptbahnhof), open Monday to Friday 8am to 6:30pm and Saturday 8am to 2pm. If you need a prescription filled during off hours, call ✆ **089/557661** for locations of open pharmacies. The information is recorded and in German only, so you may need to get someone from your hotel staff to assist you.

Safety

Munich, like all big cities, has its share of crime, especially pickpocketing and purse and camera snatching, but it is generally a safe city. Most robberies occur in the much-frequented tourist areas, such as Marienplatz and the Hauptbahnhof, which is particularly dangerous at night. Use caution and common sense.

WHERE TO STAY

Hotels in Munich are more expensive than elsewhere in Germany, and rooms are scarce (and prices higher) during Oktoberfest and when trade fairs are in town. It's a good idea to book your Munich hotel room in advance. The highest prices in this section are for rooms during Oktoberfest and trade fairs. Take note that breakfast is no longer routinely included in the price of every hotel room, especially at luxury hotels; if breakfast is offered, but for an additional charge, you can have your morning repast at one of Munich's many cafes or bakeries.

If you arrive in the city without a room, the **Fremdenverkehrsamt** (tourist office) in the main train station can book a room for you; the service is free, but the tourist office collects a 10 percent deposit of the total value of the room; the hotel then deducts this amount from your bill.

In Central Munich

Bayerischer Hof & Palais Montgelas ★★★ This is a grand hotel, in all senses of the word. It offers every amenity and service you could possibly want in a large, centrally located Altstadt hotel, including a pool, sauna, spa, cinema and a famous nightclub. The largest and oldest hotel in Munich (it will celebrate its 175th anniversary in 2014), the Bayerischer Hof is for those who want the best of traditional service and comfort—and who don't mind or even welcome the relative anonymity that comes with staying in such an enormous labyrinth (it has five inner courtyards). The double rooms here are fairly spacious, with gleaming marble bathrooms and a decor that manages to be both timeless and up-to-date. This is the kind of hotel that offers many room and suite options, some of which are spectacular (for 3,600€ a night, they should be). There are 20 luxurious suites in the adjoining Palais Montgelas. There are several dining options, too, including a Ratskeller in the vaults below the hotel, where Munich's salt was once stored. The breakfast room (always check to see whether you can get breakfast included in your room rate) is a glass-walled eyrie on the sixth floor with an outdoor terrace.

Promenadeplatz 2–6. © **800/223-6800** in the U.S. or 089/21200. www.bayerischerhof.de. 340 units. 260€–360€ double, 790€–2,000€ jr. suite. U-/S-Bahn: Marienplatz. **Amenities:** 2 restaurants, 2 bar-lounges, nightclub, pool, sauna, fitness center, cinema, WiFi (18€/day).

Cortiina ★

Located a stone's throw from Marienplatz, this boutique hotel is a pleasant and super-convient spot to park your bags in Munich's Altstadt. In fact, its that location that's the deciding factor for most guests. But there are other perks here, including suites with kitchenettes and little balconies in a building adjacent to the hotel (these are the Cortiina's most homelike accommodations). The standard double rooms are a bit on the drab side for a so-called "design hotel," but they're comfortable nonetheless, with swank, oversized bathrooms (with eco-friendly REN bath products and, in many, soothing soaking tubs). The hotel caters to many longer-stay business travelers, who appreciate the kitchenette units.

Ledererstrasse 8. © **089/2422490.** www.cortiina.com. 75 units. 159€–559€ double. U-Bahn: Marienplatz. **Amenities:** Bar; free Wi-Fi.

Creatif Hotel Elephant ★

The area around the train station is not the most picturesque section of Munich by any stretch, but it's here that you can find centrally located, value-packed hotels like this one. The family-run Creatif Hotel Elephant is one of the better options for travelers who are on a budget but still want a bit of spark in their accommodations. The rooms here are not large but they were recently redone and have a bright, simple, contemporary look and top-quality beds. The refurbed bathrooms are small, too, but completely adequate. If you're looking for a clean, comfortable, no-frills place that's a cut above the average, this is a good choice. Breakfast costs and additional 9€ but there are cafes all around where you can eat more cheaply.

Lämmerstrasse 6, Leopoldvorstadt. © **089/555785.** www.creatifelephanthotel.com. 83 units. 68€–150€ double. U-/S-Bahn: Hauptbahnhof. **Amenities:** Free Wi-Fi.

Eden-Hotel-Wolff ★

If you're arriving in Munich by train and want a nice, convenient, midrange hotel right across the street from the train station, this is your best option. From the outside, this large hotel, founded in 1890, looks a bit forbidding, but the interior has been redone with a pleasantly modern look. Most of the rooms are fairly large, and all are decorated in a comfortable, unobtrusive style that varies from room to room. Bathrooms are larger than average, with tub and shower combinations.

Arnulfstrasse 4–8. © **089/551150.** www.ehw.de. 211 units. 188€–332€ double with breakfast. U-/S-Bahn: Hauptbahnhof. **Amenities:** Restaurant; bar; concierge; exercise room; room service; spa; Wi-Fi (10€/day).

Gästehaus Englischer Garten ★★

From the ivy-covered walls of the main villa to the homey mixture of antiques, old-fashioned beds and Oriental rugs you get charm with a capital "C" at this long-established guesthouse. The service is as kindly as the atmosphere; in fact, our only complain about the place is that the bathrooms are small, with showers only. You can save a few euros by renting one of the rooms that share bathrooms. For those looking at longer stays, the guesthouse rents out 15 small apartments in a more modern annex across the street; each has a kitchenette. Breakfast costs an extra 8.50€; on nice mornings, you can eat outside in the back garden.

Liebergesellstrasse 8. © **089/383-9410.** www.hotelenglischergarten.de. 25 units. 83€–186€ double. U-Bahn: Münchener Freiheit.

Hotel Bristol München ★   Here's another hotel where the location is the star, as its centrally located and, if you're not a walker, just a hop and a skip from the the Sendlinger Tor U-Bahn stop. Built around 1960 and renovated in 2002, this efficient, modern hotel is also quite a good value, cost-wise. The rooms are fairly small, with simple, comfortable furnishings—in most cases, a wood-trimmed bed, desk and chair in a functional Scandinavian design-offset by a pale rose-pink carpet. But they have nice, little balconies and are kept spotlessly clean. Bathrooms are compact and have showers. For a quieter room, request one that faces the courtyard. The breakfat buffet costs an additional 10€.

Pettenkoferstrasse 2. *©* **089/5434-8880.** www.bristol-munich.de. 56 units. 99€–169€ double. U-Bahn: Sendlinger Tor. **Amenities:** Free Wi-Fi.

Hotel Jedermann ★   *Jedermann* means "everyman," and that translates here into a range of affordable rooms in different sizes and configurations and family-friendly prices (cribs and cots are an additional 8€,but additional beds are only 15€, which is on the low end for Munich). Other pluses include a convenient if not particularly picturesque location within easy walking distance of the train station. This pleasant, family-run hotel, established over 50 years ago, offers plain but comfortable rooms with solid wooden beds, usable work desks, and decently sized closets. Most of the rooms have roomy, shower-only bathrooms. Cheaper rooms with in-room showers but toilets down the hall also are available. The hotel serves a breakfast buffet, and if you're not traveling with a laptop or phone, you can check your e-mail on the computer in the lobby (most of but not all the rooms also have Wi-Fi access).

Bayerstrasse 95.*©* **089/543240.** www.hotel-jedermann.de. 55 units. 45€–215€ double with breakfast. U-/S-Bahn: Hauptbahnhof. **Amenities:** Free Wi-Fi.

Hotel Schlicker ★★   There are many reasons to stay at this hotel, but location is at the top of the list. Hotel Schlicker practically sits on Marienplatz, Munich's heart and soul (and where the city's famous Christmas Market is held). The famed Hofbräuhaus is almost next door, the fabulous Viktuelenmarkt, Munich's outdoor market, is around the corner, and the area is loaded with restaurants, and visitor attrctions. Plus, the Marienplatz U-Bahn station is steps away, so you can easily get anywhere in the city. The staff at this traditional hotel, established over 400 years ago and run by the same family since 1890, are extraordinarily friendly and helpful. Some of the rooms have recently been renovated and these are the ones you should ask for because the others, while perfectly serviceable, look dated. The breakfast buffet that's included in the room rate is unusually good for a hotel in this price range. Street noise on Tal can be a distraction, so consider booking a room on the quiet inner courtyard.

Tal 8. *©* **089/2428870.** www.hotel-schlicker.de. 68 units. 150€–190€ double with breakfast. U-Bahn: Marienplatz. **Amenities:** Complimentary bikes, free Wi-Fi.

Hotel Torbräu ★★   Munich's oldest hotel welcomed its first guest in 1497 and has been owned and operated by the Kirchlechner family since 1890. These are pretty sound credentials for a hotel and a good indicator that you will find a special atmosphere within…and without, too, for the long-lived hotel overlooks the medieval Isartor (gate) in the heart of the Altstadt. Because of its age and location, the Torbräu offers a cozy and close-to-everything stay. Completely refurbished in 2012, the hotel mixes the warmth of traditional wood paneling and antiques with comfortable, contemporary furniture and a light, fresh palette of colors and fabrics. Ask for a room on the fifth floor if you want an unobstructed view of the Altstadt with its church spires, or a room overlooking the Isartor if you want to enjoy the sight of that memorable landmark.

Need quiet? Ask for a room facing the courtyard. In all cases, you'll be treated to the sound of church bells in the morning, afternoon and evening, as they have done for centuries. The standard rooms and bathrooms are rather small, so you may want to upgrade to the deluxe category for some extra legroom. **Schapeau** is the hotel's excellent restaurant, and the bar has a lively happy hour. And, most importantly, the staff here seems to work overtime to help make their guests happy.

Tal 41. ✆ **089/242340.** www.torbraeu.de. 90 units. 209€–475€ double with breakfast. Closed 1 week at Christmas. U-Bahn: Isartor. **Amenities:** 2 restaurants; bar; free Wi-Fi.

Louis Hotel ★★★ This chic Altstadt hideaway is the only hotel in Munich that has rooms overlooking the lively Viktualienmarkt. But despite this marquee location it truly is a hideaway, because the hotel entrance is so unobtrusive that you pass right by and never know it's there. But if it's unobtrusive outside, the Louis is rather remarkable inside, showcasing modern European design that looks and feels effortlessly natural instead of making a "statement." The rooms are relatively large but carefully planned to maximize space (with concealed closets that pull out from the wall) and provide an aura of calm elegance. They're filled with custom loomed fabrics and carpets, fine wood and stone finishes, and handmade furniture. The Market View rooms with Juliet balconies overlooking the market square are the best; other rooms face a quiet inner courtyard. Louis is known for its exeptional Japanese restaurant, **Emiko,** just off the lobby, and its splendid summer roof terrace (the perfect place to relax with a cocktail).

Viktualienmarkt 6. ✆ **089/41119080.** www.louis-hotel.com. 72 units. 179€–639€ double. U-/S-Bahn: Marienplatz. **Amenities:** Restaurant, bar, roof terrace, free Wi-Fi.

Mandarin Oriental ★★★ Impeccable. That's the word that describes this lovely, luxurious boutique hotel across from the Hofbrauhaus and minutes away from everything in central Munich. In terms of personalized service and guest comfort, it can't be beat. The rooms are fairly large, and some have views over the red tiled roofs of Munich and its church spires. The decor here is traditional and ultra-comfortable, accessorized with fine antiques, prints and paintings.The large, marble-tile bathrooms here are noteworthy with Moulton Brown toiletries, big walk-in showers, and large bathtubs. The hotel's **Mark** restaurant has received one Michelin star for nearly a decade for its refined Bavarian cuisine. From November to January, a little rustic Alpine chalet called **Alm** is erected on the roof and becomes a wildly popular (and expensive) dining spot for Muncheners. In the summer, the rooftop terrace, the tallest spot in the Altstadt, opens up its lovely heated pool. There's also a small fitness center and spa. The rate below is a so-called rack rate; look for lower-rate specials on the hotel's website.

Neuturmstrasse 1. ✆ **089/290980.** www.mandarinoriental.com. 73 units. 775€ double. U-/S-Bahn: Marienplatz. **Amenities:** 2 restaurants; bar; bikes; concierge; exercise room; heated outdoor pool (seasonal); spa, Wi-Fi (18€/day).

Wombat's City Hostel Munich ★ Clean, safe, friendly and centrally located near the main train station, Wombat's is by far the best hostel in Munich. That's partially thanks to the relaxed but professional staff, who keep the maintenance standards high. We also laud the Wombat for offering a tad more style than most hostels. The glass-roofed, plant-filled central atrium with its hammock and brightly colored modern furniture is a nice spot for hanging out, as is the bar, which sells inexpensive drinks and food. There are bathrooms with toilets and showers in the 6-bed dorm rooms and double rooms. As in all hostels, rooms are stripped down to the essentials, but the minimalist look is warmed by polished wood floors, wood-framed beds, wooden tables, and storage areas painted with bright, lively colors. There are no curfews at Wombat's and the front desk is open 24/7. You'd be hard-pressed to find better value in this central a location.

Senefelderstrasse 1. ⓒ **089/59989180.** www.wombats-hostels.com/munich. 18€ dorm bed, 38€ double with bathroom. U-Bahn: Hauptbahnhof. **Amenities:** Bar, laundry room, free Wi-Fi in lobby.

Near Theresienwiese (Oktoberfest Grounds)

Hotel Uhland ★   This family-run hotel occupies a handsome Art Nouveau-style building that's over a century old and located just a block from Theresienwiese, the Oktoberfest fairgrounds. Hotel Uhland is an old-fashioned hotel that provides solid comfort, friendly service and great value. There's nothing hip or flashy about it, but that is part of its quiet charm. The rooms are furnished in a functional style. A buffet breakfast is included in the room rate. You can walk to the main train station in 10 minutes and Marienplatz is one stop away on the U-Bahn. During Oktoberfest the rates jump to the high end of the price range; book well in advance if that's when you'll be staying.

Uhlandstrasse 1. ⓒ **089/543350.** www.hotel-uhland.de. 30 units. 95€–214€ double with breakfast. U-/S-Bahn: Theresienwiese. **Amenities:** Free Wi-Fi.

Pension Westfalia ★   Located directly across the street from the Theresienwiese, where Oktoberfest is held, this budget pension occupies two floors in a building that dates from 1895. The rooms are comfortable if spare, with high ceilings and big windows to let in lots of light. You can save money by booking a room with a shared bathroom. A good breakfast buffet is included in the room rate. The proprietor, Peter Dieritz, and his staff are friendly and helpful. There's an U-Bahn station at the corner and Marienplatz is only two stops away.

Mozartstrasse 23. ⓒ **089/530377.** www.pension-westfalia.de. 19 units. 50€–82€ double with breakfast. U-Bahn: Goetheplatz. **Amenities:** Free Wi-Fi.

WHERE TO EAT

Munich is a city that loves to eat—and eat *big*. Homemade dumplings are a specialty, and so are all kinds of sausages (*Weisswurst* in particular) and *Leberkäse,* a large loaf of sausage eaten with freshly baked pretzels and mustard. *Schweinbraten,* a braised loin of pork served with potato dumplings and rich brown gravy, is Bavaria's answer to the north's *sauerbraten* (pot- or oven-roasted marinated beef). Inexpensive sausages, soups, and snacks are sold from outdoor stalls all around the Viktualienmarkt.

In Central Munich

Alois Dallmayr ★★ GERMAN/CONTINENTAL   In business for almost 300 years, Alois Dallmayr is the most famous delicatessen in Germany, and one of the most elegant. Downstairs you can buy fine food products; upstairs in the cafe-bistro you can order a tempting array of dishes, including herring, sausages, smoked fish, and soups and, of course, *Kaffee und Kuchen* (coffee and cake). The Restaurant is a more sophisticated dining venue, featuring daily fixed-price menus. This is also a good place to buy fine food for a picnic.

Dienerstrasse 14–15. ⓒ **089/2135100.** www.dallmayr.de. Main courses cafe-bistro 15€–38€; restaurant fixed-price menus 60€–112€. Mon–Wed 11:30am–7pm; Thurs–Fri 11:30am–8pm; Sat 9am–4pm. U-Bahn: Marienplatz.

Andechser am Dom ★ GERMAN/BAVARIAN Andechser is always packed, so be prepared to be seated at a communal table and make new friends over a glass of beer or two. This brewery-restaurant run by beermeister Sepp Krätz attracts a wide range of diner and drinkers and it is generally loud a nd occasionally boisterous. The food is typical Bavarian, not haute cuisine by any stretch, but filling and tasty. Try the *Kloster Schmaus,* sausages, dumplings, and vegetables served in the pan they're cooked in Another house specialty is *Schweinsbraten* (pork roast) in a dark beer sauce; pork knuckles with crackling are another favorite, and apple strudel is the must-have dessert. There are occasional complaints about rude service and obligatory tips being added to bills.

Weinstrasse 7A. ✆ **089/298481.** Main courses 8.50€–18€. Daily 10am–1am. U-/S-Bahn: Marienplatz.

Augustiner Grossgaststätte ★ BAVARIAN/GERMAN Located in the Altstadt on Munich's main pedestrians-only shopping street, this famous beer hall and restaurant has cavernous rooms and a genuinely good-natured and *gemütlich* (comfortable) atmosphere. Specialties include dumpling soup and roast duck with red cabbage. The house beer, Augustiner Brau, comes from one of Munich's oldest breweries, which owns the restaurant.

Neuhauser Strasse 27. ✆ **089/2318-3257.** Main courses 10€–20€. Daily 9am–midnight. U-Bahn: Karlsplatz/Stachus.

Beim Sedlmayr ★★ GERMAN/BAVARIAN It's a bit difficult to find this restaurant because it's tucked away on a sidestreet near Marienplatz and the Viktualienmarkt, but if you sleuth it out, you'll be treated to one of the more authentic Bavarian dining experiences in Munich. Expect to be seated at a communal table and expect the service to be cordial but a bit brusque because the overworked wairesses have a lot territory to cover. "At Sedlmayr" serves mouthwatering renditions of traditional Bavarian favorites, like roast pork with cracklings and dumplings, grilled *Kalbsbraten,* mushrooms served with dumplings and a creamy herb sauce, and *Kaiserschmarrn* (a kind of bread pudding with a crispy caramelized base and topped with warm apple sauce). The menu is only in German, so do a little homework before you arrive and if you aren't sure what to order, ask your server. The dining may be communal, but it's still a good idea to reserve in advance.

Westenriederstrasse 14. ✆ **089/226219.** Main courses 8€–23€. Mon–Fri 10am–11pm; Sat 9am–4pm. U-/S-Bahn: Marienplatz.

Boettners ★★ INTERNATIONAL When this century-old restaurant moved to its current location in the Altstadt, it brought its wood-paneled interior with it. The cooking is light and refined, with a French influence, but several traditional Bavarian dishes also are on the menu. Special offerings include herb-crusted lamb, beef filet, lobster stew in a cream sauce, and seasonal dishes with white truffles. The desserts are sumptuous.

Pfisterstrasse 9. ✆ **089/221-210.** Reservations required. Main courses 15€–45€; 38€ fixed-price lunch, 69€ fixed-price dinner. Mon–Sat 11:30am–3pm and 6pm–midnight. U-Bahn: Marienplatz.

Gandl ★★ ITALIAN/FRENCH At this attractive neighborhood bistro, the lunch menu leans toward Italian, but at night the cooking becomes more traditionally French and German. The Italian dishes include homemade pastas, such as spaghetti carbonara, gnocchi, and ravioli. Dinner offerings change often and seasonally, but you'll typically find fare such as entrecote with arugula salad, grilled filet of salmon, or lamb in red-wine sauce. Delicious salads and soups are always on the menu, too. Eat on the terrace if the weather's nice and don't be in a rush because the service is relaxed and unhurried. Gandl is in a pleasant residential area behind the National Theatre and is frequented mostly by locals.

St.-Anna Platz 1. ℂ **089/2916-2526.** Main courses 9€–25€; 20€–22€ fixed-price menus. Mon–Sat 9am–1am. U-Bahn: Lehel.

Glockenbach ★★ MODERN EUROPEAN   This stylish but casual and unpretentious two-story bisto-restaurant located south of the tain station in the Glockenbach neighborhood serves great breakfasts and imaginative fusion cuisine at lunch and dinner for a very reasonable price. The limited menu offerings change daily for lunch and weekly (and seasonally) for dinner. You might find curried chicken breast; Knödel with mushrooms, cherry tomatoes and egg; pasta with calf's-liver Bolognese; or ocean perch filet with potato salad.This is an excellent spot to enjoy a good, inexpensive lunch, a classy cocktail, or a delicious dessert.

Müllerstrasse 49. ℂ **089/45240622.** Main courses 12€–19€: 8€ fixed-price lunch (Mon–Fri), 35€–70€ fixed-price dinner. Daily breakfast 10am–noon, lunch noon–3pm, dinner 7–10pm. U-Bahn: Sendliger Tor.

Hofbräuhaus am Platzl ★★ GERMAN   It's not for the refined, the prissy, or the faint of heart, but it is an absolutely unique Munich experience and has been for almost 200 years. What makes it special is its enormous size and at times raucous, beer-fueled atmosphere. Yes, it's touristy. Some nights there seem to be more Americans and Asians than Germans. But if you can't go with the flow, and the din, don't step inside because you'll probably hate it. You don't have to eat; you can just order a beer and one of the giant pretzels sold by dirndl'd Frauleins who parade around the room like cigarette girls of yore. In the *Schwemme* (tap room) on the ground floor, you sit on benches at bare wood tables as a band plays and the Germans periodically burst into song, swaying back and forth in unison; a big beer garden is on this level, too. Upstairs there are a number of smaller, quieter dining rooms. The beer is Hofbrau, served by the *mass* (equal to about a liter and costing 7.60€); *Weissbier* (a light beer) is the only beer served in a smaller glass. The food is heavy and hearty with a menu that includes *Weisswürste* and several other sausages, *Schweinbraten* (roasted pork), *Spanferkel* (roast suckling pig), and the big favorite, *Schweineshaxn* (ham hocks). You gotta love it—or you won't.

Am Platzl 9. ℂ **089/290-1360.** Main courses 6.50€–18€. No credit cards. Daily 9am–midnight. U-/S-Bahn: Marienplatz.

Nürnberger Bratwurst Glöckl am Dom ★ BAVARIAN   A short walk from Marienplatz, across from the cathedral (Dom), this is the coziest and friendliest of Munich's local restaurants. You sit on wooden chairs at shared tables. *Nürnberger Schweinwurstl mit Kraut* (pork sausages with cabbage, a specialty from Nuremberg) is the dish to try. Hot dogs will never taste the same again after you've tried one of these delectable little sausages.

Frauenplatz 9. ℂ **089/295-264.** Main courses 6€–14€. No credit cards. Daily 10am–1am. U-/S-Bahn: Marienplatz.

Prinz Myshkin ★★ VEGETARIAN   If German sausages and meat dishes are getting to you, give this popular vegetarian restaurant near Marienplatz a try. The menu includes freshly made salads, macrobiotic dishes, Asian-inspired vegetarian entrees, and vegetarian *involtini*. The casseroles, soups, and pizzas generally are excellent. It's a bright, attractive place and reasonably priced.

Hackenstrasse 2. ℂ **089/265-596.** Main courses 13€–18€. Daily 11am–12:30am. U-/S-Bahn: Marienplatz.

Restaurant Mark's ★★★ FRENCH/ASIAN   The Michelin-starred Restaurant Mark in the lovely Mandarin Oriental hotel (see "Where to Stay," above) is the absolute antithesis of Munich's loud and lively beer hall restaurants, where you have to shout to be heard, share tables, and can't always be certain when your waiter (or your food) will appear. Located on the second floor and approached by a sweeping marble staircase, the Mark is quiet and elegant, with crisp linen tablecloths and a staff that at times seems to be attuned by ESP to their guests' needs. This is a restaurant that defines the fine-dining side of Munich, and a place to come when you want to enjoy a romantic evening, celebrate a special occasion, or simply to revel in top-quality food and wine served with consummate professionalism. Chef Simon Larese prepares classic French dishes inspired by the tastes and traditions of the Mediterranean—and with an occasional nod to Asia, where he worked at other Michel-starred restaurnats for many years. You can choose from a seasonally adjusted a la carte menu or a monthly changing tasting menu with 3 or 6 courses. Dinner here always begins with an *amuse bouche* to tease the palette and ends with complimentary sweets. For a starter, try the fois gras parfait with salted pear, goat cheese fcream, and brioche, or the pan-fried scallops with Alba truffle spuma and a leek-parmesan-nut crunch, or the delicious pumpkin cream soup with cinnamon flower and lobster won tons. Entrees might include poached Dover sole with potato mousseline and watercress, a seasonal saddle of venison with semolina dumpling and turnip greens with a Rouenaise sauce; or a beef tenderloin with truffle sauce, mashed potatoes and baked beans with bacon. Dessert always includes cheese and homemade chutneys or sweeter options like Vacherin (meringue filled with whipped cream, ice cream, and fruit). The sommelier will help you pair your feast with the perfect wine.

In the Mandarin Oriental, Neuturmstrasse 1. ℂ **089/29098875.** www.mandarinoriental.com. Reservations recommended. Main courses 36€–45€; 3-course menu 70€, 6-course menu 130€. Daily 7–11pm. U-/S-Bahn: Marienplatz.

Riva ★ PIZZA/PASTA   You want a simple Italian meal, pizza or pasta, and you don't want to spend a fortune in Munich's pricey Altstadt—where do you go? To Riva, just outside Marienplatz on Tal, next to the Isartor. This is an uncomplicated and uncluttered place, simple but nicely designed. Okay, maybe the music is too loud, but Riva also serves as a bar where a young crowd comes for cocktails. The menu is limited to pizza, pasta and a few salads. You can order a reasonably priced glass of wine to go with your meal, and leave quite contented, without having drained your bank account.

Tal 44. ℂ **089/220240.** Main courses 8€–13€. Mon–Sat 8am–1am; Sun noon–1am. U-/S-Bahn: Marienplatz.

Rue des Halles ★★★ FRENCH   This is one of those restaurants that you leave smiling and feeling like you've discovered something special. And you have. This airy spot in Haidhausen is Munich's oldest French restaurant—or Brasserie de Paris, as it refers to itself. It opened in 1983 and hasn't lost any of its charm or culinary acumen. And you don't have to pay fortune to enjoy a memorable meal with a glass or two of wine. The menu is wisely limited, but you will find something that suits your fancy because fish, meat, and vegetarian options are all available. If you want to share something special, start with athe Fruits de Mer (seafood) platter, with oysters, langoustines, whelks, shrimp and crab; the Moules (mussels) Mariniere de Normandy are also great, and so is the Breton boullabaisse The meat dishes with various sauces are French classics cooked to perfection: roast breast of guinea fowl with Roquefort sauce; beef cheeks confit with a Madeira sauce; duck with currant sauce; medallions of veal with green pepper sauce; and mustard-and-herb crusted rack of lamb. All of these entrees are served with seasonal vegetables. The desserts, too, are French classics: A selection of cheeses, tarte tatin (apple tart), crème brulee, and warm chocolate cake with crème anglais are tops on my list. There is also a seasonally changing 3 course menu for 23€. This is not a Michelin-starred restaurant, but you will savor every bite of your meal, the lively bistro atmosphere, and the friendly professionalism of the staff. All in all, highly recommended.

Steinstrasse 18. ✆ **089/485675.** www.rue-des-halles.de. Main courses 18€–20€; fixed-price menu 22€. Daily 6–11pm. U-Bahn: Max-Weber-Platz.

Spatenhaus ★★ BAVARIAN/INTERNATIONAL If you want to experience a Munich beer restaurant without the noise and tourist-overload found at the Hofbräuhaus—and with better food—try Spatenhaus, a well-known brewery restaurant with big windows overlooking the opera house. It serves Bavarian specialties such as veal sausages with potato salad and grilled calve's liver with roast onions; the *Bayerische Teller* (Bavarian plate) comes loaded with various meats, including pork and sausages. And if you've had enough German food for the time being, there are a handful of well-prepared Italian dishes on the menu, as well. Wash down your meal with the restaurant's own beer, Spaten-Franziskaner-Bier. The first floor dining room is more casual than the room upstairs.

Residenzstrasse 12. ✆ **089/290-7060.** Main courses 9.50€–28€. Daily 9:30am–12:30am. U-Bahn: Marienplatz.

Zum Alten Markt ★ BAVARIAN/INTERNATIONAL This snug, friendly eatery is located on a tiny square on the east side of the Viktualienmarkt, Munich's big outdoor produce market. In summer, tables are set up outside. You may begin with homemade cream of carrot soup or black-truffle tortellini in cream sauce. The chef makes a great *Tafelspitz* (boiled beef). You can also order classic dishes such as roast duck with applesauce or roast suckling pig.

Dreifaltigkeitsplatz 3. ✆ **089/299995.** Main courses 13€–17€. No credit cards. Mon–Sat 11am–midnight. U-/S-Bahn: Marienplatz.

Zum Dürnbräu ★ BAVARIAN This traditional Bavarian restaurant has a history dating back some 500 years, making it perhaps the oldest restaurant in Munich. Specialties include several beef dishes (tongue, *Tafelspitz,* filet), goose in season, and pork. You can get simple omelets or soup, too. The interior is charming and there's a lovely garden out back.

Dürngräugasse 2 (off Tal). ✆ **089/222-195.** Main courses 9.50€–15€. No credit cards. Daily 9am–midnight. U-/S-Bahn: Marienplatz.

In Schwabing

Café Ignaz ★ VEGETARIAN A Schwabing institution for nearly 3 decades, Café Ignaz is offers creative fare for both vegetarians and vegans. A variety of grains, rice, couscous and pastas are used in the daily offerings, and there are also pizzas with imaginative toppings. For dessert, try one of the soy-based cakes or pastries. During Happy Hour (Mon and Wed–Fri 3–6pm), you can order one of the restaurant's main courses for 6.90€.

Georgenstrasse 67. ✆ **089/2716093.** www.ignaz-cafe.de. Main courses 8€–11€; lunch buffet 8€. Wed–Mon 8am–10pm. U-Bahn: Josephsplatz.

MUNICH beer GARDENS & beer HALLS

Munich is famed for its breweries and beer halls, many of which have outdoor beer gardens where you can quaff their brews and order hearty Bavarian food at reasonable prices. If you'd rather nibble than dine, you can order a homemade *Brezeln* (pretzel), another Munich specialty, or a *Radl*, the large white radish that's another traditional accompaniment to beer. For a glass or mug of beer, expect to pay 5€ to 8€, depending on its size. Oom-pah-pah bands, zither players, or accordionists sometimes add to the jovial atmosphere. The beer halls and gardens are typically large and casual, with communal seating (so try not to be shy!).

Two of the city's most famous beer halls, the **Hofbräuhaus am Platzl** and **Augustiner Grossgaststätte,** are described in the "Where to Eat" section, above. Beyond those, we recommend the following:

One of Munich's largest and most popular beer gardens, **Biergarten Chinesischer Turm ★★★**, Englischer Garten 3 (© 089/383-8720; U-Bahn: Giselastrasse), is located in the Englischer Garten at the foot of the Chinese pagoda. This beer garden is open daily from May to October from 11am. to 1am. **Gaststätte zum Flaucher ★★**, Isarauen 8 (© 089/723-2677; Bus: 52), near the zoo, has tables set in a tree-shaded garden overlooking the Isar River. This beer garden is open daily from May to October from 10am to midnight; November to April, it's open Friday, Saturday, and Sunday from 10am to 9pm.

Munich's autumn **Oktoberfest** is the largest beer festival in the world, and spring is celebrated with **Starkbierzeit,** a lesser-known beer festival that heralds the end of Lent and the opening of the city's beer gardens. One of the best places to celebrate Starkbierzeit is the brewery-restaurant-beer garden **Paulaner am Nockherberg ★★**, 77 Hoch Strasse (© 089/14599120), in southeast Munich. Paulaner serves the original Starkbier, a sweet, strong brew called Salvator, and pairs it with a traditional dish of crisp-skined ham hocks served with sharp mustard. Their beer garden is a convivial spot with old chestnut trees and a playground for the kids. To reach Paulaner, take the U-Bahn to Kolumbusplatz, then bus 54 to Silberhornstrasse and streetcar 25 to the Ostfriedhof stop.

Georgenhof ★ GERMAN/INTERNATIONAL This pleasant Schwabing eatery and wine bar has a comfortably rustic interior with a wood-fired grill, but if the weather is nice, sit outside under the chestnut trees. The menu reflects seasonal specialties like *Spargel* (asparagus) in May and June and game dishes such as *Rehpfeffer* (venison) with egg *Spätzle* (German pasta) or tagliatelle with venison ragout in the fall. Grilled lamb and steak are also also smart choices here. For dessert, try the simple but delicious Bavarian cream with strawberries.

Fredrichstrasse 1. © 089/39-31-01. Main courses 11€–22€. Daily 11 am–midnight. U-Bahn: Universität.

Tantris ★★★ INTERNATIONAL Munich's most famed gastronomic pilgrimage site has been awarded a Michelin star every year for more than 40 years, and if you are deep-pocketed foodie, you should reserve your table now. This is a show spot, designed by an architect with a retro-70s interior. You will be in the hands of professionals throughout your meal, and can expect smooth, fluid, fluent service from beginning to end. The cuisine created by Chef Hans Haas changes seasonally (and daily) and is outstanding in terms of freshness, subtlety of taste and presentation. The multi-course tasting menus are the best way to sample the culinary magic of Tantris. On a tasting menu you might find Crustacean variations with curry cream, saddle of venison with red cabbage and mushrooms, turbot with bean ravioli, and banana-chocolate cake with sour cream. The excellent sommelier can recommend the perfect wine accompaniment to each dish (wine pairings are not included in the prices listed below). Your dining experience will be unforgettable, but do be prepared to pay a small fortune for it. *Note:* Tantris is in a slightly out-of-the-way spot so you'll need to take a taxi to get there.

Johann-Fichte-Strasse 7. (*C*) **089/3619590.** www.tantris.de. Reservations required. Fixed-price 4-course lunch menus 80€–120€, fixed-price dinner menus 150€–180€. Tues–Sat noon–3pm and 6:30–10:30pm. Closed Dec 22–27, Jan 1–15, public holidays, annual holidays in Jan and May. U-Bahn: Dietlindenstrasse.

EXPLORING MUNICH

Munich is one of the great sightseeing cities in Germany, bursting with first-rate museums, fascinating architecture, historic palaces, and beautiful parks. Enjoying Munich is easy, but if your time is limited, you'll have to make some difficult decisions because there is so much to see. Areas of exceptional interest for tourists are **Marienplatz and the Altstadt,** the **Museumsviertel (Museum Quarter)** and **Königsplatz.**

Attractions in the Altstadt

Marienplatz ★★★ PLAZA/SQUARE   A large pedestrian-only square in the heart of Munich's Altstadt, Marienplatz is the old heart of Munich. Chances are you'll return here again and again, because many of the city's attractions are clustered in the vicinity. On the north side of Marienplatz is the **Neues Rathaus (New City Hall),** built in 19th-century Gothic style and famous for its **Glockenspiel.** You can take an elevator to the top of the Rathaus's tower for a good view of the city center (1.50€; Mon–Fri 9am–7pm and Sat–Sun 10am–7pm). To the right of the Neues Rathaus stands the **Altes Rathaus (Old City Hall),** with its plain, 15th-century Gothic tower. Inside is the **Spielzeugmuseum,** a historical toy collection ((*C*) **089/294-001;** 3€ adults, 1.50€ children; daily 10am–5pm).

Asamkirche ★★   For a dizzying hit of Italianate Bavarian rococo church architecture at its most flamboyant, pay a quick visit this small, remarkable church that is a bit off the main tourist circuit. Multicolored marbles, gold leaf, and silver cover every square inch of the rectangular Asamkirche, built by the Asam brothers between 1733 and 1746.

Sendlinger Strasse. (*C*) **089/260-9357.** Daily 8am–5:30pm. U-/S-Bahn: Sendlinger Tor.

Bayerisches Nationalmuseum (Bavarian National Museum) ★   This museum contains three vast floors of sculpture, painting, folk art, ceramics, furniture, and textiles, in addition to clocks and scientific instruments. The objects on view are among Bavaria's greatest historic and artistic treasures, but to be honest, this isn't the most thrilling museum in terms of how the collections are displayed, and a visit can be both overwhelming and underwhelming at the same time if you try to see everything, so choose what interests you and skip the rest. A major highlight is the **Riemenschnei-der Room,** which contains works in wood by the great sculptor Tilman Riemenschnei-der (1460–1531). The museum also contains a famous collection of **Christmas Nativity cribs** from Bavaria, Tyrol, and southern Italy.

Prinzregentenstrasse 3. (*C*) **089/2112401.** www.bayerisches-nationalmuseum.de. Admission 5€ adults, 4€ students and seniors, free for children 14 and under; Sun admission for all 1€. Tues–Sun 10am–5pm (Thurs until 8pm). U-Bahn: Lehel. Tram: 17. Bus: 100.

Bier- und Oktoberfestmuseum ★   If you missed Oktoberfest, you can still experience it vicariously. The Augustiner Brewery operates this cultural and culinary

ATTRACTIONS ●
Alte Pinakothek
  (Old Masters Gallery) **6**
Altes Rathaus
  (Old Town Hall) **50**
Altes Residenztheater
  (Cuvilliés Theater) **40**
Antikensammlungen
  (Antiquities Collection) **8**
Asamkirche **21**
Bayerisches National-
  museum (Bavarian
  National Museum) **42**
Bier- und Oktoberfest-
  museum **29**
BMW Welt **1**
Deutsches Museum **25**
Deutsches Museum
  Verkehrszentrum (Trans-
  portation Museum) **14**
Englischer Garten **43**
Frauenkirche (Cathedral
  of Our Lady) **57**
Glyptothek (Museum of
  Classical Sculpture) **7**
Lenbachhaus **9**
Marienplatz **52**
Michaelskirche
  (St.Michael's) **20**
Münchner Stadtmuseum
  (City Museum) **35**
Museum Brandhorst **4**
Neue Pinakothek
  (New Picture Gallery) **3**

Neues Rathaus
  (with Glockenspiel) **53**
Peterskirche (St. Peter's) **51**
Pinakothek der Moderne **5**
Residenz (Royal Palace) **40**
Spielzeugmuseum
  (Toy Museum) **50**
Theresienwiese (Oktober-
  fest Grounds) **15**
Theatinerkirche **39**
Viktualienmarkt
  (Produce Market) **33**

HOTELS ■
Bayerischer Hof &
  Palais Montgelas **37**
Cortiina **45**
Creatif Hotel Elephant **10**
Eden-Hotel-Wolff **11**
Gästehaus Englischer
  Garten **60**
Hotel Bristol München **18**
Hotel Jedermann **13**

Hotel Schlicker **31**
Hotel Torbräu **27**
Hotel Uhland **16**
Louis Hotel **34**
Mandarin Oriental **46**
Pension Westfalia **17**
Wombat's City Hostel
  Munich **12**

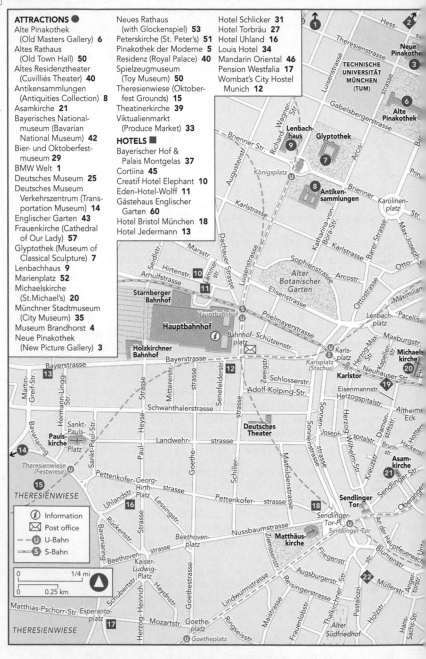

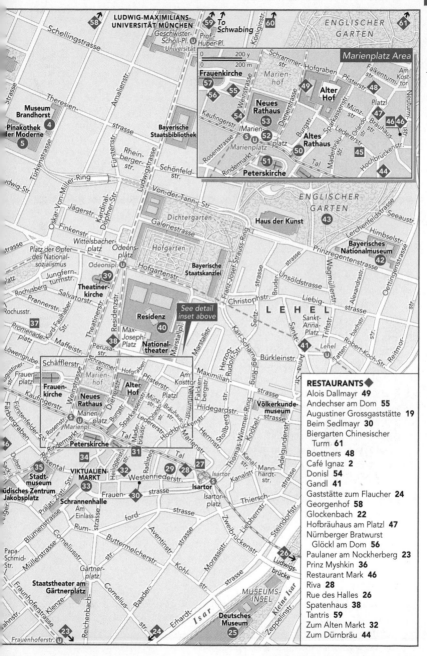

RESTAURANTS◆

Alois Dallmayr **49**
Andechser am Dom **55**
Augustiner Grossgaststätte **19**
Beim Sedlmayr **30**
Biergarten Chinesischer
Turm **61**
Boettners **48**
Café Ignaz **2**
Donisl **54**
Gandl **41**
Gaststätte zum Flaucher **24**
Georgenhof **58**
Glockenbach **22**
Hofbräuhaus am Platzl **47**
Nürnberger Bratwurst
Glöckl am Dom **56**
Paulaner am Nockherberg **23**
Prinz Myshkin **36**
Restaurant Mark **46**
Riva **28**
Rue des Halles **26**
Spatenhaus **38**
Tantris **59**
Zum Alten Markt **32**
Zum Dürnbräu **44**

MUNICH'S other FESTIVALS

Oktoberfest is Munich's most famous festival. After that 16-day beer bash, there's a lull until late November, when Marienplatz and other squares in the Altstadt gear up for the holidays with the giant **Christkindlemarkt (Christmas Market)**. Hundreds of illuminated and decorated outdoor stands sell regional craft and food specialties and hot, spiced *Glühwein*. Before Lent, from January through February, the city goes into party mode again and celebrates **Fasching (Carnival),** a whirl of colorful parades, masked balls, and revelry. After another lull comes **Starkbierzeit,** another beer-themed festival that's more of a local neighborhood affair that happens at all the city's beeer gardens and brewery restaurants. The 1-liter servings of malty Starkbier (literally, "strong beer") were originally intended to sustain the brew-brewing monks during their Lenten fast. And before you know it, all the beer gardens are open and it will soon be time for the next Oktoberfest.

combination in a building dating back to 1327. The multi-story museum explains the beer-making process and the history of the Oktoberfest. Your ticket includes a voucher for a glass of beer and a snack like the Bavarian cheese *Obatzda* with *Leberwurst* (liver sausage) or *Schmalz* (chicken fat spread over freshly baked rye bread).

After 6pm you can return to the restaurant for regional Bavarian fare such as beer-infused goulash and noodles, sausage salads and *Schnitzels*.

Sterneckstrasse 2. ✆ **089/24243941.** www.bier-und-oktoberfestmuseum.de. Admission 4€. Tues–Sat 1–5pm; beer hall Tues–Sat 6pm–midnight. U-/S-Bahn: Isartor.

Englischer Garten (English Garden) ★★★ Munich's famous city park is one of the largest (922 acres) and most beautiful city parks in Europe. Established in 1789, the Englischer Garten also is the oldest public park in the world. You can wander for hours along the tree-shaded walks, streams, and lake, and admire the view of Munich's Altstadt from the round, hilltop temple called the **Monopteros,** constructed in the 19th century. The banks of the Eisbach, the stream that runs through the park, are popular nude-sunbathing spots. A giant beer garden (open Apr–Oct) occupies the plaza near the **Chinesischer Turm (Chinese Pagoda).**

Bounded on the south by Von-der-Tann Strasse and Prinzregentenstrasse, on the west by Koönigstrasse, on the east by Lerchenfeldstrasse. Free admission. U-Bahn: Odeonsplatz.

Frauenkirche (Cathedral of Our Lady) ★ Munich's largest church, completed in the late 15th century, was a pile of smoldering rubble at the end of World War II Only its landmark twin onion-domed towers from 1525 remained standing. The rebuilt church is strikingly simple and dignified, and the view from the tower is spectacular.

Frauenplatz (near the Rathaus) 1. ✆ **089/2900820.** www.muenchner-dom.de. Free admission to church; tower 3€ adults, 1.50€ children. Church daily 7am–7pm (Fri until 6pm); tower Apr–Oct daily 10am–5pm. U-/S-Bahn: Marienplatz.

Michaelskirche (St. Michael's Church) ★ A single-nave church with a barrel-vaulted ceiling completed in 1597, St. Michael's is the largest Renaissance church north of the Alps.

Neuhauserstrasse 52. ✆ **089/231-7060.** Free admission. Mon–Sat 8:30am–7pm; Sun 6:45am–10pm. U-/S-Bahn: Marienplatz.

Münchner Stadtmuseum (City Museum) ★ Housed in a 15th-century armory, this museum chronicles Munich's history and the everyday lives of its residents. The one must-see exhibit is the *Moriskentanzer* (**Moorish dancers**), featuring ten carved and brightly painted 15th-century wooden figures. The second-floor photo museum traces the early history of the camera back to 1839. On the third-floor there's a historic collection of marionettes and hand puppets and the gallery of fairground art, which includes the oldest-known carousel horses, dating from 1820. A cafeteria in the museum's main courtyard is open daily 10am to midnight.

St. Jacobs-Platz 1. (ⓒ **089/23322370.** www.stadtmuseum-online.de. Admission 4€ adults, 2€ students. Tues–Sun 10am–6pm. U-/S-Bahn: Marienplatz.

Peterskirche (St. Peter's Church) ★ The bell tower of this 13th-century Gothic church, remodeled during the baroque era, is known locally as "Altes Peter" (Old Pete). You get a splendid view from the top, but you have to climb (and climb and climb) 306 steps to see it. The interior of the church contains baroque-era sculptures, frescoes, and a bizarre relic in the second chapel (on the left): the gem-studded skeleton of St. Mundita, who stares at you with two false eyes in her skull.

Rindermarkt 1 (near the Rathaus). (ⓒ **089/2604828.** Church free; tower 2€ adults, 1.50€ children. Mon–Sat 9am–6pm (Nov–Mar until 5pm). U-/S-Bahn: Marienplatz.

Residenz (Royal Palace) ★★ This magnificent building was the official residence of the Wittelsbach family, the rulers of Bavaria, from 1385 to 1918. Added to and rebuilt through the centuries, the palace is a compendium of various architectural styles, including German and Florentine Renaissance, and Palladian. Artisans painstakingly restored the Residenz, which was almost totally destroyed in World War II. The must-sees are the **Residenz Museum,** with arts and furnishings displayed in some 130 rooms; the **Schatzkammer (Treasury),** with 3 centuries' worth of accumulated treasures; and the **Cuvilliés Theater** (also called the **Altes Residenztheater**), a stunning rococo theater. You enter both the Residenz Museum and the Schatzkammer from Max-Joseph-Platz on the south side of the palace. On the north side of the palace is the Italianate **Hofgarten (Court Garden),** laid out between 1613 and 1617. An English-language audioguide is free with your admission.

Max-Joseph-Platz 3. (ⓒ **089/290671.** www.residenz-muenchen.de. Combination ticket for Residenzmuseum, Schatzkammer, Theater 13€ adults, 11€ seniors, free for students and children. Daily Apr–Sept 9am–6pm; Oct–Mar 10am–4pm. U-Bahn: Odeonsplatz.

Theatinerkirche ★ Named for the Theatines, a group of Roman Catholic clergy, this church is Munich's finest example of Italian baroque architecture. The church was begun by Italian architects in 1663 and was completed by German court architects about a century later. Fluted columns lining the center aisle support the arched ceiling of the nave. Every surface appears to be loaded with dollops of fanciful white stuccowork. The dome above the transept is decorated with an ornate gallery of large statues. Dark wooden pews and a canopied pulpit provide the only color in the all-white interior.

Theatinerstrasse 22. (ⓒ **089/2106960.** Free admission. Mon–Fri 10am–1pm and 1:30–4:30pm; Sat 10am–3pm. U-Bahn: Odeonsplatz.

Museumsviertel (Museum Quarter)

You could spend days exploring the four art museums that make up the Museum Quarter, also called the Kunstareal. All four are worth visiting, but the enormous **Alte Pinakothek,** with its world-class collection of Old Masters is a must-see. The smaller **Neue Pinakothek,** featuring gems from the 19th century, and the **Pinakothek der**

WATCHING THE glockenspiel

The best show on Marienplatz takes place at 11am and 9pm daily (also at noon and 5pm during the holiday seasons) when the 43-bell Glockenspiel on the 280-foot central spire of the Neues Rathaus goes through its paces. Brightly painted mechanical figures reenact two famous events from Munich's history: the knights' tournament during the 1586 wedding feast of Wilhelm V and Renate of Lorraine, and, one level below, the *Schäfflertanz* (Coopers' Dance), first performed in 1683 to express gratitude for the end of the plague.

Moderne and **Museum Brandhorst,** both in new buildings and dedicated to 20th-century art, round out this rather amazing collection of museums.

Alte Pinakothek (Old Masters Gallery) ★★★ Pinakothek means "painting gallery," and the nearly 800 paintings on display in this enormous building represent the greatest European artists of the 14th through 18th centuries. The museum is so immense that you can easily spend several days exploring the two floors of exhibits. To make the most of your time here, pick up a museum guide at the information desk, decide which paintings you particularly want to see, and then spend at least 2 to 3 hours. A free audio tour in English is available in the lobby.

Important highlights include ten paintings by **Albrecht Dürer,** including the haunting "Self Portrait with Fur-Trimmed Robe," painted in 1500 when he was 29; it's the first self-portrait ever painted by an artist. The Italian school is well represented with canvases by **Raphael, Leonardo da Vinci** and **Botticelli.** The red-walled **Rubenssaal** displays 17 large-scale canvases by the Dutch master **Rembrandt** is also well-represented; take a look at his "Self Portrait," painted in 1629 when he was 23.

Francois Boucher's loving portrait of Madame de Pompadour (1756) is a highlight from the French school. **Pieter Bruegel the Elder**'s Bosch-like "Land of Cockaigne" (1567) and "Harbor Scene with Christ Preaching" (1598) are also worth seeking out.

Barer Strasse 27. ⓒ **089/23805216.** www.pinakothek.de/alte-pinakothek. Admission 7€ adults, 5€ students and seniors; Sat 1€. Tues–Sun 10am–5pm (Tues until 8pm). U-Bahn: Theresienstrasse. Tram: 27. Bus: 100.

Neue Pinakothek (New Picture Gallery) ★★★ Housed in a postmodern building from 1981, this museum is a showcase for 19th-century German and European art, starting right around 1800. Not quite as daunting as the nearby Alte, the Neue still contains plenty to see.

The survey of 19th-century works in this museum focuses primarily on two collections. The first is German and includes Romantic works and those associated with Ludwig I, the king of Bavaria from 1825 to 1848. More important is the work by the German artist Casper David Friedrich, whose "Summer" (1807) and "Riesengebirge with Rising Fog" (1819) illuminate the Romantic style of painting. The second collection highlights important European Impressionist works, starting with Edouard Manet and continuing with canvases by Van Gogh (one of his "Sunflowers" from 1888), Monet, Goya, Munch, Degas, Renoir, and Klimt. English artists whose works are on view include Thomas Gainsborough, Joshua Reynolds, and William Turner. A tour of the highlights takes a couple of hours; an audio tour in English is free with your admission.

Barerstrasse 27 (across Theresienstrasse from the Alte Pinakothek). ℂ **089/23805195.** www. pinakothek.de. Admission 7€ adults, 5€ students and seniors; Sat 1€. Wed–Mon 10am–6pm (Wed until 8pm). U-Bahn: Theresienstrasse. Tram: 27. Bus: 100.

Pinakothek der Moderne ★★ Munich's newest museum opened in September 2002. Of the four collections housed here, the most important is the **Staatsgalerie moderner Kunst (Gallery of Modern Art),** displaying major 20th-century classics by internationally known artists including Matisse, Picasso, Gris, Ernst, Giacometti, and others, as well as a wealth of excellent German modern art represented by *Die Brücke* artists like Kirchner and Schmidt-Rotluff, and the *Blaue Reiter* group with Kandinsky, Franz Marc, and Auguste Macke. You also find sculpture, photography and video in the Modern Art collection.

The other museum holdings include the **Neue Sammlung (Craft and Design Collection),** the **Museum of Architecture** (architectural drawings, photographs, and models), and the **Graphische Sammlung (Graphics Collection),** which is not open to the general public except by request.

Barerstrasse 40. ℂ **089/23805360.** www. pinakothek.de. Admission 10€ adults, 7€ students and seniors; Sat 1€. Tues–Sun 10am–6pm (Thurs until 8pm). U-Bahn: Odeonsplatz.

> ### Museum Savings on Saturday & Sunday
>
> On Saturday, you can enjoy the treasures in all three Pinakotheks (Alte, Neue, der Moderne), Museum Brandhorst, and Schack-Galerie for 1€. On Sunday, the Glyptothek, Antikensammlungen, and the Bayerisches Nationalmuseum reduce their prices to 1€.

Museum Brandhorst ★ Paintings, sculpture, works on paper, and art installations from the mid– to late 20th century are showcased in the striking new museum which opened in 2009. The Brandhorst displays works by American artists Cy Twombley, Andy Warhol, Jean-Michel Basquiat, and Alex Katz; the controversial British artist Damien Hirst; the German painter Sigmar Polke; and features an unusual collection of books illustrated by Picasso.

Kunstareal, Theresienstrasse 35A. ℂ **089/238052286.** www.museum-brandhorst.de. Admission 7€ adults, 5€ children 5–16; Sat 1€. Tues–Sun 10am–6pm (Thurs until 8pm). U-Bahn: Königsplatz or Theresienstrasse. Bus: 100 or 154.

Königsplatz

Ludwig I (reigned 1825–48) set out to make Munich a second Athens, an endeavor best embodied in the classically inspired architecture of Königsplatz, 2 blocks south of the Museumsviertel. Here, flanking the templelike **Propyläen** monument, stand the **Antikensammlungen** and **Glyptothek,** housing the king's former collections of Greek and Roman artifacts. If antiquities don't interest you, the **Lenbachhaus** with its outstanding collection of late-19th- and early-20th-century German art is definitely worth the trip.

Antikensammlungen (Antiquities Collections) ★ An essential stop for anyone interested in ancient art, this museum's five main-floor halls house more than 650 Greek vases, from a pre-Mycenaean version carved in 3000 B.C. from a mussel shell to large Greek and Etruscan vases. If you like antiquities but ancient vases ain't your thing, opt for the more interesting Glyptothek across the square.

Königsplatz 1. ℂ **089/59988830.** www.antike-am-koenigsplatz.mwn.de. Admission 3.50€ adults, 2.50€ students and seniors; Sun 1€. Tues–Sun 10am–5pm (Thurs until 8pm). U-Bahn: Königsplatz.

Glyptothek (Museum of Sculpture) ★★ Located across from the Antikensammlung, the Glyptothek exhibits Germany's largest collection of ancient Greek and Roman sculpture. Check out the 6th-century-B.C. *kouroi* (statues of youths), the colossal "Sleeping Satyr" from the Hellenistic period, and a haunting collection of Roman portraits.

Königsplatz 3. 𝒞 **089/286100.** www.antike-am-koenigsplatz.mwn.de. Admission 3.50€ adults, 2.50€ students and seniors; Sun 1€. Tues–Sun 10am–5pm (Thurs until 8pm). U-Bahn: Königsplatz.

Lenbachhaus ★★★ This dazzling collection of late-19th and early-20th-century German Impressionist and Expressionist art reopened in 2013 after a complete refurbishment and with the addition of a new gallery wing. Lenbachhaus is an Italianate villa built by the painter Franz von Lenbach between 1887 and 1891 to serve as his residence and atelier. It houses an outstanding collection of works by the *Blaue Reiter* (Blue Rider) school of artists working in Munich before World War I. Bold colors and abstract forms characterize the work of the artists represented, including Wasily Kandinsky, Paul Klee, Franz Marc, and Gabriele Münter. Exhibitions or contemporary work are held in the new wing and in the adjacent Kunstbau.

Luisenstrasse 33. 𝒞 **089/2333200.** www.lenbachhaus.de. Admission 10€ adults, 5€ students. Tues–Sun 10am–6pm (Tues until 9pm). U-Bahn: Königsplatz.

Outside Central Munich

BMW Welt ★★ If you have any interest in the luxury brand BMW (Bavarian Motor Works), take the short trip out to Olympiapark to see the BMW Welt showroom. Architecturally, this new-car showroom is a boldly dramatic structure with soaring lines and a glass-enclosed hourglass-shaped spiral ramp that leads up to a skybridge to the museum and factory buildings that are part of the BMW Welt complex. The interior of the showroom is sinuous and sexy, showing off all the latest models like perfectly lit celebrities. This is BMW's delivery center in Germany, and there's a gallery where you can watch emotional owners picking up the keys to their new BMWs. Have a look around (it's free), and if you're a car buff, buy your ticket for the 2-hour tour of the BMW Munich Plant where you'll see the cars assembled. The company's superb collection of vintage vehicles is housed in the overpriced **BMW Museum** ★★. It's organized into categories (history, technology, racing, design) and includes motorcycles and automobiles from the company's beginning in 1929 to a hydrogen-powered roadster of the future.

Am Olympiapark 1. 𝒞 **0180/1118822.** www.bmw-welt.com. Museum admission 9€ adults, 6€ seniors and children; factory tour 6€ adults, 3€ seniors and children. Showroom daily 7:30am–midnight; museum daily 9am–6pm; factory tours Mon–Fri 8:30am–10pm. U-Bahn: Olympiazentrum.

Deutsches Museum ★★ Located on the Museumsinsel, an island in the Isar River, this is the largest science and technology museum in the world and one of the most popular attractions in Germany. Its huge collection of natural science and technoologiccal treasures includes some 15,000 exhibits in 50 departments. A few of the exhibits are interactive, and there are regular demonstrations of glass blowing, papermaking, and how steam engines, pumps, and historical musical instruments work, as well as collections of model trains, historic toys, and items of historic interest, including boats and a biplane flown by the Wright brothers in 1908. Unless you have a keen interest in science and technology, however, you may find this enormous museum enormously uninteresting because most of the objects and exhibits are displayed as relics without much dynamism in their presentation. The Verkehrszentrum, the museums new transportation museum, is far more intriguing.

Museumsinsel 1. 𝒞 **089/21791.** www.deutsches-museum.de. Admission 8.50€ adults, 7€ seniors, 3€ students. Daily 9am–5pm. U-Bahn: Schwanthalerhöhe.

VISITING THE viktualienmarkt (PRODUCE MARKET)

Located on the square of the same name, close to Marienplatz, the Viktualienmarkt has been serving Munich residents for nearly 200 years and is a wonderful place to stroll and sniff and take in the local scene. In an area the size of a city block, you find butcher shops, cheese sellers, a whole section of bakeries stocked with dozens of different kinds of Bavarian breads and rolls, fish sellers, wine merchants, dozens of produce stalls, and a beer garden. Most of the permanent stands open at 6am. and stay open until 6pm on weekdays, or until 1pm on Saturday. You can buy food at the market stalls and eat it in the beer garden if you buy a beer, a soda, water, or other beverage at the beer-garden drink stand. You can easily find the market from Marienplatz; it's bounded by Prälat-Zistl-Strasse on the west, Frauen Strasse to the south, Heiliggeiststrasse on the east, and Tal on the north.

Deutsches Museum Verkehrszentrum (Transportation Museum) ★★
How have people transported themselves for the last 200 years? You'll find out at this intriguing museum, which deals with mobility and technology, travel and urban transport. There's a wonderful collection of horse-drawn carriages. You can see "Puffing Billy," an early steam-engine locomotive from 1814, step into a passenger train from the late 19th century, and peer inside a modern high-speed ICE train. Some of the bicycles on display are 150 years old. And then there's the superlative collection of historic automobiles, including Daimlers, Opels, Mercedes, Tatas, Citroens and Bugattis. All these vehicles are exhibited in three historic exhibition halls dating from 1908 and restored to their original appearance.
Theresienhohe 14a. (C) **089/500806762.** www.deutsches-museum.de/verkehrszentrum. Admission 6€ adults, 4€children. Daily 9am–5pm. U-Bahn: Schwanthalerhöhe.

Organized Tours
BY BUS
CitySightseeing (www.citysightseeing-munich.com) offers a 1-hour **Stadtrundfahrt (City Tour)** on double-decker, open-top buses, with hop-on, hop-off service at 13 different stops. Tours depart daily (10am–5pm) about every 20 minutes from Bahnhofsplatz in front of the main train station; cost is 20€ adults, 8€ children. Buy your ticket onboard or get a discounted price online. The same company also offers daily tours to Schwabing, Nymphenburg, and Olympiapark. To go farther afield and visit major attractions in Munich's environs (such as Neuschwanstein, Ludwig II's famous castle), contact **Sightseeing Gray Line,** Schützenstrasse 9 ((C) **089/54907560;** www.grayline. com). All tours have miltilingual commentary.

BY BIKE
For a more active experience, tour Munich by bicycle with the English-speaking expats at **Mike's Bike Tours** ((C) **089/2554-3988;** www.mikesbiketours.com). The 4-hour tour (25€ adults, 18€ children) spins around the sights of central Munich, including an hour in a beer garden (lunch not included), departing daily Mar–Apr 14 and Sept–Nov 10 at 12:30pm; Apr 15–Aug daily at 11:30am and 4:30pm. All tours meet 15 minutes before setting off, under the tower of the Altes Rathaus on Marienplatz. No need to

reserve, just show up. Tour price includes bike rental and helmet. In the winter there is a Saturday tour at 12:30, reservations mandatory.

ON FOOT

Munich Walk Tours (✆ **0171/274-0204;** www.munichwalktours.de), conducted in English, include a daily 10:45am City Walk tour (also 2:45pm high season) and a 2½-hour Hitler's Munich tour (Nov–Mar daily 10:30am). Tours cost 12€ adults, 10€ under 26, free for kids under 14. All walks meet at the New Rathaus directly under the Glockenspiel on Marienplatz. No need to reserve; you pay the guide (identifiable by a yellow sign).

SHOPPING

You'll see a whole lot of shopping going on in Munich. A seemingly endless network of shopping streets rays out from **Marienplatz** and wide, pedestrian-only **Kaufingerstrasse** and **Neuhauser Strasse.** You can find anything you want here, but it's unlikely that you'll find any bargains. What you will find is high-quality, for this is a shopping society that does not spend its money on junk.

The best streets for elegant boutiques and specialty shops are **Briennerstrasse, Maximilianstrasse** (which also has the leading art galleries), **Maffeistrasse,** and **Theatinestrasse.** On these streets, all the top European couturiers and Germany's and Munich's own designers have shops: Jil Sander, Joop, Bogner, Max Dietl, and Rudolph Moshammer. Antiques devotees with deep pockets find what they want on **Ottostrasse.** The biggest concentration of shops selling secondhand goods is on **Westenriederstrasse.**

When you're shopping, remember that you will always pay more for items imported from the U.S., and less for items made or manufactured in Germany and the European Union.

Crafts

Bayerischer Kunstgewerbe-Verein ★★★   The Bavarian Association of Arts & Crafts is a showcase for Bavarian artisans and has excellent handicrafts: ceramics, glasses, jewelry, woodcarvings, pewter, and seasonal Christmas decorations. Pacellistrasse 6–8. ✆ **089/2901470.** www.kunsthandwerk-bkv.de. U-Bahn: Karlsplatz.

Prinoth ★★   Most of the woodcarvings sold here are produced in small workshops in the South Tyrol. The selection is wide-ranging, and because the shop is 6km (4 miles) west of Munich's tourist zones, prices are reasonable compared to those of shops closer to the Marienplat. You'll find a variety of Nativity figures, angels, Madonnas and other pieces. Guido Schneblestrasse 9A. ✆ **089/560378.** www.prinoth.de. U-Bahn: Laimerplatz.

Münchner Puppenstuben und Zinnfiguren Kabinette ★★   This is Germany's oldest miniature pewter foundry, dating from 1796, and it still creates traditional Christmas decorations of a type once sold to the Bavarian royal family. This store is one of the best sources in Germany for dollhouses, furniture, bird cages, and people, all cunningly crafted from pewter or carved wood. Some figures are made from 150-year-old molds that are collector's items in their own right. Maxburgstrasse 4. ✆ **089/293797.** www.mini-kabi.net. U-Bahn: Karlsplatz.

Department Stores

Kaufhof ★   This store carries everything, from men's, women's, and children's clothing to housewares, cosmetics, and much more, all at reasonable prices. Marienplatz. ✆ **089/231851.** www.galeria-kaufhof.de. U-/S-Bahn: Marienplatz.

Beer-drinkers in Munich have their festival, called Oktoberfest. And holiday shoppers have theirs, called the **Christkindlmarkt,** or Christmas Market. From late November through December, Marienplatz, the main square of the inner city, overflows with stalls selling toys, tree ornaments, handicrafts, and a mouthwatering array of traditional snacks and sweets, including gingerbread, sugarcoated almonds, fruitcakes, smoked meats, and piping hot *Glühwein,* a spiced red wine. You may not want to buy anything, but the atmosphere itself is guaranteed to put you in a festive mood.

Ludwig Beck ★★ Sometimes called the "Bloomingdale's of Munich," this upscale store on Marienplatz sells high-end clothing for women and men, cosmetics, housewares, and has what is reputedly the best classical CD selection in Germany. Am Marienplatz 11. ✆**089/236910.** www.ludwigbeck.de. U-/S-Bahn: Marienplatz.

Eyeglasses

Pupille ★ If you wear glasses, you probably know how the most fashionable and well-made frames are made in Germany. They're less expensive here, and you'll find styles that never make it to the U.S. At Pupille's, shelf after shelf of eyeglasses in all styles and sizes reveal why Germans are known for their optical products. Gärtnerplatz 2. ✆**089/2017067.** www.pupille.de.

Fashion

Dirndl-Ecke ★ "Dirndl Corner" stocks a large selection of high-quality Bavarian dirndls (traditional German dresses), folk art, and handicrafts. Am Platzl 1/Sparkassenstrasse 10. ✆**089/220-163.** U-/S-Bahn: Marienplatz.

Loden-Frey ★★★ This is the place for high-quality *loden,* a waterproof wool used for durable and long-lasting coats, jackets, and hats. Maffeistrasse 7. ✆**089/210390.** www.loden-frey.de. U-/S-Bahn: Marienplatz.

Jewelry & Watches

CADA-Schmuck ★★ Herbert Kopp, a jewelry designer, has attracted lots of media attention for the distinctive handmade jewelry that's sold here. His chic creations come in 18-carat gold or sterling silver. There is a large collection of rings, earrings, necklaces, pendants, cufflinks, and brooches. Maffeistrasse 8. ✆**089/2554270.** www.cada-schmuck.de. Tram: 19.

Hemmerle ★★ The founders of this conservative jewelry shop made their fortune designing bejeweled fantasies for the Royal Bavarian Court of Ludwig II. All pieces are limited editions, designed and made in-house by Bavarian craftspeople. The company also designs its own wristwatch, the Hemmerle. Maximilianstrasse 14. ✆**089/2422600.** www.hemmerle.de. U-/S-Bahn: Marienplatz.

Porcelain

Porzellan-Manufaktur-Nymphenburg ★★★ One of Germany's most famous porcelain factories is located on the grounds of Schloss Nymphenburg (see "Day Trips from Munich"), about 5 miles (8km) from central Munich. You can visit its exhibition and sales rooms Monday to Friday 10am to 5pm. A more central branch is in Munich's center at Odeonsplatz 1 (© **089/282428;** U-Bahn: Odeonsplatz). Nördliches Schlossrondell 8. © **089/1791970.** www.nymphenburg.com. Bus: 100.

Toys

Obletter's ★★ Established in 1825, this is one of the largest emporiums of children's toys in Munich. The two floors of inventory contain everything from folkloric dolls to computer games. Karlsplatz 11. © **089/55089510.** U-Bahn: Karlsplatz.

ENTERTAINMENT & NIGHTLIFE

Something always is going on in Munich. As southern Germany's cultural capital, Munich is renowned for its opera and symphony concerts and theater. But you can also sit back in a leafy beer garden or in a beer hall and enjoy the music and the local scene, and there are also plenty of bars and dance clubs for late-night partying. To find out what's happening in Munich, pick up a copy of *Monatsprogramm,* a monthly program guide, at the tourist office in the Hauptbahnhof or visit **www.muenchen.de** and click on "Events" or **www.muenchentickets.de.** The best way to buy tickets is to go directly to the venue's box office, or to the ticket office in the tourist office in the Hauptbahnhof.

The Performing Arts

Altes Residenztheater (Cuvilliés Theater) ★★★ Part of the Residenz palace, this historic theatre is the most beautiful in Germany. The **Bavarian State Opera** and the **Bayerisches Staatsschauspiel** perform smaller works here, in keeping with the tiny theater's intimate character. Residenzstrasse 1. © **089/21851940.** www. bayerischesstaatsschauspiel.de.

Bayerischen Staatsoper ★★★ Performing at the beautiful Nationaltheater, restored to to its 1830s grandeur, the **Bavarian State Opera** is one of the world's great opera companies and mounts a full season of grand operas with the world's greatest singers and a superlative orchestra. The productions are often anything but traditional, however. The Nationaltheater is also the home of the **Bavarian State Ballet.** Worth it just to sit in such a gorgeous space. Nationaltheater, Max-Joseph-Platz 2. © **089/21851920.** www.bayerische.staatsoper.de. U-/S-Bahn: Odeonsplatz.

Bayerisches Staatsschauspiel ★★ The Bavarian State Theater is known for its performances of the classics by Goethe, Schiller, Shakespeare, and others. Max-Joseph-Platz. © **089/21851920.** www.bayerischesstaatsschauspiel.de. U-/S-Bahn: Marienplatz.

Deutsches Theater ★★ This late-19th-century venue is mainly for musicals, but operettas, ballets, and international shows are staged as well. Schwanthalerstrasse 13. © **089/55234444.** www.deutsches-theater.de. U-Bahn: Fröttmaning.

Münchner Philharmoniker ★★★ One of Europe's great orchestras, the Munich Philharmonic Orchestra performs in Philharmonic Hall in the modern Gasteig Cultural Center. Gasteig Kulturzentrum in the Haidhausen district, Rosenheimerstrasse 5. © **089/480985500.** www.muenchnerphilharmoniker.de. S-Bahn: Rosenheimerplatz. Tram: 18 to Gasteig. Bus: 51.

Live Music

Jazzclub Unterfahrt ★★★ This is Munich's leading jazz club, attracting artists from throughout Europe and North America. The bar opens daily at 7:30pm; live music is Tuesday to Sunday 8:30pm to 1am, Friday and Saturday 7:30pm to 3am. Einsteinstrasse 42. © **089/4482794.** www.unterfahrt.de. Cover 5€–32€. U-Bahn: Max-Weber-Platz.

Mister B's ★   This small club hosts a slightly older, mellower crowd than the rock and dance clubs. Blues, jazz, and rhythm-'n'-blues combos take the stage Thursday to Saturday. Herzog-Heinrichstrasse 38. © **089/534901.** www.misterbs.de. Cover 7€–20€. U-Bahn: Goetheplatz.

Schwabinger Podium ★   This staple of the Schwabing scene offers varying live music acts, which on some nights attracts a jazz crowd; Monday nights are reserved for a local jazz outfit. Otherwise, expect cover bands and local acts. It's open Sunday to Thursday 8pm to 1am and Friday and Saturday 8pm to 3am. Wagnerstrasse 1. © **089/399482.** www.schwabinger-podium.com. Cover 7€. U-Bahn: Münchner Freiheit.

Nightclubs & Dance Halls

Bayerischer Hof Night Club ★   Down below the tony Bayerischer Hof hotel you'll find some of Munich's most sophisticated entertainment. Within one very large room is a piano bar, where a musician plays Friday and Saturday nights 7 to 10pm. Behind a partition that disappears after 10pm is a stage for the dance bands that play every night. Entrance to the piano bar is free, but there's a cover charge to the nightclub Friday to Sunday nights. The club and bar are open nightly until 3am. Daily happy hour is 7 to 8:30pm, with drinks starting at 5€. In the Bayerischer Hof hotel, Promenadeplatz 2–6. © **089/21200.** www.bayerischerhof.de. Cover to nightclub Fri–Sat 5€–50€. U-/S-Bahn: Marienplatz.

Café am Hochhaus ★   With average-priced drinks and skilled DJs, this is good, unpretentious club with a shifting music scene. On Sunday afternoon there is a gay tea dance." It's open Monday to Saturday 8pm to 3am. Blumenstrasse 29. © **089/89058152.** www.cafeamhochhaus.de. U-Bahn: Sendlinger Tor.

Nachtgalerie ★   The "Night Gallery" contains two dance halls rocking to party music and hip-hop along with house, electronica, or even rhythm 'n' blues. The club mostly attracts 20- and 30-somethings. And hosts various theme nights. There is a cover, but once inside, drinks are cheap—beginning at 2€. Nachtgalerie is open Friday and Saturday 10pm to 5am. Landsbergerstrasse 185. © **089/32455595.** www.nachtgalerie.de. Cover 10€. S-Bahn: Hirschgarten.

The Bar & Cafe Scene

Alter Simpl ★★   Back in the 1890s, Frank Wedekind, who penned the play "Spring Awakening," led a circle of artists who congregated here. Nowadays, it's a spacious "beer cafe" that's popular with students and has a great selection of food. It's open Sunday to Thursday 11am to 3am, Friday and Saturday 11am to 4am. Türkenstrasse 57. © **089/2723083.** www.eggerlokale.de. U-Bahn: Universität.

Café Puck ★   A dark-paneled retreat for students, artists, and workers, this cafe plays a variety of roles for its diverse crowd. It's a bar to students; a restaurant to the locals, who like the daily menu of German, American, and Asian dishes; and a spot where everyone can enjoy a big American breakfast. Café Puck is open daily 9am to 1am. Türkenstrasse 33. © **089/2802280.** www.cafepuck.de. U-Bahn: Universität.

Die Bank ★★   Imagine stripping the interior of a bank, adding a stage, a bar, sofas, a foosball table, local artwork, a pizza stand, and a hair salon, and you have an idea of the vibe here and the diverse crowd that comes to enjoy it all. Müllerstrasse 42 © **089/23684171.** www.die-bank.com. U-Bahn: Sendlingertor.

Havana Club ★★   This is a lively singles bar fueled by rum-based cocktails. It's open Monday to Thursday 6pm to 1am, Friday and Saturday 6pm to 3am, Sunday 7pm to 1am. Herrnstrasse 30. ℭ **089/291884.** www.havanaclub-muenchen.de. S-Bahn: Isartor.

Killians Irish Pub/Ned Kelly's Australian Bar ★   This pub/bar combo offers live music, Irish and Australian drinks and food, and coverage of sporting events, especially soccer. Both bars are open Monday to Thursday 4pm to 1am, Friday and Saturday 11am to 2 or 3am, and Sunday noon to 1am. Frauenplatz 11. ℭ **089/24219899.** www.kiliansirishpub.com. U-/S-Bahn: Marienplatz.

Sausalitos ★   For the best margaritas in town, the kind Hemingway used to slurp down in Havana, head to this welcoming Mexican cantina. If you're in your 20s, you'll fit right in. During happy hour daily from 5 to 8pm, mixed drinks are half-price. It's open Monday to Thursday and Sunday 11am to 1am, Friday and Saturday 11am to 2:30am. Im Tal 16. ℭ **089/24295494.** www.sausalitos.de. U-/S-Bahn: Marienplatz.

Schumann's Bar am Hofgarten ★★   Munich's most legendary bar has an international fan club, lots of pizazz, a history that goes back forever, and slick new premises. Schumann's is open Monday to Friday 5pm to 3am, Saturday and Sunday 6pm to 3am. Odeonsplatz 6–7, at the corner of Galerie Strasse. ℭ **089/229060.** www.schumanns. de. U-Bahn: Odeonsplatz.

Gay & Lesbian Nightlife

Munich's gay and lesbian scene is centered around the blocks between the Viktualienmarkt and Gärtnerplatz, particularly on Hans-Sachs-Strasse.

Bau ★★★   Covering two floors and drawing an international crowd, mostly men, this is Bavaria's largest gay bar. It's open nightly 8pm to 3am. Beethovenstrasse 1. ℭ **089/269208.** www.bau-munich.de. U-Bahn: Sendlinger Tor.

Inges Karotte ★★★   Located in the Glockenbachviertel (Glockenbach neighborhood), this is one of the major international gathering places for lesbians in Munich, attracting a widely diverse group of ages, professions, and interests. Cocktails begin at 5€, and happy hour is from 4 to 6pm. Disco music sometimes rules the night. Hours are Monday to Saturday 6pm to 1am, Sunday 4pm to 1am. Baaderstrasse 13. ℭ **089/2010669.** www.inges-karotte.de. U-Bahn: Frauenhofer Strasse.

Kr@ftakt ★   This is the only LGBT internet cafe in Munich, and it's been around now for over a decade. It serves a late breakfast, there's a happy hour on Wednesday from 7 to 9pm, and you can order food throughout the day. It's open Sunday to Thursday 10am to 1am, Friday and Saturday 10am to 3am. Thalkircher Strasse 4. ℭ**089/21588881.** www.kraftakt.com. U-Bahn: Sendlinger Tor.

NY Club ★★   This club is currently the most stylish and modern gay dance club in town, with a beautifully designed lounge and a high-tech dance floor. Look for special events and gay parties by searching the club's website. Sonnenstrasse 25. ℭ**089/62232152.** www.nyclub.de. Cover from 5€. U-Bahn: Sendlinger Tor.

DAY TRIPS FROM MUNICH

Dachau Concentration Camp Memorial Site (KZ-Gedenkstätte Dachau) ★★★

In 1933, shortly after Hitler became chancellor, Himmler and the SS set up the first German concentration camp on the grounds of a former ammunition factory in the small town of Dachau, 10 miles (15km) northwest of Munich. The list of prisoners at the camp included everyone from communists and Social Democrats to Jews, homosexuals, Gypsies, Jehovah's Witnesses, clergymen, political opponents, trade union members, and others. The camp was presented to the public, and shown off to visitors, as a labor camp where political dissidents and "social and sexual deviants" could be "rehabilitated" through work—hence the chilling and cynical motto that greeted prisoners as they entered the gates of the camp: ARBEIT MACHT FREI (WORK GIVES YOU FREEDOM).

The reality of what happened at Dachau, where prisoners were stripped of all human rights and dignity, and turned into slave laborers who were tortured, beaten, shot, hung, starved, lethally injected, and used for medical experiments, is the reality of the barbarism that took hold of German society during World War II and led to the Holocaust. Dachau is not an easy place to visit, but it is an important place to visit. Taking one of the 2½-hour tours, offered in English, is perhaps the best way to gain and overall understanding of the camp and how it worked.

Between 1933 and 1945, more than 206,000 mostly male prisoners from 30 countries were imprisoned at Dachau. At least 30,000 people were registered as dead during that period. However, thousands more were murdered there, even if their deaths weren't officially logged. Dachau was just one of dozens of concentration camps established by the Third Reich throughout Germany.

The SS abandoned the camp on April 28, 1945, and the liberating U.S. Army moved in to take charge the following day. They discovered some 67,000 living prisoners—all of them on the verge of death—at Dachau and its subsidiary camps.

At the **Visitor Center** you can book a tour, rent an audioguide, and visit the bookstore. Then expect to spend at least 2 to 2 to 3 hours visiting the grounds.

Much of the camp was destroyed after the war, but not all. A museum with a permanent exhibition is housed in the large building where prisoners were registered and "processed." Here, photographs, text panels (all translated into English) and documents tell the story of the camp, how it was run, who was incarcerated and killed, and who some of the personnel were—for Dachau was a training camp for Germans who wanted to work their way up the Nazi ladder. An English version of a 22-minute documentary film, "The Dachau Concentration Camp," is shown at 11:30am, 2pm, and 3:30pm.

The grounds have a bleak, haunted quality. Two barracks have been rebuilt to give visitors insight into the living conditions the prisoners endured, but these are of course sanitized versions. The camp, built to house a couple hundred prisoners, ended up holding thousands, and by the end of the war, prisoners who hadn't worked or starved to death or executed were dying of typhus and other diseases. You will also see the roll-call yard, where prisoners were brutally mustered; a bunker that was used as a camp prison and torture area; the camp road; security installations, and the crematorium area. There are Protestentant and Catholic chapels (neither denomination actively protested Hitler's policies, claiming they were "outside politics"), and Jewish Memorial, and an International Memorial.

There are still political and controversial elements to be considered at Dachau. The German government, for instance, has refused to acknowledge that the gas chambers at Dachau were used for killing prisoners, although a survivor of the camp has testified that they were. The International Memorial was meant to show versions of all the different i.d. badges that prisoners were forced to wear. Yet when the memorial was dedicated in 1968, there were objections that homosexuals were criminals and should not be represented in the memorial. The pink triangle homosexuals were forced to wear was removed from the memorial and has never been replaced, even though some 6,000 gays were imprisoned here and subjected to unusually (even for Dachau) harsh treatment. If there is one lesson to be learned at this moving memorial, it is that there is no hierarchy to suffering. Every single inmate at Dachau deserves the right to be remembered.

The camp/memorial is open Tuesday to Sunday 9am to 5pm; admission is free.

KZ-Gedenkstätte Dachau. Alte-Römerstrasse 75. © **08131/669970.** www.kz-gedenkstaette-dachau.de. Free admission; guided tours 3€; audioguides 3.50€. Daily 9am–5pm.

GETTING THERE
You can get to the camp/memorial by taking the frequent S-Bahn train S2 from the Hauptbahnhof to Dachau (direction: Petershausen), then bus no. 726 to the camp. The bus stop is marked with the name of the memorial, so you can't miss it. Expect to spend about 30 minutes to get there from Munich's main train station.

Schloss Nymphenburg (Nymphenburg Palace) ★★★

One of the most sophisticated and beautiful palaces in Europe, Schloss Nymphenburg served as a summer residence the for Bavaria's royal family, the Wittelsbachs. (Their official Munich residence was the Residenz, which you can also visit.) Located 5 miles northwest of Munich, an easy 20-minute tram ride, the palace and grounds require at least half a day if you want to see everything.

Nymphenburg was begun in 1664 and took more than 150 years to complete. In 1702, Elector Max Emanuel decided to enlarge the original Italianate villa by adding four large pavilions connected by arcaded passageways. The **Great Hall,** decorated in a vibrant splash of rococo colors and stuccowork, is the most beautiful of the grand public rooms. The south pavilion displays Ludwig I's famous **Gallery of Beauties** painted between 1827-1850 by Josef Karl Stieler. The beauties include a portrait of Lola Montez, the raven-haired dancer whose affair with Ludwig caused a scandal.

To the south of the palace buildings, in the rectangular block of low structures that once housed the court stables, is the **Marstallmuseum** with its dazzling collection of ornate, gilded coaches and sleighs, including those used by Ludwig II (the "Mad" King who built Neuschwanstein). The **Porzellansammlung (Porcelain Collection;** entrance across from the Marstallmuseum) contains superb pieces of 18th-century porcelain, including miniature porcelain copies of masterpieces in the Alte Pinakothek.

A canal runs through 500-acre **Schlosspark,** stretching all the way to the so-called **Grand Cascade** at the far end of the formal, French-style gardens. In the English-style park, full of quiet meadows and forested paths, stands the **Badenburg Pavilion,** with an 18th-century swimming pool; the **Pagodenburg,** decorated in the Chinese style that was all the rage in the 18th century; and the **Magdalenenklause (Hermitage),** meant to be a retreat for prayer and solitude. Prettiest of all the buildings in the park is **Amalienburg,** built in 1734 as a hunting lodge for Electress Amalia; the interior salons are a riot of flamboyant colors, swirling stuccowork, and wall paintings.

There are no guided tours within the palace, but you can rent an audioguide.

Schloss Nymphenburg, Schloss Nymphenburg 1. © **089/179080.** www.schloss-nymphenburg.de. Palace grounds free; admission to all attractions 12€ adults (Oct 16–Mar 8.50€), 9€ seniors (Oct 16–Mar 6.50€). Apr–Oct 15 daily 9am–6pm; Oct 16–Mar daily 10am–4pm. Badenburg and Magdalenenklause closed Oct 16–Mar.

GETTING THERE
You can get to Schloss Nymphenburg 1, 8km (5 miles) west of the city center, by taking to S-Bahn to "Laim" and then the bus marked "Schloss Nymphenburg." Another option is to take the U-Bahn to Rotkreuzplatz, then the tram to Romanplatz (a 10-min. walk west to the palace entrance). From central Munich, you can also easily reach the palace in about 20 minutes by taking tram 17 to Romanplatz.

ON & OFF THE ROMANTIC ROAD

For many travelers, Germany hits its high notes along the so-called Romantische Strasse, or Romantic Road, a scenic route that rambles through much of Bavaria. The 350km (220 miles) of specially marked lanes and secondary roads wind from the vineyard-clad hills surrounding Würzburg south through an unfolding panorama of beautiful landscapes interspersed with small medieval cities. To the south, the road rises through foothills covered with verdant pastures, lake-splashed countryside, and groves of evergreens to the dramatic heights of the Alps that divide Germany and western Austria. As if all this scenery weren't enough, these final stretches of the road lead to Linderhof and Neuschwanstein, two of the fantasy castles built by the legendary King Ludwig II in the second half of the 19th century.

Officially, the scenic route the German government drew up after World War II takes in 28 towns and villages. We take a few liberties and veer off the Romantic Road to also include some fascinating nearby places that are too good to miss—among them **Nürnberg,** a city that all in one swoop encompasses medieval and Renaissance splendor, the horrors of World War II, and the successes of Germany's postwar rebuilding. We also detour east to **Regensburg,** a little city that was untouched by the war and as result comprises one of Europe's largest swaths of medieval architecture. In the south, we wander off the Romantic Road to take in a section of the **Bavarian Alps** around Garmisch-Partenkirchen.

Although you can easily hit the high points—Würzburg, Rothernburg ob der Tauber, Nürnberg, Regensburg, and Füssen by car, bus, or train within a week—you might want to slow down and take time out to bike or hike through the Tauber Valley, see the beautiful Herrgottskirche in little Creglingen, ascend a mountaintop, or just bend your elbow in a historic tavern or two.

WÜRZBURG ★★

280km (174 miles) NW of Munich, 119km (74 miles) SE of Frankfurt, 109km (68 miles) NW of Nürnberg

For Germans, the south begins at Würzburg, a lovely city at the northern end of the Romantic Road. Unlike the quainter towns that line the Romantic Road to the south, Würzburg is a cosmopolitan place, a university town

romantic road INFO & BUS TOURS

A good source of information is the **Romantische Strasse Touristik Arbeitsgemeinschaft GbR,** Segringer Strasse 19, 91550 Dinkelsbühl (✆ **09851/ 5513487;** www.romantischestrasse.de), which officially oversees the Romantic Road and offers brochures and maps for drivers, cyclists, and walkers. A lot of bus tours ply the route, and you'll be besieged with options in Würzburg, Munich, and other cities and big towns on and near the Romantic Road. Most offer transport, guides, and overnight accommodations on trips that last anywhere from an overnight to a week, with prices from around 250€ to 1,200€. Buses operated by Romantische Strasse Touristik (www.romanticroadcoach.de)

are an economical and handy option that allow passengers to hop on and off buses that operate from mid-April to mid-October. Unlike organized bus tours, the scheme doesn't tie you to a schedule and let's you pick and choose where you want to stop along the way and for how long. A 6-month pass cost 104€, and Eurail pass holders receive a 20 percent discount. Daily departures are from Frankfurt and Füssen at 8am and from Munich at 10:30am. Do some math before purchasing, though: If you plan on visiting only one or two towns along the Romantic Road, it's probably cheaper to buy individual bus or train tickets to get there.

with 50,000 students who add life to its narrow lanes and bright squares and lend a German version of *joie de vivre.* Würzburg's appreciation of the good life becomes clear as soon as you notice the town is swathed in vineyards that climb the surrounding hillsides above its gabled rooftops. You'll also soon notice that wine merchants here sell *Bocksbeutels,* the green, narrow-necked wine bottles designed so monks could hide them under their robes.

On the night of March 16, 1945, Würzburg was leveled by a bombing raid. A plan to leave the city in ruin as a testimony to the horrors of war was scrapped and nearly every major structure has been restored, and the modern city blends in harmoniously with medieval remains and reconstructions. Würzburg isn't picture book pretty, the way Rothenburg and some other towns you'll come to on the Romantic Road are, but that doesn't district from its appeal, and there's plenty to see in a day.

Essentials
GETTING THERE
BY TRAIN The **Würzburg Hauptbahnhof** lies on several major and regional rail lines, with frequent connections to all major German cities. From Frankfurt, 30 trains arrive per day (trip time: 1 hr., 10 min.); from Munich, 20 trains (2 hr., 10 min.); from Nürnberg, 30 trains (1 hr.); and 12 trains from Stuttgart (2 hr., 15 min.). For rail information and schedules, call ✆ **01805/996633** or visit www.bahn.com.

BY BUS For bus service along the Romantic Road, see "Romantic Road Info & Bus Tours," above.

BY CAR Access is via the A7 Autobahn from north and south or the A3 Autobahn from east and west. The A81 Autobahn has links from the southwest.

The Romantic Road

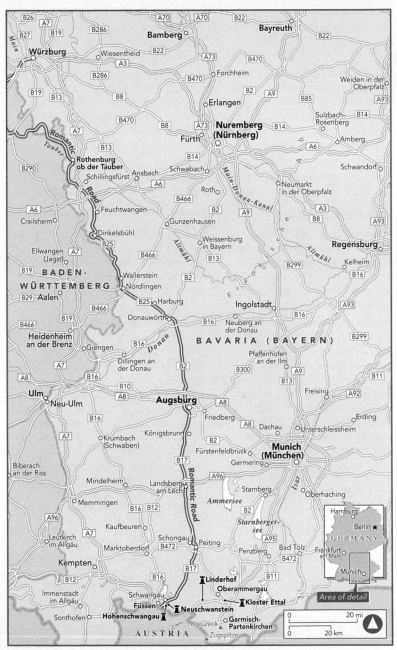

B26 A7 B286 A70 A70 B22 Bayreuth
B27 B19
Würzburg Wiesentheid B22 A73 B470 B22
A3 Bamberg
B286 B470 Forchheim Weiden in der Oberpfalz
B19 B13 B8 B2 A9 B85 A93
Erlangen
B470 B8 A73 Nuremberg B14 Sulzbach-Rosenberg B14
A7 Fürth (Nürnberg) A6 Amberg
Tauber B13 Rothenburg ob der Tauber B14 Schwabach Schwandorf
B290 Schillingsfürst Ansbach A6 Roth Neumarkt in der Oberpfalz
Crailsheim Feuchtwangen B466 B2 A9 A3 B8 A93
A6 Dinkelsbühl Weissenburg in Bayern Regensburg
Ellwangen (Jagst) A7 B25 B466 B13 B299 Kelheim
B19 BADEN- B2 B16
WÜRTTEMBERG Wallerstein Altmühl
B29 Aalen B25 Harburg Nördlingen Ingolstadt A93
B466 Donauwörth B16 Neuberg an der Donau B16 B299
Heidenheim an der Brenz Giengen B16 BAVARIA (BAYERN)
A7 Dillingen an der Donau B2 Pfaffenhofen an der Ilm B11
A8 B16 B10 Augsburg B300 A9 B13 Freising A92
Ulm A8 A8 Friedberg A8 Dachau Unterschleissheim Erding
Neu-Ulm B16 Königsbrunn B2 Munich (München)
A7 Krumbach (Schwaben) Fürstenfeldbruck Germering
Biberach an der Riss Mindelheim B17 A96 Starnberg Oberhaching
Landsberg am Lech Ammersee Isar Hamburg
Memmingen B16 B12 B2 Berlin ★
A96 Romantic Road Starnberger-see GERMANY
Leutkirch im Allgäu A7 Kaufbeuren A95 Frankfurt am Main
Kempten Marktoberdorf Schongau B472 Peiting Penzberg Bad Tölz B472 Munich
B12 B17 B11 Area of detail
Immenstadt im Allgäu B16 Linderhof Oberammergau
Schwangau Kloster Ettal
Füssen Neuschwanstein 0 20 mi
Sonthofen Hohenschwangau Kreuzeck Garmisch-Partenkirchen 0 20 km
AUSTRIA Zugspitze

137

GETTING AROUND

It's easy to cover Würzburg on foot or by tram (streetcar). A single fare is 2.20€, or else you can purchase a ticket, good for 24 hours, at any station for 4.45€. The same fare applies to buses. The no. 9 bus is especially convenient, linking the Marienberg Fortress and the Residenz palace. For information about routes and schedules, call © 0931/361352 or visit www.vvm-info.de.

VISITOR INFORMATION

The **Tourist Information Office** is in Marktplatz at Falkenhaus am Markt (© **0931/372398**). It's open April to December Monday to Friday 10am to 6pm, Saturday 10am to 2pm (May–Oct also open Sun 10am–2pm); hours January to March are Monday to Friday 10am to 4pm, Saturday 10am to 1pm. The office is next to the public library, where you can avail yourself of the restroom facilities and free Wi-Fi.

SPECIAL EVENTS The highlight of the cultural year is the annual **Mozart Festival,** www.mozartfest-wuerzburg.de, staged over the entire month of June. The venue for most of the Mozart concerts is the glorious baroque palace, the Residenz (see below).

Where to Stay

Greifensteiner Hof These bright, good sized rooms put you right in the heart of the *Altstadt* behind the Marktplatz. Each room is decorated a little differently, all with a bit of designer flair and some nice touches, such as comfy lounge chairs and fresh flowers on the bedside tables. The restaurant downstairs, the Fränkische Stuben, serves Franconian specialties and spills out to a nice terrace in good weather. A cellar wine bar stocks local vintages.

Dettelbachergasse 2. © **0931/35170.** www.greifensteiner-hof.de. 49 units. 120€–190€ double. Rates include buffet breakfast. Parking 8.50€. Tram: 1, 2, 3, or 5. **Amenities:** Restaurant, bar; free in-room Wi-Fi.

Premier Hotel Rebstock ★★ Behind a rococo facade dating from at least 1408 is a surprisingly contemporary interior that breaks out of any cookie-cutter notion of the hotel's Best Western affiliation. Some noteworthy design touches appear in the skylit rotunda downstairs and in guest quarters of all sorts of sizes and styles upstairs. Most accommodations, some of the best in town and priced accordingly, lean toward crisp, clean lines and a businesslike look, though some veer off into odd shapes and more traditional and more posh decor. The buffet breakfast is extra.

Neubaustrasse 7. © **800/528-1234** in the U.S., or 0931/30930. Fax 0931/3093100. www.rebstock. com. 70 units. 170€–280€ double. Parking 10€. Tram: 1, 3, 4, or 5. **Amenities:** Restaurant; bar; room service; Wi-Fi (free; in lobby, charge in rooms).

St. Josef ★ For an inexpensive yet pleasant place to lay your head in the Altstadt, you can't do better than these clean, no-nonsense rooms done up in crisp, modern style. The Residenz, Marktplatz, and other sights are an easy walk away, and a member of the Casagrande family is usually around to tell you what to see and how to get there.

Semmelstrasse 28–30. © **0931/308680.** Fax 0931/3086860. www.hotel-st-josef.de. 33 units. 89€–95€ double. Rates include buffet breakfast. Parking 8.50€. Tram: 1, 2, 3, or 5. **Amenities:** Restaurant; free in-room Wi-Fi.

Where to Eat

Local specialties include *Zwiebelkuchen,* similar to a quiche Lorraine, and *Frankische Mostsuppe,* a light wine soup. White Franconian wine seems to go well with just about anything that shows up on a Würzburg table.

Alte Mainmühle ★ FRANCONIAN   It's a challenge to cross the Alte Mainbrücke (Old Main Bridge) without stepping into this timbered, two-story tavern perched romantically off one side of the bridge over the rushing current. A seat on the summertime terrace comes with nice views of river traffic, the town, and the fortress, but for sheer coziness it's hard to beat the woody, fire-warmed interior. The menu ranges through a full compliment of grilled meats, fish, sausage and dumplings, and other local specialties that are more accomplished than you'd expect to find yourself enjoying sitting midstream in a river.

Alte Mainbrücke. ℂ **16777.** Main courses 8€–23€. Tues–Sat 10am–midnight. Tram: 1, 3, 4, or 5.

Backöfele ★ FRANCONIAN/GERMAN   Even the locals don't really know whether to call this place a beer hall, a wine cellar, or a restaurant, but everyone loves the cozy, stone-floored ambiance and the well-prepared traditional food served in huge quantities. A Würzburg favorite, pikeperch with noodles and a salad, is usually on the list of specials. Reservations recommended.

Ursulinergasse 2. ℂ **0931/59059.** www.backoefele.de. Main courses 7€–29€. Mon–Sat noon–11pm; Sun noon–10pm. Tram: 1 or 4.

Ratskeller Würzburg ★★ FRANCONIAN/INTERNATIONAL   This 500-year-old tavern with wood floors and frescoed walls tucked into the cellars of the Rathaus might seem like just another ho-hum rathskeller in the German tradition of a city hall cellar restaurant for its citizens, but there's a difference here. Some of the nooks and crannies are dark, paneled, and traditional, other corners of the sprawling space are chicly urbane; the menu includes a lot of tasty Franconian fare at reasonable prices—homemade sausage mixed with fried potatoes and eggs, or roast beef with noodles and fried onions—but also fans out to pastas and other international selections. Beverages stay close to home: Würzburger beer and lots of Franconian white wines. Get reservations for weekend meals.

Langgasse 1 (near the Alte Mainbrücke). ℂ **0931/13021.** www.wuerzburger-ratskeller.de. Main courses 8€–26€. Daily 11:30am–10:30pm. Tram: 1, 2, 3, or 5.

Weinhaus Zum Stachel ★ FRANCONIAN/INTERNATIONAL   No other wine house in Würzburg is as old as this one, dating from 1413. And the well-burnished tables groan under generous portions of hearty classics like rump steak with onions and freshwater fish prepared according to old family recipes. In summer, you can dine in a vine-draped outdoor courtyard, sipping wines from the restaurant's own vineyards. Reservations required.

Gressengasse 1. ℂ **0931/52770.** www.weinhaus-stachel.de. Main courses 12€–23€; 3-course meal 38€, 6-course meal 66€. Tues–Sat 11am–midnight. Tram: 1, 3, 4, or 5.

Wein und Fischhaus Schiffbäuerin ★ SEAFOOD   One of the best dining spots in the region is this combined wine house/fish restaurant, across Alte Mainbrücke on the Marienberg fortress side in an old half-timbered building. Once the residence of shipbuilders, the house now specializes in freshwater fish such as pike, carp, char, tench, trout, wels, and eel. Reservations recommended, no credit cards accepted.

Katzengasse 7. ℂ **0931/42487.** www.schiffbaeuerin.de. Main courses 16€–24€. Tues–Sat 11:30am–2:30pm and 6–11:30pm; Sun 11:30am–3pm. Closed Tues in Jun, Jul, and Aug. Tram: 2 or 4.

Exploring Würzburg

You can easily get around Würzburg on foot, though you may want to board the nunber 9 bus for the uphill climb to the Marienberg Fortress. The town center is the Marktplatz

WÜRZBURG'S master CARVER

Tilman Riemenschneider (1460–1531) lived and worked in Würzburg for 48 years, serving as both a councilor and mayor while gaining considerable fame for his sculptures and carvings. He married four times, oversaw a household of nine children and stepchildren, and owned several houses as well as vineyards. During the Peasants' Revolt of 1525, this master woodcarver sided with the rebels and incurred the wrath of the prince-bishops. As a result of his political views, Riemenschneider was imprisoned and tortured, and his hands were broken, ending his artistic career. He died shortly after being released from prison, leaving behind his incredibly expressive wood sculptures that adorn churches and museums in Würzburg and elsewhere along the Romantic Road.

(marketplace), where vendors sell produce and dispense sausages in the shadow of lovely red-and-white **Marienkapelle (St. Mary's Chapel),** built in the 14th and 15th centuries and dedicated to the city's patron saint. A few blocks to the south is another gathering spot, **Rückermainstrasse,** where an 18th-century fountain enhances the appearance of the distinctively tall and slender Rathaus (Town Hall). Just to the west, the **Alte Mainbrücke (Old Main Bridge),** completed in 1543, crosses the Main River with a flourish, adorned as it is with twelve enormous Baroque saints sculpted out of sandstone. From the end of the bridge a well-marked footpath climbs through the vineyards to the **Marienberg Fortress.** The **Residenz** is a short walk east from the Marktplatz.

Dom St. Kilian ★ CHURCH   Wuzrburg's prince-bishops worshipped and were laid to rest in this huge 10th-century church. Many of their funerary monuments line the elegantly simple nave and others reside for eternity in the Schönborn Chapel, designed by Balthasar Neumann, architect of the Residenz (see below); what you see today comes from a massive restoration effort that raised the church from ruin in the aftermath of World War II. The finest monuments are by Würzburg sculptor Tilman Riemenschneider. You will encounter him again in the Mainfränkisches Museum in the Marienberg Fortress (see below), and one of the best things about stepping in and out of Würzburg churches is seeing his work. Here his ensemble of the Magi line three pillars on the near left side of the nave. Everyone—the three magi, the Virgin Mary, even the infant Jesus—look happy, not in that remote ecclesiastical way but humanly so. Riemenschneider's great genius was capturing human empathy in wood, stone, or whatever medium he worked in. The Dom's Irish-sounding name is a tribute to St. Kilian, an Irish missionary to Franconia in the 7th century.

Domstrasse (at the end of Schönbornstrasse). ✆ **0931/3211830.** Free admission. Easter–Oct Mon–Sat 10am–5pm, Sun 1–6pm; Nov to the day before Easter Mon–Sat 10am–noon and 2–4:30pm, Sun 12:30–1:30pm and 2:30–6pm.

Festung Marienberg (Marienberg Fortress) ★ HISTORIC SITE   It's a 30-minute trek along a well-marked footpath through hillside vineyards up to this mighty fortress, affording views of the city and surrounding vineyards (bus no. 9 also climbs the hill). From 1253 to 1720 the hilltop fortress/palace, surrounded by massive bastions, was home to the prince-bishops who, beginning in 743, ruled this part of Franconia on behalf of the Holy Roman Empire. Lore, mixed with some fact, has it that Würzburg attained this important status when three martyred Irish Christian missionaries were declared saints and the city became an important pilgrimage stop and religious center; allegedly, the three met their end not in the maws of lions but at the hands of any angry wife who became resentful when they tried to convert her noble husband to Christianity and a life of poverty and celibacy. As becomes clear in the **Fürstenbaumuseum,** the tapestry-and-painting-filled residential wing of the massive complex, the prince-bishops enjoyed a lavish lifestyle that was far from modest; in adjacent galleries, town models show medieval Würzburg, along with a horrifying glimpse of the town after bombings in 1945. Another wing houses the **Mainfrän-kisches Museum (Main-Franconian Museum),** where the prized possessions are 81 wood-carved sculptures by Tilman Riemenschneider (1460–1531), the so-called master of Würzburg and one of the greatest northern sculptors of the Middle Ages. Also within the walls of the massive complex is the 8th-century **Marienkirche (St. Mary's Church),** one of the oldest churches in Germany.

Festung Marienberg. ✆ **0931/205940.** www.mainfraenkisches-museum.de. Admission to Main-fränkisches Museum 4€ adults, 2€ students, free for children 13 and under. Apr–Oct Tues–Sun 10am–5pm; Nov–Mar Tues–Sun 10am–4pm. Fürstenbaumuseum 4.50€ adults, 3.50€ students, free for children 17 and under. Apr–Oct Tues–Sun 9am–6pm. Tours of the fortress (in English and German) 3.50€ adults, 2.50€ students. Apr–Oct Tues–Sun 10am–4pm. Bus: 9.

Residenz (Palace) ★★ ARCHITECTURAL SITE   Prince-Bishop Johann Philipp Franz von Schönborn had a passion for elegance and splendor that the staid, musty salons of the Marienberg Fortress could not satisfy. So in 1720 he commissioned what over the next 50 years was to become one of Germany's grandest and most elaborate baroque palaces. Architect Balthasar Neumann (1687–1753), whose talents included a rare combination of technical skill and an eye for beauty and harmony, oversaw the design of the 350-room palace, and his masterpiece shows a unity of purpose and design unusual in structures of such size. Von Sconborn's successor, Prince-Bishop Carl Phillip von Greiffenclau, had the foresight to hire the Venetian painter Tiepolo to fresco the *Treppenhaus* (staircase), where Apollo ascends toward the upper hall, surrounded by the four corners of the world, the seasons, and signs of the zodiac, rendering a climb to the upper hall into a rather majestic event. A keen-eyed observer might note that Tiepolo worked some portraits into the Europa section, where he depicts his princely patron, as well as his son Giovanni, who accompanied him from Venice. Tiepolo also painted the frescoes in the chapel and the Imperial Hall, where he depicts, among other themes, the 1156 marriage of emperor Frederick Barbossa to Beatrice of Burgundy in Würzburg.

During the summer, a **Mozart festival** is held in the upper halls. For information, visit mozartfest.de.

Residenzplatz 2, Tor B. ✆ **0931/355170.** www.residenz-wuerzburg.de. Admission 7.50€ adults; 6.50€ students, children, and seniors. Apr–Oct daily 9am–6pm; Nov–Mar daily 10am–4pm. Guided tours in English (included in admission) 11am and 3pm. Bus: 9.

Side Trip from Würzburg
MILTENBERG ★
71km (44 miles) W of Würzburg

The reason to come to this sleepy riverside town is to get an eyeful of half-timbered buildings and medieval ambiance, minus the bus-tour hordes that descend upon some of the other Romantic Road towns. Enclosed within walls and gate towers and tucked beneath a steep wooded hill crowned by a castle, Miltenberg satisfies even the most voracious appetite for quaint townscapes.

FIGHTING THE PROTESTANT menace

Würzburg remained faithful to the Roman Catholic Church throughout the Reformation, partly through the efforts of Julius Echter von Mespelbrunn, a 17th-century prince-bishop (you'll see an elaborate tapestry tracing his family line in the Fürstenbaumuseum in the Marienberg Fortress). Von Mespelbrunn staunchly defended Würzburg against protestant incursions by banishing Lutheran preachers and demanding that public officials be Catholic. Würzburg still has a large Catholic population and is known as "the town of Madonnas" because of the more than 100 statues of its patron saint that adorn the house fronts. The best known is the baroque "Patrona Franconiae," the so-called Weeping Madonna, standing among other Franconian saints along the buttresses of the 15th-century Alte Mainbrücke.

GETTING THERE   By car from Würzburg, take the A3 west and then B469 into Miltenberg. There's at least one train connection per hour from Würzburg, and the trip takes 90 minutes.

Exploring Miltenberg

The town center is the utterly charming Marktplatz, where half-timbered houses climb hilly lanes above a fountain and flowerbeds. Atop this assemblage rises **Schloss Miltenberg;** you might have to settle for an exterior view of this white-walled, steep-roofed stronghold, as it's often shuttered; if the gates are open, cross the courtyard and climb the watchtower for a sweeping view over the town into the surrounding forest. It's open only May to October Tuesday to Friday 2 to 5:30pm, Saturday and Sunday 1 to 5:30pm. Admission is 3€ adults and 2€ for children 11 and under.

Where to Eat

If you don't want a full meal, stop by the wonderfully atmospheric 500-year-old **Weinhaus,** Marktplatz 185 (© **09371/5500**), for a beer or a taste of the local vintages.

Gasthaus zum Riesen ★★ GERMAN   A lot of locals and travelers in the know make the trip to Miltenberg just to dine in one of the region's old-time favorites, where out of the kitchen come liver dumpling soup, platters piled high with pork filets and sausages, and rump steak in dark-beer sauce. These hearty meals are accompanied by a huge choice of German beers and served in atmospheric and historic surroundings from 1190 that allegedly once hosted Emperor Frederick Barbarossa.

Hauptstrasse 99. © **09371/989948.** www.riesen-miltenberg.de. Main courses 8€–19€. Mon–Wed 11am–midnight; Thurs–Sat 11am–1am.

ROTHENBURG OB DER TAUBER ★★★

51km (32 miles) SE of Würzburg

One of Europe's best-preserved medieval gems just doesn't quit serving up a heady dose of romantic, fairytale Germany, with tall timbered houses that lean over cobbled lanes enclosed within ramparts and towers. Not surprisingly, almost everyone who comes to southern Germany follows the well-beaten path to Rothenburg to take in the scene, but that doesn't mean you shouldn't join their ranks. Or, come off-season, between September and May, or simply linger in the evening after the day trippers leave and life in this enchanting place resumes it normal pace.

Essentials
GETTING THERE
When trying to reach this gem of a town, some travelers have suddenly discovered themselves at a Rothenburg somewhere else in Germany. To avoid the confusion, make sure to ask for a ticket to "Rothenburg ob der Tauber."

BY TRAIN   Rothenburg ob der Tauber is connected with hourly trains to the junction of Steinach, which has frequent connections to Würzburg (total trip time: 1 hr.) The trip to Munich take 3 hours, 2½ hours to Frankfurt. For information, call ℂ **01805/996633** or visit www.bahn.com.

BY BUS   For bus service along the Romantic Road, see "Bus Tours of the Romantic Road," at the beginning of this chapter. Regular long-distance buses service Rothenburg from Frankfurt, Würzburg, Augsburg, and Munich, as well as Füssen. For information and reservations, call the Frankfurt terminal number (ℂ **069/7903261** in Frankfurt). Regional bus service is provided by OVF Omnibusverkehr Franken GmbH, Nelson-Mandela-Platz 18, D-90159 Nürnberg (ℂ **0911/430570;** www.ovf.de).

BY CAR   Access by car is the A7 from Würzburg.

VISITOR INFORMATION
Rothenburg Tourismus Service, on the Marktplatz (ℂ **09861/404800;** www. rothenburg.de), is open November to April, Monday to Friday 9am to 5pm, and Saturday 10am to 1pm; May to October, Monday to Friday 9am to 6pm, Saturday and Sunday 10am to 5pm.

Where to Stay

Altraenkische ★★   Six rooms in a 650-year-old house on a quiet back street pack in about as much charm and comfort for your money as you are going to find in Rothenburg, with their heavy beams, polished armoires, oil paintings, and spruce bathrooms with deep tubs. A generous breakfast next to a blue ceramic stove nicely starts off a stay. For other meals step into the *weinstub* (wine tavern) downstairs, where Franconian specialties are served next to an open fire in winter and on a romantic terrace in the summer. If you're feeling homesick, stick around on a Wednesday evening when the local English club meets at the hotel.

Kloisterhof 7. ℂ **09861/6404.** www.altfraenkische.de. 6 units. 75€–82€ double. Rates include buffet breakfast. **Amenities:** Restaurant, free in-room Wi-Fi.

Gasthof Goldener Greifen ★   A medieval mayor of Rothenburg is your host, in spirit at least, in these no-frills but comfortable accommodations in his former home. Some of the rooms are small and pretty basic, and priced accordingly, while others are a bit grander and geared to families (some sleep five) and longer stays. All have attractive and sensible furnishings, and many are enlivened with wooden ceilings and other character-supplying features. Most atmospheric is the 650-year-old common room and the breakfast room, fitted out of the mayor's office (with a toasty closet designed to keep his parchments dry). The in-house restaurant specializes in Franconian fare with tasty dishes like marinated beef, and moist roast goose leg soaked in an unforgettable gravy, and a side of red kraut and potato dumplings. Try it with the bold Taubertäler red wine from Lauda-Königshofen.

Obere Schmiedgasse 5 (off Marktplatz). ℂ **09861/228.** www.gasthof-greifen-rothenburg.de. 14 units. 65€–98€ double. Rates include buffet breakfast. Free parking. Closed Dec 22–Jan 3. **Amenities:** Room service, free in-room Wi-Fi.

Hotel Reichs-Küchenmeister ★ Just enough sense of cozy tradition makes these bright rooms extremely comfortable (with roomy armchairs, lots of blonde wood, and firm beds topped with fluffy duvets) without being stuffy or over-furnished. They're all different, vary considerably in size, and occupy a centuries-old merchant's house and a slightly less desirable (and less expensive) house across the street. A sauna, steam room, and whirlpool are welcome tonics after a day pounding the cobblestones, and a garage, soundproof windows, and a pleasant beer garden attached to the in-house restaurant are among the many other swell touches here.

Kirchplatz 8 (near St. Jakobskirche). ℂ **09861/9700.** www.reichskuechenmeister.com. 45 units. 150€–240€ double. Rates include buffet breakfast. Parking 5€ in the lot; 8€ in the garage. **Amenities:** Restaurant; bar; bikes; Jacuzzi; sauna, free in-room Wi-Fi.

Where to Eat

Stop at one of the many kiosks in town selling the local pastry called *Schneeballen* (snowballs), a round pastry coated in sugar and cinnamon. This memorable sweet is also on most dessert and snack menus in town.

Burgerkeller ★ FRANCONIAN A frescoed 16th-century cellar with vaulted ceilings that spills over to outside tables in good weather guarantees no-nonsense local cooking, along the lines of *Maultaschensuppe* (stuffed pasta in broth) and Nürnberg sausages on sauerkraut. The staff is genuinely eager to make sure that you accompany your meal with a good local wine.

Herngasse 24. ℂ **09861/2126.** Main courses 6€–12€. Thurs–Tues 11:30am–2pm and 6–9pm.

Die Blaue Sau ★★★ FRANCONIAN/INTERNATIONAL Foodies would find it a crime worthy of detention in the stocks in Rothenburg's Kriminalmuseum to pass through town without stopping this grill house for a meat-heavy take on Franconian cuisine. A casual-chic dining room, stone-walled wine cellar, and a lovely terrace are the settings for no-nonsense preparations of rib-eye, prime rib, and pork, though fresh fish and seafood also make an appearance. A 400-entry wine list is regarded as one of the best in Germany. Reservations required.

Vorm Würzburger Tor 7–9 (in Villa Mittermeirer hotel). ℂ **09861/94540.** www.villamittermeier.de. Main courses 14€–32€. Tues–Sat noon–2pm and 7–9:30pm.

Ratsstube ★ FRANCONIAN Dark wood, vaulted ceilings, and lots of copper provide a true tavern atmospheric in this character-filled old place, and its center of town location across the square from the Rathaus keep the kitchen busy throughout the day. *Sauerbraten*, game, and other local favorites fill the menu board, with some Italian interlopers. Reservations recommended.

Marktplatz 6. ℂ **09861/5511.** www.ratsstuberothenburg.de. Main courses 10€–15€. Mon–Sat 9am–10pm; Sun 9am–6pm.

Exploring Rothenburg ob der Tauber

For an excellent view over the town, take a walk on the ramparts between the massive 16th-century Spitaltor tower (at the end of the Spitalgasse) to the Klingentor tower. A circuit takes about a half-hour. At the Rödertor (Röder Gate), you can climb the tower to a small exhibition describing an air raid in 1945 that leveled a large part of the eastern end of town. Entry to the ramparts is 1.50€ for adults, 1€ for children, but opening times vary and depend on the weather.

raise a toast **TO THE *BÜRGERMEISTER***

Rothenburg's famous 17th-century drinking binge, in which the *Bürgermeister* (mayor) downed a tankard of beer to save the town, is re-enacted in a play, "Die Meistertrunk" ("The Master Draught"), first performed in 1881. These days it's part of a festival that takes place every September/October. Hundreds of citizens dress up in period costumes and, of course, drink beer.

Kriminalmuseum (Criminal Museum) ★ HISTORIC SITE   It paid to stay on the right side of the law in the Middle Ages, as these four floors devoted to medieval style law and order prove. Chastity belts, shame masks, torture devices, a beer barrel-shaped stockade for drunks, a cage for bakers whose bread was too small or too light—sadists with a historical bent will be in seventh heaven. The 1395 hospital that houses the museum was redone in 1718, giving Rothenberg its only Baroque facade.

Burggasse 3–5. ℂ **09861/5359.** www.kriminalmuseum.rothenburg.de. Admission 4€ adults, 2.80€ students, 2.40€ children 6–17. Jan–Feb and Nov daily 2–4pm; Mar and Dec 1–4pm; Apr daily 11am–5pm; May–Oct daily 10am–6pm.

Rathaus (Town Hall) ★ LANDMARK   Part Gothic, from 1240, and part Renaissance, from 1572, Rothenburg's town hall is decorated with intricate friezes, an oriel extending the building's full height, and a large stone portico opening onto the square. Give these details a look, then climb to the top of the 50m (160-ft.) tower of the Gothic hall for a view over the town and the Tauber Valley. You'll be standing where sentries once kept an eye out for fires, ringing the bell every quarter-hour to prove that they were awake and on the job.

Marktplatz. ℂ **09861/40492.** Admission: Rathaus free; tower 1.50€ adults, 1€ children. Rathaus Mon–Fri 8am–6pm. Tower Apr–Oct daily 9:30am–12:30pm and 1–5pm; Dec daily noon–3pm; Nov and Jan–Mar Sat–Sun and holidays noon–3pm.

Reichsstadtmuseum (Imperial City Museum) ★ HISTORIC SITE   In 1631, during the Thirty Years' War, the Protestant city of Rothenburg was captured by General Tilly, commander of the armies of the Catholic League. He promised to spare the town from destruction if one of the town burghers could drink down a huge tankard full of wine in one draft. *Bürgermeister* Nusch accepted the challenge and succeeded, thus saving Rothenburg. The tankard—with a capacity of 3.5 liters, more than 6 pints—is part of the historical collection of Rothenburg, housed in this 13th-century Dominican nunnery. The convent cloisters are especially well preserved, and the hall, kitchen, and apothecary show life as it was in a medieval convent. As does the barrel out front, where the nuns left bread for the poor and women left unwanted babies. The 12-panel, 1494 "Rothenburg Passion," by local painter Martinus Schwartz, depicts scenes from the suffering of Christ, and paintings by Englishman Arthur Wasse (1854–1930) present views of Rothenberg as picture perfect and romantic as today's postcards; Wasse studied art in Munich and became so enamored of Rothenburg that he spent most of the rest of his life here.

Klosterhof 5. ℂ **09861/939043.** www.reichsstadtmuseum.rothenburg.de. Admission 4€ adults, 3€ students and children 6–18, 8€ family ticket. Apr–Oct daily 10am–5pm; Nov–Mar daily 1–4pm.

St. Jakobskirche (Church of St. James) ★ CHURCH   Rothenburg lies on the pilgrim trail to Santiago de Compostella in Spain, site of the remains of St. James. This

Get Out of Town

If you want to escape the tourist hordes, rent a bike at **Rad und Tat,** Bensenstrasse 17 (*C* **09861/87984;** www.radtat.de), for about 12€ per day.

Get a map from the tourist office and follow the bike path along the Tauber River; for more information, check out cycling routes at www.germany.travel.

14th-century church, infused with mellow light from its original stained glass, has long been a stop on the route, with a relic that does justice to the role. The Reliquary of the Holy Blood (1270) is contained in a rock-crystal capsule and said to contain three drops of the blood of Jesus Christ. Würzburg sculptor Tilman Riemenschneider (ca. 1460–1531) crafted the Altar of the Holy Blood to house the shrine. The center panel depicts the Last Supper, in which you'll notice Riemenschneider adds a twist to the story. Judas, not Christ, sits at the center of the table, suggesting that God is willing to shed his grace even on sinners.

Klostergasse 15. *C* **09861/700620.** Admission 2€ adults, .50€ children. Apr–Oct Mon–Sat 9am–5:30pm, Sun 11am–5:30pm; Dec daily 10am–5pm; Nov and Jan–Mar daily 10am–noon and 2–4pm.

Shopping

Rothenburg is a good place to load up on Bavarian memorabilia. **Friese-Kabalo Kunstgewerbe OHG,** Grüner Markt 7 (*C* **09861/7166**), specializes in cuckoo clocks and also carries Hummel figurines, pewter beer steins, music boxes, and dolls. Käthe Wohlfahrt's **Weihnachtswerkstatt (Christmas Workshop),** Herrngasse 1 (*C* **098614090**), is a national institution with shops in towns around Germany and stalls at Christmas markets. Shelves are filled with everything from clothing and accessories to cuckoo clocks, but the real attractions are toys and Christmas ornaments. If you collect teddy bears, you'll love **Teddyland,** Herrngasse 10 (*C* **09861/8904;** www.teddyland.de), which stocks more than 5,000 of them, the largest teddy bear population in Germany. Bear images are printed on everything from T-shirts to bags and watches.

Side Trip from Rothenburg ob der Tauber
CREGLINGEN ★
18km (11 miles) NW of Rothenburg ob der Tauber, 40km (25 miles) S of Würzburg

Creglingen traces its history back 4,000 years and enjoyed some Middle Ages heydays when it became an important pilgrimage site. That said, the hamlet is today one of the quieter backwaters along the Romantic Road. You'll come here for only one reason, aside from seeing a tiny but pretty hamlet that evokes the Germany of long ago. That's to see the enormous and remarkable altarpiece by Tilman Riemenschneider, the master carver of Würzburg (see above), in the Herrgottskirche (Chapel of Our Lord).

GETTING THERE By car, Creglingen is 18km (11 miles) northwest of Rothenburg on L2251. Unless you're traveling by car, the only way to get from Rothenburg to Creglingen is by local buses. They're operated by **Omnibusverkehr Franken** (*C* **0931/3528940;** www.ovf.de), and from 5 to 10 a day run in either direction.

Exploring Creglingen
The **Herrgottskirche (Chapel of Our Lord),** on the road to Münster, dates from 1389 and was built where a farmer plowing his fields claimed to have found a sacred host, and the discovery was accompanied by the appearance of Jesus with a phalanx of

angels. Creglingen became a place of pilgrimage, and between 1505 and 1510, Tilman Riemenschneider was commissioned to create this extraordinarily beautiful altar with figures representing the Assumption of the Blessed Virgin framed by scenes from her life. The expressive figures catch the light in such a way that they seem animated, and the sculpture changes in appearance throughout the day with the shifting sun. The chapel can be visited daily April to October 9:15am to 6pm, and November to March Tuesday to Sunday 1 to 4pm. Admission is 2€.

If you have time to kill before the bus heads back to Rothenburg, and are into eso-terica, you might want to walk across the road to the **Fingerhutmuseum (Thimble Museum),** Kohlesmühle 6 (© **07933/370;** www.fingerhutmuseum.de), with the largest collection of thimbles in Europe. Some of them are bone rings dating from prehistoric times; others are made of brass that was smelted in Creglingen during the Middle Ages. It's open April to October Tuesday to Sunday 10am to 12:30pm and 2 to 5pm; hours for November, December, and March are Tuesday to Sunday 1 to 4pm. Admission is 2€.

NÜRNBERG (NUREMBERG) ★★

109km (68 miles) SE of Würzburg

Few cities in the world conjure such disparate images of beauty and horror. During the 15th and 16th centuries, Nürnberg enjoyed a cultural flowering that made it into the center of the German Renaissance, a northern Florence. The great Albrecht Dürer is one of many artists who produced masterpieces in the city's studios. Koberger set up his printing press here, and Regiomontanus built an astronomical observatory. Work-shops turned out gingerbread, handmade toys, and the world's first pocket watches, the Nürnberg eggs.

The art and architecture that elevated Nürnberg into one of Germany's great trea-sure-filled beauties turned out to be the city's Achilles heel. So enamored was Adolf Hitler with the Nürnberg's huge swaths of half-timbered houses, steeped and gabled rooftops, and cobbled lanes and squares that he chose to stage his massive Nazi rallies in what he considered to be the most German of German cities. Think of the "Heil Hitler-ing" masses and goose-stepping soldiers in Leni Riefenstahl in "Triumph des Willens" ("Triumph of the Will"); the film also happens to capture footage of the Führer's plane flying low over Nürnberg's maze of medieval lanes and stone towers. Attached to the city, too, are the infamous Nürnberg laws, the 1935 legislation that stripped Jews and other non-Aryans of their German citizenship and basic rights and set the stage for the Holocaust. As the ideological center of the Third Reich, the city was a choice target for Allied bombers, and on January 2, 1945, 525 British Lancasters rained fire and destruction on Nürnberg, leaving most of the historic center and sur-roundings a smoldering ruin and killing 60,000 Nürnbergers.

Nürnberg has regained its vitality, prosperity, and much of its handsome pre-war appearance. What's new blends in with the reconstructed old. In the Altstadt, sur-rounded by medieval ramparts, Gothic churches and sway-backed medieval houses rise above lively squares and line the banks of the Pegnitz River. The Hauptmarkt is the stage for Germany's largest and most famous Christmas market (said to have origi-nated when Martin Luther began giving his children Christmas presents). Amid these prosperous surroundings is a reminder of the city's day of reckoning for its World War II past: the Justice Palace, where the War Crimes Tribunal sat in 1946 and tried 21 leading Nazi war criminals for conspiracy and crimes against world peace, the rules of warfare, and humanity.

Essentials

GETTING THERE

BY PLANE   **Nürnberg Flughafen** is 6km (4 miles) north of the city center. The small airport is served by 14 airlines, with flights to dozens of other European cities. For information and schedules, call 📞 **0911/93700** or visit www.airport-nuernberg.de.

BY TRAIN   The **Nürnberg Hauptbahnhof** lies on several major German rail lines. Travel time to Frankfurt is 2 hours; to Würzburg, 1 hour; to Berlin, 5 hours; and to Munich, 1 hour. For information and schedules, call 📞 **01805/996633** or visit www. bahn.com. The station is right at the edge of the Altstadt, and a walk down Konigstrasse leads to just about anywhere you might want to go in the old city.

BY BUS   Regional service to neighboring towns within Franconia is offered by **OVF Omnibusverkehr Franken GmbH,** Nelson Mandela Platz 18 in Nürnberg (📞 **0911/430570;** www.ovf.de). For information on these or any other bus line coming into Nürnberg (or anywhere else in Franconia), contact one of the city's largest travel agents, **TUI Reise Center,** Lorenzerstrasse 19 (📞 **0911/2270000**).

BY CAR   From Munich, take the A9 Autobahn north; from Frankfurt and Würzburg, head southeast along the A3 Autobahn; from Berlin, take the A9 Autobahn south.

GETTING AROUND

Nürnberg has a **subway** system (U-Bahn) and all lines stop at the Hauptbahnhof (main railway station) and, meaning you can get just about anywhere in the city from there. Most **buses** and trams also stop at the Hauptbahnhof; bus no. 36 handily cuts through the heart of the old town. One-way fares within the city cost 2.60€. A Day Ticket Solo, valid for the entire transportation network from midnight to midnight, costs 5.10€. You can purchase tickets from machines next to major stops. For more information, call 📞 **0911/2834646** or visit **www.vag.de**.

  Walking along Konigstrasse and its extensions into the marketplace and Rathaus square—essentially, across the length of the old town from the Hauptbahnhof the Kaiserburg (the city's medieval castle)—will take you only about 30 minutes and will lead you through the city's medieval core and past most of its historic monuments. For a **taxi,** call 📞 **0911/19410.** The base fare and first kilometer cost 2.70€ each, while each additional kilometer adds on 1.35€.

VISITOR INFORMATION

Contact **Tourist Information,** Hauptmarkt 18 (📞 **0911/23360;** tourismus.nuernberg. de), Monday to Saturday 9am to 6pm. From May to October, it is also open Sunday 10am to 4pm.

Where to Stay

Burghotel ★   The pool and sauna in the cellar alone make this historic-center choice a standout, and the location near the castle just off the Hauptmarkt is especially handy for seeing the sights. Best are the large, so-called "comfort" rooms on the upper floors, furnished in pleasant contemporary style and with views over the old town; smaller "standard" rooms on lower floors are a bit dated but comfortable if rather unremarkable (built-in wooden table and chair sets in some add a bit of traditional coziness), and they're priced accordingly; you'll forgo the views but can enjoy those from the rooftop terrace.

Lammesgasse 3. 📞 **0911/238896.** www.burghotel-nuernberg.de. 55 units. 87€–217€ double. Rates include buffet breakfast. Parking nearby 6€. Tram: 6 or 9. Bus: 36 or 46. **Amenities:** Restaurant; pool; sauna; exercise room; Wi-Fi (fee).

Nürnberg

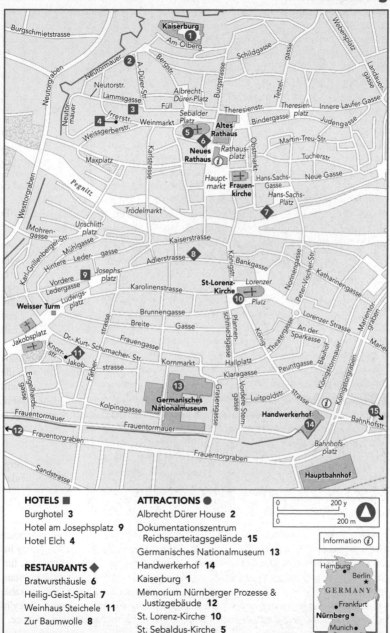

HOTELS ■
Burghotel **3**
Hotel am Josephsplatz **9**
Hotel Elch **4**

RESTAURANTS ◆
Bratwursthäusle **6**
Heilig-Geist-Spital **7**
Weinhaus Steichele **11**
Zur Baumwolle **8**

ATTRACTIONS ●
Albrecht Dürer House **2**
Dokumentationszentrum
  Reichsparteitagsgelände **15**
Germanisches Nationalmuseum **13**
Handwerkerhof **14**
Kaiserburg **1**
Memorium Nürnberger Prozesse &
  Justizgebäude **12**
St. Lorenz-Kirche **10**
St. Sebaldus-Kirche **5**

Hotel Am Josephsplatz ★★ A tall historic center house from 1675 has been thoughtfully brought up to date without losing its homey ambiance. Most of the nicely sized bedrooms are equipped with pine armoires and other comfortable, traditional furnishings. A few are more contemporary, and a few others are quite grand, with tall, frescoed ceilings and canopied beds. All have use of a sauna, exercise room, and roof terrace. Buffet breakfast is served in a series of paneled rooms off the reception area on the first level, a little lounge faces a garden on the ground floor, and all floors are connected by an elevator.

Josephsplatz 30–32. ℂ **0911/214470.** Fax 0911/21447200. www.hotel-am-josephsplatz.de. 36 units. 108€–120€ double. Rates include buffet breakfast. Parking nearby 8€–15€. **Amenities:** Exercise room; sauna; free in-room Wi-Fi.

Hotel Elch ★ A 14th-century half-timbered house just below the castle is the atmospheric setting for some of Nurnberg's most character-filled and good-value accommodations. Stylish and bright rooms are enlivened with simple contemporary furnishings, wooden floors, modern art, and colorful glass chandeliers; the occasional *elch* (elk) head also makes an appearance. A hearty buffet breakfast is served in the cozy, woody ground-floor Schnitzelria, which serves up the eponymous specialty at other meals. This place fills up quickly in any season so reserve well in advance.

Irrestrasse 9. ℂ **0911/2492980.** www.hotel-elch.com. 12 units. 89€–99€ double. Rates include buffet breakfast. Tram: 6 or 9. Bus: 36 or 46. **Amenities:** Restaurant; bar; free in-room Wi-Fi.

Where to Eat

It's easy to get a quick bite in Nürnberg. Wurst stands do a brisk business along the Königstrasse, in the Hauptmarkt, and on other main streets and squares. Nürnbergers are good cafe sitters, and even in cold weather they huddle under warmers and blankets on cafe terraces in the pedestrian zones. An especially friendly atmosphere prevails at arty **Treibhaus,** Karl-Grillenberger-Strasse 28 (ℂ **0911/223041;** www.cafetreibhaus. de; U-Bahn: Weisser Turm), which serves breakfast, sandwiches and salads throughout the day, and cocktails and light dinners at night.

Bratwursthäusle ★ FRANCONIAN It's hard to walk through the Hauptmarkt without making a stop at this friendly and authentic wursthaus that's as appealing inside as it is out, leaving you to choose between a table on the warm-weather terrace overlooking the comings and goings in the market or in one of the timbered, rustically furnished rooms inside. Wherever you sit, Nürmberg's finger-sized sausages are the thing to order, washed down with one of the many beers on tap.

Rathausplatz 1 (opposite the Rathaus). ℂ **0911/227695.** www.die-nuernberger-bratwurst.de. Reservations recommended. Main courses 6.50€–12€. No credit cards. Mon–Sat 10am–10pm. U-Bahn: Lorenzkirche.

Heilig-Geist-Spital ★★ FRANCONIAN Perched romantically above the river, Nürnberg's largest historical wine house has been in business for 650 years, serving carp, pork knuckle, and other hearty and filling Franconian fare, accompanied by more than 100 wines. Candlelight and dark paneling set the mood inside, and a fountain provides soothing sound effects for summertime dining on the terrace. Seasonal specialties include a lot of game in winter, though the stags' heads and other mounted beasts might steer you toward another choice. Reservations recommended.

Spitalgasse 16. ℂ **0911/221761.** www.heilig-geist-spital.de. Main courses 10€–18€. Daily 11am–11pm. Bus: 46 or 47.

Saving Euros

Add 2.50€ to your admission to most city museums and you can use the ticket as a day pass that will get you into other museums in Nürnberg for free on the same day. A Nürnberg card (23€) gives you admission to 10 museums and free transportation for 2 days, but you probably won't want to see all the museums (unless the Pigeon Museum hits a special chord with you) and except for the Dokumentationszentrum, it's easy to get where you want to go in Nürnberg on foot.

Weinhaus Steichele ★ FRANCONIAN/BAVARIAN   An old-time favorite with Nürnbergers serves straightforward fare in atmospheric, wood paneled, antiques-filled surroundings that don't make a single nod to being anything other than traditional. Nor do such dishes as pork roast with finger dumplings and delectable little Nürnberg sausages cooked over an open fire and served with sauerkraut. Attentive service and a tempting wine list complement a meal. The family also runs the 56-room inn that flows across the floors upstairs into a modern annex.

Knorrstrasse 2. ✆ **0911/202280.** www.steichele.de. Main courses 8€–20€. Mon–Sat 11am–midnight; Oct–May Sun 11am–3pm. U-Bahn: Weisser Turm.

Zur Baumwolle ★ FRANCONIAN   Nürnberg restaurants don't get much cozier or more welcoming than this one. Pork roast with dunplings and saukerkraut and other rustic favorites keep a loyal crowd of locals happy; you'll share tables with them in a lamp-lit, wood-beamed, low-ceilinged room and probably be encouraged to linger over an after-dinner beer or schnapps. The German-speaking staff does an admirable job of helping outsiders work their way through the choices, which usually include a tempting array of daily specials.

Alderstrasse 18–20. ✆ **0911/227003.** www.zurbaumwolle.de. Main courses 8€–15€. Mon–Fri 11:30am–3pm and 5:30–11pm; Sat 11:30am–11pm. U-Bahn: Weisser Turm.

Exploring Nürnberg

You can easily spend a full day here seeing the sights in Nürnberg. Begin as soon as you get off the train and step into the **Handwerkerhof,** just inside the walls across from the station (an underground passage leads from the station to the top of Königstrasse, the street that cuts through the old city). In this unabashedly touristic precinct of faux-medieval cottages artisans create the products for which Nürnberg has been known since the Middle Ages: glassware, pewter (often in the form of beer mugs), intricate woodcarvings, and toys; the adjoining **Historische Bratwurst-Glöcklein** is a genuinely authentic centuries-old beer hall that serves traditional Nürnberg-style bratwurst with sauerkraut and boiled potatoes. From here follow Königstrasse through the city (in many parts closed to cars) to Hauptmarkt, the central market square, filled with kiosks stacked tall with fresh produce brought in from the countryside, and from there into the adjoining Rathausplatz and up through steep streets to the castle. Along the way you'll pass the city's standout churches, St. Lorenz and St. Sebaldus.

Albrecht Dürer House ★ HISTORIC SITE   Nürnberg's only surviving 15th-century, half-timbered burgher's house also happens to have been the home of one of its most illustrious native sons, Albrecht Dürer (1471–1528). The artist lived and worked here from 1509 to 1528, and many of his etchings and woodcuts hang in rooms filled with furnishings of the period. An English-language audio tour, narrated by Dürer's wife Agnes, introduces you to the artist, who was the son of a prosperous goldsmith, achieved considerable fame and fortune, and has had a profound effect on printmaking for the past 500 years, ever since he became known throughout Europe early in his career.

Am Tiergartnertor, Albrecht-Dürer-Strasse 39. ℂ **0911/2312568.** www.museen.nuernberg.de. Admission 5€ adults, 3€ students and children 6–18, free for children 5 and under. Tues–Fri 10am–5pm, Thurs 10am–8pm, Sat–Sun 10am–6pm; July–Sept Mon 10am–5pm.Tram: 4. Bus: 36.

Dokumentationszentrum Reichsparteitagsgelände ★★ HISTORIC SITE

Adolf Hitler famously made Nürnberg the locale for his massive Nazi rallies, and he commissioned his architect, Albert Speer, to design a congress hall and assembly grounds in the grandiose, neoclassical style the Führer favored. The war prevented either from being completed, and the unfinished congress hall now houses modern, bunkerlike, concrete and brick galleries filled with photographic displays that document the rise and fall of Nazi Germany. Displays (texts are in German but translated in English-language audiotapes) chronicle Hitler's rise to power, celebrated during the Nürnberg rallies when hundreds of thousands of civilians and soldiers gathered on the adjacent Zeppelinwiese (Zeppelin Field) to listen to Hitler rant at more than 100,000 spectators enthralled by his violent denunciations. Mixed in are coverage of the Nürnberg laws, which stripped non-Aryans of their rights, and the ensuing Holocaust. The focus is on the role of propaganda in elevating Hitler to a mythic character but begs the question of how a civilized nation let itself descend to such horror. At least the center raises the issues, and it's encouraging to see the exhibits so well attended by young people for whom the war is just another part of the distant past.

Bayernstrasse 110. ℂ **0911/2315666.** www.museen.nuernberg.de. Admission 5€ adults, 3€ students and children, 5.50€ 1 adult and up to 3 children, 11€ 2 adults and up to 3 children. Mon–Fri 9am–6pm; Sat–Sun 10am–6pm. S-Bahn: 2 to Dutzendteich. Bus: 36 from the city center is the easiest way to reach the center.

Germanisches Nationalmuseum (Germanic National Museum) ★★

GALLERY   Germany's largest museum of art and culture spans the millennia to show off painting, sculpture, crafts, arms and armor, early scientific instruments—if it's part of Germany's national heritage, it's here. This bright, well-designed museum built around a Carthusian monastery and cloister, is the equivalent of the Smithsonian Institution or the British Museum, with masterpiece-filled art galleries appended. A tour begins before you even get inside the door, with the Way of Human Rights. Here 29 columns are inscribed, in different languages, with the Universal Declaration of Human Rights, adapted by the U.N. General Assembly in 1948; an oak tree stands in for those individuals who are not represented by one of the languages on the pillars, and the overall effect is especially haunting in this city that once laid such waste to human rights. No matter how pressed you are for time, find your way to the Old Master-packed painting galleries to see "Portrait Diptych of Dürer's Partents," the artist's unsentimental but tender portrait of his aging parents, possibly painted as keepsakes he could take on his extensive travels in Italy and the Netherlands.

Kartäusergasse 1 (just inside the medieval walls near the Hauptbahnhof). ℂ **0911/13310.** www.gnm.de. Admission 8€ adults, 5€ children, 10€ families. Tues and Thurs–Sun 10am–6pm; Wed 10am–9pm. U-Bahn: Opernhaus.

Kaiserburg ★ LANDMARK
For 500 years, beginning in 1050, German kings and emperors ruled from this vast fortress/palace that looms above the city from its

hidden TREASURE

It's a pleasure to come upon some lesser monuments as you walk through Nürnberg. The **Schöner Brunnen (Beautiful Fountain)** on the Hauptmarkt is a stone pyramid, 18m (60 ft.) high, from 1396 that is adorned with 30 figures arranged in four tiers. Another Hauptmarkt attraction is the **Männleinlaufen clock,** set into the facade of the 14th-century Frauenkirche; seven electors of the Holy Roman Empire glide out of the clock-works at noon and prance around Emperor Charles IV. **"The Hare, a Tribute to Dürer,"** in the medieval Tiergartnerplatz, is a 1984 sculptural reference to the artist's Junger Feldchase (Young Hare), an almost photographic-quality rendering in watercolor—here the animal is depicted quite grotesquely in bronze.

hilltop at the northern edge of the Altstadt. The Knights' Hall and Imperial Hall, with heavy oak beams and frescoed ceilings, evoke all the medieval regal splendor you'd expect from chambers where Frederick Barbarossa might have settled into domesticity between campaigns to subdue the Italian peninsula. Most telling of the social hierarchy of the times is the Imperial Chapel—actually two chapels, one above the other, arranged so an emperor could worship with his court in the airy, bright upper chapel while the lesser members of his retinue prayed in the dark, dank chamber below. The castle gardens afford views across the city rooftops that might have you agreeing with Martin Luther, who opined that "Nürnberg shines throughout Germany like a sun among the moon and stars."

Burgstrasse 13. ℭ **0911/2446590.** www.schloesser.bayern.de. Admission (including all parts of the castle) 6€ adults, 4€ students, free for children 16 and under. Apr–Sept daily 9am–6pm; Oct–Mar daily 10am–4pm. Tram: 4.

Memorium Nürnberg Prozesse & Justizgebäude (Nürnberg Trials Memorial & Courthouse) ★★ HISTORIC BUILDING

In the famous war trials that began on November 20, 1945, 21 leading Nazi war criminals were tried in Courtroom 600 before the Allied International Military Tribunal for conspiracy and crimes against world peace, the rules of warfare, and humanity. Afterward, 10 were hanged. The trials became a milestone in judicial history: For the first time in history, sentences were pronounced according to the principle of the personal responsibility of the individual. The room displays photographs and documents but is still used as a functioning court, so entrance is not guaranteed—ask the guard at the door.

Bärenschanzstrasse 72. ℭ **0911/32179372.** www.memorium-nuremberg.de. Admission 5€ adults, 3€ students and children. Wed–Mon 10am–6pm. U-Bahn: Bärenschanze.

St. Lorenz-Kirche ★ CHURCH

Every element in the largest and most majestic church in Nürnberg seems to soar heavenward, which, of course, is exactly what the architects of this Gothic edifice, begun in 1270, intended. Rows of pillars disappear into the vaulting above the nave, and "The Angelic Salutation" (1519) is suspended high above the mere mortals below; Bavarian master sculptor Veit Stoss (1450–1533) carved this colorful rendition of the Annunciation in linden wood, depicting the emotion-filled moment when the Angel Gabriel tells the Virgin Mary that she will be the mother of Christ. Similarly uplifting is a tabernacle by stone sculptor Adam Kraft, whose lacey tracery in the form of a Gothic tower rises 19m (62 ft.) into the vaulting.

Kraft's eerily lifelike self-portrait in crouching position is one of the monument's supports.

Lorenzer Platz 10. ℰ **0911/2446990.** www.lorenzkirche.de. Free admission. Mon–Sat 9am–5pm; Sun 1–4pm. U-Bahn: Lorenzkirche.

St. Sebaldus-Kirche ★ CHURCH Nürnberg's oldest church, consecrated in 1273, houses the shrine of St. Sebald, a hermit who, legend has it, was son of a Danish king who married a French princess and abandoned her on their wedding night to answer the call and come to the forests around Nürnberg to preach Christianity. Sebald's knack for turning icicles into fuel made him a hit with poor peasants who couldn't afford wood. A bit antithetical to Sebald's life of self-imposed poverty is his tomb, a splendid brass monument by Nürnberg's own Peter Vischer (1455–1529), who with the aid of his five sons labored on his finest work for 11 years. The canopy and pillars are lavishly crowded with snails, dolphins, foliage and even an image of Visher himself, a stout, bearded figure wielding the tools of his trade. The church adopted the principles of the Reformation around 1525 and became Lutheran, a coup for Martin Luther, who rightly observed that Nürnberg was "Germany's eye and ear"—a reference to the 21 Nürnberg printing presses that soon began spreading Lutheran doctrines around Germany.

Albrecht-Dürer-Platz 1. ℰ **0911/2142500.** www.sebalduskirche.de. Free admission. Jan–Mar daily 9:30am–4pm; Apr–May and Oct–Dec daily 9:30am–6pm; June–Sept daily 9:30am–8pm. Sun services 8:30 and 10am. U-Bahn: Lorenzkirche.

Side Trips from Nürnberg
BAMBERG ★★
61km (38 miles) NW of Nürnberg

You'll come to this little city, set in the rolling Franconian hills where the Regnitz River flows into the Main, for two reasons: To walk down narrow cobblestone streets to see ornate mansions, palaces, and churches, with styles ranging from Romanesque to Gothic, Renaissance to baroque, up to the eclecticism of the 19th century, and to drink beer. Bamberg and beer go together like barley and hops. The town has been called "a beer drinker's Eden" (there are more breweries here than in Munich) and the average Bamberger drinks 190 liters of beer a year, making the rest of the Germans look like teetotalers by comparison. The beverage of choice in Bamberg is *Rauchbier,* a smoked beer first brewed in 1536.

GETTING THERE You can get to the **Bamberg Bahnhof** from Nürnberg in just 1 hour on trains that run about every half hour. If you're including Bayreuth on the same day trip, you can travel between the two on direct trains that run about every hour; the trip takes about 1hour and 15 minutes. For information and schedules, call ℰ **01805/996633** or visit www.bahn.com. By car you can reach Bamberg from Nürnberg on the A73.

Exploring Bamberg
For a map and other information, stop by the **Bamberg Tourist Information Office,** near the cathedral on Geyerswörthstrasse 5 (ℰ **0951/2976200;** www.bamberg.info). Office hours are Monday to Friday 9:30am to 6pm, Saturday to Sunday 9:30am to 2:30pm (Jan–Mar closed Sun). It's an easy 10-minute walk from the train station to the Domplatz in the center of the Altstadt, or you can take one of the buses from the front of the station; buy a ticket from one of the machines for 1.70€.

Altes Rathaus ★ LANDMARK In the Middle Ages, Bamberg was two towns divided by the river: the powerful ecclesiastical town of the prince-bishopric, of which it was the capital for 800 years, and the secular town of the burghers. Determined not to play favorites between the ecclesiastical and secular sections of the city, the town authorities built this Gothic structure on its own little island in the middle of the Regnitz River, halfway between the two factions—a true middle-of-the-road (or river) political stand. From the island, you get a camera-worthy view of the old, half-timbered fishermen's cottages along the banks in so-called "Little Venice."

Kaiserdom (Imperial Cathedral) ★★ CHURCH The four towers of this massive 13th-century, hillside edifice dominate the skyline and steer you to a treasure that is reason enough to come to Bamberg. Sculptor Tilman Riemenschneider (you've met him in Würzburg; see p. 140) labored for 14 years over the tombs of Emperor Heinrich II, who erected the cathedral, and the emperor's wife, Kunigunde. A bit of storytelling in stone depicts episodes from the couple's life, including Kunigunde's suspected adultery. Veit Stoss, whose beautiful and colorful carving of the Annunciation hangs above the nave of St. Lorenz-kirche in Nürnberg (see above), carved the nativity altar in the south transept when he was close to 80; he made the altar for a church in Nürnberg at the request of his son, a prior, but when his son refused to accept Protestant doctrine the altar was rejected, removed here to Bamberg, and the elder Stoss was never paid. An equestrian statue, the Bamberger Reiter, has raised questions almost since it was unveiled in the 13th century. It's been proposed that the horseman is a German emperor or, according to the Nazis, an idealized Christian king of the Middle Ages showing the way to the eastern lands they were meant to conquer. Current thought has him as Stephen, an 11th-century Hungarian king. The cathedral also houses the only papal tomb north of the Alps, that of Pope Clement II; a bishop of Bamberg, Clement served less than a year and died, possibly from poisoning, in 1047 while traveling to Rome.

Domplatz. ✆ **0951/502330.** Free admission; Diözesanmuseum 3€ adults, 2€ students and children 8–14, free for children 7 and under. May–Oct Mon–Fri 9:30am–6pm, Sat 9:30–11:30am and 12:45–6pm, Sun 12:30–1:45pm and 2:45–6pm; Nov–Apr Mon–Sat 9:30am–5pm, Sun 12:30–1:45pm and 2:45–5pm. Bus: 910.

Neue Residenz (New Residence) ★ ARCHITECTURAL SITE The palace of the prince-bishops of Bamberg has been steeped in intrigue ever since a corpse found beneath the windows of the palace in 1815 turned out to be the body of Marshal Berthier, Napoleon's chief of staff, who retired here after Napoleon was exiled to Elba. No one knows if Berthier was murdered or committed suicide. If you wish to step inside, you can join a guided tour (in German only) that shows off Gobelin tapestries, parquet floors, baroque furnishings, and possessions of these clerics with decidedly secular tastes. Upstairs, a branch of the Bayerische Staatsgalerie (Bavarian State Gallery) houses a few of the masterpieces collected by Mad King Ludwig; among them is Lucas Cranach's almost surrealistic depiction of Abraham preparing to slay his son Isaac on God's command, set against a German backdrop complete with medieval peasants. The romantic looking, rambling half-timbered Gothic structure next to the palace is the Alte Hofhaltung, the residence of the prince-bishops until the Neue Residence replaced it in the 17th century.

Domplatz 8. ✆ **0951/519390.** www.schloesser.bayern.de. Admission 4.50€ adults, 3.50€ children. Apr–Sept daily 9am–6pm; Oct–Mar daily 10am–4pm. Bus: 910.

Where to Eat

Historischer Brauereiausschank Schlenkerla ★ FRANCONIAN Dark, rustic, and genuinely *gemütlich* (cozy), this 600-year-old beer hall is filled with long tables where locals gather for such favorites as *Bierbrauervesper* (Brewmaster's Break, with smoked meat and sour-milk cheese) and *Rauchschinken* (smoked ham). It's all washed down with the house's own hearty malt, *Rauchbier,* infused with a smoky aroma and dispensed from oak barrels.

Dominikanerstrasse 6. © **0951/56060.** www.schlenkerla.de. Main courses 7€–12€. No credit cards. Daily 9:30am–11:30pm. Bus: 910.

Zum Sternia ★ FRANCONIAN   Even older than the Schlenkeria is this wursthaus from 1380, where you can settle onto a well-burnished bench and tuck into liver dumplings and saukerkraut or a big platter of wurst. There's no question about what to drink, and your server will gladly steer you to a local brew.

Langestrasse 46. © **0951/28750.** Main courses 6€–15€. No credit cards. Daily 10am–11pm. Bus: 905 or 921.

BAYREUTH ★★

64km (40 miles) E of Bamberg, 92km (57 miles) NE of Nürnberg

Nearly everything you'll want to see in this little city set amid rolling hills is related in some way to two extraordinary past residents, Richard Wagner and Margravine Wilhelmine. The legacy of Wagner (1813–83) includes an annual festival of Wagner operas in the Festspielhaus, the concert hall he built, and Haus Wahnfried (Richard-Wagner-Museum), where the composer lived and is buried.

Even without this Wagner connection Bayreuth would stand out on the Bavarian landscapes, thanks to Margravine Wilhelmine (1709–58), sister of Prussian King Frederick the Great, a granddaughter of Britain's King George I, and an outsized personality who shaped the city's cultural and architectural landscape. A gifted artist, writer, composer, and decorator, Wilhelmine set about turning Bayreuth into a German Versailles. She commissioned the building of the *Markgräfliches Opernhaus* (Margraves' Opera House), one of the finest and best preserved Baroque theatres in Europe, and the *Neues Schloss* (New Castle), in which nearly all the rooms have retained their original Baroque and Rococo decor. She also transformed *Schloss Eremitage* (Hermitage Castle) into a glamorous country seat with a grand English-style garden. You can easily spend half a day here seeing so much creative outpouring of past centuries.

GETTING THERE   Express trains arrive from Nürnberg every hour and the trip takes about an hour. If you're including Bamberg on the same day trip, you can travel between the two on direct trains that run about every hour; the trip takes about 1hour and 15 minutes. For information and schedules, call © **01805/996633** or visit www.bahn.com. Access by car from Nürnberg is via the A9 Autobahn from the north and south. If you're traveling between Bayreuth and Bamberg, they're about 75km (44 miles) apart on the A73, about a 50-minute drive.

Exploring Bayreuth

Much of the inner city is closed to cars and the city is small enough so that you can see almost everything on foot. If you're arriving by train, however, you'll save time by taking bus no. 5 from the train station to the Festspielhaus and beginning a our there; fare is 1.60€ and you can buy tickets from machines at the bus stops. You'll need to take a bus (no. 22) or a taxi to reach Schloss Eremitage. **Tourist-Information** is in the center of town at Opernstrasse 22 (© **0921/88588;** www.tourismus.bayreuth.de), open Monday to Saturday 9am to 6pm. From May to October, it is also open Sunday 10am to 2pm.

Altes Schloss Eremitage (Hermitage) ★ ARCHITECTURAL SITE   When Bayreuth's ebullient Margravine Wilhelmine was presented with a complex of buildings as a birthday present, she transformed the previous owner's faux-hermitage into a glamorous country palace with an English-style garden and approached by a long drive lined with cypresses she had planted in honor of her brother and confidant, Frederick the Great. (Wilhelmine was a Prussian princess; her husband, Frederich, was Margrave of Bayreuth, a hereditary title passed down from the Middle Ages.) Wilhelmine gathered her salon of artists and intellectuals here (Voltaire was a visitor to Bayreuth) and she wrote her memoirs in the elaborately decorated **Chinesisches Spiegelkabinett (Chinese Mirror Chamber),** in which the shattered, fragmented pieces are said to be her response to aging and vanity.

On Rte. 22, 5km (3 miles) northeast of Bayreuth toward Weidenberg. © **0921/759690.** www. schloesser.bayern.de. Gardens free; palace 4.50€ adults, free for children 17 and under. Gardens daily 24 hr. Palace Apr–Sept daily 9am–6pm; Oct 1–15 daily 10am–4pm. Closed Oct 16–Mar. Bus: 302, 303.

Festspielhaus ★ THE PERFORMING ARTS   The operas of Wagner are dispensed like a musical Eucharist to Wagnerian pilgrims at the Festspielhaus, the opera house he built with the backing of King Ludwig II of Bavaria. Tickets to the Richard Wagner opera festival held in this huge hall, one of the largest opera houses in Europe, are almost impossible to obtain; there's an 8-year waiting list. You may, however, visit the theater on guided tours (in German) and see the huge stage capable of swallowing up Valhalla and all sorts of other innovations meant to make good Wagner's promise to fans, upon laying the cornerstone in 1872, that "they'd see the "unveiling and clear presentation of onstage images that will seem to rise up before you from an ideal world of dreams and reveal to you the whole reality of a noble art's most meaningful illusion." Productions have been a family affair almost ever since the epic 15-hour "Ring" cycle was first presented here in 1876: When the composer died in Venice, his wife, Cosima, took over, and his grandsons, Wolfgang and Wieland, have produced the operas in the post-World War II years.

Am Festspielhügel 1–2. © **0921/78780.** www.bayreuther-festspiele.de. Guided tour 5€. Tours offered in German only; English leaflets are available. Sept–May Tues–Sun at 10 and 2pm. Tours may not be given during rehearsals or at festival time. Bus: 305.

Franz-Liszt-Museum ★ HISTORIC SITE   Wagner's wife, Cosima (1837–1930), was the daughter of Franz Liszt (1811–86), the great Hungarian-born composer and piano virtuoso who revolutionized piano playing. The composer lived and died in Bayreuth, and now rests in the local cemetery. The museum shows the room where the composer died, and displays memorabilia related to his life and work.

Wahnfriedstrasse 9. © **0921/5166488.** Admission 2€. Sept–June daily 10am–noon and 2–5pm; July–Aug daily 10am–5pm. Bus: 302 or 307 to Villa Wahnfried.

Haus Wahnfried (Richard-Wagner-Museum) ★ HISTORIC SITE   King Ludwig II gave Wagner the funds to build this comfortable little manor, where he lived from 1874 until his death in Venice of a heart attack in 1883. His wife, Cosima, 24 years his junior, remained in the house for 47 more years, becoming known as the "mistress of Bayreuth." Although Cosima is credited with maintaining a firm grip on Wagnerian productions and preserving the composer's artistic intentions, she also shared his anti-Semitism and belief in the superiority of Germanic peoples. She died in 1930, just before Hitler came to power, but it's been suggested that her influence was a factor in the Nazis' appropriation of Wagnerian music. Collections in the museum include furniture, manuscripts, pianos, and Wagner's death mask, as well as the history of the Bayreuth Festival. Wagner and Cosima are buried in front of a small rotunda at the end of the garden.

Richard-Wagner-Strasse 48. 🕐 **0921/757280.** www.wagnermuseum.de. Admission 4.50€. Apr–Oct daily 9am–5pm (Tues and Thurs until 8pm); Nov–Mar daily 10am–5pm. Bus: 2.

Markgräfliches Opernhaus (Margravial Opera House) ★ THE PERFORMING ARTS   Behind the weathered wooden doors of one of the finest and best preserved Baroque theatres in Europe is an ornate interior constructed entirely of wood, glowing with vivid reds and greens and festooned with gilded stuccowork and chandeliers. The house was built under the auspices of the Margravine Wilhelmine, and formally opened by her brother, Friedrich the Great, in 1748. The theater seats 520 and is used for Bayreuth's other festival, the Musica Bayreuth, usually held late in May. Concerts are also given during the summer.

Opernstrasse. 🕐 **0921/7596922.** www.schloesser.bayern.de. Guided tours (in German only) admission 5.50€ adults, free for children 5 and under. Apr–Sept daily 9am–6pm; Oct–Mar daily 10am–4pm. Bus: 302.

Neues Schloss (New Palace) ★★ ARCHITECTURAL SITE   Margravine Wilhelmine's love of the airy, flowered Rococo style shows through in this three-story horseshoe-shaped structure completed in 1754, shortly after the Margravine and her husband came into his inheritance. The decor created by the Italian stucco-master Pedrozzi is particularly evident in the Mirror Room, the Japanese Room, and the Music Room. The creative freedom the Margravine enjoyed in Bayreuth may well have counteracted a miserable childhood at the hands of distant royal parents and a sadistic governess who came close to crippling her; she was married off to the Margrave of Bayreuth against her wishes, and his, as he was in love with her sister, and his infidelities caused her no small amount of embarrassment in the court of Bayreuth. The Margravine, her husband, and daughter are buried in the nearby Schlosskirche (Castle Church), a lovely single-aisled church painted rose-pink and decorated with stuccowork.

Ludwigstrasse (1 block from the Markgräfliches Opernhaus). 🕐 **0921/759690.** www.schloss. bayern.de. Guided tours (in German, with English leaflets available) 5.50€ adults, free for children 17 and under. Tours Apr–Sept daily 9am–6pm; Oct–Mar Tues–Sun 10am–4pm. Bus: 314.

Where to Eat

Hansl's Wood Oven Pizzeria ★ PIZZA   For a quick bite join locals who flock to this little place that's known for the best pizza for miles around, embellished with a huge choice of toppings.

Fredrichstrasse 15. 🕐 **0921/54344.** Pizzas 5€–10€. No credit cards. Daily 7am–11pm.

Oskar's ★ FRANCONIAN/INTERNATIONAL   A large central dining room, designed like a greenhouse and flooded with sunlight, and a trio of smaller, cozier, wood-paneled *Stuben* offer some of the best value in a town that's not particularly noted for reasonable prices. The kitchen serves all day into the early-morning hours, sending out lots of old-fashioned Franconian favorites, such as loin of beef with horse-radish sauce and Bayreuther-style *Klos* (potato dumplings), as well big platters of sausages, hearty breakfasts, snacks—the menu is large and the service is friendly.

Maximilianstrasse 33. 🕐 **0921/5160553.** www.oskar-bayreuth.de. Main courses 5.50€–14€. Mon–Sat 8am–1am; Sun 9am–1pm.

REGENSBURG ★★★

100km (62 miles) SE of Nürnberg, 122km (76 miles) NE of Munich

You have some compelling reasons to get off the beaten track and come to Regensburg, one of Germany's best-preserved medieval cities and the only one to remain completely unscathed by World War II bombings. Some 1,400 medieval buildings have survived and create a jumble of steep, red-tiled roofs above narrow lanes and lively squares. Strategically poised on the northernmost reaches of the Danube River, Regensburg was a Celtic settlement, then a Roman outpost known as Castra Regina, and the center from which, beginning in the 7th century, Christianity spread throughout Germany and even into central Europe via the river. Regensburg was also a major hub for trade, and by the 12th century the town was pouring its wealth into churches, towers, and some genuinely lovely houses and public buildings. Some of Regensburg's more famous contemporary residents have been Oskar Schindler, Pope Benedict, and the princely Thom und Taxis family, whose palace you can visit.

Essentials

GETTING THERE

BY TRAIN   The Regensburg **Hauptbahnhof** is on major rail lines, including Passau-Regensburg-Nürnberg and Munich-Landshut-Regensburg, with frequent connections in all directions. From Munich, more than 20 trains arrive daily (trip time: 1½ hr.); from Nürnberg, 12 direct trains daily (trip time 1 hr. 15 min.; and from Frankfurt, 7 direct trains daily (trip time: 3 hr.). For rail information and schedules, call ✆ **01805/996633** or visit www.bahn.com.

BY BUS   Regional buses service the nearby towns. For information about routes, scheduling, and prices of buses operating within the region, contact the **Regensburger Verkehrsverbund** (RVV; ✆ **0941/463190;** www.rvv.de) for information. For longer domestic or international stretches Munich or Nürnberg make better departure points.

BY CAR   Access by car is via the A3 Autobahn from east and west and the A93 from north and south.

GETTING AROUND

Nearly all places of interest to visitors are in **Regensberg's Altstadt (Old Town).** It's an easy 10-minute stroll from the Hauptbahnhof to the town's medieval core, and the walk takes you through the also-attractive 19th-century commercial district that expanded beyond the now-demolished medieval walls; almost the entire area is closed to car traffic. You can also hop onto one of the bright yellow Altstadt buses that line up along Maximilianstrasse, next to the station. One-way fare is 1€, and a day ticket valid for up to five people costs 2€ and must be purchased on the bus. Buses run at 6-minute intervals every Monday to Friday 8:30am to 8:30pm but there's no service on Saturday and Sunday.

VISITOR INFORMATION

Contact **Tourist-Information,** Rathausplatz 3 (✆ **0941/5074410;** www.tourismus.regensburg.de). Hours are year-round Monday to Friday 9am to 6pm, Saturday 9am to 4pm, and Sunday 9:30am to 4pm; between November and March, Sunday hours are 9:30am to 2:30pm.

Where to Stay

Bischofshof am Dom ★   A former ecclesiastical academy established by the bishops of Regensburg is the town's only serious contender to the Orphée (below)

when it comes to character, providing lodgings that are traditional yet surprisingly informal, even a bit quirky. Many face a sunny inner garden behind the cathedral, and all are individually decorated—some in English country house style, others dip into contemporary urbanity. An atmospheric *Weinstube* (wine bar) downstairs spills into a beer garden, taking the edge off any stuffiness the rather grandiose surroundings might suggest.

Krauterermarkt 3. © **0941/58460.** Fax 0941/5846146. www.hotel-bischofshof.de. 55 units. 138€–148€ double; 195€ suite. Rates include continental breakfast. Parking 12€. Bus: Altstadt bus or 1. **Amenities:** Restaurant; bar; free Wi-Fi.

Orphée Grosses Haus ★★★ Any one of this trio of delightful hotels would be a top choice for a stay in Regensburg. For sheer opulence it's hard to resist the **Grand Hotel Orphée** (Grosses Haus, in German), a baroque house at Untere Bachgasse 8, where ornate ceilings and elaborate furnishings will make you feel like German nobility; many of the huge rooms are suitable for families, with day beds to accommodate extra guests and plenty of parquet expanses to spare. The **Petit Hotel Orphée** (Kleines Haus, in German) at Wahlenstrasse 1 occupies the former home of a prosperous merchant clan and offers distinctive rooms individually furnished with antique washstands and bedsteads, rich fabrics, and welcoming couches and armchairs (there's no reception; you'll get the key from the Grand Hotel Orphée around the corner). **Country Manor Orphée,** Andreasstrasse 26, is across the Steinerne Brücke (Stone Bridge) from the Altstadt and spreads across the second floor of a 16th-century salt warehouse; 6 of the 10 tile-floored, casually chic apartments (all with kitchenettes) open to patios overlooking the Danube.

Grand Hotel Orphée at Untere Bachgasse 8; Petit Hotel Orphée at Wahlenstrasse 1; Country Manor Orphée at Andreasstrasse 26. www.hotel-orphee.de. © **0941/596020** for Grand Hotel Orphée and Petit Hotel Orphée; © **0941/59602300** for Country Manor Orphée. 25 units in Grand Hotel Orphée, 15 units in Petit Hotel Orphée, 10 units in Country Manor Orphée. 125€–195€ in Grand Hotel Orphée; 75€–175€ in Petit Hotel Orphée; 135€–155€ in Country Manor Orphée. Rates include continental breakfast. Parking 6€. **Amenities:** Restaurant; bar; free in-room Wi-Fi in some.

Where to Eat

Historiche Wurstkuchl ★ BAVARIAN The Historic Sausage Kitchen opened 900 years ago to feed crews building the adjacent Steinerne Brücke (Stone Bridge) and ever since has been serving the delectable little bratwursts, cooked over beechwood fires in the small kitchen. These days the place dispenses more than 6,000 sausages a day, serving 6, 8, or 10 to a platter, accompanied by house-made, grainy mustard, saukerkraut or potato salad, and bread and washed down with the house beer. In decent weather you can enjoy the feast outdoors at one of the picnic tables beneath the bridge or at other times squeeze past the kitchen into the tiny dining room. Only floodwaters put a dent in business here—they frequently close the place down, as watermarks on the walls testify.

Thundorferstrasse 3. © **0941/46621.** www.wurstkuchl.de. Platters 7.50€–12€. Cash only. Apr–Oct daily 8am–7pm; Nov–Mar Sun 8am–3pm. Bus: Steine Brücke.

Haus Heuport ★ BAVARIAN/INTERNATIONAL You'll be smitten with the views of the magnificent facade of the cathedral, but the meal, service, and surroundings—a heavy-beamed Gothic hall or sunny cobbled terrace—will also win you over. You can opt for the traditional pork roast or duck breast choices or venture into some of the kitchen's successful creative ventures, such as salmon with Tyrolean bacon or a lasagna with pike and spinach. This is a popular spot for breakfast and Sunday brunch, and the cozy ambiance plus views plus hearty fare combine for a good start to a day.

Domplatz 7. © **0941/5999297.** www.heuport.de. Reservations recommended. Main courses 7€–25€; fixed-price menu 38€, 45€ with wine pairing. Daily 9am–11pm. Bus: Altstadt bus or 1.

Restaurant Orphée ★★ FRENCH No matter how enamored you are of German cooking and Hofbrauhaus environs, take a quick trip to Paris in this delightful dining room that pronounces itself to be the most authentic French bistro east of the Rhine. Wainscoting, watercolors, wicker chairs, and the rest of the 1890s decor make good the claim, as does a big selection of homey bistro classics—from crepes to quiche to cote d'agneau, accompanied by French wines and service that, thankfully, is a lot more warmly Bavarian than snooty Parisian. This hospitable place, on the ground floor of the main house of the Hotel Orphée, is open just about all the time, welcoming guests for coffee, wine, snacks, or any meal of the day.

Unterre Bachgasse 8. (✆ **0941/52977.** www.hotel-orphee.de. Reservations recommended. Main courses 12€–30€; fixed-price dinners 40€. Mon–Sat 6–10:30pm. Bus: Altstadt bus or 1.

Exploring Regensburg

Start your explorations with a panoramic view of the roofs and spires of the Altstadt (Old Town) from the 12th-century Steinerne Brücke (Stone Bridge), built between 1135 and 1146 and spanning the Danube on 16 arches. A major engineering feat in its day, the bridge opened up land routes between northern Europe and Venice, making Regensburg a major trading center. For a quick trip back to the Middle Ages, stroll down Hinter der Grieb, an ancient alleyway lined with 15th-century houses with high towers.

Dom St. Peter's ★ CHURCH The town's most majestic edifice has towered over the Domplatz since the 13th century, though its formidable presence is deceiving—constructed with easily eroded limestone and green sandstone, this French Gothic cathedral is continually deteriorating and constantly in need of shoring up. Even the massive spires that tower high above Regensburg's red roofs are 1950s makeovers, fortified with more durable materials. Two little stone gremlins in niches on either side of the main entrance are known as "The Devil" and "The Devil's Grandmother," suggesting that evil in any guise is to be left at the door. In the cathedral beyond, salvation takes on a refreshingly humane guise. Soaring vaulting suggests a protective canopy under which all are welcome and acres of sumptuous stained glass seems to embrace the faithful in light and color; the most famous panel is of St. Peter, holding his telltale key to the kingdom, and is 1 of more than 100 images of the saint in the nave and chapels. The most popular figure, though, is the Archangel Gabriel, a happy-looking fellow affixed to a pillar near the altar with a big grin on his face, suggesting that fire and brimstone aside, divine salvation can be a pretty happy business. The cathedral is home to the world's oldest boys' choir, the 1,000-year-old Chor Dompatzen, which performs every Sunday morning at 10am mass, open to all.

Domplatz. (✆ **0941/5865500.** www.regensburger-dom.de. Free admission. Mon–Sat 8am–5pm; Sun noon–4pm. Bus: 1, 2, 6, or 11.

Domschatzmuseum and Diözesanmuseum St. Ulrich ★ HISTORIC SITE Scattered around the cathedral precincts is wealth of ecclesiastical treasures, including gold and textiles in the Domschatzmuseum, testimony to Regensburg's role as a textile center, and statuary the church has collected since the 11th century in St. Ulrich, an appropriately early Gothic building to one side of the cathedral.

Domplatz 2. (✆ **0941/51688.** Admission 3€ adults, 1€ for students and children 13 and under. Bus: 1, 2, 6, or 11.

Historisches Museum (History Museum) ★ HISTORIC SITE The Romans established a garrison town they called Castra Regrina that became their power base on the upper Danube. Though the encampment covered an area of almost 25 hectares

(62 acres), not much remains. The ancient **Porta Praetoria,** behind the cathedral, is the most impressive reminder, and through the grille beside the eastern tower you can see the original level of the Roman street, nearly 3m (10 ft.) below—which is why you often have to step down into the churches of Regensburg. Other Roman artifacts are showcased in this former monastery and include a stone tablet noting the establishment of the garrison, an altar to the god Mercury, and several Christian tombstones from the late Roman period. You'll also encounter Albrecht Altdorfer (1480–1538), a Regensburg master of the so-called Danube School; look closely at his colorful canvases of biblical scenes and you'll notice Bavarian landscapes and distinctly Germanic medieval towns in the backgrounds.

Dachauplatz 2–4. (𝄞 **0941/5072448.** www.regensburg.de/museumsportal. Admission 2.20€ adults; 1.10€ students, seniors, and children 8 to 18; 4.40€ for a family ticket; free for children 7 and under. Tues–Wed and Fri–Sun 10am–4pm; Thurs 10am–8pm.

AUGSBURG ★

150km (93 miles) SW of Regensburg, 68km (42 miles) NW of Munich,

The largest town along the Romantic Road, with a population of about 260,000, was founded some 2,000 years ago by the Roman emperor Augustus and reached its cultural heydays during the Renaissance. You probably won't want to spend a long time in Augsburg—a big industrial center, it's not as attractive and atmospheric as the smaller towns along the Romantic Road and not nearly as cosmopolitan and fun as Munich, less than an hour away. That said, Augsburg is a worth a stopover as you travel along the Romantic Road to spend a few hours exploring its churches; to see the Fuggerei, a medieval housing project for the poor; and to take in the lively ambiance of a university town.

Essentials
GETTING THERE
BY TRAIN   About 90 InterCity trains arrive here daily from all major German cities. For information, call (𝄞 **01805/996633** or visit www.bahn.com. There are 60 trains a day from Munich (trip time: 30–50 min.) and 35 from Frankfurt (3–4½ hr.).

BY BUS   For bus service along the Romantic Road, see "Bus Tours of the Romantic Road," at the beginning of this chapter.

BY CAR   Access is via the A8 Autobahn east and west. From Donauwörth, take Rte. 2 south.

VISITOR INFORMATION
Contact **Tourist-Information,** Schiessgrabenstrasse 14 (𝄞 **0821/502070;** www.regio-augsburg.de), open Monday to Friday 9am to 6pm.

GETTING AROUND   The Augsburger Verkehrs Verbund Gmbh (𝄞 **0821/157000;** www.avv-augsburg.de) oversees the public transportation in Augsburg, consisting of four tram lines and 31 bus lines. They operate daily from 5am to midnight. It's about a 10-minute walk from the station to the Rathausplatz at the center of the Altstadt (Old Town), along Prinzregentenstrasse and Grottenau Karlstrasse.

Where to Stay
You probably won't want to go out of your way to stay in Augsburg, but if you need to, you'll find the hotel scene focuses more on function than flair. A lot of international chains have outlets here, serving the city's business and convention customers.

Dom Hotel ★ A choice spot across from the cathedral is not coincidental—the rather non-descript surroundings were at one time an ecclesiastical guest house, with a roster of guests who included Martin Luther. You won't find a lot of historic ambiance in the functional rooms, though those on the top floor are tucked under the rafters and are cozily beamed. In warm weather, breakfast is served in a garden beside the town's medieval fortifications.

Frauentorstrasse 8. ✆ 0821/343930. www.domhotel-augsburg.de. 52 units. 92€–135€ double. Rates include buffet breakfast. Free parking in lot; 6€ in garage. Tram: 2. **Amenities:** Exercise room; indoor heated pool; sauna, free in-room Wi-Fi.

Privat Hotel Riegele ★ For a handy place to lay your head, you can't beat the Schmid family's tidy, good-sized rooms across from the train station. Furnishings are up to date, the premises are spotless, and the in-house Restaurant Bräustüble is a friendly tavern popular with the locals who appreciate the well-prepared traditional fare.

Viktoriastrasse 4. ✆ 0821/509000. www.hotel-riegele.de. 28 units. 89€–130€ double; extra bed 25€. Rates include buffet breakfast. Free parking. **Amenities:** Restaurant; bar; room service, free in-room Wi-Fi.

Where to Eat

Rathausplatz is lined with cafes and coffee houses, and stands sell Weisswurst, a veal and pork sausage that's a local favorite.

Bayerisches Haus au Dom ★ BAVARIAN Follow up a visit to the cathedral with lunch at this cozy, wood-paneled tavern with a good-weather beer garden. You can go the traditional route with schnitzel or sausages, or eat lightly on a selection of cold cuts and cheese. A lot of regulars take a seat on the benches just to nurse a beer or two.

Johannesstrasse 4. ✆ 3497990. www.bayerischeshaus.de. Main courses 6€–15€. Mon–Fri 11am–midnight; Sat 10am–midnight; Sun 10am–11pm. Tram: 2.

Fuggerei Stube ★ BAVARIAN Connected to the historic Fuggerei, a large, *gemütlich* dining room packs in a crowd for generous portions of sauerbraten, schnitzel, potato cream soup with mushrooms, calves' liver with apples, onions, and roast potatoes, and other satisfying traditional choices. The beer foaming out of the taps here is Storchenbräu, a local brew that keeps the conversation at the communal tables flowing.

Jakoberstrasse 26. ✆ 0821/30870. www.fuggerei-stube.de. Reservations recommended. Main courses 12€–24€. Tues–Sat 11:30am–2pm and 6–11pm; Sun and public holidays 11:30am–3pm. Tram: 1.

Exploring Augsburg

Most of the sights in Augsburg are on or near **Rathausplatz.** The town's main street, **Maximilianstrasse,** is especially attractive, lined with shops and old burghers' houses and studded with fountains by the Renaissance Dutch sculptor Adrien de Vries. Step off the avenue into the courtyard of the Damenhof, or Ladies' Court, of what was once the Fugger-Stadtpalais (Fugger City Palace), one-time home of the town's wealthiest Renaissance family.

Dom St. Maria ★ CHURCH The cathedral of Augsburg has the distinction of containing the oldest stained-glass windows in the world. These severe but colorful panels, dating from the 12th century, are in the south transept and depict Old Testament prophets. They are younger than the cathedral itself, which was begun in 944, partially Gothicized in the 14th century, later redone in the Baroque style, and remade with neo-Gothic elements in the 19th century, when many of the cathedral's artworks, including an altarpiece by Hans Holbein the Elder, were acquired to augment the Gothic ambiance.

The original 11th-century bronze doors, adorned with bas-reliefs of a mixture of biblical and mythological characters, are in the adjacent **Diözesanmuseum St. Afra** (ⓒ **0821/3166333;** www.bistum-augsburg.de), open Tuesday to Saturday 10am to 5pm and Sunday noon to 6pm. Admission is 4€ for adults, and 3€ for children and students.

Hoher Weg. ⓒ **0821/3166353.** Free admission. Mon–Sat 7am–5pm; Sun noon–5pm. Tram: 1.

Fuggerei ★★ HISTORIC SITE   During the 15th and 16th centuries, Augsburg became one of Europe's wealthiest communities, mainly because of its textile industry and the political and financial clout of its two banking families, the Welsers and the Fuggers. The Welsers have long since faded away, but the Fuggers are remembered by an unusual legacy, the Fuggerei, set up in 1519, by Jakob Fugger the Rich, to house poorer Augsburgers.

The basic tenants of Europe's oldest welfare housing, laid down in 1521, are still in force today. The nominal rent of 1€ per annum (formerly one Rhenish guilder) has not changed in more than 450 years (the city council determines who gets the break—it's based on need). The only obligation is that tenants pray daily for the souls of the founders. The Fuggerei is a miniature, self-contained town with 67 identical cottages containing 147 small apartments, a church, a fountain, and a park, surrounded by walls and gates, which are shut from 10pm to 5am and guarded by a night watchman. Franz Mozart—great-grandfather of Wolfgang Amadeus Mozart—once lived here at Mittlere Gasse 14. The house next door is now the Fuggerei Museum, where rough 16th- and 17th-century furniture, wood-paneled ceilings and walls, cast-iron stove, and bric a brac of everyday life suggest that life here might have been cheap but not luxurious.

At the end of Vorderer Lech. ⓒ **0821/3198810.** www.fuggerei.de. Museum 4€ adults, 3€ students and children. Museum Apr–Sept daily 8am–8pm; Oct–Mar daily 9am–6pm. Tram: 1.

Rathaus ★ LANDMARK   The 1620 Rathaus is a German Renaissance gem, and a formidable presence on Augsburg's main square, Rathausplatz —eight stories high and commanding one end of the vast space, it must have seemed like a skyscraper to earlier sensibilities. This rather astonishing appearance is complimented with a colorful history, including a visit from Napoleon in 1820, near-total destruction in World War II bombings, and a painstakingly accurate postwar reconstruction. Nor does this visual grandeur diminish in the main town meeting hall, the Goldener Saal (Golden Chamber), with gold-leaf coffered ceilings and huge wall frescoes, or with the adjacent Perlachturm, a soaring spire capped by a distinctive dome called an "Augsburg onion." A climb to the top rewards you with a marvelous view of the old town center.

Am Rathausplatz 2. ⓒ **0821/3242120.** Admission 2€ adults, 1€ children 7–14, free for children 6 and under. Daily 10am–6pm. Tram: 1.

St. Anna ★ CHURCH   Martin Luther stayed in this former Carmelite monastery in 1518 when he was called to Augsburg to recant his revolutionary 95 Theses before a papal emissary. Even without this historic provenance, the church is a treasure, containing paintings by Lucas Cranach (who was a friend of Luther and spent time in Augsburg), the chapel of Augsburg's beneficent Fugger family, and the Goldschmiedekapelle (Goldsmith's Chapel), where the eponymous donors are buried, surrounded by frescoes depicting Herod ordering his high priests to find Christ. Augsburg's city market is next to the church.

Im Annahof 2. ⓒ **0821/450175100.** Free admission. Daily 9am–5pm. Tram: 1.

MEET THE fuggers

By the late 1400s Augsburg had become a center of banking and finance thanks to the efforts of the Fuggers, an incredibly wealthy local family. The aptly named Jakob Fugger the Rich (1459–1529) served as the Holy Roman Empire's banker and was the financier behind the Hapsburgs, who were in debt to him to the tune of some four million ducats.

Jakob was so rich and so powerful that during an exchange with Charles I he had the temerity to say, "It is well known that without my help, Your Majesty would no longer wear the crown of the Holy Roman Empire." It was this same Jakob who founded the Fuggerei, the world's first almshouses, in exchange for the daily prayers of its impoverished residents.

St. Ulrich und St. Afra Kirche ★ CHURCH   This pair of adjoining churches commemorates the 1555 Peace of Augsburg, which recognized two denominations. Lutheran St. Ulrich occupies the assembly hall of a converted monastery and Catholic St. Afra is the more elaborate, with a magnificent altar. The two namesake saints—Ulrich was a prince-bishop and Afra a virgin martyr—spend eternity next to each other in the shared crypt.

Ulrichplatz 15. ✆ **0821/345560.** Free admission. Daily 9am–5pm. Tram: 1.

Schaezlerpalais ★ ARCHITECTURAL SITE   This 60-room mansion built between 1765 and 1770 houses the Deutsche Barockgalerie (German Baroque Gallery), showcasing 17th- and 18th-century paintings by artists active in Augsburg and its surrounding vicinity. You probably won't recognize many of the names, but there are a couple of works by Hans Holbein the Elder as well as Veronese and Tiepolo. Albrecht Dürer's portrait of Jakob Fugger the Rich does justice to the Augsburg moneyman who monopolized 16th-century German banking, not unlike the Medicis in Florence. The mansion's Festsaal is an enormous banqueting hall lavishly decorated with Rococo frescoes, stuccowork, mirrors, and wall paneling. Marie Antoinette danced away the night of April 28, 1770 here.

Maximilianstrasse 46 (facing the Hercules Fountain). ✆ **0821/3244102.** www.kunstsammlungen-museen.augsburg.de. Admission 7€ adults, 5.50€ for students, children 9 and under free. Tues 10am–8pm; Wed–Sun 10am–5pm. Tram: 1.

GARMISCH-PARTENKIRCHEN ★★

97km (60 miles) SW of Munich, 117km (73 miles) SE of Augsburg

You might come to these two side-by-side villages that make up Germany's top Alpine resort to ski, to hike, to climb, or simply to gaze at some spectacular mountain scenery. A lot of European yuppies and aristocratic types also come here just to be seen, because making a wintertime appearance is Garmisch is still de rigueur in some social circles. Unless you plan on strapping on a pair of skis to test your mettle on a high-altitude run, the biggest thrill you're likely to have is ascending the Zugspitze, Germany's highest mountain, via cog railway and cable car. For that matter, seeing country folk in traditional dress, or mountain chalets bedecked with window boxes, or cattle plodding through the village lanes can be a bit of a thrill, too. Garmisch-Partenkirchen makes a nice way station on your travels between the Romantic Road towns to the north and Ludwig's castles, just to the west of here.

FOOTLOOSE ON THE hohenwege

Alpine hiking is a major summertime attraction in Garmisch-Partenkirchen. People come from around the world to roam the mountain paths (called Hohenwege, or "high ways"), enjoy nature, and watch animals in the forest. A network of funiculars and cable cars ascend to various points in the mountains where you can hike and admire the panoramic views.

An easily accessible destination is the 1,240m (4,070-ft.) **Eckbauer peak,** which lies on the southern fringe of Partenkirchen. You can take a chairlift to the top, have a drink at the Berggasthof (a guesthouse or cafe, usually in a high-altitude and rural location) and in less than an hour make the descent on relatively easy trails through a forest. The cable car departs year-round from the **Eckbauerbahn** (*℗* **08821/3469;** www.eckbauerbahn.com), adjacent to the ski stadium in Garmisch. A round-trip fare costs 12€ for adults, 7€ for children ages 6 to 16, and free for children 5 and under.

The rugged **Alpspitz region** begins about 1.6km (1 mile) southwest of Garmisch. The Kreuzeckbahn carries you up and across a rugged landscape to the lowest station of the Hochalm cable car, which then takes you up to a 1,050m-high (6,500-ft.) summit called Osterfelderkopf. The hiking trails skirt areas of wildflowers, unusual geologic features, and lush alpine meadows. Return to Garmisch on the Alpspitzbahn, a scenic 10-minute descent above gorges, cliffs, and grassy meadows. Cable cars run year-round approximately every half-hour 8:30am–4:30pm (Mar–June until 5pm, July–Aug until 5:30pm). Round-trip fare 21€ adults, 16€ kids 6–15.

Another hearty hike is through the **Partnachklam,** a gorge with a roaring stream at the bottom and sheer cliff walls rising on either side of the trail. Take the Graseck Seilbahn from its departure point at the bottom of the gorge, less than 1km (½ mile) south of Garmisch's ski stadium, and get off at the first station. The 3-minute cable car ride costs 6€ per person each way and operates from 7am to 10pm, midnight on weekends.

The tourist office supplies maps and info on these and other routes.

Essentials
GETTING THERE
BY TRAIN The **Garmisch-Partenkirchen Bahnhof** lies on the major Munich-Weilheim-Garmisch-Mittenwald-Innsbruck rail line, with frequent connections in all directions. With a change in Weilheim, you can reach Garmisch-Partenkirchen in about 2 hours from Augsburg. For information and schedules, call *℗* **01805/996633** or visit www.bahn.com. Mountain rail service to several plateaus and the Zugspitze is offered by the **Bayerische Zugspitzbahn** at Garmisch (*℗* **08821/7970;** www.zugspitze.de).

BY BUS Both long-distance and regional buses through the Bavarian Alps are provided by **RVO Regionalverkehr Oberbayern,** Finkenstrasse 3, in Garmisch-Partenkirchen (*℗* **08821/948274;** www.rvo-bus.de).

BY CAR Access is via the A95 Autobahn; exit at Eschenlohe.

VISITOR INFORMATION
Contact the **Verkehrsamt,** Richard-Strauss-Platz 2 (*℗* **08821/180700;** www.garmisch-partenkirchen.de). It's open Monday to Saturday 8am to 6pm, and Sunday and holidays 10am to noon. The tourist office arranges free bookings in local guesthouses.

GETTING AROUND

You don't need a car here, but having one makes getting around a little easier. A free municipal bus runs every 15 minutes from 6am to 8pm between the Bahnhof (train station) and Marienplatz, Garmisch's main square. A network of 10 funiculars and cable-cars departing from the train station and the borders of the town carry visitors up local peaks.

Where to Stay

A lot of townsfolk have gone into the *Gästehäus* (guesthouse) business, offering rooms in their homes, usually for 30€ to 50€per person with breakfast. The tourist office provides a list.

Gasthof Fraundorfer ★ You can't miss the frescoed facade depicting a family feast right in the middle of Partenkirchen. The subjects might be the Fraundorfers themselves, who've been welcoming guests into their cozy rooms and restaurant for more than 150 years. Furnishings are playfully Bavarian, with four-poster beds and polished wooden tables in some and sleigh beds (with colorful luges used as footboards) and fanciful log furniture in others. Some of the larger units can accommodate up five guests.

Ludwigstrasse 24. ✆ **08821/9270.** www.gasthof-fraundorfer.de. 31 units. 86€–98€ double; 115€–192€ family room for 2–5 people. Rates include buffet breakfast. Free parking. **Amenities:** Restaurant; room service; sauna; free Wi-Fi in most rooms.

Hotel-Gasthof Drei Mohren ★ A big chalet on the quiet side of Partenkirchen offers large, cozy accommodations with handsome, modern furnishings. The generous perks include big balconies overlooking the mountains in most and a restaurant and beer garden downstairs.

Ludwigstrasse 65. ✆ **08821/18974.** www.dreimohren.de. 8 units. 140€–140€ double. Rates include buffet breakfast. Free parking. **Amenities**: Restaurant; free in-room Wi-Fi.

Hotel Hilleprandt ★ A cozy, tranquil chalet near the train station lays on the Bavarian hospitality. An attractive garden and cozy living room provide plenty of space to relax, but the real treat is sitting on your own balcony and taking in the sweep of the surrounding mountains. Rooms are bright and nattily done up in a modern Bavarian style, with lots of warm wood.

Riffelstrasse 17. ✆ **08821/943040.** www.hotel-hilleprandt.de. 13 units. 94€–130€ double. Rates include buffet breakfast. Free parking. **Amenities:** Restaurant; exercise room; Jacuzzi; room service; sauna; free Wi-Fi in lobby.

Where to Eat

Braustuberl ★ BAVARIAN It doesn't get much more atmospheric than this 350-year-old brew pub where the cozy rooms are filled with well burnished rustic furnishings and the walls are covered in frescoes. There's even a pretty, good-weather beer garden out back. The kitchen lives up to its end of the deal with simple, well-prepared local specialties of the schnitzel-with-noodles variety.

Fürstenstrasse 23. ✆ **08821/2312.** www.braeustueberl-garmisch.de. Main courses 8€–16€. Daily noon–11pm.

Café Riessersee ★★ BAVARIAN/INTERNATIONAL It's a nice walk up to this cafe/restaurant on the shores of a small emerald-green lake, and this casual eatery in a waterside resort is also on the cable car route up to the Zugspitze. A late, leisurely weekend lunch in summer is accompanied by zither music, and fresh fish and game are on the dinner menu.

Riess 6 (3km/2 miles from the center of town). ⓒ **08821/95440.** www.riessersee.de. Main courses 9€–21€. Daily 11:30am–9pm.

Gasthof Fraundorder ★ BAVARIAN   One of the town's most seasoned family of innkeepers shows off their hospitality in these large, tourist-friendly rooms where old photos of mountain scenes cover the walls and the food is hearty and uncompli- cated (sausage, ham hocks with sauerkraut, and the like). Yodelers, musicians, and dancers provide Bavarian entertainment nightly, but the hokey antics don't distract the kitchen from sending out genuinely good and filling fare. The guest rooms upstairs are likewise satisfactory (see above).

Ludwigstrasse 24. ⓒ **08821/9270.** Main courses 8€–14€. Wed–Mon noon–2:30pm and 6–10pm.

Exploring the Area

The 1936 Winter Olympics put Garmisch-Partenkirchen on the map, with a lot of Nazi fanfare stealing the show from the athletes. The most famous competitor to emerge from the games was Norwegian figure skater Sonja Heine, whose twirls on the ice at the Olympic Ice Stadium earned her three gold medals, launched a Hollywood career, and made her a favorite of gossip columnists (her affairs with boxer Joe Louis and actors Tyrone Power and Van Johnson, along with her vile temper and Nazi sympa- thies, supplied plenty of juicy material). You can take a spin yourself on the three public rinks (Adlerstrasse 25, ⓒ **08821/753291;** 4.20€ adults, 2.40€ kids 6–15; public skating daily July to mid-May 11am–4pm). The Ski Stadium, with two ski jumps and a slalom course, is on the slopes at the edge of town. In 1936, more than 100,000 people watched the events in this stadium, and the World Cup Ski Jump is held here every New Year's Day.

An especially pleasant in-town excursion is along the pine-scented Philosopher's Walk at the edge of Partenkirchen, with views to the peaks that form a backdrop to the 18th-century Chapel of St. Anton.

TO THE TOP OF THE ZUGSPITZE ★★★

The tallest mountain in Germany, soaring 2,960m (9,700 ft.) above sea level, lures view seekers up its craggy slopes on a tremendously popular thrill ride. The only chal- lenge is deciding how to make the ascent, but whichever way you go, you'll be treated to phenomenal mountain views all the way up, at the top, and on the way down—pro- vided, of course, it's not snowing or the mountain is otherwise enshrouded in cloud cover, in which case the trip is pointless. One way begins on the Zugspitzbahn (cog railway), which departs from its own depot behind Garmisch-Partenkirchen's main railway station. The train travels uphill, past boulder-strewn meadows and rushing streams, to the Zugspitzplatte, a high plateau with sweeping views, where you transfer to a cable car, the Gletscherbahn, for a 4-minute ride up to the summit. The second way is to take the Zugspitzbahn for a shorter trip, disembarking at the Eibsee Sielbahn (Eibsee Cable Car), which carries you to the top. Round-trip tickets allow you to ascend one way and descend the other, in order to enjoy the widest range of spectacular views. When you reach the top, you can linger on a sunny cafe terrace before making the descent. Round-trip fares are 42€ for adults, 32€ for ages 16 to 18, and 23€ for ages 6 to 15; fares increase by about 10€ in the popular summer season. For more informa- tion, contact the **Bayerische Zugspitzbahn,** Olympiastrasse 27, Garmisch-Parten- kirchen (ⓒ **08821/7970;** www.zugspitze.de).

A HIKE TO KONIGSHAUS AM SCHACHEN ★

Perhaps with Wagner's music ringing in your ears—or, okay, "The Sound of Music"—you can hike through Alpine meadows up to the remote mountainside lodge that in 1872 King Ludwig II had built in a style that crosses a Swiss chalet with a Greek temple. The ground-floor rooms resemble those of a simple mountain dwelling, but upstairs is the "Türkische Saal" (Turkish Hall), a Moorish fantasy out of "The Arabian Nights" where low divans surround a fountain. Ludwig would sit here in Eastern attire in the company of his hookah-smoking retinue. The effect is all the more extravagant considering that teams of workers had to cart all the building materials up the mountainside. More than 1,000 species of Alpine flora grow in an adjacent botanical garden. The only way to reach the lodge is by a well-marked trail that makes a fairly easy, 10km (6-mile) ascent up the mountain. Once up there, admission is by guided tour (in German only, but guides will usually explain things in English if you ask), at 11am, 1pm, 2pm, and 3pm. 4.50€ adult, 3.50€ children, kids under 14 free; www.schloesser. bayern.de. Allow at least half a day for the hike and your time at the lodge.

Side Trip from Garmisch-Partenkirchen

OBERAMMERGAU ★

20km (12 miles) N of Garmisch-Partenkirchen

No one could ever accuse the residents of this pretty town set in a wide mountain valley of sitting around doing nothing. They put on a world-famous passion play every 10 years and in the meantime make intricate wood carvings and paint the fronts of their houses with utterly charming frescoes. You can stroll through this beehive of activity in about an hour, but you'll want to spend most of your time here just outside of town at Schloss Linderhof, the most aesthetically pleasing of King Ludwig's castles.

GETTING THERE   An unnumbered bus goes back and forth between Oberammergau and Garmisch-Partenkirchen; check with **RVO Regionalverkehr Oberbayern** in Garmisch-Partenkirchen (© **08821/948274;** www.rvo-bus.de). By car, take the A95 toward Munich and exit at Eschenlohe.

EXPLORING OBERAMMERGAU

The citizens of Oberammergau have a long tradition of painting frescoes on their houses, an ages-old approach to curb appeal known as *Lüftmalerei.* Some are based on scenes from "Hansel and Gretel," "Little Red Riding Hood" (at Ettaler Strasse 48 and 41, respectively) and other fairy tales, while others depict beer hall joviality and other typical snippets from Bavarian life. The most famous, though, is a reverential rendering of Jesus coming before Pilate in the frescoes on Pilatushaus, at Ludwig-Thoma-Strasse 10 (the headquarters of a carvers' and artisans' workshop).

For alpine experiences and great views, whisk up Berg Laber, the mountain that rises to the east of the town, and Berg Kolben, to the west. The 10-minute ascent up Berg Laber via an enclosed cable-gondola costs 17€ per person (© **08822/4770;** www. laber-bergbahn.com) for a single trip, but if you're outdoorsy, you might prefer the open-air ride up Berg Kolben via chairlift (© **08822/4760;** www.kolbensesselbahn. com) for 9.50€ round trip. The Berg Kolben cable car runs from December through October, and the chairlift is open for rides from spring into November but requires lift and run passes during the busy ski season.

The **Oberammergau Tourist Information Office** is at Eugen-Papst-Strasse 9A (© **08822/922740;** www.oberammergau.de). It's open Monday to Friday 8:30am to 6pm, and Saturday 9am to noon and 1 to 5pm.

Kloster Ettal ★ RELIGIOUS SITE   Located in a high, narrow, alpine valley, the vast Benedictine monastery of Ettal was founded in 1330 by Emperor Ludwig IV of Bavaria. The most noticeable features of its Lady Chapel are the elaborate facade and dome, part of an exuberant 18th-century makeover by Enrico Zucalli, an 18th-century Swiss architect with a passion for the Italian Baroque. The church's Italian connections go back to its origins, to a statue of the Virgin by the sculptor Giovanni Pisano (1250 – c. 1315), whose works grace so many churches throughout Tuscany. That such a grandiose church should be standing in such a relatively isolated spot harks back to its popularity as a place of pilgrimage, a magnet for the faithful who hiked through the valley to honor the Virgin Mary, the patroness of heavily Catholic Bavaria. Early visitors were shown hospitality with the cloister's much-loved liqueur and beer, both named Ettaler for a nearby peak, and you may have some, too, in the adjoining Braustuberl.

3km (2 miles) south of Oberammergau (along the road to Garmisch-Partenkirchen). ✆ 08822/740. www.kloster-ettal.de. Free admission. Daily 7am–8pm. Buses from Oberammergau leave from the Rathaus and the Bahnhof once per hour during the day.

Passiontheater (Passion Theater) ★ THE PERFORMING ARTS   Oberammergau put on its first *Passionspiele* (Passion Play) in 1634 to give thanks for being spared from the plague and has been staging the16-act drama depicting Christ's journey to the Cross almost ever since. The whole town participates, with a cast of 2,000 (actors must be natives or have lived in the town for at least 20 years) and non-actors working behind the scenes to build sets and sew costumes—one thing they don't do is make wigs or beards, since appearance-altering props are not allowed in this realistic portrayal. In extreme adherence of the age-old theatrical ploy to always leave the audience wanting more, they stage the 5½-hour epic only once every decade (in years that end in 0) in a much-anticipated season that runs from mid-May to early October. The theater does not remain dark in the years between performances; it's a much-attended venue for other drama, film, and music, and behind-the-scenes tours show off stage mechanics and the costumes and sets used for the big show. Tickets for the guided tours (some in English) include admission to the Pilatushaus workshops (see below) and the sophisticated little Oberamagau Museum, where exhibits show off the town's woodcarving and also include rotating exhibits, often of contemporary German artists working in various media.

Passionswiese 1. ✆ 08822/92310. Admission 8€ adults, 3€ children. Daily 9:30am–5:30pm.

Schloss (Castle) Linderhof ★★ ARCHITECTURAL SITE   In 1869, King Ludwig II transformed a former royal hunting lodge into a small, dazzling-white château meant to resemble the Petit Trianon at Versailles. The ornate exterior is restrained when compared to the interior, which is a riot of Neo-Rococo flashiness, glittering with gold leaf, mirrors, crystal chandeliers, and contrivances like a dining table designed to rise from the kitchens at mealtimes so the king would not have to deal with servants and could carry on, undisturbed, conversations with his imaginary dinner companions Louis XV and Marie Antoinette. Ludwig was nocturnal and spent his nights lounging and reading in the Hall of Mirrors, where the candlelight seemed to be reflected endlessly, clouding the lines between reality and unreality, not unlike the king's state of mind. The park, with its formal French gardens, is more appealing than the overwrought interiors and fascinating for its fanciful playfulness. Here, as in Neuschwanstein down the road (p. 176), you're left to wonder if Ludwig was a

SHOPPING FOR woodcarvings

Oberammergau is world famous for its woodcarving, but know before you buy you should keep in mind that even some of the most expensive "handmade" pieces may have been roughed in by machine prior to being finished off by hand. If you're a serious shopper, make your first stop the village woodcarver's school, the **Pilatushaus,** Ludwig-Thoma-Strasse 10 (© **08822/949511**), to learn the hallmarks of quality you should be looking for. You can watch local carvers, painters, and sculptors as they work from June to October, Tuesday to Sunday from 3 to 5pm. Two reliable shops with a wide range of carvings are **Holzschnitzerei Franz Barthels,** Schnitzler-gasse 4 (© **08822/4271**), and **Toni Baur,** Dorfstrasse 27 (© **08822/821**), both with a sophisticated inventory of woodcarvings crafted from maple, pine, and linden.

dreamer or just plain mad. He would retreat to the Moorish Kiosk to indulge his Arabian Nights fantasies (also played out at Konigshaus Am Schachen, above Garmisch-Patrenkirchen; see above) smoking a *chibouk* (a Turkish tobacco pipe) and having his retinue treat him as an Asian prince. In the Grotte (Grotto), an artificial cave with stalagmites and stalactites designed to re-create stage sets for Wagner's opera "Tannhäuser," he would be rowed over a waterfall-fed lake in a swan-shaped boat; his pet swans glided beside him and special lighting effects simulated the illumination in the Blue Grotto on Capri.

Bus line 9622 runs between Oberammergau (from the railway station) and Schloss Linderhof six times per day, beginning at 10:25am; the last bus leaves Linderhof at 6:56pm. Round-trip fare is 13€. For bus information, call **RVO Bus Company** (© **08821/948274;** www.rvo-bus.de) at their regional office in Garmisch-Partenkirchen. If driving from Oberammergau follow the signs to Ettal, about 5km (3 miles) away, and then go another 5km (3 miles) to Draswang; from there follow the signs to Schloss Linderhof.

Linderhof 12. © **08822/92030.** www.schlosslinderhof.de Admission to palace and grotto by guided tour only, some in English, 8.50€ adults, 7.50€ seniors/students (1€ less in winter). Parking 2€. Apr–Oct 15 daily 9am–6pm; Oct 16–Mar 10am–4pm. Closed Nov 1; Dec 24, 25, 31; Jan 1; park buildings closed Oct 16–Mar.

FÜSSEN ★

60km (37 miles) NW of Garmisch-Partenkirchen, 92km (57 miles) S of Augsburg, 119km (74 miles) SW of Munich

This little town at the southern terminus of the Romantic Road in the foothills of the Bavarian Alps is a workhorse compared to the show ponies down the road, the castles at Neuschwanstein and Hohenschwangau. But Füssen is more than just a jumping-off point and makes quite an attractive showing on its own with a cluster of gabled houses sheltering on medieval lanes beneath the Hohes Schloss, a fine Gothic castle. If you're arriving by train, you'll be traveling in good historic company: Richard Wagner used to take the train down here to visit his patron, King Ludwig II. And should you need reminding that this is an old town, the main shopping street, Reichenstrasse, follows the main street of a Roman garrison, Via Claudia.

Essentials
GETTING THERE
BY TRAIN   Trains run between Garmisch-Partenkirchen and Füssen every hour and a half and the trip takes just under 2 hours. For information, call 🕾 **01805/996633** or visit www.bahn.com.

BY BUS   For bus service along the Romantic Road, see "Bus Tours of the Romantic Road," at the beginning of this chapter. Regional service is provided by **Regional-verkehr Oberbayaern** (🕾 **089/551640;** www.rvo-bus.de), which runs 19 buses a day to the royal castles, costing 2.10€ for the 8-minute trip.

BY CAR   The trip from Garmisch-Partenkirchen to Füssen by car is via the B23 and the B17 and takes about an hour.

VISITOR INFORMATION
Contact the **Kurverwaltung,** Kaiser-Maximilian-Platz 1 (🕾 **08362/93850;** www. fuessen.de). Hours vary but are usually Monday to Friday 8:30am to 6:30pm, Saturday 9am to 2:30pm, and Sunday 10am to noon in summer; and in winter Monday to Friday 9am to 5pm and Saturday 10am to noon.

Where to Stay

Altstadt-Hotel zum Hechten ★   The same family has run this spotless guest-house just below the castle for generations but their notion of old-fashioned Bavarian hospitality goes well beyond flowerboxes at the windows. Rooms are smartly streamlined and almost contemporary in design, with sleek low-lying furnishings interspersed with some traditional pieces. Some have balconies, and all have use of a sauna and solarium.

Ritterstrasse 6. 🕾 **08362/91600.** www.hotel-hechten.com. 35 units. 94€–100€. Rates include buf-fet breakfast. **Amenities:** Restaurant, sauna, free in-room Wi-Fi.

Feriengasthof Helme ★   A traditional Bavarian guesthouse outside Schangau, just below King Ludiwg's extravaganza, supplies endless views of the mountains (and glimpses of the famous castles) and makes the most of its pretty Alpine setting, with balconies, a sunny cafe terrace downstairs, and all sorts of outdoor activities on tap. Decor in each of the individually decorated rooms takes a nice neutral tack, with lots of handsome wood, though a Ludwig room veers off into some mural-heavy extrava-gance. The in-house restaurant serves Bavarian specialties.

Mitteldorf 10 (about 5km/3 miles east of Füssen). 🕾 **08362/9800.** www.hotel-hechten.com. 10 units. 76€–118€. Rates include buffet breakfast. MC. **Amenities:** Restaurant, free in-room Wi-Fi.

Steig Mühle ★   Owners and hosts Gunter and Hedwig Buhmann provide a mod-ern take on Bavarian charm in their chaletlike guesthouse, with large, functional rooms that open onto a view of a lake or mountains; a few have some nice flourishes, like wooden ceilings or canopied beds, and many have their own balconies. This is a smart base for touring the castles, but your hosts also provide info on hiking, mountain bik-ing, and all sorts of other activities as well.

Alte Steige 3. 🕾 **08362/91760.** www.steigmuehle.de. 24 units. 68€–70€ double. Rates include buffet breakfast. No credit cards. Free outside parking; 3€ in garage. From Füssen, take Rte. 310 toward Kempten, a 5-min. drive. **Amenities:** Sauna, free Wi-Fi in public areas.

Where to Eat

Altstadt-Hotel zum Hechten ★ BAVARIAN   These comfy lodgings in the center of town extend hospitality to an inviting stube-style restaurant that adheres to the mantra if it's not from the region, it's not worth serving, or as they say it here, "everything that comes into our pots, come from our waters, fields and meadows." Schnitzel with noodles and venison goulash, served in a pleasant, paneled dining room, will amply fortify you for a walk in the surrounding mountains.

Ritterstrasse 6. ℂ **08362/91600.** www.hotel-hechten.com. Main courses 8€–18€. Daily 10am–9:30pm.

Fischerhütte ★ SEAFOOD/BAVARIAN Four paneled, old-fashioned dining rooms and a summertime beer garden at the edge of a little mountain lake are the perfect setting for a fish meal. Not all the choices here will be local—though the pan-fried trout from nearby streams is a surefire hit with locavores—but North Atlantic lobster and garlicky Provencal bouillabaisse are delicious nonetheless, and a few meat-heavy Bavarian specialties also appear on the menu.

Uferstrasse 16, Hopfen am See (5km/3 miles northwest of Füssen).ℂ **08362/91970.** www.fischer huette-hopfen.de. Reservations recommended. Main courses 12€–28€. Daily 10am–9:30pm.

Hotel Hirsch ★ BAVARIAN *Hirsch* in German means stag, and the name has more to do with the game-in-season menu than any attempt at hunting-lodge decor, which instead achieves a light, airy look with lots of blonde furniture. Ever-changing menus in the Bierstube and more formal dining room often include some memorable standouts like wild duck and trout from local rivers. Upper floors house bright, comfortably appointed and traditionally furnished bedrooms; doubles rent from around 100€.

Kaiser-Maximilian-Platz 7. ℂ **08362/93980.** www.hotelhirsch.de. Main courses 10€–18€; fixed-price menu 20€. Daily 11:30am–2pm and 6–9:30pm.

Zum Schwanen BAVARIAN A flavorful blend of Swabian and Bavarian cuisine ranges farther afield into Eastern Europe. So, along with homemade sausage and roast pork, the kitchen also prepares goulash, paprika rice, and some other hearty, non-local dishes that nonetheless seem well suited to the mountain environs. Service is attentive, and portions are generous.

Brotmarkt 4.ℂ **08362/6174.** Main courses 7€–18€. Tues–Sat 11:30am–2pm and 6:30–10pm.

Exploring Füssen

A popular walk from Füssen along a well-marked trail leads to the **Lechfall,** a waterfall less than a kilometer (½ mile) south of town. A pedestrian footbridge spans the falls, located where the Lech River squeezes through a rocky gorge and over a high ledge.

Hohes Schloss ★ HISTORICAL SITE The aptly named "High Castle," surrounded by formidable white walls and reached from the parish church below by a steep lane, was once the summer residence of the prince-bishops of Augsburg. While the coffered Rittersaal (Knight's Hall) suggests pomp and ceremony, the courtyard frescoes, providing the illusion of many more gables and windows than are actually there, add a refreshingly light touch to the otherwise somber surroundings. The princely chambers house paintings and sculptures by 15th- and 16th-century Bavarian masters, including the Sippen Altar panels from 1510, showing eight chilling scenes of plague and war.

Magnusplatz.ℂ **08362/903164.** www.fuggerei.de. Museum 3€, free for children under 13. Apr–Oct Tues–Sun 11am–4pm (Oct–Mar 2–4pm).

St. Mangkirche ★ CHURCH Magnus himself, an 8th-century Irish missionary, founded this abbey on the site of his wilderness cell, and he's buried here—or was, as his bones went missing some time in those dark ages and all that remains is a tiny sliver of clavicle that hangs above the altar. Some of the former monks' cells and some rather grand frescoed halls house the **Heimatmuseum,** one of the world's stellar collections of lutes and violins. Europe's first lute maker's guild was founded in Füssen in the 16th century. For the next 3 centuries the town was renowned for its violin makers, whose equipment is also on show. The Chapel of St. Anne is frescoed with a macabre *Totentanz* or "dance of death," a popular medieval European allegorical theme in which corpses succumb to a violin-playing specter, proving, less the faithful ever forget it, that death comes to us all.

Town center. Abbey: ℭ **08362/6190.** Admission by free tours (in German) on Tues and Thurs at 4pm and Sat at 10am (hours vary greatly throughout year; check with the tourist office). Heimatmuseum: ℭ **08362/903146.** Admission 3€. Apr–Oct Tues–Sun 10am–5pm, Nov–Mar Tues–Sun 1–4pm. Chapel of St. Anne: Free admission. Apr–Oct Tues–Sun 10am–5pm, Nov–Mar Tues–Sun 1–4pm.

Side Trip from Füssen
WIESKIRCHE ★★

One of the world's most exuberantly decorated buildings was created by Dominikus Zimmermann (1685–1766), an architect and stuccoist who worked on this Rococo masterpiece with his brother, Johann Baptist, a frescoist, from 1746 to 1754. A decade or so before work began, it was noticed that a rough-hewn statue of Christ (being scourged at the pillar) was crying. Pilgrims began flocking to the site in a remote mountain meadow, and the Zimmermans were commissioned to create a proper shrine. Behind a rather sober facade, the light-flooded interior with its enormous cupola shimmers with a superabundance of woodcarvings, gilded stucco, columns, statues, and bright frescoes. The overall effect is to make the supernatural seem present, as indeed seems to be the case for those who claim to have been cured of various ailments while praying in front of the statue. The great Dominikus was so enchanted with his creation that he built a small home in the vicinity and spent the last decade of his life here.

A bus heading for the church leaves Füssen Monday to Friday six times per day (once per day on the weekend); check the timetable at the station for bus information or ask at the Füssen tourist office (see above). If you're driving, follow B17 23km (14 miles) north from Fussen to Steingaden, and signs from there indicate the way 3km (2 miles) south to Wies. The church is open daily from 8am to 6pm in summer and 8am to 8pm in summer (ℭ **08862/501;** www.wieskirche.de).

NEUSCHWANSTEIN ★★★ & HOHENSCHWANGAU ★

7km (4 miles) E of Füssen

Just east of Füssen are the two "Royal Castles" of Hohenschwangau and Neuschwanstein. Maximilian II built Hohenschwangau atop a medieval ruin in 1836; his son, King Ludwig II, began the extravagantly romantic Neuschwanstein on an adjoining hilltop in the 1860s. These two royal castles combine fantasy and beautiful settings amid Alpine peaks and valleys and will probably be your most memorable stop along the Romantic Road.

Most fanciful of the two is multi-turreted Neuschwanstein, perched high on a crag and the ultimate fantasy creation of Ludwig, the strange, self-obsessed monarch who has become one of the legendary figures in Bavarian history. Neuschawanstein was one of many excesses that eventually threatened to bankrupt the kingdom, and in 1886, at age 41 and before his castle was completed, Ludwig was declared insane. Three days later, he was found drowned in Lake Starnberg on the outskirts of Munich, along with the physician who had declared him unfit. It has never been determined if Ludwig was murdered or committed suicide. He has been the subject of biographies, films, plays, and even a musical, and his dream castle has drawn millions of visitors to this part of Bavaria over the years.

Essentials

GETTING THERE   By Bus   Nineteen buses a day arrive from Füssen (see above). **By Car**   Head east from Füssen along the B17.

VISITOR INFORMATION   Information about the region and the castles is available at the **Kurverwaltung,** Kaiser-Maximilian-Platz 1, Füssen (℡ **08362/93850**). Hours vary but are usually Monday to Friday 8:30am to 6:30pm and Saturday 9am to 2:30pm in summer; in winter, hours are Monday to Friday 9am to 5pm and Saturday 10am to noon. Information is also available at the **Kurverwaltung in the Rathaus,** Münchenerstrasse 2, Schwangau (℡ **08362/938523**), open Monday through Friday from 9am to 5pm and Saturday from 10am to 1pm.

Visiting the Royal Castles

The royal castles of Hohenschwangau and Neuschwanstein are the most popular tourist attractions in Germany, receiving nearly a million visitors a year. Be prepared for long lines (sometimes up to 3 hr.) in the summer, especially in August. To save yourself time, try to arrive as soon as the castles open in the morning.

A ticket office near the parking lot of the castles sells tickets for both Hohenschwangau and Neuschwanstein. You can see the castles only on guided tours, which last about 35 minutes each. Tours in English are available throughout the day. A tour number and entry time are printed on your ticket. A digital sign informs you when your tour is ready. When the time comes, feed your ticket into the turnstile in front of the respective castle. The tour guide will meet you inside. *Note:* It is imperative to arrive by the time indicated on your ticket; otherwise, you will have to go back to the kiosk at the base and pick up a new ticket and start all over again.

HOHENSCHWANGAU ★

Ludwig II's father, Crown Prince Maximilian (later Maximilian II) purchased the 12th-century castle of the knights of Schwangau in 1832 and had it completely restored in faux medieval style. This decorative scheme comes to the fore in the Hall of the Swan Knight, named for the wall paintings depicting the saga of Lohengrin (a Germanic hero associated with the swan; the name of the castle literally translates as High Swan County Palace). Ludwig II spent much of his joyless childhood at Hohenschwangau with his strait-laced father and his mother, Queen Maria of Prussia. As a young man he received Richard Wagner in its chambers; the music room on the second floor contains copies of letters between Ludwig II and the composer, and the grand piano on which the two played duets.

Although Hohenschwangau has the comfortable air of a home, the heavily Gothic halls and chambers recall knights' castles of the Middle Ages. Maximillian's restorations were part of a 19th-century European craze for re-creating medieval settings—his son would take the concept to new extremes with Neuschwanstein, on an adjoining mountaintop.

Hohenschwangau, Alpseestrasse (☎ **08362/930830**), is open April to September daily 8am to 5:30pm, and October to March daily 9am to 3:30pm. Admission is 12€ for adults and 8€ for students and children 12 to 15; children 11 and under enter free. Several parking lots serve both castles.

NEUSCHWANSTEIN ★★★

Reaching Neuschwanstein involves a steep half-mile climb from the parking lot at Hohenschwangau Castle (see above). You may take a bus to Marienbrücke, a bridge that crosses over the Pöllat Gorge at a height of 90m (300 ft.). From that vantage point, you, like Ludwig, can stand and meditate on the glories of the castle and its panoramic surroundings. If you want to photograph the castle, do it from here instead of at the top of the hill, where you'll be too close for a good shot. It costs 1.80€ for the bus ride up to the bridge or 1€ to return. From Marienbrücke, it's a 10-minute walk to Neuschwanstein castle. This footpath is very steep.

The traditional way to reach Neuschwanstein is by horse-drawn carriage; this costs 6€ for the ascent and 3€ for the descent. *Note:* Some visitors have complained about the rides being overcrowded and not at all accessible for those with limited mobility. Also note there is no guarantee of arrival time and if you miss your timed entry, you're out of luck. Our recommendation is to avoid the ride unless you have plenty of time to wait in line and make the ascent before your timed entry into the castle.

King Ludwig II's folly floats in the clouds atop a rugged hilltop above little villages and mountain lakes, his romantic homage to the Middle Ages and to the Germanic mythology evoked in the music of Richard Wagner. As Ludwig wrote to the composer, "It will also remind you of 'Tannhäuser' (Singers' Hall with a view of the castle in the background), 'Lohengrin' (castle courtyard, open corridor, path to the chapel). . . ." He began work on the castle in 1868, shortly after the death of his grandfather, Ludwig I, left him with a considerable private fortune. Construction continued for 17 years until the king's sudden death in 1886, when all work stopped, leaving a part of the interior uncompleted. Ludwig watched the construction of his dream palace through a telescope from neighboring Hohenschwangau. Between 1884 and 1886, the king lived in Neuschwanstein on and off for 170 days. He was at Neuschwanstein when he received news of his dethronement, on the basis of mental instability. Three days later he was found dead.

Just as Ludwig built Neuschwanstein to recreate legend, his ersatz version of a distant past has become the iconic European castle—appropriated most famously by Walt Disney as Cinderella's Castle. It's no accident that one of Ludwig's designers was the Wagnerian set designer Christian Janck, who ensured that almost every room suggest legend and saga. The king's study is decorated with painted scenes from the medieval legend of Tannhäuser. Murals in the king's bedroom portray the doomed lovers Tristan and Isolde (a mood reinforced by scenery—through the balcony window you can see a waterfall in the Pöllat Gorge, with the mountains in the distance). The Sängerhalle (Singer's Hall) takes up almost the entire fourth floor and is modeled after Wartburg castle in Eisenach, the site of song contests in the Middle Ages; frescoes depict the life of Parsifal, a mythical medieval knight. Ludwig's illusions of grandeur come quite forcibly to the fore in the unfinished Throne Rome, designed to resemble a Romanesque basilica, with columns of red porphyry and a mosaic floor and frescoes of Christ looking down on the 12 Apostles and 6 canonized kings of Europe.

After you leave the guided tour, you can make your way down to the enormous kitchens of the castle. The automatic grills and huge stoves are indicative of technological innovations used throughout the castle that include running water, flush toilets, central heating, electric buzzers to summon servants, even telephones.

The castle is open year-round. In September, Wagnerian concerts and other music is performed in the Singer's Hall. For information and reservations, contact the tourist office, **Verkehrsamt,** at the Rathaus in Schwangau (① **08362/938523**). Tickets go on sale in early June and sell out rather quickly. The castle can be visited only on one of the guided tours (offered in English), which are given daily year-round, except November 1; December 24, 25, and 31; January 1; and Shrove Tuesday. April to September, tours are given 8am to 5pm, and October to March, times are 9am to 3pm. Tours leave every 45 minutes and last 35 minutes. Admission is 12€ for adults, 8€ for students and seniors over 65, and free for children 14 and under. A combination ticket for both castles is 22€ for adults and 15€ for children 14 and under. For more information, visit www.neuschwanstein.com.

HEIDELBERG & THE BLACK FOREST

Southwestern Germany has long inspired legends, soothed romantic sensibilities, and delighted travelers, and little wonder. Ancient castle ruins in the midst of thick woodlands, lovely and atmospheric towns and cities, valleys carpeted with vineyards, dark forests and shimmering lakes—it's all here. Aside from an overload of scenery, these landscapes also offer the heavy-on-atmopshere ambiance of an old university town (Heidelberg); soothing thermal baths (in sophisticated Baden-Baden); cozy Black Forest town ambiance (on the cobbled lanes of Freiburg); even shiny vintage cars (in Stuutgart's Mercedes-Benz and Porsche museums).

HEIDELBERG ★★★

89km (55 miles) S of Frankfurt

This ancient university town on the Neckar River enjoys a reputation as an enchanted purveyor of wine and romance, song and student life, fun and frivolity. It drew 19th-century German Romantics, who praised and painted it; Mark Twain, who cavorted in its lively streets and made cynical observations in "A Tramp Abroad"; and fans of the 1924 operetta "Student Prince," set in Heidelberg (and with a rousing chorus, "Drink, drink, drink" that is still an anthem for many young residents and their visitors). A little less poetically, this attractive city of 135,000 inhabits also housed a U.S. army base for many decades after World War II, helping ensure its popularity with Americans. Heidelberg was ravaged by French invaders during the 30 Years War in the 17th century yet was relatively unscathed in World War II, and the Altstadt (Old Town) looks much as it did a century or two ago, with a lot of architectural landmarks from the later Middle Ages and early Renaissance still standing. Historically, though, Heidelberg is young at heart; the oldest university in Germany is based here, dating to 1386. Some 28,000 students impart a palpable energy to the narrow lanes and lively inns of the Altstadt. While great mouments and museums are thin on the ground in Heidelberg, this youthful aura and romantically historic ambiance will no doubt make your time here memorable.

Heidelberg

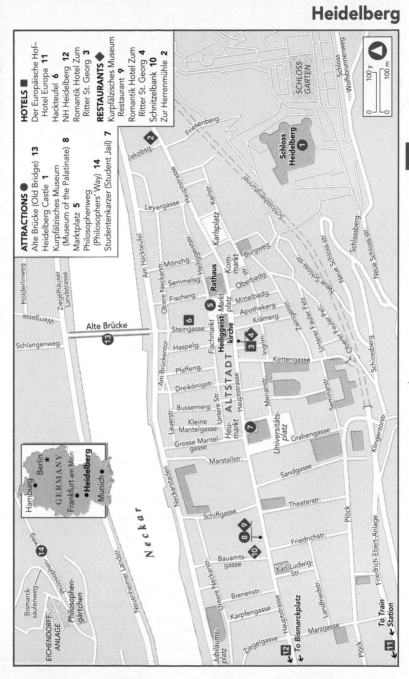

ATTRACTIONS ●
Alte Brücke (Old Bridge) **13**
Heidelberg Castle **1**
Kurpfälzisches Museum
(Museum of the Palatinate) **8**
Marktplatz **5**
Philosophenweg
(Philosophers' Way) **14**
Studentenkarzer (Student Jail) **7**

HOTELS ■
Der Europäische Hof-
Hotel Europa **11**
Hackteufel **6**
NH Heidelberg **12**
Romantik Hotel Zum
Ritter St. Georg **3**

RESTAURANTS ◆
Kurpfälzisches Museum
Restaurant **9**
Romantik Hotel Zum
Ritter St. Georg **4**
Schnitzelbank **10**
Zur Herrenmühle **2**

0   100 y
0   100 m

SCHLOSS-
GARTEN

Schloss
Wolfsbrunnenweg

Schloss

Schloss Heidelberg **1**

Friesenberg

Jakobsg.

Leyergasse

Haupstrasse

Karlstr.

Karlsplatz

Schlossbergtunnel

Schlossberg

Neue Schloss-str.

Neue Schloss-str.

Mönchg.

Heiliggeiststr.

Burgweg

Korn-markt

Semmelsg.

Rathaus

Oberbadg.

Fischerg.

Markt-platz **5**

Mittelbadg.

Apothekerg.

Kramerg.

Steingasse **6**

Fischmarkt

Heiliggeist-kirche

3 4

Ingrimstr.

Zwingerstr.

Unter-Faller Pelz

Obere Neckarstr.

Haspelg.

ALTSTADT

Haupstrasse

Kettengasse

Merianstr.

Seminarstr.

Schlossberg

Alte Brücke **13**

Am Brückentor

Pfaffeng.

Dreikönigstr.

Obere Faule Pelz

Klingentorstr.

Schlangenweg

Hölderlinweg

Werrgasse

Ziegelhäuser Landstrasse

Am Hackteufel

Bussemerg.

Lauerstr.

Kleine Mantelgasse

Grosse Mantel-gasse

Unter Str.

Heu-markt

7

Universitäts-platz

Grabengasse

Marstallstr.

Sandgasse

Neckarstaden

Theaterstr.

Plöck

Schiffgasse

Friedrichstr.

Friedrich-Ebert-Anlage

8 9

10

Bauamts-gasse

Karl-Ludwig-Str.

Bienenstr.

Haupstrasse

Karpfengasse

Landfriedstr.

To Train Station **11**

Neckar

GERMANY
Hamburg
Berlin ★
Frankfurt am Main
Heidelberg
Munich

EICHENDORF-ANLAGE

Bismarck-säulenweg

Philosophenweg **14**

Philosophen-gärtchen

Neuenheimer Landstr.

Unter Neckarstr.

Jubiläums-platz

Ziegelgasse

Marzgasse

Plöck

To Bismarckplatz **12**

2

179

Essentials

GETTING THERE

BY PLANE The nearest major airport is Frankfurt (see chapter 9), with a direct bus link to Heidelberg. The shuttle bus between Frankfurt and Heidelberg costs 20€ per person. Call ☏ **0621/651620** or visit www.ics-logistik.de for shuttle information.

BY TRAIN Heidelberg's **Hauptbahnhof** is a major railroad station, lying on the Mannheim line, with frequent service to both regional towns and major cities. From Frankfurt, 26 direct trains arrive per day (trip time: 1 hr.); travel time to and from Munich is about 3½ hours. For information, call ☏ **01805/996633** or visit www.bahn.de.

BY BUS Regional bus service is provided by BRN Busverkehr Rhein-Neckar at Heidelberg (☏ **06221/60620;** www.brn.de).

BY CAR Motorists should take the A5 Autobahn from the north or south.

GETTING AROUND

Heidelberg is crisscrossed with a network of trams and buses, many of which intersect at the Bismarckplatz in the town center. Bus nos. 31 and 32 travel frequently between the railway station and the Universitätsplatz, in the Altstadt. The Altstadt's lanes run off either side of the Hauptstrasse, the long, pedestrian-only thoroughfare that stretches from the Marktplatz all the way to Bismarckplatz in the new town. Bus or tram fares cost 2.20€ for a single ride.

VISITOR INFORMATION

The **Heidelberg Tourist Bureau,** Willy-Brandt-Platz 1 (☏ **06221/19433;** www. heidelberg-marketing.de), is open April to October Monday to Saturday 9am to 7pm, and Sunday 10am to 6pm; and November to March Monday to Saturday 9am to 6pm.

Where to Stay

Der Europäische Hof-Hotel Europa ★★★ Heidelberg's best, and one of the finest in Germany, seems to do everything right and makes it all seem effortless. Lounges are comfortably plush and attractive; guest rooms, ranging over an old wing and a newer extension, are enormous and beautifully furnished with a nice mix of old-fashioned comfort and contemporary accents, lit by crystal chandeleers and equipped with sumptuous marble baths. Service is unfailingly attentive while unobtrusive and personable. A multilevel, rooftop spa includes a large indoor pool and state of the art gym, and the wood-paneled grill room serves French fare that's as sophisticated as the surroundings. You'll pay a bit more to stay here than in other Heidelberg lodgings, but you'll be staying in style you're not going to find many other places in the world.

Friedrich-Ebert-Anlage 1. ☏ **06221/5150.** www.europischerhof.com. 118 units. 148€–384€ double. Rates include breakfast. Parking 19€. Tram: Bismarckplatz. **Amenities:** 2 restaurants; bar; babysitting; concierge; health club & spa; indoor heated pool; room service; Wi-Fi (fee).

Hackteufel ★★ A guesthouse right in the heart of the Altstadt, between the Marketplace and Old Bridge, offers some of the sprucest, most comfortable lodgings in town. Each of the 12 rooms is different, but most are extra large and embellished with wood floors, beams, dormers, and plenty of nice traditional wood furnishings; number 12 is a cross-beamed garret with a castle view and number 8 is a commodious suite with a terrace. Downstairs is a handsome restaurant and wine bar that serves snacks and drinks throughout the day and traditional specialties at mealtimes, accompanied by lots of cozy ambiance.

Steingasse 7. ☏ **06221/905380.** www.hackteufel.de. 12 units. 120€–170€ double. Rates include buffet breakfast. **Amenities:** Restaurant, bar; free in-room Wi-Fi.

IS THE HEIDELBERG CARD a money saver?

The short answer is: not usually. Yes, the **Heidelberg Card** offers discounts on attractions and free use of public transportation. But since most of what you want to see in Heidelberg is within walking distance and there aren't many attractions you'll be paying to see, the card will probably be a money saver only if you're staying a tram or bus ride away from the Altstadt or will be going back and forth to the Hauptbahnhof frequently.

Transport-wise, you'd have to make three round trips on the bus or tram within a 2-day period to break even.

If you still would like to purchase it, know that cards valid for any consecutive 2-day period cost 13€ per person; cards valid for any consecutive 4-day period go for 16€ per person. A family card valid for two adults and two children 15 and under for any consecutive 2-day period sells for 28€.

NH Heidelberg ★   A courtyard that was once filled to the brim with kegs of beer is now the glass-filled atrium of these smart lodgings at the far edge of the Altstadt, where bright, commodious business-style rooms range through a restored former brewery and modern wing, all nicely done in traditional-meets-modern decor. The Bräustüberl, serving Bavarian specialties, is the most popular of the three in-house restaurants, among many perks that also include a spa and health club. This business-oriented hotel often has weekend and summer specials that can make the spiffy rooms some of the best lodging bargains in Heidelberg.

Bergheimer Strasse 91. ✆ **06221/13270.** www.nh-hotels.com. 174 units. 82€–225€ double. Parking 15€. Tram: 22. Bus: 35. **Amenities:** 3 restaurants; bar; health club and spa; room service; Wi-Fi (fee).

Romantik Hotel Zum Ritter St. Georg ★   The glorious German Renaissance façade right on the Marktplatz is a Heidelberg landmark, and the old inn behind the welcoming doors is a Heidelberg institution. The large, high-ceilinged rooms and suites in the front of the house do justice to the surroundings, and the others off the rambling back corridors are smaller and perfectly comfortable, done in an unremarkable but pleasing contemporary style. A stay here puts you right in the heart of the Altstadt, and just a flight of stairs away from the Ritter's wonderful in-house restaurant (see below).

Hauptstrasse 178. ✆ **06221/1350.** www.ritter-heidelberg.de. 37 units. 118€–176€ double. Bus: 31, 32, or 35. **Amenities:** 3 restaurants; room service; free in-room Wi-Fi.

Where to Eat

Kurpfälzisches Museum Restaurant ★ GERMAN   The baroque Palais Morass not only houses museum exhibits but is also the setting for a pleasant meal, served in a baronial dining hall, some smaller rooms, and a garden next to a splashing fountain in good weather. The cuisine is a bit more pedestrian than the surroundings, with pizzas sharing space on the menu with schnitzels and other traditional fare.

Hauptstrasse 97. ✆ **06221/24050.** www.restaurantkurpflzischesmuseumheidelberg.com. Reservations required. Main courses 16€–19€. June–Sept Sun–Thurs 11am–11pm, Fri–Sat 11am–midnight; off season Sun–Thurs 11am–3pm and 5:30–10pm, Fri–Sat 11am–11pm. Bus: 31 or 32.

Romantik Hotel Zum Ritter St. Georg ★★★ GERMAN/INTERNATIONAL An atmospheric and very grown-up dining room occupies the ground floor of the city's most decorative Renaissance-era landmark, where high-ceilings, paneling, frescoes, and Persian carpets provide lovely old world surroundings for a menu to match. Rumpsteak with cream sauce, roasted venison, calf's livers with apples and onions, Kurpfälzer (a so-called farmer's treat of liver dumplings and sausages served on potatoes and sauerkraut) are among the many local specialties that seasoned waiters serve on starched linens. One of the advantages of staying in one of the comfortable rooms upstairs (see above) is lingering late over a meal in this memorable dining room without worrying about moving on.

Hauptstrasse 178. ☏ **06221/1350.** www.ritter-heidelberg.de. Reservations recommended. Main courses 10€–23€. Daily noon–2pm and 6–10pm. Bus: 31, 32, or 35.

Schnitzelbank ★ GERMAN   The well-worn tables here are workbenches from the days when the premises were a barrel factory. These days the business is wine, with an emphasis on local varieties and sold by the glass, but you can also dine well on the namesake schnitzels, of course, along with lots of other tavern mainstays.

Bauamtsgasse 7. ☏ **06221/21189.** www.schnitzelbank-heidelberg.de. Main courses 8€–12€. Daily noon–11pm.

Zur Herrenmühle ★ GERMAN/INTERNATIONAL   A 17th-century grain mill with thick walls, antique paneling, and heavy beams doesn't skimp on atmosphere, and the cuisine does justice to the surroundings. Fresh fish, grass-fed lamb, and homemade pastas appear in classic preparations served with more flair than is the norm in Heidelberg restaurants, and the vine-covered courtyard is the city's most atmospheric setting for summertime meals.

Hauptstrasse 237. ☏ **06221/602909.** www.herrenmuehle-heidelberg.de. Reservations recommended. Main courses 16€–26€; fixed-price menu 29€. Mon–Sat 6–11pm. Closed last 2 weeks of Mar. Bus: 33.

Exploring Heidelberg

You'll spend most of your time in Heidelberg on or near the south bank of the Neckar River, probably not venturing too far beyond the **Marktplatz (Marketplace)** at the center of the Altstadt. On market days (Wed and Sat mornings), stalls overspilling with fresh flowers, fish, and vegetables surround the Rathaus and the **Heiliggeistkirche (Church of the Holy Spirit)**, a stark, late-Gothic structure from around 1400. Gone from the nave is the dividing wall that was a sign of Heidelberg's conciliatory approach the Reformation: For more than a century both Protestants and Catholics used separate ends of the church. No such compromise tactics spared the Heiliggeistkirche and most of the rest of Heidelburg from the rampaging French troops of King Louis XV, who in 1690 pillaged the interior, along with the graves of the city's prince-electors. You'll want to cross the gracefully flowing Neckar River at least once during stay, walking over the **Alte Brücke (Old Bridge),** a handsome, twin-towered stone span from 1788 (destroyed in 1944 by German troops trying to halt the advance of the Allied army and rebuilt 2 years later). After a stop in front of the raffish **Brückenaffe (Bridge Ape)**—touch the mirror he's holding for wealth, his outstretched fingers to ensure a return to Heidelberg, and the mice that surround him to ensure progeny—continue up the **Schlangenweg (Snake Path)** to the **Philosophenweg (Philosophers' Way).** This 2km (1.25-mile) walking trail above the north bank of the Neckar provides memorable views of the castle, the river, and the Altstadt. The amble ends at the the **Philosophengärtchen (Philosophers' Garden),** where the river valley's mild climate nurtures Japanese cherries, cypresses, lemons, bamboos, rhododendrons, gingkos, yucca trees, and other warm-weather plants.

HISTORIC STUDENT drinking clubs

Heidelberg's most famous and revered student tavern, **Zum Roten Ochsen (Red Ox Inn),** Hauptstrasse 217 (© **06221/ 20977;** www.roterochsen.de; bus: 33), opened in 1703. For six generations, the Spengel family has welcomed everybody from Bismarck to Mark Twain. It seems that every student who has attended the university has left his or her mark (or initials) on the walls, and every tourist in town eventually finds his or her way here, too. Meals go from 9€ to 17€. The tavern is open from April to October Monday to Saturday 11:30am to 2pm and 5pm to midnight, November to March Monday to Saturday 5pm to midnight.

Next door is **Zum Sepp'l,** Hauptstrasse 213 (© **06221/23085;** www.zumseppl.de; bus: 11 or 33), open since 1634, the second most famous drinking club in Heidelberg and another perennial crowd pleaser. It's filled with photographs and carved initials of former students, along with memorabilia that ranges from old Berlin street signs to Alabama license plates. Meals cost 8€ to 18€. It's open Monday to Friday noon to 11pm, and Saturday and Sunday 11:30am to 3:30pm and 5pm to midnight.

Dorfschänke, Lutherstrasse 14 (© **06221/419041;** www.dorfschnke-hd.com; tram: 5 or 23, bus: 31), doesn't have the same pedigree as these two old taverns, having just opened in 1908, but it's been packed ever since and accompanies its beer selections witih some serious food, including *Flammkuchen,* a square pizza with onions and cheese—a bit like tarte flambée, minus the lardons. It's open daily, 5pm to midnight. Meals cost 8€ to 18€.

Heidelberg Castle ★★★ HISTORIC SITE Perched enticingly above the Altstadt, set amid woodlands and terraced gardens, Heidelberg's half-ruined castle has impressed everyone from kings and princes to the poet Goethe, novelists Victor Hugo and Mark Twain, and millions of visitors for whom the red sandstone walls clinging to the green hillside are the epitome of German romanticism. Even in ruin one of the great Renaissance landmarks of northern Europe suggests beauty, grandeur, and long vanquished empires—in this case a division of the Holy Roman Empire known as the County Palatine of the Rhine, whose prince electors lived here from the 13th century.

Elizabeth, the teenaged daughter of English King James I who married prince elector Frederick V and came to Heidelberg in 1605, entered the castle through the portal named for her, Elizabeth's Gate, as visitors still do. The soulless salons of the heavily restored Friedrichsbau, the early-17th-century palace where the young couple took up residence, are less evocative than the shells of most of the rest of the compound's royal enclaves, laid waste to in 1690 by the French troops of Louis XV and finished off by a disastrous lightning strike. Enough gables and arches remain to suggest the grandeur of the place, and a multilanguage audioguide does a good job of filling in the missing pieces.

An especially noteworthy relic is the Great Cask, aka the Heidelberg Turn, a symbol of the exuberant life of the prince electors enjoyed. The vulgar vessel was built in 1751 to store more than 208,000 liters (55,000 gal.) of wine but failed to impress Mark Twain, who wrote, "An empty cask the size of a cathedral could excite but little emotion in me." The Chemist's Tower houses the Apothekenmuseum (Pharmaceutical Museum) and the old chambers quite engagingly spotlight the importance of German pharmaceutical research (much of it conducted at Heidelburg University) with utensils, laboratory equipment, and a re-created chemist's shop from the 18th and 19th

WHERE beer drinking IS A RELIGION

In the Middle Ages, monks were the world's great brew meisters, making the "liquid [that] does not break the fast"— that is, you could drink all the beer you wanted to. It's pretty well established that beer-drinking is a religion in Hedielberg, so it's only natural that the tradition continues at the brewery **Brauerei zum Klosterhof**, part of Heidelberg's 12th-century Neuburg Abbey, on the banks of the Neckar River about 2km (1 mile) east of the Altstadt. To this day, 15 monks live in the monastery and oversee the production of organic beer, including the popular HeidALEberg Red Summer Ale. You can see the brewery, taste the beer, enjoy some grilled sausages and dumplings, and tour the abbey on tours arranged by **Heidelberg Tourism** (*(C)* **06221/5840200;** www.heidelberg-marketing.de); they cost from 20€ to 24€, depending on how much you eat.

centuries. The castle's perennial crowd pleaser are the views that stretch across the old town and down the Neckar Valley. You can enjoy them 24 hours day, since the castle courtyard is always open, as is the shady Schlossgarten.

You can reach the castle by several routes. The Bergbahn (mountain train) whisks you up from the Kornmarkt in a flash (tickets to the castle include the train ride). A paved road gradually winds up the Neue Schlossstrasse past told houses perched on the hillside, while the steeper Burgweg walk climbs uphill from Kornmarkt.

Schlossberg. *(C)***06221/872-7000.** 5€ (includes tram ride to and from castle). 1-hr. guided tours in English 4€; audio tours 4€. Admission ticket is good for 24 hr. and is required daily 8am–5:30pm; castle precincts open 24 hr.

Kurpfälzisches Museum (Museum of the Palatinate) ★ MUSEUM

In the salons of the baroque Palais Morass, Heidelberg's very long history comes to the fore with artifacts that include a cast of the jawbone of Heidelberg Man, an early human who lived in Europe and Africa until 250,000 years ago and is thought to be the direct ancestor of homo sapiens; the original (stored at the university) was unearthed near Heidelberg in 1907. Nearby are some remarkably well preserved wooden beams from a Roman bridge across the Neckar. Other displays may or may not help you understand the complex, strife-torn history of the Palatinate, as a large swath of southwestern Germany was once known, while the collection's standout, the Altar of the Apostles by Tilman Riemenschneider from 1509, alone justifies the price of a ticket. If you're traveling on to Wurzburg (p. 140), you'll encounter this master carver again and see more of his uncanny talent for embellishing religious scenes with emotion and compassion.

Hauptstrasse 97. *(C)* **06221/5834020.** www.museum-heidelberg.de. Admission 3€ adults, 1.80€ students and children 17 and under. Tues–Sun 10am–6pm. Bus: 31, 32, or 35.

Studentenkarzer (Student Jail) HISTORIC SITE

It's ironic that one of the few parts of the august university that Count Palatinate Ruprecht I established in 1386 open to the public are these rough cells where unruly and drunken students were once incarcerated. (If laughter and screaming disrupt your sleep in an Altstadt hotel, you may wish the practice were still in force.) Prisoners bedecked the walls and even the ceilings with graffiti and drawings, including portraits and silhouettes, until the last ones left in 1914. Despite the need to control rowdiness, even the curmugeonly Mark Twain commented that "idle students are not the rule" in Heidelberg. Germany's oldest university, officially known as the Ruprecht-Karls-Universität Heidelberg and centered around the Universitätsplatz, has produced 55 Nobel Prize winners.

Augustinergasse 2. *©* **06221/543593.** Admission 3€ adults, 2.50€ students and children 14 and under. Ticket includes entry for the University Museum and Old Auditorium. Apr–Sept Tues–Sun 10am–6pm; Oct Tues–Sun 10am–4pm; Nov–Mar Tues–Sat 10am–4pm. Bus: 31, 32, or 35.

ALONG THE NECKAR

From Heidelberg, you can float up the Neckar River past wooded hillsides and the occasional castle to **Neckarsteinach** or **Hirschorn,** two picturesque riverside villages. There are usually four or five round-trips daily, and you need not return on the same boat. Trips between Heidelberg and Neckarsteinach cost 13€ round-trip, and those between Heidelberg and Hirschhorn cost 20€ round-trip. Boats are operated by the **Rhein-Neckar-Fahrgastschiffahrt GmbH,** Stadthalle, Heidelberg (*©* **06221/20181;** www.rnf-schifffahrt.de).

You can also follow the river on the Neckar Valley Cycle Path. The route begins at the source in the south near Villingen-Schwenningen and continues 375km (233 miles) to the confluence of the Rhine at Mannheim. Along the way, you'll pass castles, manor houses, vineyards, country inns, and old towns; a popular outing from Heidelberg follows the river through vineyards and the Odenwald Forest toward Eberbach, about 35km (21 miles) east. You can rent a bike from **Radhof,** at the Hauptbanhof, for about 18€ a day (www.fahrrad-heidelberg.de).

Side Trip from Heidelberg

STUTTGART

126km (78 miles) SE of Heidelberg

Stuttgart, a city of about 600,000, is ground zero for German engineering. The neon-lit logos of Mercedes, Porsche, and Zeiss optical equipment light up the sky. Yet, in that German way of never getting too far away from grass roots and nature, a lot of greenery takes the hard edges off all this industry and technology. Vineyards sweep down hillsides into the outskirts, and the forested banks of the Neckar River cut a swath right through town. Softening the Stuttgart image, too, are several much respected art collections and a lot of high-brow culture (the Stuttgart Ballet is world renowned). Stuttgart is not a vacation spot, but you can easily fill up a satisfying day here on an easy outing from Heidelberg, just 45 minutes away by train.

GETTING THERE   Stuttgart has rail links to all major German cities, with frequent connections. The train station is directly north of the historic area. About 25 direct trains run between Heidelberg and Stuttgart daily (trip time: 45 min.). Twenty-seven daily trains run from Munich (trip time: 2½ hr.), and 19 trains run from Frankfurt (trip time: 1½ hr.). For information, call *©* **01805/996633** or visit www.bahn.de. Access by car is via the A8 Autobahn east and west or the A81 north and south.

Exploring Stuttgart

Historically, the center of Stuttgart clusteres around **Schillerplatz,** where a bronze statue of the poet and playwright, who was born near Stuttgart, presides over a sea of cobblestones. The modern Rathaus faces the old **Marktplatz,** where vendors in open stalls sell flowers, fruit, and vegetables. You'll be able to walk to most sights within the center city, though you'll have to rely on the efficient bus and U-bahn system to get to the automobile museums and other outlying sights. A single ride between points that fall within Stuttgart's historic core on the city's bus or U-bahn costs 2.20€. Rides to the outlying districts vary but began at 2.60€ and go up the farther out you travel. If you plan moving around a bit, consider buying a *Tageskarte* (day ticket), which costs 6.30€ and is valid for a day of unlimited transport within the city core and also within zones 1 (central Stuttgart) and 2 (immediate suburbs). For more information about the city's transport system, its routes, and its prices, call ✆ **0711/19449** or visit www.vvs.de.

If you're drawn to crowds and drinking, you might want to plan a visit to coincide with the **Stuttgart Wine Festival** in late August, when wine lovers converge to taste a selection of more than 350 Württemberg wines, or the 16-day **Stuttgart Beer Festival,** beginning in late September. This 200-year-old tradition, the second largest beer fest in Germany after Munich's Oktoberfest, includes a grand procession of horse-drawn beer wagons and as many as 20,000 eager participants, many donning traditional costumes for the occasion. Stuttgart also plays host to a lively late-November and December **Christmas Market (Weihnachtsmarkt),** one of the oldest and largest in Europe, with about 230 decorated stalls selling gifts, mulled wine, and cinnamon waffles.

Information about transportation, sightseeing, and hotels is available at the **i-Punkt,** Königstrasse 1A (✆ **0711/22280;** www.stuttgart-tourist.de), which is open year-round Monday to Friday 9am to 8pm, Saturday 9am to 6pm, and Sunday 11am to 6pm.

Altes Schloss and Württembergisches Landesmuseum (Old Castle and Württemberg Regional Museum) ★ HISTORIC SITE/MUSEUM

For many visitors, the highlight of one of Stuttgart's oldest standing structures, a moated castle built in the 13th century and redone in the 16th century in Renaissance style, is the spectacle of two rams locking horns every hour on the hour on the clock face high above the courtyard. Step through the massive castle doors to find a treasure trove of all things Swabian, Swabia being the ancient lands of which Stuttgart was long the capital. Cases show off the crowns of the kings, 14th-century swords, and some other extraordinary but not altogether unexpected treasures, along with some stunners of local design, like a cooly contemporary-looking silver tea service from the late 19th century and an 18th-century automaton, a wind-up, gold-leafed bird that struts and prances. The archological collections display a wealth of artifacts left behind by past residents over the millennia, including a stone mammoth carved by local cave dwellers as long as 35,000 years ago and a treasure trove of jewelry unearthed in Celtic graves. Shedding light on more recent cultures is a riveting exhibition of local living rooms and household artifacts from the 19th through 20th centuries.

Schillerplatz 6. ✆ **0711/2793498.** www.landesmuseum-stuttgart.de. Admission 4.50€ adults, 3€ students, free for children 13 and under. Tues–Sun 10am–5pm. U-Bahn: Schlossplatz.

Gottlieb Daimler Memorial ★ HISTORIC SITE/MUSEUM

Gottlieb Daimler converted the garden house behind his villa just outside Stuttgart into a workshop and it was here that the world's first internal-combustion engine began spinning in 1883. Daimler and his partner, Wilhelm Maybach, worked in such secrecy that a suspicious gardener, convinced his boss was a counterfeiter, summomed the police to the premises. Daimler was soon fitting his engine onto bikes and into coaches and moved his workshop to a nearby factory, where his mechanics perfected the automobiles that were eventually manufactured by Mercedes-Benz, one of the world's most enduring luxury brands. Daimler's covert workshop now houses drawings, photographs, and models of an airship and motorboat that he invented.

Taubenheimstrasse 13. ✆ **0711/569399.** Free admission. Tues–Fri 2–5pm; Sat–Sun 11am–5pm. U-Bahn: Kursaal.

Kunstmuseum Stuttgart (Stuttgart Art Museum) ★★ MUSEUM

Yet another standout art collection, designed by Berlin architects Hascher and Jehle, is

Stuttgart

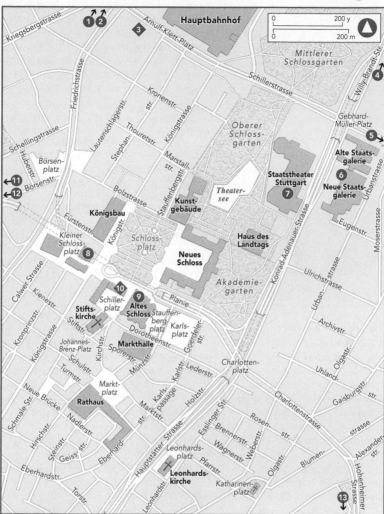

Hauptbahnhof

0 ___ 200 y
0 ___ 200 m

Kriegsbergstrasse
Arnulf-Klett-Platz
Mittlerer Schlossgarten
Friedrichstrasse
Schillerstrasse
Willy-Brandt-Str.
Schellingstrasse
Kronenstr.
Thouretstr.
Königstrasse
Lauterschlagerstr.
Stephan
Börsen-platz
Börsenstr.
Huberstr.
Oberer Schloss-garten
Gebhard-Müller-Platz
Alte Staats-galerie
Neue Staats-galerie
Urbanstrasse
Mösersstrasse
Marstall-str.
Stauffenbergstr.
Bolzstrasse
Staatstheater Stuttgart
Fürstenstr.
Königsbau
Kunst-gebäude
Theater-see
Eugenstr.
Kleiner Schloss-platz
Königstr.
Schloss-platz
Neues Schloss
Haus des Landtags
Konrad-Adenauer-Strasse
Calwer Strasse
Kienestr.
Stifts-kirche
Schiller-platz
Altes Schloss
Stauffen-berg-platz
Planie
Akademie-garten
Ulrichstrasse
Urban
Archivstr.
Olgastr.
Kronprinzstr.
Königstrasse
Stiftstr.
Kirchstr.
Dorotheenstr.
Karls-platz
Goerdeler-str.
Markthalle
Johannes-Brenz-Platz
Schulstr.
Spörerstr.
Münzstr.
Karlstr.
Lederstr.
Charlotten-platz
Uhland-
Gaisburgstr.
Turmstr.
Neue Brücke
Markt-platz
Karls-passage
Holzstr.
Charlottenstrasse
strasse
Alexander-str.
Schmale Str.
Rathaus
Nadlerstr.
Marktstr.
str.
Esslinger Str.
Brennerstr.
Weberstr.
Rosen-
str.
Hirschstr.
Steinstr.
Geiss- str.
Eberhard-
Leonhards-platz
Wagnerstr.
Pfarrstr.
Olgastr.
Blumen-
Hohenheimer Strasse
Eberhardstr.
Torstr.
Leonhards-kirche
Katharinen-platz
Hauptstätter Strasse
Leonhardstr.

ATTRACTIONS ●

Altes Schloss and Württembergisches Landesmuseum (Old Castle and Württemberg Regional Museum) **9**
Birkenkopf **12**
Fernsehturm (Television Tower) **13**
Gottlieb Daimler Memorial **4**
Kunstmuseum Stuttgart (Stuttgart Art Museum) **8**
Liederhalle **11**

Mercedes-Benz Museum **5**
Porsche Museum **2**
Staatsgalerie (State Gallery of Stuttgart) **6**
Staatstheater **7**
Weissenhofsiedlung (Weissenhof Estate) **1**

RESTAURANTS ◆

Alte Kanzlei **10**
Zeppelin-Stüble **3**

Hamburg
Berlin ★
GERMANY
Frankfurt am Main
Stuttgart
Munich

187

housed in a filigree glass cube surrounding a rough-hewn limestone inner core. Taking center stage are 19th- and 20th-century works by artists from southern Germany; the paintings, many depicting the brutality of war, by Otto Dix (1891–1969) are particularly compelling. Many of his works were burned by the Nazis, though some of them were hidden by an art dealer and not uncovered until 2012. The museum was highly supportive of Dix in the post-war years and has the most important collection of his works in the world. If you're wondering what the fuss is all about, check out his "Gross Stadt" ("Big City") triptych, depicting decadent urbane life in the 1920s. The top floor, a cafe open to the public, provides a panoramic view of Stuttgart and its surrounding hills.

Kleiner Schlossplatz 1. ⓒ**0711/2162188.** www.kunstmuseum-stuttgart.de. Admission 6€ adults, 4€ students, free for children 12 and under. Tues–Sun 10am–6pm (Fri until 9pm). U-Bahn: Schlossplatz.

Mercedes-Benz Museum ★ MUSEUM   All curves and glass, this automotive showcase designed by Dutch superstar architects Ben van Berkel and Caroline Bos is as dynamic as the automobile to which it pays homage. Among the 160 vehicles parked on nine floors are the Daimler Reitwagen from 1885, the world's first motorized bicycle, and a fleet of Mercedes-built race cars, from 1899 Blitzen-Benz to the 1980s Sauber Mercedes. The cars that steal the show, though, are the sleek icons of luxurious automobile passenger travel—the long, lean 500 K convertible from 1936, the 1950s Gullwings, and even the classic family sedans will have you riding down the road in style, if only in your dreams, long after you leave.

Mercedesstrasse 100. ⓒ **0711/1730000.** www.museum-mercedes-benz.com. Admission 8€ (4€ after 4:30pm), 4€ ages 15–17 (2€ after 4:30pm), free for children 14 and under. Tues–Sun 9am–6pm. S-Bahn: 1 to Gottlieb-Daimler-Stadion; then walk to the entrance of the plant, where you'll be taken on a special bus to the museum.

Porsche Museum ★ MUSEUM   Bold, dynamic, eye-catching—and that's just the architectural statement that houses 80 legendary cars that are the legacy of Ferdinand Porsche. One of Germany's great automotive pioneers set up a factory in Zuffenhausen, an industrial suburb, in 1931, launching a business that would become world famous for its sporty serial autos and racing cars. (The Volkswagen was also launched here in 1936 and was often called the "Rounded Porsche.")

Exhibits change frequently and are designed to be viewed in 90 minutes, with the cars set off in stark displays to ensure they take center stage. Most of Porsche's milestone-vehicles are always on dispay, including Formula 1 champions and the legendary Porsch 911, the company's two-door flagship. Tours of the factory show how a car is built, with gigantic robotic claws lowering finished bodies onto drivetrains and chassis. You'll also see how fenders, engines, and dashboards come together to make what many consider to be the world's most beautiful automobiles.

Porscheplatz 1. ⓒ**0711/91125685.** www.porsche.com/museum. Admission 8€ (4€ after 5pm), 4€ ages 15–17 (2€ after 5pm), free for children 14 and under. Factory tours in English, times vary (check with information desk). Museum Tues–Sun 9am–6pm. S-Bahn: Neuwirtshaus/Porscheplatz.

Staatsgalerie (State Gallery of Stuttgart) ★★ MUSEUM   A fine museum that opened as part of the royal art school in 1843 houses works spanning some 550 years. Among many early masterpieces is Hans Memlings's "Bathsheba at Her Bath" (from around 1440), a brilliant piece of portraiture in which the artist captures beads of moisture on his subject's brow and her long hair twisted into a knot; bathing Bathsheba, believed to represent the cleansing act of baptism, provided artists with a church-sanctioned means to paint the naked female body. Your reflections on this work and those by other old masters, who were revolutionary in their time, might enhance your appreciation of the

HIT THE heights

The 217m (712-ft.) **Fernsehturm (Television Tower),** capped with a red-and-white transmitter, soars above a forested hillock south of Stuttgart. It was designed and built in 1956 using radically innovative applications of aluminum and prestressed reinforced concrete, and served as a prototype for larger towers in Toronto and Moscow. A 150m (490-ft.) elevator ride delivers you to a cafe, bar, restaurant, observation platform, and displays detailing the tower's construction. Food is served daily 10am to 8pm. The entrance is at Jahnstrasse 120, Stuttgart-Degerloch (✆ **0711/232597;** www.fernsehturm-stuttgart.com). Admission is 5€ adults, 3€ children, and the tower is open daily, 9am to 10:30pm. Take tram 15 from the center.

For a more bucolic view of Stuttgart, climb to the top of the 510m (1,670-ft.) **Birkenkopf,** west of the city, topped off with debris dumped here after World War II to make it the tallest hill in Stuttgart—a green reminder that bombing attacks leveled 60 percent of the city, sparing not a single landmark or historic structure. After the 20-minute walk to the top, you'll be rewarded by a view of the rebuilt city and the surrounding Swabian Hills, covered with vineyards and woods. Bus 92 will drop you at the trailhead.

adjoining New State Gallery, a controversial addition with an undulating façade designed by the British architect James Stirling and completed in 1984. Galleries surrounding a glass rotunda house a collection of 19th- and 20th-century works that has made the museum into a noted repository of modern art. Picasso's "Inclined Head of a Woman" and Matisse's "La Coiffeur" are among many works from the early 20th century, with Mondrian, Gris, Braque, and many other European artists of the time well represented. Curators worked throughout the latter part of the century to reconstitute collections lost to World War II and Nazi purges, with admirable results: Max Beckmann's "Self Portrait with Red Scarf" is one of relatively few early works of the artist to survive, and the museum has also brought together a sizable number of other works by the Bauhaus school and Blue Rider group, much vilified by the National Socialists.

Konrad-Adenauer-Strasse 30–32. ✆ **0711/470400.** www.staatsgalerie.de. Admission 7€ adults, 5€ students, free admission on Wed. Wed and Fri–Sun 10am–6pm; Tues and Thurs 10am–8pm. U-Bahn: Staatsgalerie.

Weissenhofsiedlung (Weissenhof Estate) ★ ARCHITECTURAL SITE

Architecture buffs will want to pay a visit to this housing estate built for a building exhibition in 1927. Walking through the estate you see houses created by architects such as Ludwig Mies van der Rohe (Am Weissenhof 14–29), Le Corbusier (Rathenaustrasse 1–3), and Hans Scharoun (Hölzweg 1). Many of the houses represent the functional style that was being promoted by the Bauhaus school of art and design. Displays in the small **Architektur-Galerie,** Am Weissenhof 30 (✆ **0711/257-1434;** www.weissenhofgalerie.de), provide information about the project and the architects involved; the gallery is open Tuesday through Saturday 2 to 6 p.m. and Sunday noon to 5 p.m.; walking tours are available on Saturdays at 11am (call first to confirm). To reach the Weissenhof Estate, take a taxi or the U-Bahn line 7 to the Killesberg-Messe stop and walk northeast around the Messe into the residential neighborhood. For a private architectural tour by an English-speaking city guide/taxi driver, call **Anselm Vogt-Moykopf** at ✆ **0172/740-1138** (www.stadtrundfahrt-stuttgart.de).

SUEVI & studs

You encounter the word "Swabia" a lot in Stuttgart. Swabia (Schwaben in German) is the name for a medieval duchy now contained within the federal state of Baden-Württemberg in southwestern Germany, of which Stuttgart is capital. The name comes from Suevi, the original inhabitants, who were conquered by the Franks in the A.D. 5th century. The name "Stuttgart" comes from a stud farm owned by Luidolf, Duke of Swabia, and son of Emperor Otto the Great. With Stuttgart as its capital, Swabia has been a leader of German industry for decades, but the region also is renowned for its scenic countryside. To the north, the Schwäbische Wald (Swabian Forest) stretches to the Schwäbische Alb, a wedge of limestone upland south of Stuttgart. Forests sweep south to the Bodensee, also part of Swabia, and west to the Danube River. The smaller Neckar River flows past Heidelberg and Stuttgart through a vineyard-covered valley.

Where to Eat

Alte Kanzlei ★★ SWABIAN   Occupying a section of the Altes Schloss (Old Castle) on a corner of Stuttgart's most atmospheric square, the cobbled Schillerplatz, these atmospheric, high-ceilinged rooms dispense traditional Swabian dishes. Some perennial favorites are *Maultaschen* (pasta stuffed with ham, egg, spinach, or other fillings), *Zwiebelrostbraten* (roast beef topped with onions), and Fladelsuppe, literally, pancake soup, beef broth flavored with strips of salted, crepelike pastry. A cafe section serves breakfast and lighter meals and spills onto the terrace, making this perbennial favorite even more popular in warmer months.

Schillerplatz 5A. (© **0711/294457.** www.alte-kanzlei-stuttgart.de. Main courses 10€–20€. Daily 10am–midnight (Fri and Sat until 1am). U-Bahn: Schlossplatz.

Zeppelin-Stüble ★ SWABIAN   Another stop for Swabian fare—which is what you should eat while in Stuttgart—is an elegant and antiques-filled dining room across from the train station in the Steigenberger Graf Zeppelin hotel, an outlet of a German chain. The food stays close to old Swabian recipes and dispels any notions of generic hotel dining rooms; *Schwäbischer Sauerbraten* (a Swabian version of marinated beef) and other classics are often accompanied by *Spätzle* with roasted onions and buttered bread crumbs.

In the Steigenberger Hotel Graf Zeppelin, Arnulf-Klett-Platz 7. (© **0711/2048184.** Reservations recommended. Main courses 11€–21€. Mon–Sat 11:30am–2:30pm and 6–10:30pm. U-Bahn: Hauptbahnhof.

The Performing Arts

Stuttgart is so close to Heidelberg (only 40 min. by train) that you may want to consider spending an evening at one the city's highly regarded cultural events; listings and tickets are available from the tourist office, and the magazine "Lift," available at newsstands, lists all the happenings around Stuttgart. **Staatstheater (State Theater),** Oberer Schlossgarten (© **0711/202090;** S-Bahn: Hauptbahnhof), is home to the highly regarded **Stuttgart Ballet** and the **Staatsoper (State Opera).** Classical and other concerts are given in the **Liederhalle,** Schloss-Strasse (© **0711/2167110;** U-Bahn: Liederhalle/Berlinerplatz), home to the Stuttgarter Philharmoniker and the Radio Symphony Orchestra.

BADEN-BADEN ★★

88km (55 miles) SW of Heidelberg

The notion of the old-fashioned European spa town lives on in Baden-Baden, where the bath-conscious Roman emperor Caracalla came to ease his arthritic aches 2,000 years ago. Queen Victoria, Kaiser Wilhelm I, Napoleon III, Berlioz, Brahms, and Dostoevsky are among the elite who put Baden-Baden on the map as the most elegant and sophisticated playground in Germany. Tolstoy even set a scene in "Anna Karenina" here. Baden-Baden still evokes an aura of privilege, though there's nothing stuffy about this lively little city that tumbles across green hillsides above darting streams. You can join a well-heeled European crowd and soak in the waters, see the sights and some world-class art, stroll and hike, attend a performance in one of Germany's most acclaimed concert halls, even try your luck in the casino. You can easily visit Baden-Baden on a day trip from Heidelberg, but after so much exposure to the thermal waters and evergreen-scented fresh air, you may not want to venture any farther than a bed in one of the resort's pleasant hotels.

Essentials

GETTING THERE By Train Baden-Baden is on major rail lines connecting Frankfurt and Basel, and Stuttgart and Munich. Trains to and from Heidelberg run about every half hour and the trip takes about an hour. For information, call ℂ **01805/996633** or visit www.bahn.de. The railway station is at Baden-Oos, northwest of town, well outside the city center but well connected by buses just outside the entrance.

By Car Access to Baden-Baden is via the A5 Autobahn north and south or the A8 Autobahn east and west. The drive south from Frankfurt takes an hour at most; from Munich, it's about 4 hours.

GETTING AROUND Bus no. 201, which runs at 10-minute intervals, interconnects most of the important sites with the railway station, about 5km (3 miles) from the center. One-way fare is 2.40€, and tickets are sold from machines and from drivers. The **City-Bahn** (ℂ **07221/991-998;** www.citybahn.de) is a sightseeing train that makes stops at all of Baden-Baden's major attractions. The train runs daily from 9:30 a.m. to about 5 p.m., making stops at the Kurhaus, Lichtentaler Allee, the Caracalla Baths, and other spots. Tickets cost 6.50€ for adults and 3.50€ for children 5 to 15, and 15€ for families of two adults and two childrn. English commentary is available on a headset.

VISITOR INFORMATION For information, contact **Tourist-Information,** Schwarzwaldstrasse 52 (ℂ **07221/275200;** www.baden-baden.com), Monday to Saturday 9am to 6pm and Sunday 9am to 1pm.

Where to Stay

Hotel am Markt ★ Rates at this tidy house on the old marketplace seem out of line with what's offered—as in, they're amazingly low given the comfort of the pleasantly modern, colorful guest rooms, some with nice outlooks over the old town. Rooms are the lower floors are a little grander than those at the top of the house, where ceilings are bit low; singles share bathrooms, while some of the doubles have toilets only and shared showers down the hall. Breakfast is served on a tiny terrace cafe in front with petunia-filled window boxes, and a snug, wood-ceilinged breakfast room is a pleasant place to start the day at other times.

Marktplatz 18. ℂ **07221/27040.** Fax 07221/270444. www.hotel-am-markt-baden.de. 27 units, 12 with bathroom or shower. 65€–68€ double without bathroom or shower; 82€–88€ double with bathroom or shower. Rates include buffet breakfast. Parking 4€. Bus: 201. **Amenities:** Cafe, free in-room Wi-Fi.

Hotel Schweizer Hof ★   A lot of old fashioned charm is on tap in these high-ceilinged, nicely furnished rooms right in the center of things. It's not posh, but spotless and friendly, and has atmosphere to spare. The place has been hosting guests who come to take the waters for decades, and offers some attractive multi-day package rates to accommodate them. A large garden is the perfect place to relax after a session at the baths.

Lange Strasse 73. ℂ **07221/30460.** www.schweizerhof.de. 34 units. 102€–115€ double. Rates include buffet breakfast. Bus: 201. Opposite the Festspielhaus. **Amenities:** Bar; free Wi-Fi in some rooms.

Rathausglöckel ★★   A 16th-century house near the Rathaus and Friedrichsbad and Caracalla baths goes the traditional route with cozy, wood-floored guest rooms that are as distinctive as the centuries-old surroundings. All are good-size, and some of the family-oriented suites are truly substantial; rooms on the upper floors have nice views of the rooftops of the old town, and so does a nice terrace at the top of the house.

Steinstrasse 7. ℂ **07221/90610.** www.rathausgloeckel.de. 20 units. 110€–137€ double. Rates include buffet breakfast. Bus: 201. **Amenities:** Restaurant, bar; free in-room Wi-Fi.

Where to Eat

Löwenbräu ★ GERMAN/BAVARIAN   Baden-Baden, of course, is not in Bavaria, but that doesn't mean Bavarian specialties served amist kitschy mountain decor don't have a big following here—not in the least becase the hearty servings of sausages and offerings from the "pork-knuckle grill" are affordable, accompanied by a good selection of beer, and served on a nice linden-shaded terrace and in a beer garden in good weather.

Gernsbacher Strasse 9 (in the Altstadt). ℂ **07221/22311.** www.loewenbru-baden-baden.de. Main courses 11€–27€. Daily 10am–11pm. Bus: 201.

Rathausglöckel ★★ GERMAN   This cozy 16th-century house on one of the stepped streets around the Rathaus might be Baden's most welcoming restaurant. A couple of low-ceilinged, beamed, candlelit rooms on the ground floor of a similarly charming hotel (see above) specialize in local comfort food, of the beef broth with dumplings and bratwurst on braised onion sauerkraut variety. Racks of lamb, duck breasts, and other haute entrees are accompanied by generous portions of gratins and noodles. Service is as polished as the well-burnished wood tables.

Steinstrasse 7. ℂ **07221/90610.** www.rathausgloeckel.de. Reservations recommended. Main courses 12€–23€. Mon–Sat 5–11pm; Sun noon–10pm. Bus 201.

Stahlbad ★★ CONTINENTAL   These elegantly low-key, painting-hung rooms in the center of town suggest the parlors of a refined German home, but the menu at one of Baden-Baden's best and most popular old mainstays sticks to some homey classics like fried goose slices with red cabbage and dumplings and veal kidneys in a mustard sauce with potato puree. The surroundings are especially tranquil in the summer, when the dining room expands to a flowery terrace.

Augustaplatz 2. ℂ **07221/24569.** www.stahlbad.com. Reservations recommended. Main courses 15€–30€. Tues–Sun noon–2pm and 6–10pm. Bus: 201.

Exploring Baden-Baden

Baden-Baden isn't a demanding place in terms of monuments and landmarks. The pace is relaxed, and the streets are geared toward pleasurable strolls. The time-honored center of activity is Lichtentaler Allee, an elegant park promenade lined with rhododendrons, azaleas, roses, and ornamental trees set along the bank of the narrow Oosbach River (called the Oos; pronounced *ohs*). At the north end of the promenade are the formally landscaped grounds of the Kurgarten and the neoclassical Kurhaus, built in the 18th century as a "Promenade House," where the rich and prominent came to see and be seen. It's been the hub of Baden-Baden's social scene ever since, used for receptions and galas, and one wing houses Baden-Baden's casino (see below). You'll also want to step into the Trinkhalle (Pump Room) for a sip of the medicinal waters that have been bubbling up for more than 17,000 years and have a look at the frescoes depicting Black Forest legends.

Caracalla-Therme ★ SPA   These slightly radioactive waters, rich in sodium chloride, bubble up from artesian wells at a temperature of about 160°F (70°C). Bathers usually begin in cooler pools, working up to the warm water. The baths also have a sauna area, with foot baths and sun baths. You must wear bathing suits in the pools, but everyone goes nude in the saunas.

Römerplatz 1. ✆ **07221/275940.** www.carasana.de. Admission 15€ for 2 hr., 18€ for 3 hr., 21€ for 4 hr. Daily 8am–10pm. Bus: 201.

Friedrichsbad ★★ SPA   Leave your clothing and any notions of modestly at the door of the so-called Old Baths, built from 1869 to 1877 at the behest of Grand Duke Friedrich von Baden. The German notion of *Freikörperkultur,* or Free Body Culture, is the house rule here, and bathing attire is not allowed in the domed, mosaic-covered chambers. On some days the facilities are coed, and on others men and women bathe separately. Following the Roman-Irish method that combines thermal waters and warm air, it takes about 3 hours to follow the complete routine, which involves a shower, two saunas, an optional brush-massage soaping, thermal steam baths, and three freshwater baths ranging in temperature. At the end of the routine you're encouraged to drift off to sleep beneath a warm blanket in a dimly lit rotunda. After experiencing the Friedrichsbad, you'll better understand what Mark Twain meant when he said, "Here at Baden-Baden's Friedrichsbad you lose track of time in 10 minutes and track of the world in 20."

Römerplatz 1. ✆ **07221/275920.** www.carasana.de. Admission 23€ without soap-brush massage, 35€ with soap-brush massage. Daily 9am–10pm.

Sammlung Frieder Burda ★★ MUSEUM   The scion of a famous publishing family, Frieder Burda spent nearly 4 decades amassing this amazing collection of some 580 works of modernist and contemporary art, housed in airy glass premises designed by New York architect Richard Meier. German expressionists, from Ernst Ludwig Kirchner to Max Beckmann, are well represented, and American abstract expressionists Willem de Kooning, Mark Rothko, and Jackson Pollock also make a showing. Picassos, sculptures by Joan Miro and Niki de Saint-Phalle, and canvases by such contemporary artists as Anselm Kiefer round out this collection that is all the more extraordinary because you don't expect to come upon so many modern masterpieces in a place as old world and out-of-the-way as Baden-Baden. The building itself is an attraction, a stunning white cube surrounded by reflecting pools and parkland.

Lichtentaler Allee 8B. ✆ **07221/398980.** www.museum-frieder-burda.de. Admission 9€ adults; 7€ students, children, and seniors. Tues–Sun 10am–6pm.

avant-garde BADEN-BADEN

If you think Baden-Baden is just another stodgy European spa, ponder this. Way back in 1927, the city's Kurhaus hosted the German Chamber Music Festival. Some avant-garde upstarts stole the show: Composer Kurt Weill and playwright/director Bertolt Brecht premiered their collaboration "Mahagonny Songspiel," an intoxicating blend of contemporary classical styles, jazz, and cabaret starring Weill's wife, the singer/actress Lotte Lenya. The three became major forces in 20th-century theater and film. Lenya is most fondly remembered by American audiences for her role in the James Bond thriller "From Russia with Love," in which she plays Rosa Klebb, a villainous Russian agent with a venom-laced blade stashed in the toe of her shoe. The music they introduced to the Baden-Baden audiences that night in 1927 ushered in the antiopera, opera-like works that defy convention and include such modern classics as "Three Penny Opera," "Company," "West Side Story," and "Rent." The tune that brought the house down, "Alabama Song," is a perennial favorite, and one of the Doors' biggest hits.

The Performing Arts & Nightlife

Baden-Baden has a busy annual schedule of concert, dance, and dramatic performances. A lot of events are held in the 1870s **Kurhaus,** Kaiserallee 1 (✆ **07221/9070;** www.kurhaus-baden-baden.de); one wing hosts Baden-Baden's casino, the **Spielbank** (see "The Casino," below).

The baroque **Theater am Goetheplatz,** Goetheplatz (✆ **07221/932700;** www. theater.baden-baden.de), presents opera, ballet, and drama productions. It opened auspiciously with the world première of the Berlioz opera "Beatrice et Benedict" in 1862. The **Philharmonie Baden-Baden (Philharmonic Orchestra of Baden-Baden)** usually performs in one of the largest concert halls in Germany, the **Festspielhaus,** in the Alter Bahnhof. In the summer Baden-Baden hosts **Musikalischer Sommer Festival,** usually conducted during an 8-day period in mid-July, as well as many outdoor concerts in greenspaces around town. For tickets to any cultural or musical event within Baden-Baden, contact either the tourist office (✆ **07221/275200**), which sells tickets on its premises, or the **Ticket Service Trinkhalle,** in the Trinkhalle on Kaiserallee (✆ **07221/932700**).

THE CASINO

Spielbank ★ GAMBLING Marlene Dietrich, the glamorous German film star, once remarked, "The most beautiful casino in the whole world is in Baden-Baden— and I have seen them all." The casino has been hosting those who like to flirt with lady luck for more than 200 years. Dostoevsky is said to have written "The Gambler" after he lost his shirt, and almost his mind, at the tables here. The casino rooms were designed in the style of an elegant French château. Jackets and ties for men are mandatory, as is evening wear for women. To enter during gambling hours, you must possess a valid passport or identification card and be at least 21 years old.

The historic gaming rooms may be viewed daily 9:30am to noon on a tour costing 5€ for adults, 3€ for children 15 and under. For those who want to gamble later, a full day's ticket is available for 3€. The minimum stake is 5€, but visitors are not obligated to play. Hours are daily noon to 2am (Fri–Sat until 3am). Kaiserallee 1. ✆ **07221/30240.** www.casino-baden-baden.de. Bus: 1.

FREIBURG IM BREISGAU ★★

111km (69 miles) SW of Baden-Baden

The largest city unofficial capital of the Black Forest lives up to its role with an outrageously picturesque Altstadt (Old Town) full of gabled, half-timbered houses nestling in a plain below high mountain peaks. Although surrounded by alpine scenery, Freiburg enjoys the benefits of warm air currents that come up from the Mediterranean. Summer days can get very hot, but a mountain breeze called the *Höllentaler* flows down into the town like clockwork twice every night between 7 and 7:30 and 9 and 9:30pm to cool things down. The Altstadt's splashing fountains and shallow, fast-flowing streams called *Bächle* (little brooks) that run alongside the streets in stone-lined channels are also time-honored cooling systems. In spring Freiburg bursts with springtime blooms while snow still covers the surrounding peaks, and in autumn, the smell of new wine fills the narrow streets even as snow is already falling on those nearby summits. On the subject of wine: 1,600 acres of vineyards surround the city, and winegrowing always requires celebrations. On the last weekend in June, a 4-day public wine-tasting festival takes place in the Münsterplatz, the square in front of Freiburg's magnificent Gothic cathedral.

Essentials

GETTING THERE   By Train   Trains arrive from Frankfurt almost every half hour (trip time: 2 hr.) and also half hourly from Baden-Baden, about an our away. For information, call 𝓒 **01805/996633** or visit www.bahn.de.

By Bus   Long-distance bus service is provided by **Südbaden Bus GmbH,** Central Bus Station, Freiburg (𝓒 **0761/3680388;** www.suedbadenbus.de), with service from Freiburg to EuroAirport Basel-Mulhouse; and by **EuroRegioBus** (𝓒 **0761/3680388**), which has a bus between Freiburg and the French cities of Mulhouse and Colmar.

By Car   Access by car is via the A5 Autobahn north and south.

GETTING AROUND   Freiburg is well served by buses and trams, the latter running in the inner city. A one-way fare costs 2.20€; a 24-hour day pass is 5.40€. For schedules and information, or to buy passes, go to **VAG Plus-Punkt,** Salzstrasse 3 (𝓒 **0761/4511500;** www.vag-freiburg.de), in the Altstadt. Hours are Monday to Friday 8am to 7pm and Saturday 8:30am to 4pm. Most of the city's public transportation network shuts down from 12:30 to 5:30am.

VISITOR INFORMATION   For tourist information, contact **Freiburg Tourist Board,** Rathausplatz 2–4 (𝓒 **0761/3881880;** www.freiburg.de). The office is open June to September Monday to Friday 8am to 8pm, Saturday 9:30am to 5pm, and Sunday 10am to noon (Oct–May Mon–Fri 8am–6pm, Sat 9:30am–2:30pm, and Sun 10am–noon).

Where to Stay

Many restaurants in Freiburg, including those listed below, also rent rooms.

Oberkirch ★   A 200-year-old tavern on busy Münsterplatz also rents comfortable, old-fashioned rooms, some with views of the cathedral and market and all enjoying a nice terrace above the square. It's said you'd have to be a priest to stay in a better location in Freiburg. Some rooms are above the restaurant and others in an adjacent building, and all are different with plenty of warmth and character, enhanced with canopied beds, elaborate headboards, foral wallpapers, crystal chandileers, and other decorative touches best suited to those not looking for generic or minimalist surroundings.

Münsterplatz 22. *©* **0761/2026868.** http://eng.hotel-oberkirch.de. 26 units. 139€–159€ double. Rates include buffet breakfast. Tram: 1, 4, or 5. **Amenities:** Restaurant; free in-room Wi-Fi.

Rappen ★ From the inside this charming inn in the pedestrians-only Altstadt has a lot more cozy Black Forest ambience than many Freiburg hotels. Wrought-iron hanging sign, little dormer windows in its steep roof, window boxes, and shutters are a lot more atmospheric than the rooms, pleasantly and comfortably furnished in a fairly generic style. Ask for a room with a view of the cathedral and your eyes won't really be on the room decor anyway.

Münsterplatz 13. *©* **0761/31353.** Fax 0761/382252. www.hotelrappen.de. 18 units, 13 with bathroom. 124€–150€ double. Rates include buffet breakfast. Parking 9€. All trams stop 20m (70 ft.) behind the hotel. Tram: 1, 2, 3, or 5. **Amenities:** Restaurant; room service; TV, Wi-Fi (free).

Zum Roten Bären ★★ With parts dating from 1120, one of the oldest buildings in Freiburg claims to be the oldest inn in Germany. The vaulted cellar, some evocative stone work, and a smattering of antiques are faithful to the provenance, though the innkeepers have spared any attempt to be quaint in favor of plain contemporary decor in most rooms, and it's a bit dated at that. High-ceilinged rooms in the orginal building have the most ambiance, and the best overlook a tranquil courtyard. Rooms in a new addition are stylish and nicely furnished in sleek contemporary style, but if it's medieval atmosphere you're after, ask for one of the more traditional rooms.

Oberlinden 12, near Schwabentor. *©* **0761/387870.** www.roter-baeren.de. 25 units. 158€–197€ double. Rates include buffet breakfast. Parking 9€. Tram: 1. **Amenities:** Restaurant; room service; sauna; Wi-Fi (in some areas, fee).

Where to Eat

For a beer and snack, stop by **Hausbräuerei Feierling,** Gerberau 46 (*©* **0761/243480;** www.feierling.de), a brewpub with a beer garden across the street. You can get a plate of sausages for about 7€, along with salads or some more substantial fare.

Oberkirch's Weinstube ★★ GERMAN It's hard to to find more atmospheric surroundings than this old city-center *Weinstube* (wine tavern) with a monumental, ceiling-high ceramic stove made with ornate decorative tiles and rich wood paneling. Local legend has it the place wouldn't be here if in centuries past the owner hadn't put out a blaze by emptying the contents of his wine cask. The food here is old-fashioned, too—tasty soups, meat dishes (veal schnitzel, pork filets in morel cream sauce), poultry, and game in season, all served in large helpings. Summertime dining is on a terrace overlooking the minster.

Münsterplatz 22. *©* **0761/2026868.** Fax 0761/2026869. www.hotel-oberkirch.de. Reservations recommended. Main courses 13€–25€. Mon–Sat noon–2pm and 6:30–9:30pm. Closed for 2 weeks in Jan. Tram: 1, 2, 3, or 5.

Weinstub/Hotel Sichelschmiede ★ GERMAN Another top Freiburg spot for picturesque dining has a biergarten-terrace on a small square flanked by a rushing Bächle (little brook) and shaded by horse-chestnut trees. In cooler months the action moves into wood paneled, beamed, and fire-warmed rooms inside. These are excellent settings in which to try some local Zwiebel (onion) dishes, a specialty of the region. Zwiebelschmelze is especially memorable—a spinach-and-vegetable-filled ravioli covered with sautéed onions. A simpler Vesperkarte (late-evening menu) is available from 10pm to midnight.

MapInsel 1. *©* **0761/35037.** www.sichelschmiede.de. Main courses 8€–15€. Daily noon–midnight.

A monster münster IN THEIR MIDST

The minster is almost as rich a repository of secular concerns as it is a sacred precinct, a phenomenon you'll notice even before you step through the massive portals—one of the gargoyles peering down from the tower's roof has its backside turned toward the archbishop's house across the square, supposedly a sign of the architect's contempt for the city fathers. Markings on the façade were used as gauges to keep medieval vendors honest and make sure they were selling bread that met the criterior for length and height. Commerce also makes an appearance in the 13th- and 14th-century stained glass, where the guilds who funded them ensured pretzels, tools, and other signs of their crafts were incorporated into the designs. Likewise, scenes in the panels of Hans Holbein's magnificent altarpiece include the donor's sons, daughters, deceased wife, grandchildren, and decreased wife, giving all a little push toward eternal salvation.

Zum Roten Baren ★★ GERMAN   One of the best kitchens in Freiburg serves wonderfully prepared dishes using local ingredients in one of the city's most authentically atmospheric dining rooms. Pay special attention to the seasonal dishes, such as Spargel (white asparagus), available in May and June, or roasted goose, served in November and December. The Spargelpfannkuchen is asparagus served with a special pancake, cooked ham, and Hollandaise sauce. A young Rivaner wine, grown on the nearby Kaiserstühl vineyards, is a light, fruity accompaniment.

In the hotel Zum Roten Bären, Oberlinden 12 (just inside the Schwabentor). ℰ **0761/387870.** www.roter-bren.de. Main courses 10€–22€. Daily noon–2pm and 7–10pm.

Exploring Freiburg

Augustiner Museum ★ MUSEUM   Some outstanding pieces of art from the Middle Ages are arranged throughout a 13th-century Augustine church and monastery that's been beautifully restored to show off the pieces to their best effect. Weathered red sandstone sculptures of 10 Old Testament prophets that once adorned the tower of the Minster are dramatically arrayed in two rows of the former nave, beneath gargoyles depicting the Seven Deadly Sins. The minster's medieval gold and silver has been brought here for safekeeping, and the collection's greatest treasure is "Miracle of the Snows" by Matthias Grünewald (1470–1528), depicting a miraculous August snowfall in 4th-century Rome. Little is known about Grünewald and all but 10 of his paintings were lost at sea when they were being carted off to Sweden as booty during the Thirty Years War; his great masterpiece, the Isenheim Altarpiece, is in Colmar, just across the border in France.

Augustinerplatz. ℰ **0761/2012531.** www.augustinermuseum.de. Admission 6€ adults, free for children 17 and under. Tues–Sun 10am–5pm. Tram: 1.

Freiburg Münster (Minster) ★★ CHURCH   You get a sense of the magnificence of this cathedral long before you reach the doors and catch glimpses of the spire, a masterpiece of filigree stonework that has risen above the roofs of Freiburg for almost 8 centuries. Jacob Burckhardt, the 19th-century Swiss historian of art and culture, said it "will forever remain the most beautiful spire on earth," and so far, his words appear to be holding true. The tower's longevity and miraculous survival during World War II bombing raids are attributed not to divine intervention but to some sound

THE bächle OF FREIBURG

Freiburg's Altstadt has many lovely old fountains and a unique system of streams called **Bächle (little brooks)** that date back to the 12th century. First devised to keep the city clean and to help fight fires, the brooks channel water from the Dreisam River through the old university town and help to keep it cool in the hot summer months. You can see the Bächle running alongside many Altstadt streets. According to local folklore, if you step in a Bächle, you will marry a person from Freiburg.

13th-century engineering and the use of lead anchors. Those early masterminds never saw the enormous church completed, as it took 4 centuries before the last stones were put in place and the cathedral's style had transformed from Romanesque to Gothic. The carvings around the main doors are lessons in stone, intended to teach the illerate parables from the Old and New Testaments. Inside are two of the great masterpieces of Germany's so-called Northern Renaissance, both altarpieces, one by Hans Baldung (1484–1545) and the other by Hans Holbein (1497–1543), probably the most renowned German artist of his time. Baldung's is a monumental 12-paneled portrayal of the Coronation of the Virgin with scenes from her life, all rendered in the bright colors and showing the tranquil expressions that are hallmarks of this artist who learned his craft from the great Albrecht Dürer. Only two panels of Holbein's work remain, depicting the Adoration of the Shepherds and the Three Magi; the other pieces were allegedly destroyed when Holbein's Catholic imagery fell out of favor during the Protestant Reformation.

In Münsterplatz, across from the cathedral, is the brick-red **Kaufhaus (Customs House),** a medieval emporium with an arcaded balcony and hands down the most colorful and charming structure in Frieburg. The four statues above the balcony are of Hapsburg emperors, who ruled Freiburg for 4 centuries, until the early 19th century.

Münsterplatz. ℭ **0761/202790.** www.freiburgermuenster.info. Admission: Cathedral free; tower 2€ adults, 1€ students, free for children 14 and under. Cathedral year-round Mon–Sat 10am–5pm; Sun 1–7:30pm. Tower May–Oct Mon–Sat 9:30am–5pm, Sun 1–5pm; Nov–Apr Wed–Sat 9:30am–5pm. Tram: 1, 2, 3, or 5.

Museum für Neue Kunst ★ MUSEUM   It's well worth spending half an hour or so in this small modern art collection that delivers some surprises with a few 20th-century masterpieces. Among the best are works by Otto Dix, who once lived on nearby on Constance and is best known for his depictions of the brutality of war, and Oskar Kokoshka, the Austrian born expressionist who's canvases are explosions of color and movement.

Marienstrasse 10A. ℭ **0761/2012581.** www.museen.freiburg.de. Admission 3€ adults, 2€ students, free for children 6 and under. Tues–Sun 10am–5pm. Tram: 1, 2, 3, or 5.

Schlossberg ★ ACTIVITY   From the Schwabentor (see below), a pathway climbs up this hill that provides good views of the cathedral. You can also ascend the Schlossberg from the Stadtgarten (City Gardens) by cable car (ℭ **0761/39855;** round-trip fare 3€, operates June–Sept 10am–7pm, Oct–Jan 11:30am–6pm).

Schwabentor (Swabian Gate) ★ LANDMARK   One of two surviving gates from the Middle Ages, when Freiburg was a walled city, the Schwabentor dates from around 1200. Paintings on the tower include one of St. George, the city's patron saint. The neighborhood around the Schwabentor is called the Insel (Island) because rushing streams, called Bächle (p. 195), surround it and is the most picturesque quarter in Freiburg, with narrow cobblestone streets and old houses once inhabited by fishermen and tanneries.

Side Trips from Freiburg

THE SCHWARZWALD (BLACK FOREST) ★★

The Black Forest, about 145km (90 miles) long and 40km (25 miles) wide, runs parallel to the Rhine, which serves as a boundary with Switzerland to the south and France to the west. The Bodensee (Lake Constance) adjoins the forest to the east. For the Germans the mountainous, legend-filled, pine- and spruce-filled forest is a favorite place to escape into nature. The name "Black Forest" comes from the Romans, who thought the dark swaths of trees sweeping across the mountainus landscapes looked black.

Here are two ways to explore the Black Forest from Freiburg, a drive and an excursion by train or bus to the nice little woodsy town of Triberg.

Driving Through the Upper Black Forest

From Freiburg, you can make an easy 145km (90-mile) circuit through a scenic part of the Black Forest and be back in time for dinner. Along the way, you pass some of the forest's highest peaks and two of its most beautiful lakes.

From Freiburg, head south on Kaiser-Joseph-Strasse to Günterstal and follow the narrow, twisting road to **Schauinsland.** From the parking lot, you can climb 91 steps to an observation tower for a panoramic view toward the Feldberg, a nearby peak. The area also has easy hiking trails. Continue south to the hamlet of **Todtnau,** where you find a 1.6km-long (1-mile) footpath to an impressive series of waterfalls. (You need about an hour to get to the falls and back.) From Todtnau, pick up B317 west to Utzenfeld and follow the narrow road northwest to the **Belchen,** a famous mile-high peak. An enclosed gondola, the **Belchen Seilbahn,** Belchenstrasse 13 (© **07673/888-280**), takes you to the peak for one of the most spectacular views in the Schwarzwald. From the grassy summit you can see the Feldberg and other nearby mountains, green hillside pastures, tile roofs in small villages, and the vast Rhine plain to the west. Give yourself about 90 minutes for the gondola ride and a stroll on the summit; the cable car operates daily from 9:30 a.m. to 5 p.m. The round-trip costs 6.50€ for adults, 4.50€ for children.

From the Belchen, backtrack to Utzenfeld and follow B317 east to Feldberg, where another enclosed gondola, the **Feldbergbahn** (© **07655/8019**), takes visitors to the 1,450m (4,750-ft.) summit of a peak called **Seebuck.** The round-trip takes about an hour, and on a clear day, you can see the highest peaks of the Alps to the south. The cable car operates daily from 9 a.m. to 4:30 p.m.; the round-trip ride costs 6.80€ for adults, 4.80€ for children.

Continue on B317 east and turn south on B500 to **Schluchsee,** one of the loveliest of the Black Forest lakes. From Schluchsee, head back north along B500 to **Titisee,** another popular Black Forest lake. From Titisee, you can return to Freiburg by heading west along B31.

TRIBERG ★

48km (30 miles) NE of Freiburg

Triberg, deep in the heart of the Black Forest, claims to be the birthplace of the cuckoo clock, so if you're in the market for a traditional timepiece, this is the place to find it. You'll also find many little shops selling woodcarvings, music boxes, and other local

STOPS FOR clocks

Clock watchers with a car and time on their hands may want to drive the scenic Deutsche Uhrenstrasse (German Clock Rd.) through the Black Forest from Villingen-Schwenningen to Bad Duerrheim, find more about the route at www.deutsche-uhrenstrasse.de. Triberg is one of the stops on the 320km (200-mile) circuit, along which you find all kinds of museums and sights related to clocks. One of the most interesting stops is the **Deutsches Uhrenmuseum (German**

Clock Museum), Robert-Gerwig-Platz 1, Furtwangen ((C) **07723/920-117;** www.deutsches-uhrenmuseum.de). In addition to the world's largest collection of Black Forest clocks, the museum has timepieces from all around the world and from all eras. The museum is open daily April through October from 9am to 6pm, and November through March from 10am to 5pm. Admission is 4€ for adults, 2.50€ for students.

crafts. The big natural attraction is **Wasserfälle Gutach (Gutach Falls),** the highest cataracts in Germany. You can reach Triberg by train along a scenic stretch of railway, making the town a good target for nondrivers. Be warned, though, that Triberg is virtually overrun with tour buses in summer.

GETTING THERE   The Triberg Bahnhof is on the picturesque Schwarzwaldbahn rail line connecting Konstanz, Singen, Villingen, and Offenburg, with frequent connections in all directions; you'll change in Offenberg when coming from Freiburg. Call (C) **01805/996633** or visit www.bahn.de for schedules and information. Regional bus service in the Black Forest area is provided by **SBG Südbaden Bus GmbH,** located in the nearby town of Furtwangen ((C) **07723/19449;** www.suedbadenbus.de). Access by car is via the A5 Autobahn north and south; exit at Offenburg and then follow the signs along Rte. 33 south.

Exploring Triberg

When you get to town you may want to make a stop at the **tourist office,** Wallfahrtstrasse 4 ((C) **07722/866490;** www.triberg.de); it's open year-round daily 10am to 5pm (summer until 6pm).

It's easy to find **Wasserfälle Gutach (Gutach Falls),** also known as Triberg Falls, in which the Gutach River spills some some 160m (525 ft.) downhill in seven misty and poetically evocative stages: Signs all over town point to DEUTSCHLAND'S HOCHSTE WASSERFÄLLE (Germany's Highest Waterfalls). The falls are accessible only on foot, and only between April and late October. (The rest of the year, snow makes trails dangerously slippery, and access to the falls is closed.) It takes no more than half an hour of moderate climbing to reach the falls, and you can replenish your reserves in a cafe and restaurant at the bottom that serves bracing, rib-sticking German food and big portions of Black Forest cake. You might be disappointed to discover the falls are more of a tourist attraction than a pristine natural wonder: They're illuminated at night, and at any time a kiosk collects an entrance charge of 3.50€ for adults, 2€ for students and children ages 8 to 17, free for children under 8.

Schwarzwald-Museum Triberg, Wallfahrtstrasse 4 ((C) **07722/4434;** www.schwarzwaldmuseum.com), pays homage to Black Forest traditions with displays of handicrafts, furnishings, and, of course, clocks and clock making. A working model of the famed Schwarzwaldbahn railway chugs across the Black Forest, through spectacular

The Black Forest

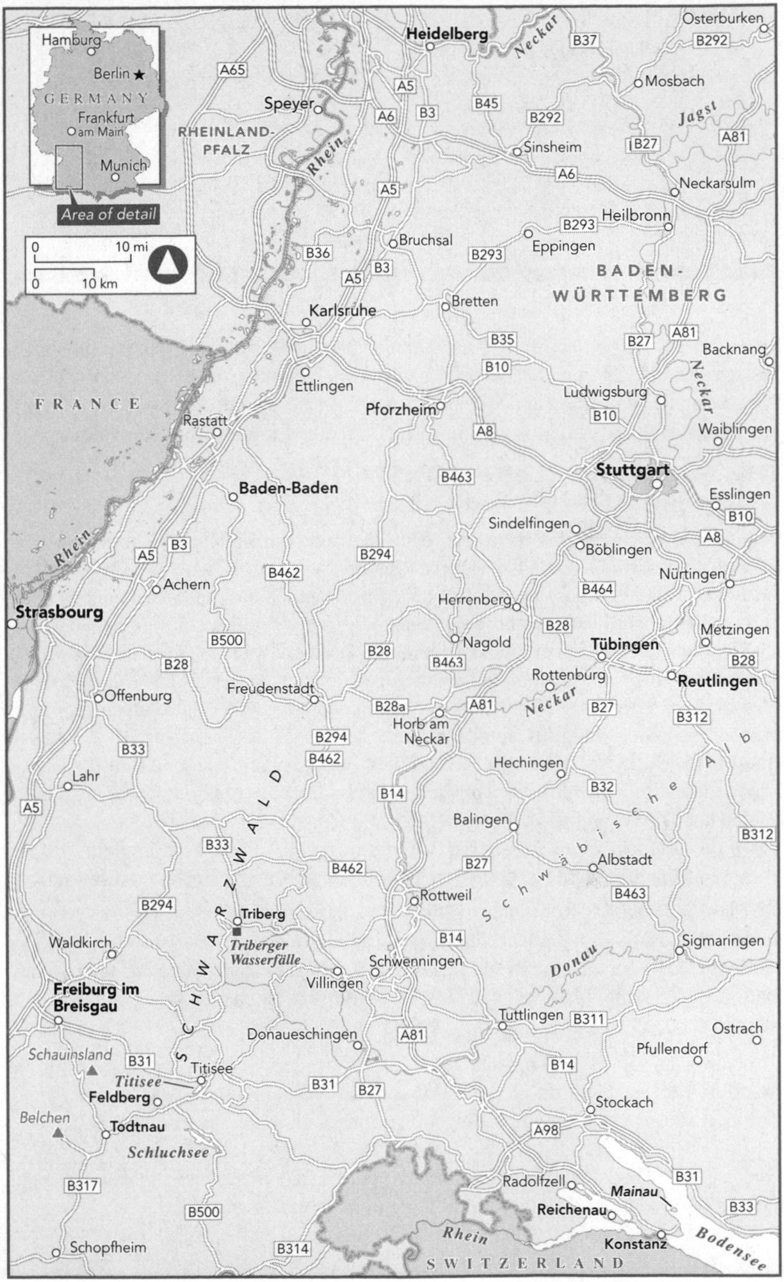
Hamburg
Berlin
GERMANY
Frankfurt am Main
Munich
Area of detail
0 10 mi
0 10 km
Heidelberg
Neckar
Osterburken
Mosbach
Jagst
Speyer
RHEINLAND-PFALZ
Rhein
Sinsheim
Neckarsulm
Heilbronn
Bruchsal
Eppingen
BADEN-WÜRTTEMBERG
Bretten
Karlsruhe
Backnang
Ettlingen
Ludwigsburg
Pforzheim
FRANCE
Rastatt
Waiblingen
Stuttgart
Baden-Baden
Esslingen
Sindelfingen
Böblingen
Achern
Nürtingen
Herrenberg
Strasbourg
Metzingen
Nagold
Tübingen
Rottenburg
Reutlingen
Offenburg
Freudenstadt
Horb am Neckar
Hechingen
Lahr
Schwäbische Alb
Balingen
SCHWARZWALD
Albstadt
Rottweil
Triberg
Triberger Wasserfälle
Waldkirch
Sigmaringen
Schwenningen
Donau
Villingen
Freiburg im Breisgau
Tuttlingen
Ostrach
Donaueschingen
Pfullendorf
Schauinsland
Titisee
Feldberg
Stockach
Belchen
Todtnau
Schluchsee
Radolfzell
Mainau
Reichenau
Konstanz
Bodensee
Schopfheim
SWITZERLAND
A5
A6
A8
A65
A81
A98
B3
B10
B14
B27
B28
B28a
B31
B32
B33
B35
B36
B37
B45
B292
B293
B294
B311
B312
B314
B317
B462
B463
B464
B500

FROM cake TO sausage: BLACK FOREST TREATS

The famous Schwarzwälder Kirschtorte (Black Forest Cherry Cake), the thick, chocolaty cake flavored with cherry preserves, is one of the specialties of this region that's so close to France and Switzerland and something of a culinary crossroads. If you want to sample other regional specialties, look for Zwetchgentorte (plum pastry), Zwiebelkuchen (onion tart), Schwarzwald Schinken (Black Forest smoked ham), meat and fowl dishes with creamy sauces, and wild game such as venison and boar. Most restaurants make their own Hauswurst (sausage) and guard the recipe.

scenery; parts of the electrified route, completed in 1873, still cover 150km (90 miles), passing through 39 tunnels and over 2 viaducts. The museum is open daily May to September 10am to 6pm, and October to April 10am to 5pm. Admission is 5€ adults and 3€ students and children ages 5 to 17; it's free for children 4 and under enter free.

THE BODENSEE (LAKE CONSTANCE) ★★
Konstanz is 125km (78 miles) SE of Freiburg

German speakers call this enormous body of water the Bodensee, but elsewhere in Europe it's known as Lake Constance. Whatever you call it, it is the largest lake in Germany–15km (9 miles) across at its widest point and 74km (46 miles) long. Because of its mild, generally sunny climate and natural beauty, the Bodensee is considered by the Germans to be a kind of inland Riviera. The northern shore is German; Switzerland and Austria share the western and southern portions of the lake's 258km (160 miles) of shoreline. The Rhine flows into the lake from the Swiss Alps, which rise up in majestic splendor along the southern shore, and leaves at **Konstanz,** continuing on from there to the North Sea. In the summer, holidaymakers descend on the shores, where vineyards slope down to crowded marinas, and charming old towns bask in the golden sun. You even find subtropical vegetation growing in sheltered gardens.

On this day trip we're suggesting that you travel east from from Freiburg to get a glimpse of the lake from the pretty old town on its northwestern shores, Konstanz.

GETTING THERE   Konstanz is 125km (78 miles) east of Freiburg on B31, and the scenic drive through the Black Forest takes about 1½ hours. The train trip between Freiburg takes about 2½ hours and requires at least one change. Konstanz tourist information is at Bahnhofplatz 13 (© **07531/13-30-30;** www.konstanz.de).

Exploring Konstanz & the Lake
Crowding the tip of a peninsula right on the border with Switzerland, Konstanz straddles both banks of the Rhine. Adding to this scenic advantage is a great deal of medieval charm, supplied by twisting streets, pretty churches, and two Rhineside towers that are remnants of the town's walls. The Altstadt escaped bombing by Allied Forces during World War II with a simply ploy: Residents left their lights on at night, making bombardiers think they were flying over neutral Switzerland.

You can see the town in about half an hour, beginning on the Münsterplatz for a look at the Münster (Cathedral), begun in the 11th century and not completed until the 17th, and just to the south, the Rathaus, with a painted facade. Then head towards the harbor and stroll along the Seeufer (Lake Shore), an attractive promenade that passes the port, public gardens, a casino, dozens of cafes and restaurants. The historic lakeside Konzil-gebäude (Council Building) hosted the Council of Constance between 1414 and 1418, the only papal conclave ever held north of the Alps (Hafenstrasse 2). You may want to board one of the ferries in the harbor for a trip to one of two nearby islands; **Bodensee-Schiffsbetriebe,** Schützingerweg 2, Lindau (© **08382/2754-810;** www.bsb-online. com), provides ferry service on the lake.

Insel Reichenau (Reichenau Island) ★ RELIGIOUS SITE   In 724 St. Pirmin founded the first Benedictine monastery east of the Rhine on this little island, only 5 sq. km (2 sq. miles), which later became a center for the production of illuminated manuscripts. Three churches are the main attraction: The late-9th-century St. Georg-skirche (Church of St. George) in Oberzell is remarkable for its harmonious design and wall paintings from about A.D. 1000; the oak roof frame of the Munster St. Maria and Markus (Church of St. Mary and Mark) in Mittelzell, the chief town on the island, is believed to be the oldest in Germany, created from oaks that were felled around 1236; and the Stiftskirche (College Church) St. Peter in Niederzell on the western tip of the island has wall paintings from the 12th century.

Mainau ★★★ PARK/GARDEN   On this almost tropical island 6km (4 miles) north of Konstanz, palms and orange trees grow and fragrant flowers bloom year-round, practically in the shadow of the snow-covered Alps. The late Swedish Count Lennart Bernadotte is credited with this luxuriant botanical oasis, with greenhouses, seasonal gardens, and an arboretum. Palms, citrus and fruit trees, orchids, azaleas, rhododendrons, tens of thousands of tulips in the spring, and roses in the summer fill the gardens and hothouses, and butterflies from throughout the world flit and flutter through the Butterfly House. The count's family resides in the ancient castle, once a stronghold of the Knights of the Teutonic Order, and oversee the island paradise he established. A number of restaurants—including a formal restaurant, a cafe, and a sausage grill—are tucked into scenic locations around the island. The gardens are open year round from sunrise to sunset. You can reach Mainau either by tour boat from Konstanz or by walking across the small footbridge connecting the island to the mainland, north of the city. Admission is 18€ for adults, 11€ for students and children, 37€ for families, free for children 12 and under. For more information, call © **07531/3030** or visit www.mainau.de.

FRANKFURT, COLOGNE & THE RHINELAND

For about 2 centuries now, the mighty Rhine has attracted visitors from around the world, who come to enjoy the romantic scenery of hilltop castles, medieval towns, and vineyard-covered slopes. The **Rhineland,** the area along the river's west bank, is a treasure-trove for tourists, with **Cologne,** the Rhineland's largest and most important city, sitting right on the river. Possessing the largest cathedral in Germany and filled with a fascinating assortment of museums and cultural venues, Cologne makes a wonderful headquarters for exploring the Rhineland. There are many day trip options from Cologne, including **Aachen,** one of Germany's oldest cities, the **Mosel Valley,** covered with meticulously tended vineyards, and river trips on the **Mittelrhein (Middle Rhine),** the river's most scenic stretch, where you can glide by castle-crowned summits, stop at riverside wine towns, and finally see that rock—the Loreley—that you've heard so much about.

But this chapter begins not on the Rhine but on one of its tributaries, the Main, and in another city, **Frankfurt,** because Frankfurt-am-Main is where so many journeys to Germany begin and end. Frankly, Frankfurt is not as appealing as Cologne, which lies 117 miles northwest and is less than an hour away by train. Frankfurt, with its high-rise towers and emphasis on business and banking, lacks Cologne's human scale, historic charm, and fun-loving heart. But it has several renowned museums, is a shopping mecca, and a transportation hub for all of Germany. Like Cologne, Frankfurt offers a host of nearby and easily accessible day trips, including the historic town of **Mainz,** the spa town of **Wiesbaden,** and the beautiful **Rheingau wine district.**

FRANKFURT-AM-MAIN ★

Sometimes called "Mainhattan" because of its skyscraper-studded skyline, Frankfurt is Germany's fifth-largest city. Many travelers get their first introduction to Germany in this city because the Frankfurt airport serves as the country's main international hub. And that's a shame, because although there are cultural and financial riches here, the city itself is not particularly memorable.

As with just about every city in Germany, you have to figure World War II into the equation of modern-day Frankfurt-am-Main. After major

9

The Rhineland

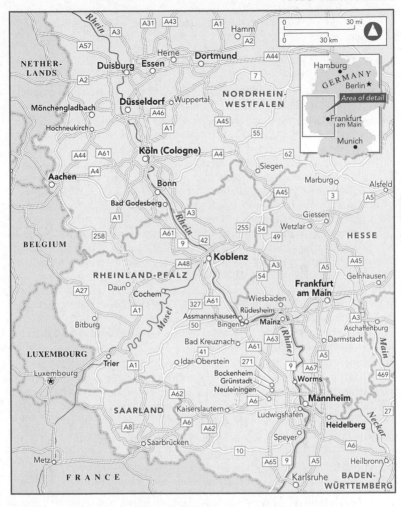

destruction in World War II, Frankfurt was rebuilt in a way that salvaged a small portion of its once-extensive Altstadt (Old Town), but otherwise turned, in architectural terms, to the future instead of the past. Visitors looking for a romantic or atmospheric piece of Old Germany will not find it in this fast-paced and cosmopolitan metropolis. Instead, Frankfurt is a city representative of modern, business-oriented Germany. It has been a major banking city since the Rothschilds opened their first bank here more than 200 years ago and has long been the financial center not only of Germany but also of the entire European Union, home of the Bundesbank, Germany's central bank, and the Central Bank of the EU. More banks maintain headquarters here than anywhere else in German city, a fact that helps account for all those designer skyscrapers (including the Commerzbank Tower, the tallest building in western Europe) with their somewhat

9

FRANKFURT, COLOGNE & THE RHINELAND

Frankfurt-am-Main

bland and anonymous corporate facades. The huge € sign that stands on Willy-Brandt-Platz in front of the opera house can be regarded as the city's logo.

Visitors will find several excellent museums in Frankfurt, but if your time in Germany is limited, you may want to hop on a fast train right below the airport and head to Cologne instead.

Essentials

GETTING THERE

BY PLANE   **Flughafen Frankfurt/Main** (ⓒ **069/6901;** www.frankfurt-airport.de) lies 11km (7 miles) from the city center. Europe's busiest airport and Germany's major international gateway, this airport serves more than 110 countries worldwide, with direct flights from many U.S. and Canadian cities. The airport has a full array of stores, restaurants, banks, a bus terminal, several car-rental offices, and two railway stations.

The long-distance **DB Rail Terminal,** conveniently located below the airport, links the airport to cities throughout Germany and neighboring countries. Regional and local trains operate from the **Regional Station** directly below Terminal 1. What this means is that you can fly into Frankfurt, hop on a train right at the airport, and be on your way to any destination in Germany.

The simplest method for getting into the city from the airport is by **S-Bahn** (light rail). **S8** and **S9** trains (direction Offenbach or Hanau) take you directly to Frankfurt's Hauptbahnhof (main railway station) in about 10 minutes. A one-way ticket costs 4.50€. Tickets are available from the RMV ticket machines.

Buses into the city stop in front of Terminal 1 on the arrivals level and in front of Terminal 2 on Level 2. Some airlines offer special shuttle-bus services to Frankfurt from the airport; check when you purchase your ticket.

A **taxi** from the airport to the city center costs about 25€ and takes about 20 minutes. Taxis are available in front of the terminals.

BY TRAIN   Frankfurt's **Hauptbahnhof** (main train station) is the busiest train station in Europe, with connections to all major German and European cities. **Tourist Information Hauptbahnhof,** opposite the main entrance (ⓒ **069/2123-8800**), is open Monday to Friday from 8am to 9pm, and Saturday and Sunday until 6pm. For train travel information, contact **Deutsche Bahn** (ⓒ **11861;** www.bahn.com).

BY CAR   The A3 and A5 autobahns intersect near Frankfurt's airport. The **A3** comes in from the Netherlands, Cologne, and Bonn and continues east and south to Munich. The **A5** comes from the northeast and continues south to Heidelberg and Basel, Switzerland. From the west, **A60** connects with **A66,** which leads to Frankfurt.

The Neighborhoods in Brief

ALTSTADT

The **River Main** divides Frankfurt. Most of the historic sights and several museums are found in the Altstadt on the north bank. Concentrated in the **city center** around the Altstadt are hotels, restaurants, and nightlife. The Altstadt contains an even older section referred to as the **Innenstadt,** or Inner City. The **Hauptbahnhof** is located at the western edge of the city center. As you

walk out of the station, Baselerstrasse is on your right and heads south toward the River Main. You have a choice of streets heading east to the Altstadt: Münchner Strasse leads directly into **Theaterplatz,** with its opera house; Taunusstrasse goes to three of the major Altstadt squares in the southern part of the city—**Goetheplatz, Rathenauplatz,** and the **Hauptwache.**

WESTEND

The exclusive Westend district, west of the Altstadt, is a residential and embassy quarter. It was the only part of Frankfurt that was not destroyed during the Allied bombing of the city in World War II. The huge, modern Frankfurt **Messe** (trade-fair convention center) is considered part of the Westend.

MUSEUMSUFER

The embankment (*Ufer*) along the river's south side, is the site of many prominent museums, some of them housed in former riverside villas.

SACHSENHAUSEN

This district on the south side of the river, is a popular entertainment quarter filled with Frankfurt's famous apple-wine taverns.

GETTING AROUND

BY FOOT   After you arrive in the Altstadt, you can easily get everywhere, including the Museumsufer on the opposite bank of the river, on foot.

BY PUBLIC TRANSPORTATION   A network of modern U-Bahn (subways), **Strassenbahn** (streetcars), and **buses,** administered by the **RMV** (**Rhein-Main Verkehrsverbund;** ℂ **069/19449;** www.vgf-ffm.de), links Frankfurt. All forms of public transportation can be used interchangeably at a single price based on fare zones. Tickets are good for 1 hour on routes going in the same direction. Purchase your tickets at ticket counters or from the coin-operated machines found in U-Bahn stations and next to tram and bus stops. The ticket machines have user screens in English to guide you through the process. A one-way single ticket (*Einzelfahrkarte*) within the city center costs 2.20€ for adults, 1.35€ for children.

BY TAXI   To call a taxi, dial ℂ **069/230001.** You can also get a cab at one of the city's clearly designated taxi stands, or by hailing one on the street (the car's roof light will be illuminated if it's available). Taxis charge by the trip and by the number of passengers, without extra surcharges for luggage. The initial charge is 2.50€; each kilometer costs 1.70€.

VISITOR INFORMATION

Tourist Information Hauptbahnhof, opposite the main entrance of the train station (ℂ **069/2123-8800;** www.frankfurt-tourismus.de), is open Monday through Friday 8am to 9pm and Saturday through Sunday 9am to 6pm. **Tourist Information Römer,** Römerberg 27 (ℂ **069/2123-8800**), in the Altstadt, is open Monday through Friday 9:30am to 5:30pm and Saturday through Sunday 10am to 4pm.

Where to Stay

Frankfurt is an expensive, business-oriented city, and you can save a bundle by booking one of the air-hotel packages available from major airlines. Note that hotel rates can almost double when there is a major trade fair going on.

Art-Hotel Robert Mayer ★★   This artfully decorated Westend hotel is within walking distance of Frankfurt's trade-fair complex. The building dates from 1905, but the rooms were completely redone in 1994, when 11 artists were hired to lend their individual visions to each of the 11 bedrooms; one was inspired by Frank Lloyd Wright, another looks Italian postmodern with pop art. You get the,er, picture. All the rooms are comfortable and stylish. Many restaurants are nearby.

Robert-Mayer-Strasse 44. ℂ **069/9709100.** www.arthotel-frankfurt.de. 11 units. 99€–275€ double with breakfast. U-Bahn: Bockenheimer Warte: **Amenities:** Free Wi-Fi.

Two special tickets help you save money on public transportation in Frankfurt: A **Tageskarte** (day ticket) good for unlimited travel inside Frankfurt's central zone, costs 5.60€ for adults and 3.35€ for children. You can buy this ticket from the ticket machines. The **Frankfurt Card,** available at the city's tourist offices, allows unlimited travel anywhere within the greater Frankfurt area, transport on the airport shuttle bus, a reduction on the tourist office's sightseeing tour, and half-price admission to many of the city's museums. The cost is 8.70€ for a 1-day card and 13€ for a 2-day card.

Hotelschiff Peter Schlott ★   You'll be rocked to bed, like a baby in a cradle in this 1950's era riverboat, now permanently moored in the Frankfurt suburb of Höchst. All of them have washbasins, 10 have tiny showers, but none has a private toilet. As you might imagine, everything is cabin-size and pretty basic (some rooms are just a cut above a hostel), but if you love boats you'll enjoy hearing the waters of the Main lapping beneath your window. The ship's narrow and steep staircases are not easy to navigate if you have lots of luggage or difficulty walking. There's a nice cafe and restaurant on board.

Mainberg. ⓒ **069/3004643.** www.hotel-schiff-schlott.de. 19 units. 65€–100€double with breakfast. S-Bahn: Höchst. **Amenities:** Restaurant, free Wi-Fi.

The Pure ★★   White on white on more white (with some dark wood and orange thrown in for accenting)—that about sums up the decor at this uber-hip, Zen property. If you like modern decor, you'll think this place is stunning (most do). But in the end, no matter how trendy it is, a good hotel must provide efficient service and a good bed, and The Pure is a winner there as well.

Niddastrasse 86. ⓒ **069/710-4570.** www.the-pure.de. 50 units. 140€–200€ double with breakfast. U-Bahn: Hauptbahnhof. **Amenities:** Restaurant, bar, fitness center, free Wi-Fi.

Where to Eat

In recent years, Frankfurt has become, along with Berlin and Munich, one of Germany's great dining capitals, with restaurants that offer an array of richly varied cuisines—at predictably steep rices. But there are places where you can to eat well for less. The *Apfelwein* (apple wine) taverns in Sachsenhausen on the south bank of the Main, tend to serve traditional Hessian dishes such as *Rippchen mit Kraut* (pickled pork chops with sauerkraut), *Haspel* (pigs' knuckles), and *Handkäs mit Musik* (strong, cheese with vinegar, oil, and chopped onions; not recommended for honeymooners). One condiment unique to Frankfurt is *grüne Sosse,* a green sauce made from seven herbs and other seasonings, chopped hard-boiled eggs, and sour cream, usually served with boiled eggs, boiled beef *(Tafelspitz),* or poached fish.

Exedra ★ GREEK/MACEDONIAN   Behind an ornate 19th-century facade is one of the best Greek restaurants in Frankfurt. All the menu offerings are reliably good. The grilled lamb with feta-cheese sauce and grilled sweet peppers, and the pan-fried veal with white-wine and lemon sauce are both excellent. As for ambiance, it's a large and fairly plain taverna, but with big windows overlooking the street. Exedra also serves as a cafe-bar in the early mornings.

Heiligkreuzgasse 29. ⓒ **069/287397.** Main courses 10€–20€. Mon–Fri 8:30am–midnight; Sat–Sun 4pm–midnight. U-Bahn: Konstablerwache.

Haus Wertheym ★ GERMAN/HESSIAN Wertheym operates three old-fashioned, atmospheric, and relatively inexpensive restaurants in the Altstadt: **Restaurant Haus Wertheym,** a half-timbered house on a cobblestone street just west of the Römer; **Historix** (*℃* **069/29-44-00;** Saalgasse 19), an apple-wine tavern right across from it; and **Römer-Bembel,** a larger tavern with outdoor tables right on Römer square (*℃* **069/28-83-83**). Wood paneling and antique accessories decorate the interiors of all three. The menus favor traditional dishes such as Frankfurter sausages, pork Schnitzels (breaded cutlets), Frankfurter *Hacksteak* (chopped steak), and a good *Tafelspitz* (boiled beef) that comes with the restaurant's trademark green sauce. The waiters can be brusque when the places are busy.

Fahrtor 1. *℃* **069/28-14-32.** Main courses 8€–24€. Daily 11am–11pm. U-Bahn: Römer.

Restaurant Français ★★★ FRENCH It's a dress-up affair at the Restaurant Francais (men are requested to wear coats and ties) but that seems in keeping with the dining experience at this stylish and well heeled eatery in the grand Steigenberger Frankfurter hotel. Does it have the best French cooking in Germany? Many think so and we'll say that the Chef Patrick Bittner's food is creative, delicious, and beautifully presented. To sample the full range of flavors, go for the seven-course tasting menu (you can also order three-, four-, five-, or six-course fixed-price menus). Your starter might be Alsatian goose liver with apricots and artichokes or a cream of celery soup with scampi, followed by Scottish partridge with grapes and raddichio, or Breton turbot with celery red onions. (The menu changes weekly.) Desserts are refined and delectable—which is how you might describe the entire experience. An expert sommelier is on hand to recommend the perfect wine accompaniment.

In the Steigenberger Frankfurter Hof, Am Kaiserplatz. *℃* **069/21502.** www.restaurant-francais.de. Reservations required. Main courses 38€–48€; fixed-price menus 74€–135€. Mon–Fri noon–1:45pm and 6:30–10:30pm. U-Bahn: Willy-Brandt-Platz.

Tiger Gourmet Restaurant/Palastbar-Restaurant ★★★ INTERNATIONAL What came first, the first-class variety show or the first-class restaurant? Well, this 190-seat venue has been playing two shows a night for 25 years old, but the gourmet restaurant only took off in 2000 when Andreas Kroliks' cooking was awarded a Michelin star. Eating here, as at Restaurant Francais, can be very pricey, but if you combine it with watching the show, it gives you a totally unique and very high-caliber dining-entertainment experience that goes way beyond supper-club standards. There is a 6-course seasonal tasting menu and other multi-course menus that show off Kroliks culinary talents (or you can order a la carte). In season, you might encounter a fresh "fruits of the sea" menu featuring hamachi, Arctic char, and a medley of other fresh fish dishes. There are vegetarian entrees, as well. More people tend to eat in the larger and less elaborate Palast-Resaurant, but it's kind of like business class as opposed to first-class. The service here is deftly professional and the show (see Tigerpalast, below) is comparable to Cique de Soleil but on a very small stage.

Heiligkreuzgasse 16–20. *℃* **069/9200220.** www.tigerpalast.com. Reservations required. Gourmet Restaurant main courses 45€–65€, fixed-price menus 110€–135€. Palastbar-Restaurant main courses 25€–38€. Gourmet Restaurant Tues–Sat 7pm–midnight. Palastbar-Restaurant Tues–Sun 5pm–1am. U-Bahn: Konstablerwache.

Exploring Frankfurt

You can explore Frankfurt's compact Altstadt and Innenstadt on foot. Nearly all the main sights lie within the boundaries of the old town walls (which today form a stretch of narrow parkland around the Altstadt) or are just across the river along the **Museumsufer (Museum Embankment),** where several museums are located along **Schaumainkai,** the street that runs directly parallel to the river Main.

MUSEUMS ON MUSEUMSUFER

Several of Frankfurt's best and most-visited museums are found across the river from the Altstadt along the Main embankment on a street called Schaumainkai. The Eisener Steg, an old iron bridge, spans the river, connecting the Altstadt to Museumsufer.

Deutsches Architekturmuseum (German Architecture Museum) ★

MUSEUM   Housed in a pair of 19th-century villas, this museum isn't for everyone, but will intrigue those with an interest in architecture or urban planning. On display is a collection of 19th- and 20th-century architectural plans and models, examples of international modern architecture, and a series of exhibits showing how human dwellings have evolved over time in different parts of the world.

Schaumainkai 43. ℂ **069/21238844.** Admission 6€ adults, 3€ students and children. Tues–Sun 11am–6pm (Wed until 8pm). U-Bahn: Schweizer Platz.

Deutsches Filmmuseum (German Film Museum) ★★ MUSEUM   Deutsches

Filmmuseum is one of the two top film museums in Germany (the other is in Berlin). The first-floor galleries chronicle the history of the German and European filmmaking industry with examples of moviemaking equipment and models illustrating how special effects are shot (highlights include Emile Reynaud's 1882 Praxinoscope, Edison's 1889 Kinetoscope, and a copy of the Lumière brothers' Cinematograph from 1895). Old German films play continuously on the second floor.

Schaumainkai 41. ℂ **069/21238830.** Admission 2.50€ adults, 1.30€ students and children. Tues and Thurs–Fri 10am–5pm; Wed and Sun 10am–7pm; Sat 2–7pm. U-Bahn: Schweizer Platz.

Liebieghaus (Liebieg Sculpture Museum) ★★ MUSEUM   This important

museum, housed in an elegant 19th-century villa, displays superb sculptures of the human face and form created over a 1,500-year period. There's an intimacy and expressiveness in some of these pieces that is both timeless and somehow elevating. Each piece is beautifully displayed, which adds to the aesthetic pleasure of a trip here.

The Liebighaus collection includes noteworthy pieces from ancient Egypt, Greece, and Rome, and from medieval and Renaissance Europe. In the medieval section, look for the 11th-century carving of the Virgin and Child created in Trier, the expressive 16th-century Madonna created by Tilman Riemenschneider, the brilliant woodcarver from Würzburg (for more on his work, and where it's found, see chapter 7), Andrea

Frankfurt

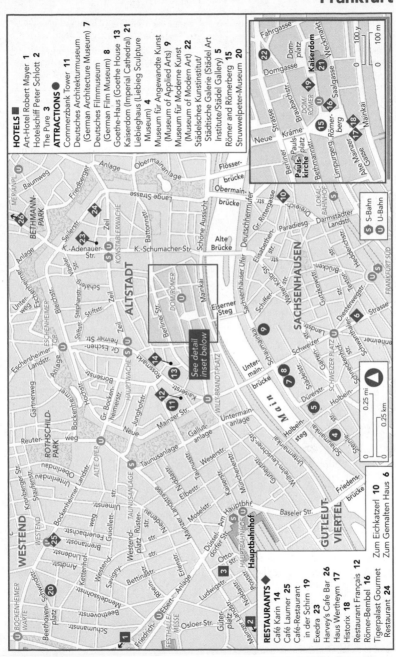

HOTELS ■
Art-Hotel Robert Mayer **1**
Hotelschiff Peter Schlott **2**
The Pure **3**

ATTRACTIONS ●
Commerzbank Tower **11**
Deutsches Architekturmuseum
(German Architecture Museum) **7**
Deutsches Filmmuseum
(German Film Museum) **8**
Goethe-Haus (Goethe House) **13**
Kaiserdom (Imperial Cathedral) **21**
Liebieghaus (Liebieg Sculpture
Museum) **4**
Museum für Angewandte Kunst
(Museum of Applied Arts) **9**
Museum für Moderne Kunst
(Museum of Modern Art) **22**
Städelsches Kunstinstitut/
Städtische Galerie (Städel Art
Institute/Städel Gallery) **5**
Römer and Römerberg **15**
Struwwelpeter-Museum **20**

RESTAURANTS ◆
Café Karin **14**
Café Laumer **25**
Café-Restaurant
in der Schirm **19**
Exedra **23**
Harvey's Cafe Bar **26**
Haus Wertheym **17**
Historix **18**
Restaurant Français **12**
Römer-Bembel **16**
Tigerpalast Gourmet
Restaurant **24**
Zum Eichkatzerl **10**
Zum Gemalten Haus **6**

S S-Bahn
U U-Bahn

211

Guided Tours

A good way to see Frankfurt, especially when your time is limited, is by the **daily guided tour** offered by the city's tourist offices. The 2½-hour bus tour, in English, picks up passengers at 2pm from Touristinfo Römer (Römerberg 27, in the Altstadt; ✆ **069/2123-8800**) and at 2:15pm from Touristinfo Hauptbahnhof (opposite the main entrance of the train station). From April through October, an additional tour leaves from the Römer at 10am and from the train station at 10:15am The tour covers the entire city and includes a trip to the Goethe House and, in the summer, the top of the Commerzbank tower, Frankfurt's tallest skyscraper. The cost is 26€ for adults, 21€ for students, and 10€ for children ages 6 to 10. Buy tickets at the tourist offices.

della Robbia's altarpiece of the Assumption, and the 16th-century Black Venus with Mirror. Give yourself at least an hour to see the major works.

Schaumainkai 71. ✆ **069/21238617.** Admission 7€ adults; 5€ seniors, students, and children. Fri–Tues 10am–5pm; Wed–Thurs 10am–9pm. U-Bahn: Schweizer Platz.

Museum für Angewandte Kunst (Museum of Applied Arts) ★ MUSEUM Two buildings—one an early-19th-century villa, the other a 1985 structure designed by architect Richard Meier—house this enormous collection of European, Asian, and Islamic objects. The museum has outstanding collections of glassware (including 15th-c. Venetian pieces), German rococo furnishings, and porcelain.

Schaumainkai 17. ✆ **069/2123-4037.** Admission 5€ adults, 2.50€ students and children. Tues–Sun 10am–5pm (Wed until 9pm). U-Bahn: Römer.

Städelsches Kunstinstitut/Städische Galerie (Städel Art Institute/ Städel Gallery) ★★★ MUSEUM   The Städel is Frankfurt's most important art gallery, and one of the the the top museums in Germany, bringing together noteoworthy collections of painting, sculpture, and drawings from medieval to modern Europe, and a photography collection that spans the entire spectrum of photographic art. The first floor features French Impressionists such as Renoir and Monet, along with German painters of the 19th and 20th centuries, including Tischbein's famous Portrait of Goethe in the Campagna in Italy. If you're short on time, the second floor displays an outstanding collection of Flemish primitives, 17th-century Dutch artists, and 16th-century German masters, such as Dürer, Grünewald, and Memling. One of the most impressive paintings is Jan van Eyck's "Madonna" (1433). A large altarpiece and an impish nude Venus represent the work of Lucas Cranach. In the Department of Modern Art hang works by Francis Bacon, Dubuffet, Tapies, and Yves Klein.

Schaumainkai 63. ✆ **069/605-0980.** 10€ adults, 8€ children 9–16. Tues and Fri–Sun 10am–5pm; Wed–Thurs 10am–9pm. U-Bahn: Schweizer Platz.

OTHER ATTRACTIONS IN FRANKFURT

Commerzbank Tower ★ ARCHITECTURAL SITE/VIEW   The outdoor observation deck on the 56th floor of this gleaming, cylindrical tower in the city center provides a spectacular panorama of Frankfurt and the entire region. The building, constructed in 1997, is the tallest building in Western Europe.

Neue Mainzer Strasse 52–58. ✆ **069/36504777.** Admission 4.60€. Sun–Thurs 10am–9pm (until 7pm in winter); Fri–Sat 10am–11pm (until 9pm in winter). U-Bahn: Willy-Brandt-Platz.

Goethe-Haus (Goethe House) ★ MUSEUM/HISTORIC SITE   Johann Wolfgang von Goethe (1749–1832), Germany's greatest writer, was born in this spacious,
light-filled house and lived here until 1765, when he moved to Weimar. Reconstructed
after wartime damage, the ocher-colored house still manages to convey the feeling of
a prosperous, tranquil home life in bygone days. The interior decoration reflects the
baroque, rococo, and neoclassical styles of the 18th century. Paintings of friends and
family adorn the walls. The room where Goethe wrote is on the second floor; the room
next door displays one of his most cherished childhood possessions, a puppet theater.
Annexed to the house is the modern, glass-fronted Goethe-Museum. Of interest to
Goethe specialists, the museum contains a library of books, manuscripts, graphic artworks, and paintings associated with Goethe and his works.

Grosser Hirschgraben 23–25. ✆ **069/138800.** Admission 5€ adults, 2.50€students, 1.50€ children.
Mon–Sat 10am–6pm; Sun 10am–5:30pm. U-/S-Bahn: Hauptwache.

Kaiserdom (Imperial Cathedral) ★ CHURCH   The famous dome-topped west
tower of the Kaiserdom (also known as Bartholomäus-Dom/Cathedral of St. Bar-
tholomew) dominates the Altstadt. The highly ornamented tower dates from the 15th
century and is built of red sandstone. Construction on the cathedral began in the 13th
century and went on to the 15th, but the structure wasn't entirely completed until 1877.
The church gained cathedral status in the 14th century when it became the site of the
election of the emperors (called Kaisers in Germany) of the Holy Roman Empire.
Later, between 1562 and 1792, the Kaisers also were crowned here, so the church
became known as the Kaiserdom. Previous coronations had taken place in Aachen
Cathedral. Destroyed by Allied bombs in 1944, the cathedral was painstakingly rebuilt
in 1953. The layout is a fairly simple Gothic hall-church with three naves and a transept. The **Dom Museum** in the church's 19th-century cloister, exhibits coronation
robes of the imperial electors. The oldest vestments date from the 1400s.

Domplatz. ✆ **069/29703236.** Church free; Dom Museum 2€ adults, 1€ children. Church daily
9am–noon and 2–6pm; Dom Museum Tues–Fri 10am–5pm, Sat–Sun 11am–5pm. U-Bahn: Römer.

Museum für Moderne Kunst (Museum of Modern Art) ★ MUSEUM   The
Germans are great collectors of modern and contemporary American art from the New
York School, and museums reverentially displaying the works of Andy Warhol and
other big-name American artists are found throughout the country. This is one of them,
and if you are interested in the works of major American artists since the 1950s, you
will enjoy the painting collections on display here. The big, bold works by Americans
Roy Liechtenstein, Claes Oldenburg, Warhol and George Segal tend to steal the show
from the modern German artists (Joseph Beuys, Lothar Baumgarten, Herbert Brandl)
whose works are also on permanent display. The museum serves as a useful tool to
tune in on current trends in international contemporary art. Located 1 block north of
the cathedral in the Altstadt, the MMK opened in 1991 in a postmodern building
designed by Austrian architect Hans Hollein. The massive triangular structure, with its
projecting and receding window openings, stands in stark contrast to everything
around it. A pleasant cafe-restaurant is on the premises.

Domstrasse 10. ✆ **069/212-0447.** Admission 7€ adults, 3.50€ students. Tues–Sun 10am–5pm
(Wed until 8pm). U-Bahn: Römer.

Römer and Römerberg ★★ HISTORIC SITE   As early as the Stone Age,
people occupied this high ground that was later settled by the Romans. After Germanic
tribes conquered the Romans, the settlement fell into ruins and was forgotten until

construction workers in the 20th century stumbled across its ancient remains. But from then to now, this area in Frankfurt's Altstadt has always played a prominent role in the life of the city, both physically and psychically. The Altstadt centers around three Gothic buildings with stepped gables, known collectively as the Römer—the German word for Roman, and perhaps an oblique reference to the Holy Roman Empire and Holy Roman Emperor who, from the 10th to the 16th centuries, was crowned in the nearby Kaiserdom. These houses, just west of the cathedral, originally were built between 1288 and 1305 and then bought by the city a century later for use as the Rathaus (Town Hall). After his coronation in the Kaiserdom, a new emperor and his entourage paraded westward to the Römer for a banquet. In the **Kaisersaal (Imperial Hall),** on the second floor of the center house, you can see romanticized images of 52 emperors sculpted in the 19th century to celebrate the thousand-year history of the Holy Roman Empire. Medieval city officials and their families watched plays and tournaments from a specially built gallery on the **Nikolaikirche (St. Nicholas Church),** the small chapel in front of the city hall. The chapel has a 35-bell carillon that plays at 9:05am, 12:05pm, and 5:05pm. **Römerplatz,** the square in front of the Römer, is one of Frankfurt's most popular spots, with a series of rebuilt half-timbered buildings housing cafes and restaurants. In December, it becomes the site of Frankfurt's giant **Christmas Market.** The elaborate facade of the Römer, with its ornate balcony and statues of emperors, overlooks the **Römerberg (Roman Hill).**

Römer. Kaisersaal ⓒ**069/21234814.** Admission 2€. Daily 10am–1pm and 2–5pm. U-Bahn: Römer.

Shopping

As you might expect, this big, modern, wealthy and international city serves as a shopping Mecca for the entire region. The **Zeil,** reputedly the busiest shopping street in Germany, is a pedestrian zone between the Hauptwache and Konstablerwache. It's loaded with department stores, clothing shops, shoe stores, boutiques of all kinds, restaurants, cafes and people. The **Hauptwache,** in the center of Frankfurt, has two shopping areas, one above and one below ground. **Schillerstrasse,** another pedestrian zone, lies between Hauptwache and Eschenheimer Turm, near the stock exchange. Walking from Schillerstrasse northeast toward Eschenheimer Tor, you pass many elegant boutiques and specialty shops. Southwest of the Hauptwache is **Goethestrasse,** with exclusive stores evocative of Paris or Milan.

Höchster Porzellan Manufaktur ★★ CHINA & GLASSWARE   If you're looking for a special piece of porcelain, this store contains one of Germany's largest inventories of Höchst porcelain, called "white gold" and manufactured for the past 260 years. Am Kornmarkt/Berliner Strasse 60. ⓒ**069/295-299.** www.hoechster-porzellan.de. U-Bahn: Römer.

Nightlife

Frankfurt may be big and cosmopolitan, but it lacks the spit and spirit that animates the nightlife in places like Berlin and even nearby Cologne. It's not dull, exactly, but it's geared to banking and bankers rather than the young and young at heart. But that's not to say that you won't be able to find anything to do after dark. You will—but not with the choices you'd find in other German cities. For details about what's happening in Frankfurt, pick up **"Journal Frankfurt"** at newsstands throughout the city. **"Fritz"** and **"Strandgut,"** both free and available at the tourist office, also have listings. To purchase tickets for major cultural events, go to the venue box office (*Kasse*) or to the **Touristinfo** office at the main train station or in the Römer. One of the best ways to spend an evening is at an apple-wine taverns in Sachsenhausen (see below).

STRUWWELPETER: A VERY naughty BOY

He's a memory now, but up until World War II, the image of Struwwelpeter, with his enormous shock of hair and Edward Scissorhands-length fingernails, was ingrained in the nightmares of every German child and many children throughout the world. (Struwwelpeter's grotesque hair and fingernails were the result of his bad-boy behavior.) Published in 1844, Struwwelpeter was the creation of Heinrich Hoffman (1809–94), a Frankfurt physician who wrote gruesomely moralistic children's stories. The illustrated story became one of the most popular "children's books" in Germany and was translated into 14 languages (in England, Struwwelpeter became "Shockheaded Peter"). The entertaining **Struwwelpeter-Museum,** Schirn, Römerberg, Bendergass 1 (© **069/281-333**), displays original sketches and illustrations with copies of the book (and its classic image of Struwwelpeter) from many different countries. Admission is free; the museum, located alongside the Schirn Gallery, is open Tuesday to Sunday 11am to 5pm.

THE PERFORMING ARTS

Alte Oper ★★ CONCERT HALL When the Alte Oper (Old Opera House) opened in 1880, critics hailed the building as one of the most beautiful theaters in Europe. Destroyed in the war, the Alte Oper didn't reopen until 1981. Today the theater, with its golden-red mahogany interior and superb acoustics, is the site of frequent symphonic and choral concerts, but opera is not performed here. Opernplatz. © **069/1340400.** www.alteoper.de. U-Bahn: Alte Oper.

Oper Frankfurt/Ballet Frankfurt ★★ PERFORMING ARTS VENUE This is Frankfurt's premier showcase for opera and ballet. Willy-Brandt-Platz. © **069/134-0400.** www.oper-frankfurt.de. U-Bahn: Willy-Brandt-Platz.

English Theater ★★ THEATER This long-establish theater presents English-language musicals, comedies, dramas, and thrillers. Kaiserstrasse 52. © **069/24231620.** www.english-theatre.org. U-Bahn: Hauptbahnhof.

Tigerpalast ★★★ CABARET/THE PERFORMING ARTS This is the most famous cabaret in Frankfurt. Shows take place in a small theater, where guests sit at tiny tables to see about eight different acts (you can also have dinner before or after the twice-nightly shows, see Tiger Gourmet Restaurant under "Where to Eat," above) Each show, a kind of small-scale Cirque de Soleil with an overall theme and a roster of every-changing artistes ranging from gymnasts and acrobats to magic tricks and musicians, lasts 2 hours with breaks for drinks and snacks. You don't need to know German to enjoy the show, which is excellent family-style entertainment. Heiligkreuzgasse 16–20. © **069/289691.** www.tigerpalast.de. U-Bahn: Konstablerwache.

CAFES, BARS & CLUBS

Café Karin ★★ CAFE This unpretentious cafe with art-filled walls, old wooden tables, daily newspapers, and cafe food, is a good place to stop for coffee, a glass of wine or beer, or a light meal. Grosser Hirschgraben 28. © **069/295-217.** U-Bahn: Hauptwache. Mon–Sat 9am–midnight; Sun 10am–7pm.

Café Laumer ★★ CAFE A classic German *Kaffeehaus* with a large garden, Café Laumer serves some of the best pastries in town. It's had plenty of time to perfect its recipes since it's been around since 1919. Bockenheimer Landstrasse 67. © **069/727912.** Mon–Sat 9:30am–7pm; Sun 10am–7pm. U-Bahn: Westend.

SACHSENHAUSEN & THE apple-wine TAVERNS

Sachsenhausen, the district south of the River Main, has long been known for its taverns where *Apfelwein*, not beer, is the special drink. At an apple-wine tavern, everyone sits together at long wooden tables and, sooner or later, the singing starts.

Apfelwein (pronounced *ebb*-el-vye in the local dialect) is a dry, alcoholic, 12-proof apple cider. The wine always is poured from a blue-and-gray stoneware jug into glasses embossed with a diamond-shaped pattern. The first sip may pucker your whole body and convince you that you're drinking vinegar. If drinking straight Apfelwein is too much for you, try a *Sauergespritzt* (sour spritzer), a mixture of Apfelwein and plain mineral water, or a *Süssgespritzt* (sweet spritzer), Apfelwein mixed with lemonade-like mineral water.

Although available year-round, Apfelwein also comes in seasonal versions. *Süsser* (sweet), sold in the autumn, is the dark, cloudy product of the first pressing of the apple harvest. When the wine starts to ferment it's called *Rauscher*, which means it's darker and more acidic. You're supposed to drink Süsser and Rauscher straight, not mixed.

The Apfelwein taverns in Sachsenhausen display a pine wreath outside when a new barrel has arrived. The taverns usually serve traditional meals; hard rolls, salted bread sticks, and pretzels for nibbling are on the tables, too. What you eat, including the snacks, goes on your tab. The following are traditional Apfelwein taverns; all of them are *Gartenlokale*, meaning they move their tables outside in good weather:

Zum Eichkatzerl, Greieichstrasse 29 (*©* **069/617-480**), open Thursday to Tuesday from 3pm to midnight. **Fichtekränzi,** Wallstrasse 5 (*©* **069/612-778**), open Monday to Saturday from 5pm. to midnight. **Zum Gemalten Haus,** Schweizer Strasse 67 (*©* **069/614-559**), open Wednesday to Sunday from 10am to midnight; closed mid-June to the end of July.

On Saturdays, Sundays, and holiday afternoons throughout the year, you can hop on the **Ebbelwei-Express** (*©* **069/21322425**), an old, colorfully painted trolley, and ride all through Frankfurt and over to the apple-wine taverns in Sachsenhausen. The entire route takes about an hour and costs 6€ for adults and 3€ for children up to 14. The fare includes a glass of apple wine (or apple juice). You can buy tickets from the conductor. Catch the trolley at Römer, Konstablerwache, or the main train station; service starts about 1:30pm and ends about 5pm.

Café-Restaurant in der Schirn ★★ CAFE   Located in the Schirn Museum in the heart of the Altstadt, this stylish steel, glass, and granite see-and-be-seen cafe-bar-restaurant has outdoor tables in summer. The restaurant, under Chef Michael Frank, is completely organic. Römerberg 6A. *©* **069/291732.** Tues–Sun 10am–10:30pm; bar open until midnight. U-Bahn: Römer.

Harvey's Cafe Bar ★ CAFE/BAR   This popular and pleasantly relaxed cafe and bar with outdoor seating in summer draws a mixed gay-straight crowd and occasionally features live disco bands on the weekend. Bornheimer Landstrasse 64. *©* **069/497303.** Daily 10am–1am. U-Bahn: Hauptwache.

La Gata ★★ CAFE/BAR   The most upfront lesbian bar in Frankfurt looks like a rustic English pub and serves soups and snacks as well as cocktails. Seehofstrasse 3. © **069/614581.** Daily 8pm–midnight (Fri–Sat from 9pm). U-Bahn: Südbahnhof.

Luna ★★ BAR   A hip bar that's always packed with young professionals, this is the sort of place where singles mix as true mixologists—bartenders who know a thing or two about grasshoppers, juleps, champagne fizzes, and tropical coladas—work their magic. Stiftstrasse 6. © **069/294774.** Sun–Thurs 7pm–2am; Fri–Sat 7pm–3am. U-Bahn: Hauptwache.

Nachtleben ★★ CAFE/BAR/DANCE CLUB   The name means "nightlife," and this is one place where you can party until the wee hours. There's a cafe-bar upstairs and a disco downstairs that plays hip-hop, funk, soul, and house. Kurt-Schumacher-Strasse 50. © **069/20650.** Mon–Sat 11:30am–4am; Sun 7pm–2am. U-Bahn: Konstablerwache.

Day Trips from Frankfurt
WIESBADEN, MAINZ & THE RHEINGAU WINE DISTRICT
Frankfurt is close and convenient to many historic towns and scenic regions in western Germany. On a day trip you can visit the ancient cathedral town of Mainz, the popular spa town of Wiesbaden, and the Rheingau, one of Germany's great wine-producing areas. The itinerary below is a driving tour—but it can also be done by train.

Getting There
The itinerary begins in **Mainz,** about 43.5km (27 miles) southwest of Frankfurt (about 40 min. by train). From Mainz you can continue by car, boat or train to Bingen. If you're driving from Frankfurt, take the A66.

Mainz ★★
This ancient city lies on the west bank of the Rhine at its confluence with the Main (the river that flows through Frankfurt). Founded by the Romans around 13 B.C. it played a key role in the empire's strategic string of forts and defenses along the Rhine. Situated at the intersection of the Rheinhessen and Rheingau wine regions, Mainz today is a bustling wine town that celebrates the grape with annual wine festivals on the first week in August and September. You can pick up a map and at the **tourist information center** (Brückenturm am Rathaus; www.touristic-mainz.de). Put the **Altstadt (Old Town)** at the top of your sightseeing list and head first to the 11th-century **Dom (Cathedral),** Marktplatz (www.mainz-dom.de). This venerable red-sandstone edifice, which since the 11th century has served as the church of the Archbishop of Mainz, is the most important Catholic cathedral in Germany after Cologne. Its oldest parts are early Romanesque in style, but, as with the cathedral at Aachen (p. 235), later Gothic additions obscure some of its great age. After admiring the cathedral, head to the nearby **Stephenskirche (Church of St. Stephen)** to see the stained-glass windows by Marc Chagall, installed in 1978. The world-changing achievements of native son Johanes Gutenberg, inventor of the movable-type printing press, are chronicled at the **Gutenberg Museum** (Liebfrauenplatz 5; www.gutenberg museum.de). Free admission to cathedral; tours (in German) Mon, Wed, Fri-Sun 2pm, 5€; tours in English by special request at cathedral information kiosk. Mon-Fri 9am-6:30pm (Nov–Feb until 5pm), Sat 9am-4pm, Sun 12:45-3pm and 4-6:30pm (Nov–Feb until 5pm).

From Mainz, take A60 and then A643 across the Rhine to Wiesbaden, 21km (13 miles). It's a 15-minute train ride (schedules at www.bahn.com), or you can go by boat (schedules at www.k-d.de).

Wiesbaden ★

Wiesbaden is one of Germany's most popular spa towns—second only to Baden-Baden in the Black Forest. To understand just what a German spa experience is all about, head over to the massive, modern **Kaiser Friedrich Therme,** Langgasse 38–40 (✆ **0611/1729660;** www.wiesbaden.de; 10€–23€; daily 8am–10pm), for a relaxing sauna or a swim in one of the several thermal pools. For a good meal—and some fun spa-town people-watching—head over to **Käfer's Bistro,** Im Kurhaus (✆ **0611/536200;** main courses 14€–24€; daily 11:30am–1am), a popular spot located in the town's stately Kurhaus (and casino), a long-established center of social life in the spa town. The seasonally changing menu has many healthy choices, including fresh salads, as well as traditional Rhineland cuisine.

From Wiesbaden, head west along the north bank of the Rhine for 50km (31 miles) to **Rüdesheim ★**, described below under "Day Trips from Cologne." You can also travel this section by train in about 30 minutes. This part of the day trip takes you through the Rhinegau.

This part of the day trip takes you through the **Rheingau wine district ★★★**, a 45km (27-mile) stretch of the Rhine Valley west of Wiesbaden. Vineyards on terraced hllsides have produced wine here since Roman times. The wind-sheltered southern slopes of the Taunus range, on the river's northern bank, get plenty of sunshine and comparatively little rain, conditions the Romans recognized as perfect for grape-growing. The Rheingau wine grapes produce a delicately fruity wine with a full aroma. Eighty percent of this wine comes from the Riesling grape, and wine fans consider Rheingau Rieslings to be among the best white wines made anywhere.

From Rüdesheim you can continue north along the Middle Rhine, described under "Day Trips from Cologne" or return to Frankfurt (about 1 hr. by car or train) or Cologne (about 2 hr. by car or train).

COLOGNE (KÖLN) ★★★

It's difficult not to like Cologne. Visitors to this lively metropolis on the Rhine, Germany's fourth-largest and oldest city, are immediately struck by Cologne's cheek-by-jowl juxtaposition of the very old with the very new. You can see Roman ruins in an underground parking garage, a dizzyingly ornate Gothic cathedral beside a modern museum complex, and a humble Romanesque church wedged in among luxury shops. On a 10-minute walk in Cologne, you can traverse 2,000 years of history.

Cologne—spelled *Köln* in Germany and pronounced *koeln*—offers far more than Germany's largest cathedral, although that is spectacular and reason enough to visit. The range of Cologne's museums and the quality of their collections make Cologne one of the outstanding museum cities of Germany. Music, whether it's a symphony concert in the modern philharmonic hall, an opera at the highly regarded opera house, or a boisterous outdoor concert in the Rheinpark, is likewise a vital component of life here. The city also is famous as the birthplace of eau de cologne.

Cologne traces its beginnings to 38 B.C., when Roman legions set up camp here. As early as A.D. 50, the emperor Claudius gave the city municipal rights as capital of a Roman province. In addition to its substantial Roman legacy, the city boasts 12 major Romanesque churches. Older than the cathedral, the churches drew medieval pilgrims from all across Europe to "Holy Cologne," one of the most important pilgrimage cities in medieval Christendom.

Cologne

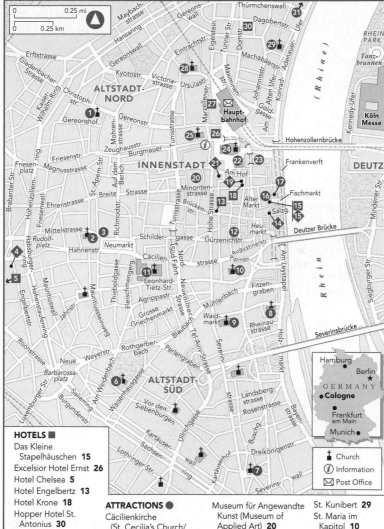

HOTELS ■
Das Kleine
    Stapelhäuschen **15**
Excelsior Hotel Ernst **26**
Hotel Chelsea **5**
Hotel Engelbertz **13**
Hotel Krone **18**
Hopper Hotel St.
    Antonius **30**
Station - Hostel for
    Backpackers **27**

RESTAURANTS ◆
Brauhaus Pütz **4**
Brauhaus Sion **19**
Das Kleine
    Stapelhäuschen **15**
Früh am Dom **21**
Sünner im Walfisch **14**

ATTRACTIONS ●
Cäcilienkirche
    (St. Cecilia's Church/
    Schnütgen Museum) **11**
Dom (Cathedral) **24**
Gross St. Martin **16**
Käthe Kollwitz Museum **3**
KD (Köln-Düsseldorfer
    Rheinschiffahrt/Rhine
    Boat Excursions) **17**
Kölner Seilbahn
    (Cologne Cable Car) **31**

Museum für Angewandte
    Kunst (Museum of
    Applied Art) **20**
Museum Ludwig **23**
Römisch-Germanisches
    Museum (Roman-
    Germanic Museum) **22**
Schnütgen Museum **11**
St. Andreas **25**
St. Aposteln **2**
St. Georg **9**
St. Gereon **1**

St. Kunibert **29**
St. Maria im
    Kapitol **10**
St. Maria
    Lyskirchen **8**
St. Panteleon **6**
St. Severin **7**
St. Ursula **28**
Wallraf-Richartz
    Museum **12**

✝ Church
ⓘ Information
✉ Post Office

carnival **IN COLOGNE**

Many cities throughout Germany have Christmas markets, but only the traditionally Catholic cities celebrate carnival—a time when the weather may be gray, but spirits are high. Cologne's Carnival, the city's "fifth season," is one of the most eagerly anticipated events in Germany. The season officially lasts from New Year's Eve to Ash Wednesday. During this period, Cologne buzzes with masked balls, parades, and general delirium. Natives call this celebration *Fasteleer* or *Fastelovend*. We highly recommend visiting at this time---just make sure to book a room in advance.

Like Munich, Cologne is a city that likes to have fun, and a huge student population keeps it buzzing and vital. The Kölner themselves are refreshingly relaxed and down-to-earth in how they enjoy their city. Ancient traditions are annually renewed in the city's raucous pre-Lenten Carnival (called *Fasching*), a time of masked balls, parades, and general delirium. When the weather turns warm, visitors and citizens alike stroll along the Rhine promenades and flock to outdoor taverns and restaurants to enjoy the pleasures of a *Kölsch,* Cologne's unique and delicious beer, and a substantial meal of hearty Rhineland cuisine.

Essentials
GETTING THERE

BY TRAIN   Cologne is a major rail hub, so reaching the city from anywhere in Germany or the rest of Europe is easy. Frequent daily trains arrive from Berlin (trip time: 5½ hr.), Frankfurt (trip time under 1 hr.), and Hamburg (trip time: 4½ hr.). The Cologne **Hauptbahnhof** (main train station) is in the heart of the city. For schedules, call **Deutsch Bahn** at ✆ **11861** or visit www.bahn.com.

BY PLANE   Cologne's airport, **Konrad-Adenauer-Flughafen Köln/Bonn** (✆ **02203/40-40-01;** www.airport-cgn.de), is located 14km (9 miles) southeast of the city. Direct flights arrive from most major European cities. The fastest and simplest way to get into the city is by taking an **S-Bahn train** (S-13) from the airport train station directly to the Cologne main train station. The trip takes 20 minutes; the fare is 3€. A **taxi** from the airport to the city center costs about 30€.

BY CAR   Cologne is easily reached from major German cities. It's connected north and south by the **A3** Autobahn and east and west by the **A4** Autobahn.

The Neighborhoods in Brief

ALTSTADT

The major sights of Cologne, including the mighty cathedral and the most important museums, are all located in the Altstadt (Old Town), the restored and much altered medieval core of the city. The Altstadt spreads in a semicircle west from the Rhine to a ring road that follows the line of the 12th-century city walls (demolished, except for three gateways, in the 19th c.). The center of the Altstadt is the **Innenstadt (Inner City),** the historical heart of Cologne, where the Romans built their first walled colony.

NEUSTADT

The ring road and a greenbelt in the southwest (the location of the university) girdle Neustadt, the "new" part of town dating from the 19th century.

BELGISCHES VIERTEL (BELGIAN QUARTER)

Called the Belgian Quarter because its street names refer to Belgian cities and provinces, this inner-city neighborhood just west of the Altstadt doesn't have tourist attractions but it's popular with students and has some good, non-touristy cafes and restaurants.

DEUTZ

The area across the river, on the Rhine's east bank, is called Deutz. Besides providing the best views of the cathedral-dominated Cologne skyline, Deutz is where you find the **Köln Messe** (trade-fair grounds) and the **Rhinepark.** The city's early industrial plants were concentrated in Deutz, and many of them are still there.

GETTING AROUND

The compact and pedestrian-friendly Altstadt, where you find the cathedral and most of the major attractions, is most easily explored on foot. The city also has an excellent **bus, tram, U-Bahn** (subway), and **S-Bahn** (light rail) system. A **CityTicket,** good for a single one-way fare within the inner city is 1.90€ for adults, 0.95€ for children. Purchase tickets from the automated machines (labeled *Fahrscheine*), from bus drivers, or at the stations. Be sure to validate your ticket before entering; validation machines are in stations and on buses. For information about public transportation, call VRS at ℰ **01803/504-030** or visit **www.kvb-koeln.de.**

Taxi meters start at 3€ plus 1€ if you hail a taxi from the street; the fare rises 1.55€ to 1.70€ per kilometer thereafter, depending on time of day. To order a taxi, call **Taxi-Ruf** at ℰ **0221/19410.**

VISITOR INFORMATION

For tourist information, go to the **Köln Tourismus Office,** Kardinal-Höffner-Platz 1 (ℰ **0221/22130400;** www.cologne-tourism.com), a few steps from the cathedral. The office has city maps, a room-rental service, and information on city attractions, including tours. It's open Mon-Sat 9am to 8pm, Sun 10am-5pm.

Where to Stay

Das Kleine Stapelhäuschen ★ The two town houses that make up this very old-fashioned and atmospheric hotel stand on a corner of a historic square, right on the Rhine in one of the busiest sections of the Altstadt. On the ground floor there's a long-established wine restaurant (see "Where to Eat"), somewhat unusual in beer-drinking Cologne. The rooms differ according to what building you're in. The "newer" one has rooms created in the 1960s—comfortable but pretty plain. Rooms in the older building are also fairly basic but not lacking in a kind of creaky-floored, old-fashioned charm, some with beamed ceilings (the one at the top still has the crane that was once used to haul goods and furniture up and down). Most of the small bathrooms have showers; a few have tubs, too. You can easily walk everywhere in the Altstadt from here. Just be aware that voices and laughter from the surrounding restaurants can go on until after midnight. Alas, no wifi is offered.

Fischmarkt 1–3. ℰ **0221/272-7777.** www.kleines-stapelhaeuschen.de. 31 units. 64€–115€ double with breakfast. U-Bahn: Heumarkt. **Amenities:** Restaurant.

Excelsior Hotel Ernst ★★★ Walk out of the train station in Cologne and you stare up, mesmerized, at the enormous cathedral, one of the architectural wonders of Europe. You can see the cathedral from some of the rooms in the grand Excelsior Hotel Ernst, founded in 1863. But that's not the only masterpiece on view: The breakfast room contains a Gobelins tapestry, and the walls of the public areas are hung with works by big names (like Van Dyck). The art is set off by gleaming and elegant public rooms with marble floors and beautiful finishes. Guest rooms are swank (especially those in the newly refurbished Hanseflügel wing), with high ceilings, French windows (often with Juliet balconies), fine linens and such nice perks as a complimentary mini-bar (filled with excellent German beer). Bathrooms throughout are large and luxurious, but the bathrooms in the Hanseflügel wing are truly astounding, with big marble-clad tubs and huge rain showers. Both of the hotel's restaurants—the traditional **Hanse Stube** and Asian-fusion **Taku**—are noteworthy gourmet destinations. This is one of the few luxury hotels that includes breakfast in the room rate, and it's a sumptuous affair. Hotel Excelsior Ernst also stands out for its incredibly friendly and helpful staff (the hotel has one of the highest staff-to-guest ratios of any hotel in Germany).

Trankgasse 1–5. ℰ **0221/2701.** www.excelsiorhotelernst.de. 152 units. 265€–440€ double with breakfast. Parking 25€. U-Bahn: Hauptbahnhof. **Amenities:** 2 restaurants; exercise room; business center; sauna, Wi-Fi (22€ per day).

Hotel Engelbertz ★ Kindly service and a top Alstadt location (right off Hohes-trasse, Cologne's main shopping street, and 5 min. from the cathedral and train station) keep this modest, family-run hotel filled with repeat visitors. The large, comfortable rooms are decorated in a light, cheery, modern style and have bathrooms with tub or shower. Yes, it's bit dated, but very well-run.

Obenmarspforten 1–3. ℰ **0221/2578994.** www.hotel-engelbertz.de. 40 units. 80€–160€ double with breakfast. U-Bahn: Heumarkt. **Amenities:** Wi-Fi (1€/day).

Hotel Chelsea ★★ You wouldn't guess from the simple entrance or lobby how well-designed the rooms are in this winner of a hotel. Spread out over five floors, guestrooms come in a wide array of sizes—from affordable rooms with shared bath (38€ for a single) to doubles, suites amd apartments with balconies or skylights—but all of them share the same design aesthetic, which provides a pleasing, comfortable, uncluttered environment with art on the walls, modern furniture and well-designed fixtures. Like many German hotels, this family-owned establishment is not completely smoke-free, so if you're a non-smoker, be sure to specify that you want a non-smoking room. The staff here is unusually friendly and helpful. There's a great on-site cafe. The hotel is in the so-called Belgian Quarter of Cologne, near the university, an easy 10-minute tram and/or U-Bahn ride from the main train station.

Jülicherstrasse 1. ℰ **0221/207150.** www.hotel-chelsea.de. 35 units. 95€–145€ double. U-Bahn: Rudolfplatz. **Amenities:** Restaurant; bar, free Wi-Fi.

Hotel Krone ★ Clean, simple, central—that's what Hotel Krone has going for it. It's a small, efficient, modern hotel in the heart of the Altstadt, close to the cathedral, the Rhine, and many museums and restaurants. The decor has not been updated, but it's comfortable and completely serviceable. The plain-Jane rooms have usable desks and small bathrooms with tub/shower. Breakfast is included in your room rate.

Kleine Budengasse 15. ℰ **0221/92593150.** www.hotel-krone-koeln.de. 95€–179€ double with breakfast. U-Bahn: Hauptbahnhof. **Amenities:** Free Wi-Fi.

Hopper Hotel St. Antonius ★ This five-story hotel is about a 10-minute walk from Cologne's train station, cathedral and Altstadt along the Rhine promenade. It's modern, minimalist and, most importantly, comfortable. On that last point, many of the rooms here are larger than average and feature a calm, uncluttered look, with lovely hardwood floors, contemporary teakwood furniture, and state-of-the-art technology. Each has a compact, marble-clad bathrooms, most of them with showers only. A couple of rooms on the top floor have little balconies. The staff is professional and

KÖLSCH: COLOGNE'S trademark BEER

Even if you don't like beer, you'll probably like Kölsch (pronounced *koehlsch*), a dry, delicious, top-fermented beer that's brewed only in Cologne. Kölsch has an alcohol content of about 3 percent (most other types of German beer have an alcohol content ranging from 4 percent to 6 percent). If you go to any of the taverns in town, you can order a Kölsch from one of the blue-aproned waiters, called a *Köbes*. The waiters always serve the beer in a tall, thin glass, called a *Stangen*, which they bring you in a special carrier called a *Kölschkranz*. Expect to pay about 2€ for a small glass of Kölsch on tap.

helpful, the breakfast is good (enjoy it in the courtyard when the weather's nice). As in many German hotels, there's no a/c here, so in hot weather you'll need to open your window (request a courtyard-facing room if you want more quiet) and use the fan.

Dagobertstrasse 32. ℗ **0221/16600.** www.hopper.de. 54 units. 145€–210€ double with breakfast. U-Bahn: Hauptbahnhof. **Amenities:** Bar; free Wi-Fi.

Station Hostel for Backpackers ★ Located next to the train station and Cologne cathedral, with all the main sights in Cologne just a few minutes' walk away, this hostel has a better location that most hotels in Cologne, for a fraction of the cost. The rooms are comfortable if spare, with good beds and strong showers. The staff is friendly and helpful and there's no curfew. Breakfast is available (you pay only for what you eat) and you can do your laundry—everything a backpacker wants.

Marzellenstrasse 44–56. ℗ **0221/9125301.** www.hostel-cologne.de. 48€–55€double. U-Bahn: Hauptbahnhof/Dom. **Amenities:** Bar, free lockers, free Wi-Fi.

Where to Eat

Although several highly rated restaurants have established themselves here in recent years, Cologne is not a city particularly known for its gourmet dining. Rather, it's a place for conversation and drinking, generally over enormous portions of typical Rhineland fare in crowded restaurants that are *gemütlich* (cozy) rather than elegant.

To eat and drink as the Kölner do, visit one of the city's old tavern-restaurants. Local dishes generally include *Halver Hahn* (a rye bread roll with Dutch cheese), *Tatar* (finely minced raw beef mixed with egg yolk, onions, and spices and served on bread or a roll), *Kölsch Kaviar* (smoked blood sausage served with raw onion rings), *Matjes-filet mit grünen Bohnen* (herring served with green butter beans and potatoes), *Hämchen* (cured pork knuckle cooked in vegetable broth), *Himmel und Äd* (apples and potatoes boiled and mashed together and served with fried blood sausage), and *Speckpfannekuchen* (pancakes fried in smoked bacon fat).

Brauhaus Pütz ★ GERMAN/RHINELAND Pütz is a neighborhood brewery-restaurant in the Belgian Quarter, near the university. It's a small, non-touristy place where locals come for a good meal and a glass of delicious Kölsch, and consequently it's more "authentic" than the larger brewery-restaurants in the Altstadt, and less expensive. The food is all traditional Kölner fare: herring filets (in cream or freshly marinated) with fried or boiled parsley potatoes and onions; homemade goulasch with brown bread; *Himmel und Üd* (mashed potatoes and applesauce with blood sausage and fried onions); or *Mettwurst,* a smoked, mince pork sausage. The atmosphere is unfussy, with wooden tables and brick walls: very real and very good value.

Engelbertstrasse 67. ✆ **0221/211166.** Main courses 9€–17€. Mon–Thurs noon–midnight; Fri–Sat noon–1am; Sun 4:30pm–11:30pm. U-Bahn: Rudolfplatz.

Brauhaus Sion ★ GERMAN/RHINELAND If you want a traditional Bräuhaus where the beer is good, the wood paneling a little smoky with age, and the food portions inexpensive and generous, Sion is the place. The main courses are traditional and filling Rhineland fare, such as *Riesenhämchen* (boiled pigs' knuckles) with sauerkraut, Bockwurst (sausage) with potato salad, or *sauerbraten* (pot- or oven-roasted marinated beef) with an almond-raisin sauce. The Bräuhaus also has a few rooms upstairs that it rents out; a double with bathroom and breakfast goes for 60€. Credit cards not taken.

Unter Taschenmacher 5. ✆ **0221/257-8540.** Main courses 10€–16€. Daily 11am–11pm. U-Bahn: Heumarkt.

Das Kleine Stapelhäuschen ★★ GERMAN/FRENCH This popular and cozy wine restaurant (and hotel, see "Cologne Hotels") opens onto the old fish-market square and the Rhine, just a few minutes' walk from the cathedral. Although the wine is the main reason for coming here (the local Rhine wines are that special), you won't be disappointed with the food. You can't go wrong with simple, local favorites like grilled pork chops with sauerkraut and mashed potatoes or *sauerbraten* with potato dumplings. There are always daily specials to choose from.

Fischmarkt 1–3 (Am Rheinufer). ✆ **0221/2727777.** Main courses 10€–28€. Tues–Thurs 6–10:30pm; Fri–Sun noon–2:30pm and 6–10:30pm. Closed Dec 22–Jan 10. Tram: Heumarkt.

Früh am Dom ★★ GERMAN/RHINELAND This big, busy Bräuhaus near the cathedral is the best all-around spot for atmosphere, economy, and hearty portions. You can eat in the upstairs or downstairs dining rooms (upstairs, on the ground floor, is better), with a different German specialty offered every day of the week. (A menu in English is available.) A favorite dish is *Hämchen,* a Cologne specialty of smoked pork knuckle served with sauerkraut and potato purée. Other specialties include *Sauerkrautsuppe* (sauerkraut soup) and *Kölsch Kaviar* (blood sausage with onion rings). Früh-Kölsch, the tavern's beer on tap, has a 1,000-year-old brewing tradition. In summer, this tavern also has a beer garden. Sorry, credit cards not accepted.

Am Hof 12–18. ✆ **0221/26130.** www.frueh.de. Main courses 10€–20€. Daily 8am–midnight. U-Bahn: Hauptbahnhof.

Sünner im Walfisch ★ GERMAN/RHINELAND Set back from the Rhine in the Altstadt, this 17th-century step-gabled inn with a black-and-white timbered façade is a good choice for atmospheric dining—especially if you are interested in trying the traditional dishes of Cologne. How about *Himmel und Äd* (fried blood sausages with fried onions, mashed potatoes and apple sauce), the *Sudhausteller* (grilled pork knuckles in brown beer sauce, cabbage and fried potatoes), or Rhenish sauerbraten (braised pork with raisin sauce and potato dumplings)? There are vegetarian dishes as well. No credit cards accepted.

Salzgasse 13. ✆ **0221/2577879.** www.walfisch.net. Reservations required. Main courses 14€–22€. Mon–Thurs 5pm–midnight; Fri 3pm–midnight; Sat–Sun 11am–midnight. U-Bahn: Heumarkt.

Exploring Cologne

Cologne cathedral and all the major museums are found in the Altstadt. After a day of sightseeing, round off your visit with a stroll along the Rhine promenade in Deutz. *Note:* Museums in Cologne are generally closed on Monday.

THE TOP ATTRACTIONS

Dom (Cathedral) ★★★ CHURCH   This enormous and enormously remarkable structure is the star of Cologne, the city celebrity with top billing. Considering how much time passed during the construction of this gigantic edifice, the largest cathedral in Germany and all of northern Europe, it's a wonder that the Gothic facade is so stylistically coherent. More than 600 years elapsed from the laying of the cornerstone in 1248 to the placement of the last finial on the south tower in 1880. Upon completion, Cologne cathedral was the tallest building in the world, its twin filigreed spires rising to a height of 157m (515 ft.). Overwhelming is the simplest way to describe it—as you'll discover when you step inside.

The cathedral was built to enshrine holy relics—in this case, relics of the Three Kings or Magi—which had been stolen from a church in Milan by Emperor Frederick Barbarossa. These relics, which drew pilgrims to Cologne throughout the Middle Ages, are still housed in the **Dreikönigschrein (Shrine of the Three Magi),** a glass case at the end of the cathedral choir. The giant reliquary is a masterpiece of goldsmith work dating from the end of the 12th century. The **choir,** which can be visited only on guided tours, was consecrated in 1322 and contains original, richly carved oak stalls, screen paintings, and a series of statues made in the cathedral workshop between 1270 and 1290. The famous **Three Kings windows** in the clerestory were installed in the early 14th century. In addition to some magnificent Renaissance-era stained-glass windows in the north aisle, and German artist Gerhard Richter's darkly shimmering stained-glass windows in the south transept, installed in 2007, the cathedral has only two other conspicuous treasures. The **Gero Cross,** hanging in a chapel on the north side of the choir, is a rare monumental sculpture carved in Cologne in the late 10th century and reputedly the oldest large-scale crucifix in the Western world. On the south side of the choir is Stephan Lochner's altarpiece, "Adoration of the Magi" (c.1445). The painting is a masterpiece of the Cologne school—Italian in format, Flemish in the precision of its execution.

The cathedral's **Schatzkammer (Treasury)** is rather disappointing, and you aren't missing much if you skip it. If, on the other hand, you're in reasonably good shape, climb the 509 stairs of the 14th-century south tower (entry through the Portal of St. Peter) for an inspiring view of the city and the Rhine. The cathedral is now a UNESCO World Heritage Site.

Domkloster. ✆ **0221/9258-4730.** www.koelner-dom.de. Admission to cathedral free; treasury and tower combined 5€ adults, 2.50€) children and students; tower 2€ adults, 1€ children and students; tour 7€ adults, 5€ students and children. Daily 6am–7:30pm.; tower 9am–5pm; treasury 10am–6pm. English-language tours Mon–Sat 11am, 12:30, 2, 3:30pm and Sun 2, 3:30pm. U-Bahn: Hauptbahnhof/Dom.

Käthe Kollwitz Museum ★★ MUSEUM   This museum is devoted to the works of Berlin-born Käthe Kollwitz (1867–1945), Germany's most celebrated female artist of the 20th century. The works displayed here reveal Kollwitz's deep emphathy with suffering caused by war, hunger and political upheaval, evoking universal emotions, both tender and disturbing. The collection includes drawings, sketches, and sculpture.

Neu-Markt 18–24. ✆ **0221/2272363.** www.museenkoeln.de. Admission 4€ adults, 2€ seniors and students. Tues–Fri 10am–6pm; Sat–Sun 11am–6pm.

Kölner Seilbahn (Cologne Cable Car) ★ ACTIVITY/VIEW   For the best panoramic view of the the the city of Cologne, take a ride on the first and only cable-car system in Europe designed to span a major river. In operation since 1957, the enclosed gondolas cross the river beside the Zoobrücke (Zoo Bridge) between the Rheinpark in

COLOGNE'S romanesque CHURCHES

Cologne has a dozen important Romanesque churches, all within the medieval city walls. During the Middle Ages, these churches were important destinations for the pilgrims who flocked to "Holy Cologne" to venerate relics of the Three Kings and various Christian martyrs. Devastated during World War II, all 12 of the churches were later restored, often with interior changes, and together they represent the rich architectural legacy of early medieval Cologne. If you have the time, and an interest in architectural history, Cologne's Romanesque churches are worth seeking out. Keep in mind, however, that not all of them are open daily, or open only for a limited period.

The 12th-century church of **St. Ursula,** Ursulaplatz (U-Bahn: Hauptbahnhof), the patron saint of Cologne, is on the site of a Roman graveyard. Legend has it that St. Ursula was martyred here with her 11,000 virgin companions in about 451. The story inspired countless medieval paintings and sculptures, and drew pilgrims in droves. The **shrine room of St. Ursula** (2€ admission) is a rather remarkable combination of medieval sculpted wooden busts in niches with upper walls and ceiling decorated with bones.

St. Panteleon, Am Pantaleonsberg 2 (U-Bahn: Poststrasse), built in 980, has the oldest cloister arcades remaining in Germany. Elliptically shaped and twin-towered **St. Gereon,** Gereonsdriesch 2–4 (U-Bahn: Christophstrasse), contains the tomb of St. Gereon and other martyrs, with 11th-century mosaics in the crypt. **St. Severin,** Severinstrasse 1 (U-Bahn: Severinstrasse), originated as a 4th-century memorial chapel; the present church dates from the 13th to the 15th centuries. **St. Maria im Kapitol,** Kasinostrasse 6 (U-Bahn: Heumarkt), on the site where Plectrudis, the wife of Pippin, built a church in the early 8th century, has a cloverleaf choir modeled on that of the Church of the Nativity in Bethlehem. **St. Aposteln,** Neumarkt 30 (U-Bahn: Neumarkt), and **Gross St. Martin,** on the Rhine in the Altstadt (U-Bahn: Heumarkt), also have the cloverleaf choir design. **St. Georg,** Am Waidmarkt (U-Bahn: Poststrasse), the only remaining Romanesque pillared basilica in the Rhineland, contains an impressive forked crucifix from the early 14th century. **Cäcilienkirche (St. Cecilia's Church),** Cäcilienstrasse 29 (U-Bahn: Neumarkt), is the site of the **Schnütgen Museum** (see above). **St. Andreas,** near the cathedral (U-Bahn: Hauptbahnhof), contains a wealth of late-Romanesque architectural sculpture. The remaining two Romanesque churches are on the Rhine: **St. Kunibert,** Kunibertskloster 2 (U-Bahn: Hauptbahnhof), and **St. Maria Lyskirchen,** Am Lyskirchen 12 (U-Bahn: Heumarkt), both of 13th-century origin.

Deutz and the zoo. You get a great view of the massive cathedral and the river traffic along the Rhine. The trip takes about 15 minutes each way.

Riehler Strasse 180. ℂ **0221/547-4184.** www.koelner-seilbahn.de. Mar 15–Oct daily 10am–6pm. Round-trip ticket 6.50€ adults, 3.70€ students and children. U-Bahn: Zoo/Flora.

Museum für Angewandte Kunst (Museum of Applied Art) ★

MUSEUM   The treasures on display in this museum include furniture, home decor, and crafts from the Middle Ages to the present day. The Art Nouveau room is particularly impressive. On the ground floor and mezzanine, the exhibits, exclusively from the 20th century, include rooms and furniture by Finnish architect Alvar Aalto, German architect Mies van der Rohe, and the American designer Charles Eames, among others. Give yourself about an hour to see everything.

An der Rechtsschule. ℭ**0221/23860.** www.museenkoeln.de. Admission 6€ adults, 3.50€ children 6–12. Tues–Sun 11am–5pm. U-Bahn: Hauptbahnhof.

Museum Ludwig ★★★ MUSEUM   Dedicated to 20th-century and contemporary art, Museum Ludwig opened in 1986 in a choice location right behind the cathedral. Exhibits represent nearly every major artist and art movement of the 20th century, and the collection includes one of the world's largest collections of Picasso paintings, ceramics, and works on paper. The **Agfa-Foto-Historama,** a museum within the museum, is devoted to the history of photography. Give yourself at least an hour, more if you love modern art.

Bischofsgartenstrasse 1. ℭ **0221/22126165.** www.museenkoeln.de. Admission 10€ adults, 7€ seniors and students. Tues–Sun 10am–6pm. U-Bahn: Dom/Hauptbahnhof.

Römisch-Germanisches Museum (Roman-Germanic Museum) ★★ MUSEUM   Cologne's history, and the fabric of the city today, is inextricably bound with the history of Rome. The museum was built around the magnificent **Dionysius mosaic,** produced in a Rhineland workshop in the 3rd century and discovered in 1941 by workers digging an air-raid shelter. Towering over the mosaic, which extols the joys of good living (something the Kölner are still good at), is the tomb of Lucius Poblicius, constructed around A.D. 40 for a Roman officer; it is the largest antique tomb ever found north of the Alps.

The museum's exhibits explore themes in the ldaily lives of the ancient Romans in Cologne: religious life, trade and industry, the cult of the dead, and so on. The museum covers the period that extends from the Stone Age to the period of Charlemagne (9th c.). On the second floor, you can see a superlative collection of Roman glassware and a world-renowned collection of Roman jewelry. On the lowest level, devoted to the daily life of the Romans, there's an ancient black-and-white mosaic floor covered with swastikas. Centuries before the symbol became ominously identified with the atrocities of the Third Reich, the swastika—probably Indian in origin—was a symbol of good luck and happiness, and was known in Latin as the *crux gamata.* You need at least an hour to browse through the entire museum.

Roncalliplatz 4. ℭ **0221/22124438.** www.museenkoeln.de. Admission 7€ adults, 3.50€ seniors and students. Tues–Sun 10am–5pm. U-Bahn: Hauptbahnhof.

Schnütgen Museum ★★★ MUSEUM   The medieval period in Cologne, starting in the 12th century and lasting into the 16th, saw a blossoming of art and architecture that was nothing short of amazing. This was the period when construction of the massive cathedral was begun and when the city's 12 Romanesque churches were built. Cologne was a major pilgrimage site, and art—nearly always sacred in nature—flourished with superb woodcarvers, stonecarvers, stained-glass makers, and painters. This is the art that you will see in the strangely undervisited Schnütgen Museum, housed in a rather forbidding looking modern building that

---

Saving with a KölnCard

The money-saving **KölnCard** costs 9€ for 24 hours (18€ for 48 hr.) and enables you to travel throughout the city's transportation network and get reduced-price entry to museums and other attractions. You can buy it at the tourist information center.

Cologne (Köln)

incorporates the graceful Romanesque church of St. Cäcilien (St. Cecilia, patron saint of music) within its walls. A must for anyone interested in Cologne's medieval artistic heritage, the museum houses a small, splendid sampling of sacred art from the early Middle Ages to the baroque. The surprisingly expressive sculptures and images in stained glass will give you an idea of the artistic blessings bestowed upon "Holy Cologne." Outside, around the back, a skeleton has been spray-painted on the walled-in western portal of the church. Called simply "Tod" (Death), this oddly engaging work is by the Zurich graffiti artist Harald Nägele.

Cäcilienstrasse 29. ℭ **0221/22122310.** www.museenkoeln.de. 6€ adults, 3.50€ seniors and students. Tues–Sun 10am–5pm (Thurs until 8pm). U-Bahn: Neumarkt.

Wallraf-Richartz Museum ★★★ MUSEUM   The Wallraf-Richartz Museum is one of the country's greatest repositories of art from the Middle Ages to the late 19th century. On the first floor, you find an outstanding collection of paintings by the medieval Cologne school (most done between 1330 and 1550). Many of the paintings and altarpieces depict legends from the lives of martyred saints who became identified with the "Holy Cologne" of the Middle Ages, St. Ursula in particular. The Renaissance section includes works by Albrecht Dürer and Lucas Cranach. A memorable collection of 17th-century Dutch and Flemish paintings holds pride of place on the second floor, including major works by Rubens and Rembrandt. In addition to important French and Spanish works, the museum boasts a rich collection of 19th-century paintings, with major pieces by the German Romantic painter Caspar David Friedrich, Gustave Courbet, Edvard Munch, Auguste Renoir, and Vincent van Gogh, among scores of others. Give yourself about 2 hours if you want to browse through all the galleries.

Obenmarspforten. ℭ **0221/22121119.** www.museenkoeln.de. Admission 12€ adults, 8€ seniors and students. Tues–Sun 10am–6pm; Thurs until 10pm. U-Bahn: Hauptbahnhof.

Shopping

The first *Füssgänger* (pedestrians-only) shopping zones in Germany originated in Cologne and present a seemingly endless and interconnected conglomeration of shops and shopping arcades.

   Hohe Strasse, the main north-south street in Roman times, is now Cologne's busiest commercial drag, jammed every day except Sunday with shoppers, musicians, organ grinders, snack shops, and fruit sellers. On Hohe Strasse and its surrounding streets, you find all the major international designer-clothing boutiques; stores selling silver, fine jewelry; and the big department stores. **Schildergasse** is where you find international men's fashions, fine leather bags and purses, and French, German, and Italian designer shoes.

Filz Gnoss ★★ SPECIALTY SHOPPING   One specialty shop worth knowing about is Filz Gnoss, a long-established family business that manufactures and sells all manner of personal and household accessories made out of felt. You'll find comfortable and durable felt slippers, hats, bags, table runners, chair coverings and more.

Apostelnstrasse 21. ℭ **0221/257010.** www.filz-gnoss.de. U-Bahn: Neumarkt.

Nightlife

One of Germany's major cultural centers, Cologne offers a variety of performing arts and nightlife options. To find out what's going on in the city, pick up a copy of **Monats Vorschau** at newsstands). You can purchase tickets at a venue's box office *(Kasse),* at the **Tourist Information Office,** or at **Köln MusikTicket,** Roncalliplatz 4, next to the cathedral (ℭ **0221/2801;** www.koelnticket.de; U-Bahn: Hauptbahnhof).

COLOGNE FROM COLOGNE: no. 4711

Any kind of toilet water is now called "eau de Cologne," or simply "cologne," but *Echt Kölnisch Wasser* (real eau de Cologne) remains the official designation of origin for the distinctive toilet waters created in the city of Cologne. **4711 Haus,** Glockengasse 4711 (ℂ **0221/9250450;** www.4711.com; U-Bahn: Neumarkt), sells the orange-and-lavender-scented water first developed in Cologne in 1709 by Italian chemist Giovanni Maria Farina. The Müh-lens family, another early producer of *Kölnisch Wasser,* also lived and worked in this house at no. 4711. The street number eventually became the trade-mark name for their product. You can buy 4711 cologne in all sizes and shapes, as soap, and even as premoist-ened towelettes.

THE PERFORMING ARTS

Kölner Philharmonie (Philharmonic Hall) ★★★ THE PERFORMING ARTS   Completed in the late 1980s, and located behind and below the Roman-Ger-manic Museum, Cologne's philarmonic hall is the home of two fine orchestras: the **Gürzenich Kölner Philharmoniker** and the **Westdeutscher Rundfunk Orchestra (West German Radio Orchestra).** The hall also presents pop and jazz programs. Bischofsgartenstrasse 1. ℂ **0221/2801.** www.koelner-philharmonie.de. U-Bahn: Hauptbahnhof.

Oper Köln (Cologne Opera) ★★★ THE PERFORMING ARTS   The Rhine-land's leading opera house, designed by Wilhelm Riphahn and opened in 1957 after the original opera house was destroyed by Allied bombs, is underoing a major refurbish-ment that will keep it closed until 2015. Along with improving the acoustics and bring-ing the technical and stage infrastructure up to state-of-the-art standards, the project will renew the plaza and adjacent Schauspielhaus (Theater), all part of Riphahn's postwar architectural ensemble. Until the house reopens, opera performances will be held at different venues around Cologne. The website provides complete performance and location details. Offenbachplatz. ℂ **0221/22128400.** www.operkoeln.de.

THE BAR, CLUB & MUSIC SCENE

E-Werk ★★★ THE CLUB & MUSIC SCENE   This dance club and concert hall housed in a former power plant has been going strong for years and shows no sign of letting up. Check the website to see what's going on when and make it a point to visit if you want to experience Cologne's hippest club vibe. Schanzenstrasse 28. ℂ **0221/9627910.** www.e-werk-cologne.com. U-Bahn: Keupstrasse.

Klimperkasten ★★ LIVE MUSIC/BAR   Also known as Papa Joe's Biersalon, this intimate jazz and piano bar has live music every night beginning around 8pm. Alter Markt 50–52. ℂ **0221/2582132.** www.papajoes.de. U-Bahn: Hauptbahnhof.

Loft ★★ THE CLUB & MUSIC SCENE   International groups and solo artists perform most nights of the week at this music hub created in a musician's apartment near the Cologne Messe. The website will give you details of who's performing and opening hours. Wissmannstrasse 30. ℂ **0221/952155.** www.loft-koeln.de. U-Bahn: Liebigstrasse.

Hotelux ★ CAFE/BAR   Pretending you're in Russia is a whole lot easier than actu-ally living there, and this bar-cafe-club perpetrates the fantasy with Soviet-style decor mixed with Russian food, vodka and beer. Von Sandt Platz 10. ℂ **0221/241136.** www. hotelux.de. Tues–Sun from 8pm. U-Bahn: Deutz.

Cologne is a major embarkation point for Rhine cruises. Even if you don't have time for a long Rhine cruise, you can enjoy a trip on the river aboard one of the many local boats. From late March through October, **KD** (Köln-Düsseldorfer Deutsche Rheinschiffahrt), Frankenwerft 15 (✆ **0221/208-8318;** www.k-d.com), offers several boat tours of the Rhine from Cologne. The KD ticket booth and boarding point is right on the river, a short walk south from the cathedral.

The 1-hour **Panorama Rundfahrt** tour is a pleasant way to see the stretch of Rhine immediately around Cologne—don't particularly scenic, since the river hereabouts is pretty industrialized, but you will get a view of the Cologne skyline with its cathedral and church spires. The tour departs daily at 10:30am., noon, 2pm, 3:30pm, 5pm and 6p:30m. Prerecorded commentary in English plays on both of these sightseeing cruises.

9

Gloria ★★ GAY & LESBIAN BARS If you're looking for a LGBT venue with food, drink and music, this long-established and straight-friendly cafe and concert stage should be at the top of your list. The cafe generally opens a couple of hours before the performances. Check out the website to find out what's going on. Apostelnstrasse 11. ✆ **0221/660630.** www.gloria-theater.com. U-Bahn: Neumarkt.

Day Trips from Cologne

Cologne is ideally situated for exploring western Germany, an area that includes the famous wine-growing regions along the Rhine and Mosel valleys, the ancient city of Aachen, and the Mittelrhein, the most scenic stretch of the river.

THE MIDDLE RHINE ★★★

Germany has many important rivers, but for 2,000 years the Rhine has served as the principle artery between southern and northern Europe. The mighty, myth-laden Rhine (spelled *Rhein* in German) originates in southeastern Switzerland, flows through the Bodensee (Lake Constance), and forms Germany's southwestern boundary as it continues its 1,320km (820-mile) journey west, north, and northwest to the North Sea.

The most scenic section of the Rhine, with the legendary Loreley rock and many hilltop castles, is the **Middle Rhine (Mittelrhein)** between Koblenz and Rüdesheim. This stretch of the **Rhinetal,** or Rhine Gorge, with its vineyards, forests, and castle-topped crags, has been designated a UNESCO World Heritage Site. You can enjoy the sights along the Middle Rhine by taking a river cruise departing from Koblenz. *Note:* There are many ways to explore the Rhine by boat besides the itinerary listed here. If you want a longer Rhine cruise, you can travel from Cologne south to Bonn and all the way to Mainz. You'll find seasonal timetables and itineraries at **www.k-d.de**.

Essentials

GETTING THERE By Train & Boat To make the itinerary work as a day-trip from Cologne, you first need to take a train to **Koblenz,** about 85km (53 miles) southeast of Cologne (1 hr. by train). From Koblenz, a boat operated by **KD** (✆ **0221/20881;** www.k-d.de) departs at 9am (Apr–Oct) and travels down the Rhine to Rüdesheim, one of the main Rhineside wine towns, arriving at 1:15pm. From Rüdesheim you can retirn to Koblemz by boat (departing 2:15pm or 4:15pm), or take a train all the way back to Cologne (about 2½ hr.). B sure to check current train (www.bahn.com) and boat schedules before you depart.

Sights along the Middle Rhine

For over 2,000 years the Rhine has played a huge role in the history of Germany and Europe, serving as a means of transportation, communication and cultural exchange between the south and the north.From Koblenz south to Alsace, the Rhine Valley's sheltered sunny slopes covered with vineyards almost makes it look like a northern extension of Italy. This part of the Rhineland but has been fundamentally formed by the culture of wine, as reflected in its economy, traditions, and festivals.

The excursion boat from Koblenz sails down this famous stretch of the Rhine, known as the **Rheintal,** or Rhine Gorge, passing the Rheingau winegrowing region (see "Day Trips from Frankfurt," above) and stopping at riverside wine towns along the way. (You can also travel by boat up the Rhine, starting your trip in Mainz, Rüudesheim, or Bingen.) As you head south from Koblenz, highlights are:

The fortress of **Marksburg,** one of two surviving medieval fortifications on the Middle Rhine, towers above **Braubach** on the right (west) bank. **Rhens,** on the left (east) bank, is where the German Emperors were enthroned after being elected in Frankfurt and crowned in Aachen Cathedral. **Oberspay** and **Niederspay,** now incorporated into a single town, contain more timber-framed houses than anywhere on the Middle Rhine. **Boppard,** located below a horseshoe loop in the river, originated as a Roman way-station and was replaced in the 4th century by a military fort. Across the river on the right bank is **St. Goarshausen,** with its castle of Neu-Katzenelnbogen.

As you continue towards Oberwesel, the valley landscape begins to transition from soft clay-slate to hard sandstone, creating a series of narrows, the most famous of which is the **Loreley,** the most over-rated rock formation in the world. This stretch of river was once hazardous for shipping and inspired legends of the Lorelei, a golden-haired beauty who sat on the rocks combing her hair and was so entrancing that she lured sailors to their deaths. This area is also reputed to be the place where the fabulous treasure of the Niebelungs lies hidden. Looking at the Loreley today, you may scratch your head and wonder what all the fuss was about.

Oberwesel, on the river's left bank, has preserved a number of fine early houses, as well as two Gothic churches, the medieval Schönburg castle, and its medieval town wall. **Kaub** and its environs contain a number of monuments, among them the **Pfalzgrafenstein castle,** the town wall of Kaub itself, and the terraced vineyards, created in the Middle Ages. **Bacharach,** at the entrance of the Steeger valley, contains many timber-framed houses and retains its medieval appearance.

Just before the 5km (3-mile) long **Bingen Pforte (Bingen Gate),** a section of the river widened in the 19th and 20th centuries, there are two small wine towns. **Bingen** on the left bank and **Rüdesheim** on the right (the excursion boat stops at both). Rüdesheim is dominated by the 12th-century **Brömserberg fortress.** The vineyards of the **Rüdesheimer Berg** (mountain) are among the best in the Rheingau.

RÜDESHEIM ★★

Although the excursion boat continues on to Mainz, Rüdesheim is a good place to disembark and have a stroll before heading back to Cologne. With its old courtyards and winding alleyways lined with half-timbered houses, Rüdesheim is the quintessential Rheingau wine town. The vineyards around the village date back to the Roman times and produce a full-bodied Riesling and *Sekt* (sparkling wine). Rüdesheim is also the scene of the annual August **wine festival,** when the old taverns on narrow **Drosselgasse (Thrush Lane)** are crowded with visitors from all over the world. Drosselgasse has been called "the smallest but the happiest street in the world."

The **Rheingauer Weinmuseum,** Rheinstrasse 2 (© **06722/2348;** www.rheingauer-weinmuseum.de), in Bromserburg Castle, traces the history of the grape and has an exhibition of wine presses, glasses, goblets, and drinking utensils from Roman times to the present. Admission is 5€ for adults, 3€ for children, with an extra charge for wine tastings. The museum is open mid-March to October daily 10am to 6pm.

Located next to their own vineyards, **Gasthof Krancher,** Eibinger-Oberstrasse 4 (© **06722/2762;** www.gasthof-krancher.de), is a homey guesthouse that serves regional German food, mostly Rhinelander specialties.

The beautifully carved 17th-century facade of **Hotel und Weinhaus Felsenkeller,** Oberstrasse 39–41 (© **06722/94250;** www.ruedesheim-rhein.co), suggest the traditional ambience you'll find within. Sample Rhine wine in a room with vaulted ceilings and murals or, if the weather is nice, enjoy regional Rhineland cuisine on the terrace. The hotel-restaurant is closed from November to Easter.

THE MOSEL VALLEY ★★

Winding through the steep slopes of the Eifel and Hunsruck hills in the German state of Rheinland-Palatinate, the Mosel Valley follows the course of the Mosel River for more than 60km (100 miles) between **Trier** and **Koblenz,** where the Mosel's waters flow into the Rhine. The valley encompasses thousands of acres of vineyards, a full 10 percent of the national total. The beautiful scenery, fine wine, Roman ruins, medieval castles, and riverside towns with cobble streets and half-timbered houses make the Mosel Valley a prime area for exploration. As with the previous Rhine itinerary, this day trip begins in Koblenz, where the Rhine and the Mosel rivers converge.

Essentials

GETTING THERE   By Train & Boat   If you're headquartering in Cologne and want to enjoy a boat cruise down the Mosel River, the easiest way is to take a train to **Koblenz,** about 85km (53 miles) southeast of Cologne (1 hr. by train). From Koblenz, a boat operated by **KD** (© **0221/20881;** www.k-d.de) sails down the Mosel to **Cochem,** 51km (32 miles) southwest of Koblenz. From Koblenz, boats depart (May–Oct) at 9:45am, arriving in Cochem at 3pm A return boat departs Cochem at 3:40pm, arriving in Koblenz at 8pm. Check current train (www.bahn.com) and boat schedules online before you go.

Cochem ★★

Cochem, about halfway down the Mosel River from Koblenz. is a medieval riverside town surrounded by vineyards, and a popular spot for wine tastings and festivals. For information on events in the town, stop in at the **tourist information office,** Endertplatz 1 (© **0267/60040;** May–Oct Mon–Fri 9am–5pm, Sat 9am–1pm, Sun 10am–noon), or visit www.cochem.de.

If you're driving through the Mosel Valley, Cochem is your best choice for an overnight stopover between Koblenz and Trier. You can also reach Cochem by train from either of those cities.

Cochem's biggest attraction, and the most photographed sight along the Mosel River, is **Reichsburg Cochem** (© **02671/255;** open daily mid-Mar through Nov 9am–5pm; 4.50€ adults, 2.50€ students and children), a restored 11th-century castle at the top of the hill behind the town.

Both a hotel and a wine restaurant, **Alte Thorschenke,** Brückenstrasse 3, 56812 Cochem (© **02671/7059;** 84€–105€ double w/breakfast), is one of the oldest and best-known establishments along the Mosel. The half-timbered structure, originally built in 1332, added a modern wing and became a 35-room hotel in 1960.

Mosel-Wein-Woche (Mosel Wine Week), celebrating the region's wines with tasting booths and a street fair, begins the first week of June. The similar **Weinfest** takes place the last week- end of August. From late November through December 21, Cochem dresses itself up for the **Weihnachtsfest (Christ- mas Festival)** that features a daily Christmas market.

For a fine meal, drive to **Enterttal,** 1.6km (1 mile) northwest of Cochem, and dine at **Weissmühle im Enterttal,** Endertstrasse 1 (℗ **02671/8955;** main courses 15€–25€; daily noon–2pm and 6–9pm). Try the trademark dish of fresh trout stuffed with herbs, baked, and kept warm at your table with a hot stone.

AACHEN (AIX-LA-CHAPELLE) ★

64km (40 miles) W of Cologne

The ancient Imperial City of Aachen (Aix-la-Chapelle) is inseparably connected with the Emperor Charlemagne (748–814), who in 800 was crowned Emperor in Rome and became the first emperor of western Europe since the demise of the Roman Empire. Charlemagne selected this spot at the frontier where Germany, Belgium, and the Neth- erlands meet as the center of his vast Frankish empire. Visitors come to visit Char- lemagne's cathedral, where subsequent Holy Roman emperors were crowned, the Altstadt with its impressive Rathaus, and to relax in the hot spring baths that have been used since Roman times.

Essentials

GETTING THERE   By Train   The trip from Cologne to Aachen's **Hauptbahnhof** (main train station) takes only 45 minutes; trains depart frequently throughout the day. For schedules and train information, call ℗ **01805/996633** or visit www.bahn.com.

VISITOR INFORMATION   For a map and general information on the town, stop in at the **Tourist Office Aachen** on Friedrich-Wilhelm-Platz (℗ **0241/1802960;** www. aachen.de). Office hours are Monday to Friday 9am to 6pm, Saturday 9am to 2pm. From April to December the tourist office is also open on Sunday 10am to 2pm.

GETTING AROUND   From the train station, it's a 15-minute walk to the cathedral precincts. Or take a bus from in front of the station; tickets are 1.90€.

Where to Eat

Elisenbrunnen ★ CAFE/GERMAN   A long-established institution, this cafe-res- taurant just behind the Elisenbrunnen is a great spot to relax with coffee, pastry or a light meal—especially if the weather's nice and you can sit outside on the terrace overlooking the garden. Inside, it's casual and a bit on the well-heeled side. Enjoy fresh salads, soups, baked potatoes with various toppings, or heartier Rhineland fare.

Friedrich-Wilhelm-Platz 14. ℗ **0241/94313490.** www.eb-aachen.de. Main courses 5€–15€. Daily 9:30am–11pm.

Magellan ★ TURKISH/MEDITERRANEAN   A large, casual, family-friendly restaurant-cafe-bar built next to the old city walls near the Rathaus, Magellan offers an

9

FRANKFURT, COLOGNE & THE RHINELAND

Aachen (Aix-la-Chapelle)

sweet specialty: PRINTEN FROM AACHEN

Aachen is famous for its *Printen*, a cake-like cookie (*Lebkuchen*) made with honey and spices and frosted with white or dark chocolate. A bag of Printen makes a great gift...if there are any left by the time you get home. **Printen Bäackerie**

Klein, Münsterplatz 15 (www.printen.de; daily 10am–5pm), is conveniently located right outside the cathedral and sells this delicious sweet local treat in a variety of sizes and containers.

all-purpose menu of Turkish *mezes,* Italian pizzas and pastas, grills and fresh salads. The food is good and the prices moderate. There's an outdoor terrace where you can sit in nice weather. Magellan is on the so-called "Student Mile" where there are many clubs and bars, and later in the evening it becomes more of a bar scene.

Pontstrasse 78. ℂ **0241/4016440.** www.magellan-ac.de. Main courses 7.50€–12€. Daily 10am–1am.

Ratskeller ★★ GERMAN/INTERNATIONAL   Solid, tasty food served in a historic setting: That's the appeal of the Ratskeller, though you have two choices on *how* to dine here. The actual Ratskeller beneath the Rathaus is more formal and expensive (so good for a special occasion). Today, it boasts an attractive, contemporary look with white masonry walls, columns, a black granite floor, and formal table settlings. But many choose the charming Postwagen, a two-story timbered structure attached to the side of the building, that's cramped and cozy, with creaking floors and simple wooden booths and tables. You'll eat well at both. On the Ratskeller menu, Chef Maurice de Boer has upped the ante and focuses on international-style gourmet cooking using fresh local ingredients (foie gras and Canadian lobster, main courses of braised veal cheeks and cutlets, Scottish beef, and fish.) Choices in the Postwagen are more traditionally Rhenish and include sausage salad, *Himmel und Äd* (blood sausage with mashed potatoes and apples), and *sauerbraten.*

Markt 40, Am Markt (in the Rathaus). ℂ **0241/35001.** www.ratskeller-aachen.de. Reservations required in Ratskeller. Ratskeller main courses 21€–27€; fixed-price menus 40€–50€. Postwagen main courses 11€–21€. Ratskeller daily noon–3pm and 6–10pm. Postwagen daily 11am–10pm.

Exploring Aachen

Aachen's **Altstadt** (Old Town), the area you want to explore, is surrounded by a ring road.Tthe **Hauptbahnhof** is on the southern part of the ring. From Bahnhofplatz in front of the station, walk north on Bahnhofstrasse to **Theaterstrasse,** and turn left, or northwest. This will bring you to the giant **Theater Aachen,** a postwar reconstruction of the city's original 1825 theater, opera and concert hall. From here, head northwest to **Friedrich-Wilhelm-Platz,** where you'll find the tourist office and the **Elisenbrunnen,** a colonnaded neoclassical building that sits atop Aachen's famous thermal springs. The sulphury-smelling water spills out into shallow pools behind the building, where you'll find the **Elisengarten,** a landscaped garden area where recent archaeological excavations of Aachen's Roman and medieval past are on view in a glass-walled pavilion. You'll see the spires of the **Dom (Cathedral)** to your northwest. Just north of the cathedral is **Marktplatz (Market Square),** the main square in Aachen's Altstadt, and the site of the Gothic **Rathaus (Town Hall).** The **Carolus Thermen,** the city's thermal bath and pool complex (open to the public), is northeast of the Altstadt, just beyond the ring road, in the The **Stadtgarten (City Park).**

Dom (Cathedral) ★★★ CHURCH Between A.D. 792 and 805, as part of his now vanished palace, Emperor Charlemagne built what's called the **Palatine Chapel,** or the **Octagon.** This eight-sided, two-tiered, domed structure clad in multi-colored marbles is the first part of the cathedral that you enter, and the oldest. Consecrated by the Pope in 805, it was the first large church building to be constructed in western Europe since the demise of the Roman Empire. Stylistically it's an amalgamation of classical, Byzantine and pre-Romanesque architecture. Charlemagne's throne, the simple stone *Königsstuhl,* one of the most venerable monuments in Germany, is on the chapel's second level and can only be seen on a guided tour.

The soaring Gothic style, imported from France, was used when the cathedral's **choir** was constructed some 600 years later. Visitors aren't allowed to enter this section, which contains ttwo treasures: **Charlemagne reliquary,** an ornate gold box created in 1215 for the emperor's remains, and the gold **pulpit of Henry II** (ca. 1014), decorated with antique bowls, ivory carvings, chess figures and reliefs of the evangelists.

From 936 to 1531, when the ceremony moved to Frankfurt cathedral, the Holy Roman emperors were crowned in Aachen's cathedral.

The newly redone cathedral **treasury** is worth visiting to see the famous silver and gilt bust of Charlemagne and the golden reliquaries associated with him and other venerated figures.

Klosterplatz 2. ℂ **0241/47709127.** www.aachendom.de. Cathedral free; treasury and guided tours 5€ adults, 4€ seniors and students. Cathedral daily 7am–7pm (Jan–Mar until 6pm). Treasury Mon 10am–1pm; Tues–Sun 10am–5pm.

Rathaus (Town Hall) ★ LANDMARK/ARCHITECTURAL SITE Some 500 years after Charlemagne's death in 814, the Aachen Rathaus was built on the site of the emperor's ruined palace. Part of the ancient palace structure can still be seen in the so-called Granus Tower at the east side of the hall. After a fire in 1656, the fadade of the building was redone in the baroque style and decorated with stucco statues of 50 German rulers, 31 of whom had been crowned in Aachen. Standing in relief in the center are the "Majestas Domini," the two most important men of their time in the Holy Roman Empire, Charlemagne and Pope Leo III. (The building was restored after suffering serious damage during World War II.) Inside, on the second floor, you can visit the **Coronation Hall** where coronation banquets took place from 1349 to 1531, when the coronation site was moved to Frankfurt. The hall contains a 17th-century life-size statue of Charlemagne, reproductions of the imperial crown jewels (originals are in Vienna) and the Charlemagne frescoes, painted in the 19th century by Alfred Rethel, illustrating the victory of the Christian Franks over the Germanic heathens.

Am Markt. ℂ **0241/4327310.** Admission 5€ adults, 2.50€ students and children. Daily 10am–6pm.

Center Charlemagne

In late 2014 a new city museum will open in Aachen. The **Center Charlemagne,** Katschhof (ℂ **0241/4324919;** www.aachen.de; 5€ adults, 3€ students/children; Tues–Sun 10am–6pm), located between the cathedral and Rathaus, presents a historical overview of Aachen and is the starting point of a designated "Route Charlemagne" that links all the significant buildings and museums in Aachen.

Carolus Thermen ★ SPA   If you have the time, this is a fun and relaxing way to spend a couple of hours in Aachen. For over 2,000 years, the warm mineral waters that flow from thermal springs below the town have been used for health and relaxation. This bath complex in the Stadtgarten features outdoor and indoor pools, water features, a sauna area, spa treatments and restaurants. Lockers and towels are included with your admission.

Guided Tours

From April through December, 90-minute guided tours of Aachen's Altstadt are offered in English every Saturday at 11am, departing from the Tourist Information office at the Elisenbrunnen; cost is 8€.

Stadtgarten, Passstrasse 79. Ⓒ **0241/182740.** www.carolus-thermen.de. Admission (up to 2½ hr.) 11€–12€ without sauna, 22€–24€ with sauna. Daily 9am–11pm.

Couven Museum ★ MUSEUM   Home decor of the upper middle classes from the rococo to the Biedermeyer eras is displayed in period rooms in this lovely house in the Altstadt.

Hühnermarkt 17. Ⓒ **0241/4324421.** Admission 5€ adults, 3€ students/children. Tues–Sun 10am–6pm.

Suermondt Ludwig Museum ★ MUSEUM   The museum displays an impressive collection of medieval German sculpture, 17th-century Dutch and Flemish paintings, and.modern works from the 1920s and 1930s.

Wilhelmstrasse 18. Ⓒ **0241/479800.** www.suermondt-ludwig-museum.de. Admission 5€ adults, 3€ students and children. Tues–Fri noon–6pm (Fri until 8pm); Sat–Sun 11am–6pm.

PLANNING YOUR TRIP TO GERMANY

Germans are famously organized, and travelers will be wise to follow their example in doing a little advance planning for a trip to Germany, from how to get there and around to where to stay.

GETTING THERE

By Plane

Lufthansa (℃ **800/645-3880** in the U.S., 800/563-5954 in Canada, or 01805/805805 in Germany; www.lufthansa.com) operates the most frequent service from North America, with service from almost 20 cities. Given the quality of the fleet and service, as well as timeliness, a flight on Lufthansa is a good kickoff to a trip to Germany.

American Airlines (℃ **800/443-7300;** www.aa.com) flies nonstop from Chicago, Dallas, and other U.S. hubs to Frankfurt daily, and American's flights connect easily with ongoing flights to many other German cities on Lufthansa or British Airways. **Delta Airlines** (℃ **800/241-4141;** www. delta.com) offers daily nonstop service to Frankfurt from Atlanta, Cincinnati, and New York's JFK; nonstop to Munich from Atlanta; nonstop to Berlin from JFK; and connecting service to Hamburg. **United Airlines** (℃ **800/538-2929;** www.united.com) offers daily nonstops from Los Angeles, New York, and Chicago to Frankfurt and Munich. **Air Berlin** (℃ (866/ 266-5588; www.airberlin.com) flies from Chicago, Los Angeles, Miami, New York, and other U.S. cities to Berlin.

From London, **British Airways** (℃ **0870/8509850;** www.british airways.com) and **Lufthansa** (℃ **01805/805805;** www.lufthansa.com) are the most convenient carriers to the major German cities. **British Midland** (℃ **0870/6070555;** www.flybmi.com) has daily flights to Cologne, Düsseldorf, Frankfurt, Hamburg, and Munich. **Ryanair** (www.ryanair.com) is among discount airlines offering low-cost service from Britain to dozens of German cities.

By Train

Many passengers travel to Germany by train from other European cities. (See "Getting Around," below, for information on purchasing rail passes.)

From **London,** your fastest option is to take the English Channel to Brussels and from there, a high-speed train to your destination within Germany. Travel time to Cologne is 4 hours and 45 minutes; from London to Berlin, 9 hours; and from London to Munich, between 9 and 10 hours, depending on the day of the week. You can purchase tickets through **Eurail** (www. eurail.com).

GETTING AROUND

By Plane

From Frankfurt and other German gateways, most **Lufthansa** (✆ **800/645-3880** in the U.S., or 800/563-5954 in Canada; www.lufthansa.com) destinations in Germany can be reached in an average of 50 minutes. All German cities with commercial airports have an airport shuttle service, offering reduced fares and fast connections between the city center and the airport. Departure points are usually the airlines' town offices and the city's main rail terminal. Luggage can be checked at the DB (Deutsche Bahn/German Rail) baggage counter at the airport for delivery to the railroad station at your ultimate destination.

By Train

You'll find that the trains of **German Rail** (**DB Rail;** ✆ **0800/1507090;** www.bahn. com) deserve their good reputation for comfort, cleanliness, and punctuality. All are modern and fast, and all cars are nonsmoking. A snack bar or a dining car, serving German and international cuisine as well as good wine and beer, can usually be found on all trains except locals. Accompanying baggage can be checked for a nominal fee; suitcases, baby carriages, skis, bicycles, and steamer trunks are permitted as baggage.

Germany's high-speed rail network, known as **InterCity Express (ICE),** is among the fastest in Europe—their trains reach speeds of 280kmph (174 mph), making transits north to south and across the country in half a day or less. ICE trains have adjustable cushioned seats and individual reading lights, and are equipped with Wi-Fi (for a fee). Bars, lounges, and dining rooms are available, too. About 20,000 slightly slower **InterCity (IC)** passenger trains offer express service between most large and medium-size German cities. A network of **EuroCity (EC)** trains connecting Germany with 13 other countries offers the same high standards of service as those of IC.

InterCity Night (ICN) trains operate between Berlin and Bonn, Berlin and Munich, Hamburg and Frankfurt, and other German cities. Trains depart between 10 and midnight with arrival the next morning between 7 and 8am. The ICN offers first and tourist class. Sleeping accommodations in first class include single or double compartments with shower and toilet, and they are equipped with key cards, phones for wake-up service, luggage storage, and other amenities. Tourist class offers reclining seats as well as berths is four- or six-person compartments. The ICN is equipped with a restaurant and bistro car, and a breakfast buffet is included in the first-class fare. Advance reservations are mandatory for all sleeping accommodations.

German Rail issues tickets for the ICN and also makes reservations. Eurail and German Rail pass holders are accepted on this train but have to pay for the seat or sleeper reservation and for meals. Children 3 and under travel free, provided they do not require a separate seat; those between 4 and 12 are charged half fare.

You can get complete details about **German Rail** and the many plans it offers, as well as information about Eurail passes, at **Eurail** (www.eurail.com).

GERMAN RAIL TOURIST PASSES **Eurail and German Rail Passes** offer several options beginning with 3 days and going up to 3 months. For example 3 days of travel in 1 month costs 247€ first class or 188€ second class. The German Rail

Twinpass, for two adults (they do not have to be married and can be of the same sex) traveling together in first or second class represents a 50 percent savings over single prices. A German Rail Youth Pass is valid only for persons younger than 26 years of age and is available only in second class; German Rail Passes for kids ages 6 to 11 are half the adult price. The passes also entitle the bearer to additional benefits, such as free or discounted travel on selected bus routes operated by **Deutsche Touring/ Europabus,** including destinations not serviced by trains, or excursions along particularly scenic highways such as the Romantic Road. The pass also includes travel on **KD German Line steamers** (day trips only) along the Rhine, Main, and Mosel.

WHERE TO BUY RAIL PASSES   Order Eurail and German Rail Passes from **Eurail** (www.eurail.com).

By Car

Competition in the European car-rental industry is fierce, so make sure you comparison shop. Players include **Avis** (*✆* **800/331-1212;** www.avis.com), **Budget** (*✆* **800/472-3325;** www.budget.com), **Hertz** (*✆* **800/654-3001;** www.hertz.com), **Kemwel Drive Group** (*✆* **877/820-0668;** www.kemwel.com), and **Auto Europe** (*✆* **800/223-5555;** www.autoeurope.com). You can often rent a car in one German city and return it to another for no additional charge. You may also rent a car through **Eurail** (www.eurail.com); they offer a German Rail 'n Drive option that gives you 2 days of unlimited train travel and 2 days of Hertz car rental within one month. You can purchase extra days for both train travel and car rental.

There are some advantages to **prepaying rentals** in your native currency before leaving home. You get an easy-to-understand net price, the rental process is more streamlined, and you can avoid unpleasant surprises caused by sudden unfavorable changes in currency exchange rates. Remember, however, that if you opt to prepay and your plans change, you'll have to go through some rather complicated paperwork for changing or canceling a prepaid contract.

DRIVING RULES   In Germany, you drive on the right side of the road. Both front- and back-seat passengers must wear safety belts. Children 5 and younger cannot ride in the front seat.

Easy-to-understand international road signs are posted, but travelers should remember that road signs are in kilometers, not miles. In congested areas, the speed limit is about 50kmph (about 30 mph). On all other roads except the autobahns, the speed limit is 100kmph (about 60 mph).

In theory, there is no speed limit on the autobahns (in the left, fast lane), but many drivers going too fast report that they have been stopped by the police and fined, and the government recommends a speed limit of 130kmph (81 mph). German motorists generally flash their lights if they want you to move over so they can pass. You must use low-beam headlights at night and during fog, heavy rain, and snowfalls, and you must stop for pedestrians in crosswalks; they have the right of way.

Note: Drinking while driving is a very serious offense in Germany. Be sure to keep any alcoholic beverages in the trunk or other storage area.

BREAKDOWNS/ASSISTANCE   The major automobile club in Germany is **Automobilclub von Deutschland (AvD),** Lyoner Strasse 16, 60528 Frankfurt (*✆* **069/660600;** www.avd.de). If you have a breakdown on the autobahn, you can call from one of many emergency phones, spaced about a mile apart. If you don't belong to an auto club, call *✆* **01802/222222.** In English, ask for "road service assistance." Emergency assistance is free, but you pay for parts and materials.

DRIVER'S LICENSES   American drivers, and those from E.U. countries, need only a domestic license to drive. However, in Germany and throughout the rest of Europe, you must also have an international insurance certificate, known as a *carte verte* (green card). Any car-rental agency will automatically provide one of these as a standard part of the rental contract, but it's a good idea to double-check all documents at the time of rental, just to be sure that you can identify the card if asked by border patrol or the police.

PARKING   Parking in the center of most big towns is difficult, expensive, and often impossible. Look for parking lots and parking garages outside the center, identified by a large P; in some larger cities, signs on the way into town indicate how much space is available in various lots or parking garages. Most parking lots use an automated ticket system. You insert coins or credit cards to purchase time.

By Bus

An excellent, efficient bus network services Germany. Many buses are operated by **Bahnbus** (www.*bahnbus*.com), which is owned by the railway. These are integrated to complement the rail service. Bus service in Germany is particularly convenient during slow periods of rail service, normally around midday and on Saturday and Sunday. German post offices often operate local bus services (contact local post offices for schedules and prices).

By Boat

The mighty Rhine is Germany's most traveled waterway. Cruise ships also run on the Main River between Mainz and Frankfurt; on the Danube from Nürnberg to Linz (Austria), going on to Vienna and Budapest; and on the Mosel between Cochem and Trier. A good place to begin investigating the many options, with lists of operators, cruise line reviews, and loads of other information, is Cruise Critic (www.cruisecritic.com). Canal barge cruises are a way to see a rarely viewed part of Germany. Many German itineraries focus on Berlin and the Mecklenburg lakes, and the "Mosel Cruise," from Trier to Koblenz. A good overview of trips, as well as cruise packages, are available from **European Barging** (© 888/869-7907; www.europeanbarging.com).

ACCOMMODATIONS STRATEGIES

In Germany's large cities, like Berlin and Munich, booking your hotel room ahead is essential, especially if you're going to be in Munich during Oktoberfest or any major city during a large trade fair or special event.

Booking ahead isn't as important in the rest of Germany, but it's still a good idea, particularly when you're going to be spending a Friday or Saturday night in places that are popular getaways for Germans, such as Dresden, the Black Forest, the Rhine and Mosel valleys, and the Bodensee (Lake Constance).

Tourist information centers, located in or near the main train stations in all German cities and towns, can help you find a room. Some charge nothing; others charge a small fixed fee (usually no more than 4€); and others charge 10 percent of the first night's hotel rate, but you get that back at the hotel, so the service ends up costing nothing. Most tourist information centers also have a free directory of local accommodations. All have high standards, controlled by hotel associations, regional tourist associations, and local tourist boards.

But you shouldn't only be thinking about accommodations in terms of hotels. Short-term apartment and house rentals can be economical and often provide travelers with more space and a more-authentic travel experience. In some cases you'll rent through an agency and in others directly from the owner of the property, who may or may not be near at hand to offer assistance during your stay. Among the companies offering these sorts of stays are **Airbnb** (www.airbnb.com); **Drawbridge to Europe** (☎ 541/482-7778; www.drawbridgetoeurope.com); **HomeAway** (www.homeaway. com); and **VRBO** (www.vrbo.com).

SPECIAL-INTEREST TRIPS & TOURS

SPECIALTY ESCORTED TOURS   **Brendan Worldwide Vacations** (☎ 800-421-8446; www.brendanvacations.com) offers escorted tours of German Christmas markets, as does **Maupintour** (www.maupintour.com). **Reformation Tours** (800/303-5534, www.reformationtours.com) leads excursions to cathedrals, monasteries, and sites associated with Martin Luther. **Alpenventures World War II Tours** (888/991-6718; www.worldwar2tours) visits naval bases and other sites associated with the war. You can taste beer in Munich, Bamberg, and other cities with **BeerTrips. com** (406/531-9109, www.beertrips.com) and tour the Rhine and Mosel vineyards with **Wine Tours of the World** (888/635-8007; www.winetoursoftheworld.com).

LEARNING VACATIONS   **Road Scholar** (800/454-5788; roadscholar.com) offers travelers 55 and older university-based courses on art, history, culture and other subjects that provide insight into Germany. Fees for the programs, usually two weeks long, include airfare, accommodations, meals, tuition, tips, and insurance. Good sources for language schools in Germany are **Languages Abroad** (www.languagesabroad.com), **Languages Directory** (www.language-directory.com), **Language School Abroad** (www.goabroad.com).

BIKING   Germany is excellent biking terrain. **Classic Adventures** (☎ 800/777-8090; www.classicadventures.com) leads bike tours along the Romantic Road and other scenic routes. **Euro-Bike and Walking Tours** (800/575-1540; www.austin-lehman.com) leads bike trips in Bavaria. **Cyclists Touring Club** (44-844/736-8450; www.ctc.org.uk) organizes bike trips in Bavaria and along the Rhine and Mosel.

WALKING & HIKING   **E.E.I. Travel** (800/927-3876; www.eeitravel.com) combines walking trips with cultural tours in southern Germany. It's estimated that Germany has more than 80,000 marked hiking and mountain-walking tracks, and the **Deutschen Wanderverband** (tel. 0561/938730; www.wanderverband.de) offers details about trails, shelters, huts, and addresses of hiking associations in various regions. The **Deutscher Alpenverein** (tel. 089/140030; www.alpenverein.de) owns and operates 50 huts in and around the Alps that are open to all mountaineers; it also maintains a 15,000km (9,300-mile) network of Alpine trails. The best Alpine hiking is in the Bavarian Alps, especially the 1,240m (4,070-ft.) Eckbauer, on the southern fringe of Garmisch-Partenkirchen. The tourist office supplies hiking maps and details.

ATMs In German cities, you can easily find 24-hour ATMs in airports, train stations, and outside banks. Cirrus (© **800-424-7787;** www.mastercard.com) and Plus (© **800-843-7587;** www.visa.com/atms) are the most popular networks. Remember that many banks impose a fee every time you use a card at another bank's ATM, and that the fee can be higher for international transactions. In addition, the bank from which you withdraw cash may charge its own fee. Despite the fees, ATM withdrawals are usually less costly than transactions made at Bureaux du Change and other commercial exchanges.

Business Hours Most banks are open Monday to Friday 8:30am to 1pm and 2:30 to 4pm (Thurs to 5:30pm). Money exchanges at airports and border-crossing points are generally open daily from 6am to 10pm. Most businesses are open Monday to Friday from 9am to 5pm and on Saturday from 9am to 1pm. Store hours can vary from town to town, but shops are generally open Monday to Friday 9 or 10am to 6 or 6:30pm (Thurs to 8:30pm). Saturday hours are generally from 9am to 1 or 2pm, except on the first Saturday of the month, when stores may remain open until 4pm. In shopping malls and major shopping districts in larger cities, some stores open on Sunday from noon to 5pm.

Customs You can take into Germany most personal effects and the following items duty-free: one video camera or two still cameras with 10 rolls of film each; a portable radio, a tape recorder, and a laptop PC, provided they show signs of use; 400 cigarettes, 50 cigars, or 250 grams of tobacco; 2 liters of wine or 1 liter of liquor per person 18 and over; fishing gear; one bicycle; skis; tennis or squash racquets; and golf clubs.

Returning U.S. citizens who have been away for at least 48 hours can bring back, once every 30 days, US$800 worth of merchandise duty-free. You'll be charged a flat rate of 4% duty on the next US$1,000 worth of purchases. Be sure to have your receipts handy. On mailed gifts, the duty-free limit is US$200. With some exceptions, you cannot bring fresh fruits and vegetables into the United States. For specifics on what you can bring back, download the invaluable free pamphlet *Know Before You Go* online at www.cbp.gov.

For a clear summary of Canadian rules, you can download the booklet *I Declare* at www.cbsa-asfc.gc.ca/publications. It is issued by Canada Border Services Agency (© **800/461-9999** in Canada, or 204/983-3500; www.

cbsa-asfc.gc.ca). Canada allows a C$750 exemption, which can be used only once a year and only after an absence of 7 days. You're allowed to bring back duty-free one carton of cigarettes, one can of tobacco, 40 imperial ounces of liquor, and 50 cigars. In addition, you're allowed to mail gifts to Canada valued at less than C$60 a day, provided they're unsolicited and don't contain alcohol or tobacco (write on the package "Unsolicited gift, under C$60 value"). You should declare all valuables on the Y-38 form before departing Canada, including serial numbers of valuables you already own, such as expensive foreign cameras.

Disabled Travelers Germany is relatively hospitable for travelers with disabilities. Most large cities and many smaller ones provide elevator access to subways, ramps and lifts on buses and streetcars and at museums and other public facilities, and wheelchair-accessible taxis. The local tourist offices can issue permits for drivers to allow them access to parking areas for people with disabilities. Many hotels, especially newer ones, are equipped to meet the needs of those with disabilities, and some have specially equipped rooms for the disabled. Many restaurants, including many of the more expensive ones, are wheelchair accessible. Keep in mind, though, that throughout the country some historic sights may not be properly equipped for travelers with disabilities.

Organizations that offer assistance to travelers with disabilities include MossRehab (© **800/225-5667;** www.mossresourcenet.org), which provides a library of accessible-travel resources online; Society for Accessible Travel & Hospitality (SATH; © **212/447-7284;** www.sath.org), which offers a wealth of travel resources for all types of disabilities and informed recommendations on destinations, access guides, travel agents, tour operators, vehicle rentals, and companion services; and the American Foundation for the Blind (AFB; © **800/ 232-5463** or 212/502-7600; www.afb.org), a referral resource that provides information on traveling with Seeing Eye dogs.

Access-Able Travel Source (© **303/232-2979;** www.access-able.com) offers a comprehensive database on travel agents from around the world with experience in accessible travel; destination-specific access information; and links to such resources as service animals, equipment rentals, and access guides. Many travel agencies offer customized tours and itineraries for travelers with disabilities. Among them are Flying Wheels Travel (© **888/451-5006** or

507/451-5005; www.flying-wheelstravel.com) and Accessible Journeys (© **800/846-4537** or 610/521-0339; www.disability-travel.com). The "Accessible Travel" link at Mobility-Advisor.com (www.mobility-advisor.com) offers a variety of travel resources to persons with disabilities.

Doctors Contact the International Association for Medical Assistance to Travelers (IAMAT; © **716/754-4883** or 416/652-0137; www.iamat.org) for lists of local, English-speaking doctors. You can find listings of reliable medical clinics in Germany at the International Society of Travel Medicine (www.istm.org).

Drinking Laws Officially, you must be 18 to consume any kind of alcoholic beverage in Germany. Bars and cafes rarely request proof of age. Drinking while driving, however, is treated as a very serious offense.

Electricity In most places, the electricity is 220 volts AC (50 cycles). Much of your electronic gear (including laptops) have built-in converters but you will need a transformer for any device without one. Be sure to pack an adapter (a plug that fits the German socket. Many hotels will supply these.

Embassies & Consulates The following embassies and consulates are in Berlin. The embassy of the United

States is at Pariser Platz 2 (© **030/83050;** http://germany.usembassy.gov; U-Bahn: Brandenburger Tor), open Monday to Friday 8:30am to 3pm. The U.K. Embassy is at Wilhelmstrasse 70 (© **030/204570;** http://ukingermany.fco.gov.uk/de; U-Bahn: Anhalter Bahnhof), open Monday to Friday 8am to 4:30pm. The Australian Embassy is at Wallstrasse 76–79 (© **030/ 8800880;** www.germany.embassy.gov.au/beln/home.html; U-Bahn: Spittelmarkt), open Monday to Thursday 8:30am to 5pm and Friday 8:30am to 4:15pm. The Canadian Embassy is at Leipziger Platz 17 (© **030/203120;** www.canadainternational.gc.ca; U-Bahn: Potsdamer Platz), open Monday to Friday 9am to noon. The Irish Embassy is at Jägerstrasse 51 (© **030/220720;** www.embassyofireland.de; U-Bahn: Uhlandstrasse), open Monday to Friday 9:30am to noon and 2:30 to 3:45pm. The New Zealand Embassy is at Friedrichstrasse 60 (© **030/ 206210;** www.nzembassy.com; U-Bahn: Friedrichstrasse), open Monday to Friday 9am to 1pm and 2 to 5:30pm.

Emergencies Throughout Germany the emergency number for police is © **110;** for fire or to call an ambulance, dial © **112.**

Family Travel Admission prices for attractions throughout Germany are reduced for children ages 6 to 14. Kids younger than 6

almost always get in for free. If you're traveling with children, always check to see whether the attraction offers a money-saving family ticket, which considerably reduces the admission price for a group of two adults and two or more children. The same is true for public transportation: Low-priced family or group tickets usually are available. On trains, children ages 6 to 11 pay half the adult fare, and children younger than 6 travel free.

Gay & Lesbian Travelers Germany is one of the most "developed" countries in the world when it comes to gay pride, gay culture, and gay tourism. If you are *schwul* (gay) or *lesbisch* (lesbian), you'll find plenty to do in Deutschland. Berlin, Munich, Hamburg, Frankfurt, and Cologne all have large gay communities, but gay life flourishes outside the big cities, too. A network of gay or gay-friendly restaurants, cafes, stores, bars, dance clubs, and community centers exists throughout the country, in small towns and large.

Gay and lesbian couples (or friends) qualify for family tickets on public transportation in many Germany cities. With most family, or Gruppen (group) tickets, all that matters is that two (or more) individuals travel together.

Every summer, parades and special events celebrate gay pride. Berlin holds its annual Gay & Lesbian Street Festival in

mid-June, celebrates its Christopher Street Day and Parade around the third weekend in June, and stages its famous Loveparade in mid-July. Munich celebrates Christopher Street Day in mid-July. Hamburg celebrates with a Gay Pride Parade and Festival around June 8 to 10. Cologne's Christopher Street Weekend usually is the first weekend in June. Frankfurt's Christopher Street Weekend takes place around the third weekend in July.

Health Germany should not pose any major health hazards. The heavy cuisine may give some travelers mild indigestion, so you might want to pack an over-the-counter medicine and moderate your eating habits. The water is safe to drink throughout Germany; however, don't drink from mountain streams, no matter how clear and pure the water looks, to prevent contact with giardia and other bacteria.

German medical facilities are among the best in the world. If a medical emergency arises, your hotel staff can usually put you in touch with a reliable doctor. If not, contact the American embassy or a consulate; each one maintains a list of English-speaking doctors. Medical and hospital services aren't free, so be sure that you have appropriate insurance coverage before you travel.

Pack prescription medications in your carry-on luggage and carry them in

their original containers, with pharmacy labels—otherwise they might not make it through airport security. Carry the generic name of prescription medicines, in case a local pharmacist is unfamiliar with the brand name.

Insurance For travel overseas, most U.S. health plans (including Medicare and Medicaid) do not provide coverage, and the ones that do often require you to pay for services upfront and reimburse you only after you return home.

Canadians should check with their provincial health-plan offices or call Health Canada (*℡* **866/225-0709;** www.hc-sc.gc.ca) to find out the extent of their coverage and what documentation and receipts they must take home if they are treated overseas.

Travelers from the U.K. should carry their European Health Insurance Card (EHIC), which replaced the E111 form as proof of entitlement to free/reduced-cost medical treatment abroad (*℡* **0845/605-0707;** www.ehic.org.uk). Note, however, that the EHIC covers only "necessary medical treatment"; for repatriation costs, lost money, baggage, or cancellation, travel insurance from a reputable company should always be sought. Call *℡* **0870/033-9985** or visit www.travelinsurance-web.com for quotes from several companies.

Internet & Wi-Fi Many hotels, cafes, and retailers have Wi-Fi "hot spots," as do most libraries in Germany. Many hotels also offer in-room Wi-Fi (noted in our listings), others in the lobby and other public areas. To find cybercafes, increasingly rare, check www.cybercaptive.com and www.cybercafe.com.

Mail Street mailboxes are painted yellow. It costs 1.70€ for the first 5 grams (about ⅕ oz.) to send an airmail letter to the United States or Canada, and 1€ for postcards. Letters to the U.K. cost .70€.

Mobile Phones In Germany, a mobile phone is called a Handy (pronounced as it's spelled). If your cellphone is on a GSM system, and you have a world-capable multiband phone, you can make and receive calls across Germany and the rest of Europe. Just call your wireless operator and ask for "international roaming" to be activated on your account. Having an unlocked phone enables you to install a cheap, pre-paid SIM card (found at a local retailer) in Germany. (Show your phone to the salesperson; not all phones work on all networks.) You'll get a local phone number and much lower calling rates.

Although you can rent a phone from any number of German sites, including kiosks at airports and at car-rental agencies, it's often more cost-effective if you rent the phone before you leave home. Two reliable wireless rental companies are InTouch USA

(*℃* **800-872-7626;** www.intouchglobal.com) and RoadPost (*℃* **888-290-1606** or 905-272-5665; www.roadpost.com).

Money & Costs The euro (€) is the single European currency of Germany and other participating countries. Exchange rates of participating countries are locked into a common currency fluctuating against the dollar. Prices in Germany are moderate, especially compared to those in large cities in the U.S. and Britain, and you generally get good value for your money. Travelers can expect to pay as little as 100€ or even less for a decent hotel room, 40€ for a modest dinner for two, 2.50€ for a cup of coffee, and around 8€ for admission to major galleries.

In Germany, American Express, Diners Club, MasterCard, and Visa are commonly accepted, with the latter two cards predominating. Note that many banks now assess a 1% to 3% "transaction fee" on all charges you incur abroad (whether you're using the local currency or your native currency).

Passports Citizens of the U.S., Canada, Ireland, Australia, New Zealand, and the U.K. do not require visas for visits of less than 3 months.

Police Throughout the country, dial *℃* **110** for emergencies.

Safety Overall, the security risk to travelers in Germany is low. Violent crime is rare, but it can occur, especially in larger cities or high-risk areas such as train stations. Most incidents of street crime consist of theft of unattended items and pickpocketing. Take the same precautions against becoming a crime victim as you would in any city.

Report the loss or theft abroad of your passport immediately to the local police and the nearest embassy or consulate. If you are the victim of a crime while in Germany, in addition to reporting to local police, contact the nearest embassy or consulate for assistance. The embassy/consulate staff, for example, can assist you in finding appropriate medical care, contacting family members or friends, and explaining how funds could be transferred. Although the investigation and prosecution of the crime is solely the responsibility of local authorities, consular officers can help you understand the local criminal-justice process and find an attorney if needed

Senior Travel Members of AARP (*℃* **888/687-2277;** www.aarp.org), may get discounts on hotels at some major international chains, and car rentals from most major firms. Anyone 50 and over can join. In general, though, travelers should not expect to find a treasure-trove of senior discounts in Germany. Even some typical at-home discounts—such as those for museum entrance fees and public transport fares—are usually not available to non-resident seniors.

Smoking Check before lighting up. In general, you cannot smoke in most restaurants and many bars in Germany, but these rules are in a continuous state of flux and vary by federal state—in some cases smoking is banned by law and enforced. In other cases the official law is not enforced in bars of a certain size, or after the kitchen closes at restaurants that are open late and morph into a bar-like setting as the night goes on. Throughout the country, smoking is banned in all public buildings and on transport.

Taxes As a member of the European Union, Germany imposes a tax on most goods and services known as a value-added tax (VAT) or, in German, Mehrwertsteuer. Nearly everything is taxed at 16%, including vital necessities such as gas and luxury items such as jewelry; the tax is factored into the price. Food and books are taxed at 7%. VAT is included in the prices of restaurants and hotels. Stores that display a tax-free sticker will issue you a Tax-Free Shopping Check at the time of purchase. When leaving the country, have your check stamped by the German Customs Service as your proof of legal export. You can then get a cash refund at one of the Tax-Free Shopping Service offices in the major airports and many train stations and some of the bigger ferry terminals. Otherwise, you must send the checks to Tax-Free Shopping Service, Mengstrasse 19, 23552 Lübeck, Germany. There is no airport departure tax.

Telephones The country code for Germany is 49. To call Germany from the United States, dial the international access code 011, then 49, then the city code, then the regular phone number. Note: The phone numbers listed in this book are to be used within Germany; when calling from abroad, omit the initial 0 in the city code.

For directory assistance: Dial ✆ **11837** if you're looking for a number inside Germany, and dial ✆ **11834** for numbers to all other countries. For operator assistance: If you need operator assistance in making a call, dial ✆ **0180/200-1033.**

To call the U.S. or Canada from Germany, dial 01, followed by the country code (1), then the area code, and then the number. Alternatively, you can dial the various telecommunication companies in the States for cheaper rates. From Germany, the access number for AT&T is ✆ **0800/8880010,** and for MCI, ✆ **0800/8888000.** USA Direct can be used with all telephone cards and for collect calls. The number from Germany is ✆ **013/00010.** Canada Direct can be used with Bell Telephone Cards and for collect calls; this number from Germany is ✆ **013/00014.**

Tipping If a restaurant bill says Bedienung, that means a service charge has already been added, so just round up to the nearest euro. If not, add 10% to 15%. Bellhops get 1€ per bag, as does the doorperson at your hotel, restaurant, or nightclub. Room-cleaning staffs get small tips in Germany, as do concierges who perform some special favors.

Toilets Use the word "Toilette" (pronounced twah-leh-tah). Women's toilets are usually marked with an f for Frauen, and men's toilets with an h for Herren. Expect to pay 1€ to use public facilities.

Visitor Information All cities and nearly all larger towns in Germany have tourist offices; we include these for all cities and towns we cover. The German National Tourist Board headquarters is at Beethovenstrasse 69, 60325 Frankfurt am Main (✆ **069/751903;** www.germany-tourism.de or www.cometogermany.com). The website provides listings for offices abroad.

Index

See also Accommodations and Restaurant indexes, below.

General Index

A

B

C

D

Accommodations

Restaurants